OUTLINES
OF
CEYLON HISTORY

MAHA VIHARA AT DAMBULLA.

OUTLINES OF CEYLON HISTORY

DONALD OBEYESEKERE

ISBN : 978-93-5324-499-6 (HB)

First Published, Colombo, 1911

Published, 2020

Published by

Facsimile Publisher
12 Pragati Market
Ashok Vihar, Ph-2
Delhi-110052
E-mail: books@facsimilepublisher.com

Printed at: G. Print Process, Delhi.

Outlines of Ceylon History

Author: Donald Obeyesekere

OUTLINES

OF

CEYLON HISTORY

By

DONALD OBEYESEKERE,

M.A. (Trin. Coll. Cantab.), Barrister-at-Law (Inner Temple),
President of the Ceylon Social Reform Society, M.R.A.S. (C.B.), F.R.C.I.,
etc., etc.

"Breathes there a man with soul so dead
Who never to himself hath said
This is my own, my native land."

SCOTT.

PRINTED & PUBLISHED BY
THE "TIMES OF CEYLON," COLOMBO.
LONDON OFFICE: 27, MINCING LANE, E.C.

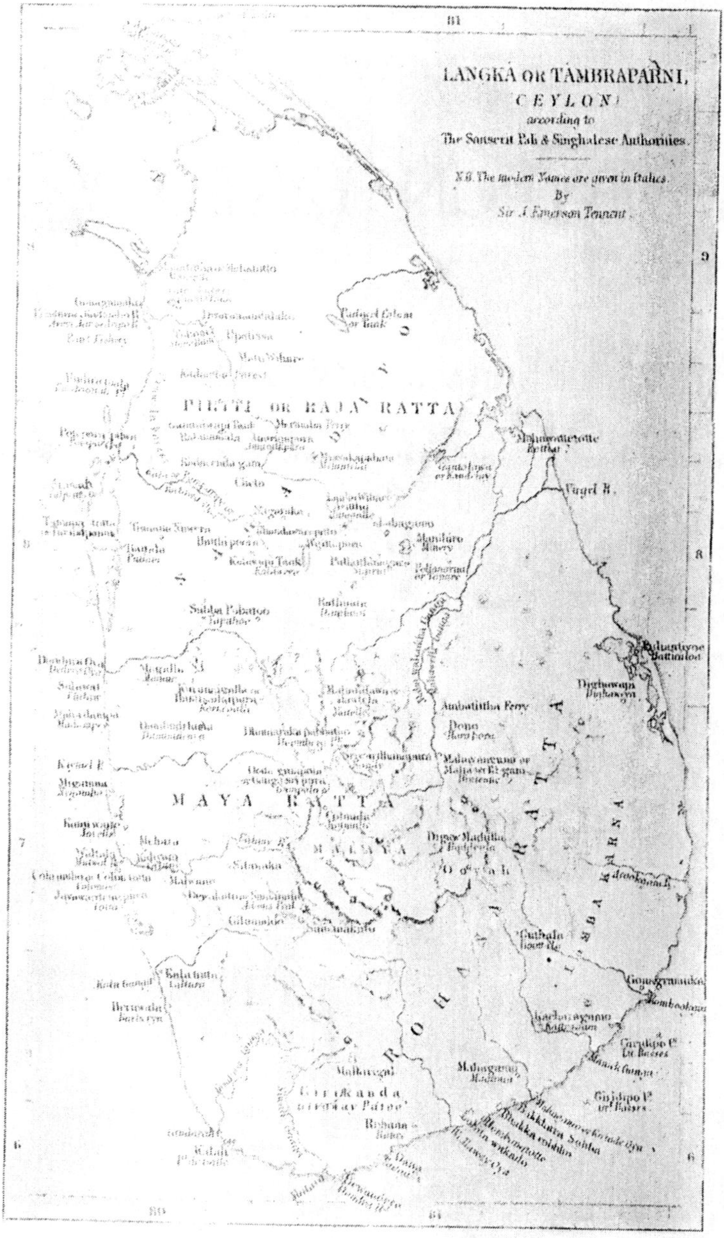
LANGKA OR TAMBRAPARNI,
CEYLON
according to
The Sanscrit Pali & Singhalese Authorities.
N.B. The modern Names are given in Italics.
By
Sir J. Emerson Tennent.
PIHITI OR RAJA RATTA
MAYA RATTA
ROHANA
Batticaloa
Dighawapi
Mahagama
Girikanda
Kalatutta
Colombo

DEDICATED TO

THE YOUTH OF CEYLON

IN THE HOPE THAT THE AWAKENING IN THEM
OF A CONSCIOUSNESS OF THEIR PAST MAY
SPUR THEM ON TO ENDEAVOUR TO
BE WORTHY OF THE TRADITIONS
OF THEIR FOREFATHERS.

ERRATA.

Page 5, in line 24, Singhababu should read Singhabahu.
" 61, Sanghatissa should read Sanghatissa I.
" 72, Upatissa should read Upatissa I.
" 86, තිදුනොළබා should read තිදීනොලබා (දු should be දී)
" 88, Upatissa III. should read Upatissa II.
" 94, Sanghatissa should read Sanghatissa II.
" 95, Mogallana should read Mogallana III.
" 100, lines 17, 18, and 19 should read :—The dagoba built at the Thuparama by Kings Devanampiatissa and Kuda Aggabodhi is said to have been levelled with the ground and deprived of all the rich offerings which it contained.
" 102, Dappula II. should read Dapula I.
" 109, Aggabodhi III. should read Aggabodhi VII.
" 113, Dappula III. should read Dappula II.
" 115, Dappula IV. should read Dappula III.
" 125, Abon-zeyd should read Abou-zeyd.
" 143, Jaya Bahu should read Jaya Bahu I.
" 166, Veligama = Weligama.
" 194, Jaya Bahu I. should read Jaya Bahu II.
" 231, Wimala Dharma should read Wimala Dharma I.
" 271, Toot should read tooth.
" 314, Charge should read change.

PREFACE.

AT an interview accorded by H. E. Sir Henry Blake on 2nd July, 1906, to a deputation of the Ceylon Social Reform Society, on the question of the teaching of Ceylon History in the local schools being raised, the objection was taken by the Acting Director of Public Instruction that there was no suitable school-history available; and he held out a promise to do all he could to further the study of the subject as soon as such a book was brought into existence.

I have accordingly devoted almost all my leisure to the production of such a work, as I believe will not only be of use in the schools, but will also interest the general reader; and I shall consider my labour well rewarded if it would but assist the youth of the country to acquire some knowledge of their past.

It has been truly said by Emerson that "a man is what he thinks himself to be." And when we possess a history such as most peoples in the world would envy, it is sad to think that the study of the subject has for the past century received little or no attention in the Government schools.

I have to express my obligation to Mr. P. E. Pieris, M.A., L.L.M., C.C.S., for reading through the proof sheets of that portion of my work which relates to the European period.

The works from which my information has been mainly derived are the following:—

The *Mahâwansa*.—L. C. Wijesinghe's Trans. Colombo, 1889.

The *Rajavaliya*.—Contained in Edward Upham's Trans. of the "Sacred and Historical books of Ceylon." London, 1833.

The *Rajaratnacara*.— Do. do. do.

"*A Contribution to the History of Ceylon translated from the Pujavuliya*" by B. Gunasekara. Colombo, 1895.

The *Nikâya Sangrahawa*.—C. M. Fernando's Trans. Colombo 1908.

The *Attanagaluwansa* in Sinhalese edited by W. A. Samarasekara. Colombo, 1903.

The *Rájataranggini*.—J. C. Dutt's Trans. Calcutta, 1879.

The *Sidath Sangarawa.*—James de Alwis' Trans. Colombo, 1851.

"*Sketches of Ceylon History*" by P. Arunachalam. Colombo, 1906.

"*Ancient Ceylon*" by J. Parker. London, 1909.

"*Ceylon*" by Emerson Tennent, 2 vols. London, 1859.

"*Buried Cities of Ceylon*" by S. M. Burrows. Colombo, 1905.

"*Numismata Orientalia*" by T. W. Rhys Davids. London, 1877.

"*The Dipavansa and Maháwansa and their historical development in Ceylon*" by Wilhelm Geiger. Trans. by Ethel Coomaraswamy. Colombo, 1908.

"*Ceilao*" by Ribeiro. Trans. by P. E. Pieris. Colombo, 1909.

"*The History of Ceylon, from the earliest times to 1600 A.D., as related by Joao de Barros and Diogo do Couto.*" Trans. by Donald Ferguson, and contained in the Journal of the Asiatic Society of Ceylon, Vol. XX., No. 60. Colombo, 1909.

"*Correspondence between Rája Sinha II. and the Dutch*" by Donald Ferguson, contained in the Journal of the Asiatic Society of Ceylon, Vol. XVIII., No. 55.

"*A Description of the great and most famous Isle of Ceylon*" by Philippus Baldaeus. Contained in the English Trans. in Vol. III. of Churchill's "Collection of Voyages." London, 1672.

"*An Historical relation of the Island of Ceylon in the East Indies, etc.,*" by Robert Knox. London, 1817.

"*The Dutch in Ceylon, 1602-1757.*" Trans. by F. H. de Vos, and contained in the Journal of the Asiatic Society of Ceylon, Vol. XI., No. 38. 1889.

"*The Age of Srí Parákrama Báhu VI. (1412-1467)*" by Edward W. Perera, contained in the Journal of the Asiatic Society of Ceylon, Vol. XXII., No. 63. 1910.

"*The History of Ceylon from the earliest period to the year MDCCCXV., etc.,*" by Philalethes, M.A. Oxon. London, 1817.

"*An Historical, Political and Statistical Account of Ceylon and its Dependencies*" by Charles Pridham, in 2 vols. London, 1849.

"*Mediæval Singhalese Art*" by Ananda K. Coomaraswamy. London, 1908.

"*Description and Conquest of Ceylon*" by Henry Marshall. London, 1846.

"*Eleven Years in Ceylon*" by Major Forbes, 2 vols. London, 1840.

"*Recent Disturbances and Military Executions in Ceylon*" by Lieut.-Col. J. Forbes. London, 1849.

"*Account of the Interior of Ceylon and of its Inhabitants with Travels in that Island*" by Dr. Davy. London, 1821.

RAJAGIRIYA,
MARCH, 1911.

CONTENTS.

MAP OF ANCIENT INDIA.

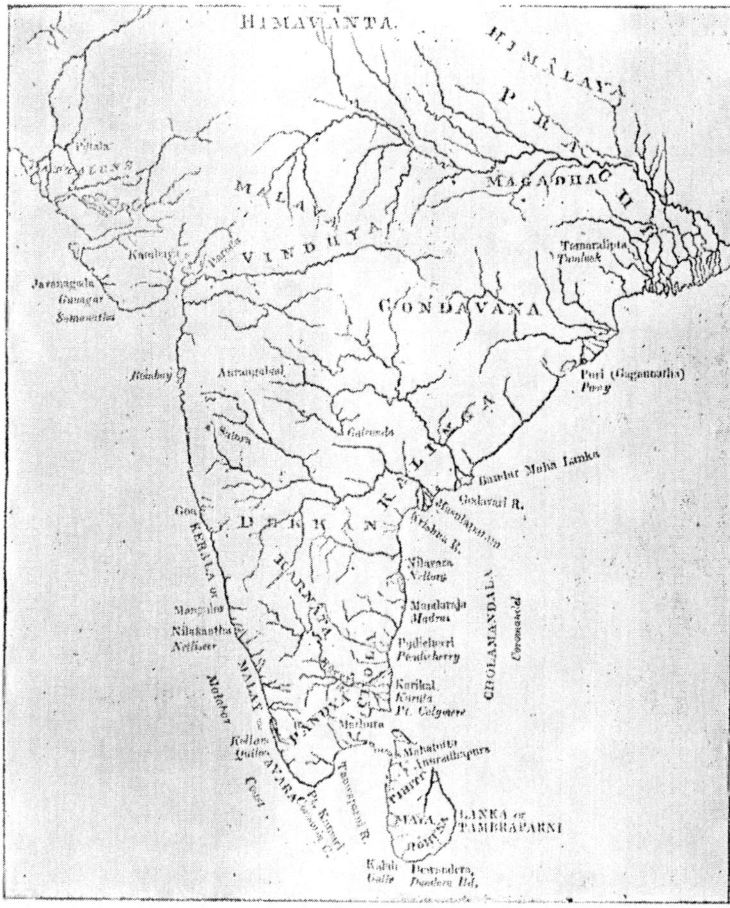

HISTORY OF CEYLON.

THE primitive history of Ceylon is enveloped in fable, yet there is perhaps no country in the world that has such a long continuous history and civilisation. Her stupendous religious edifices more than two thousand years old and, in extent and architectural interest, not second to the structures of Egypt, and her vast irrigation works, attest the greatness and antiquity of her civilisation. Her rich products of nature and art, the beauty of her scenery, her fame as the home of a pure Buddhism, have made her from remote times the object of interest and admiration to contemporary nations. Merchants, sailors, and pilgrims have in diverse tongues left records of their visits, which confirm in a striking manner the ancient native chronicles which Ceylon is almost singular among Asiatic lands in possessing.

Ceylon, it is believed, was part of the region of Ophir and Tarshish of the Hebrews, from which King Solomon's navy supplied him with "gold and silver, ivory, apes, and peacocks": i Kings x. 22. To the ancient Greeks and Romans the Island was known by the name of Taprobane, by which name it is described by Onesicritus, Diodorus, Siculus, Ovid, Strabo, Pliny, Ptolemy and others—a name, too, familiar to English readers through Milton:—

> "Embassies from regions far remote,
> From India and the golden Chersonese,
> And from utmost Indian isle, Taprobane."

The name is a corruption of "Tambapanni," one of the names given to Ceylon in the Sinhalese chronicles. It is explained in the *Mahawansa* (i. p. 33) as derived from Tambapanayo (copper-palmed), having been given to the Island by Wijeya and his followers, who, "exhausted by sea-sickness and faint from weakness, had landed out of their vessel supporting themselves on the palms of their hands pressed on the ground......... hence their palms became copper-coloured" (tambapanayo), a fanciful explanation. On the opposite coast of India there is a river still called Tamraparni, and the name may have been brought to Ceylon by the early Tamil settlers, a common practice among colonists in ancient and modern times. Virgil in his Æneid makes Æneas, on landing in Italy, express surprise at seeing a little Troy, another Pergamus and another river Xanthus.

> "........... parvam Trojam, simulataque magnis
> Pergama, et arentem Xanthi cognomine rivum
> Adgnosco. ...." (Virg. Æneid iii. 349.)

How many English and Scotch names of places have been introduced into Ceylon by British Colonists. The Arabs called Ceylon "Serendib" and the Portuguese "Ceilao." The names are probably derived from Sinhala or Sihalam (changed to Selan and Seren) and Dwipa (an island) changed to "dib." To the inhabitants of the neighbouring Continent of India it was known centuries before the Christian era by the name of Lanka (the resplendent), the name it still bears among the native inhabitants, both Sinhalese and Tamil. The Siamese have added the honorific Tewa, calling the Island Tewa Lanka, "divine Lanka." To the Chinese Ceylon was "the Island of Jewels," to the Greeks "the land of the hyacinth and the ruby," to the Indian Buddhist "the pearl upon the brow of India."

The traditions respecting the Island are many and curious. The orthodox Buddhist believes that every one of the four Buddhas of the present cycle from Kakusanda to Gautama visited Ceylon and instructed its inhabitants, and that Gautama Buddha left on Adam's Peak his foot-print as an undying memorial of his third and last visit. The Hindus claim the foot-print as that of Siva whose shrine was probably established there or revived by Samana or Lakshmana, one of the heroes of Ramayana and the reputed guardian of the peak. From him it was called Samana-kuta even prior to the visit of the second Buddha, and is still called Samanala by the Sinhalese. The Mohammedans, continuing a tradition inherited from some of the early Christians, are equally positive that the foot-print is that of Adam, and that Ceylon was the cradle of the human race—the elysium provided for Adam and Eve to console them for the loss of Eden—a tradition which somewhat softened the bitterness of the exile of Arabi Pasha and his fellow-Egyptians during their internment in the Island from 1883 to 1901.

The earliest Indian tradition about Ceylon is recorded in the *Skanda Purana*, the story of the rise and fall of a mighty and wicked Titan, for whose overthrow Skanda or Kartikeya, the god of war and wisdom, was incarnated. The echoes of that contest live in a remote forest shrine in the south-eastern corner of the Island, called after him Kartikeya Gráma or Kataragama, where, after his victory, he wooed and won a chieftain's daughter, who shares with him the worship of millions from Cashmere to Ceylon, and with whom the Sinhalese priests (Kapuralas) of the shrine proudly claim kinship. The southern bank of the Kalutara river near its mouth (Kalutara South railway station) is still locally called Velapura, the city of the lance god (the lance being his favourite weapon) and marks the limit of his territory, while the opposite bank of the river is assigned to his enemies, and is called Desestara, a corruption of Devasatru (the enemies of the gods).

The next Indian tradition, later by many centuries, is that of the *Ramayana*, the celebrated epic of Valmiki, which relates the abduction of Sita, a North Indian Queen of Ravana, King of Ceylon, the invasion of Ceylon by her husband Rama, and his recovery of her after a sanguinary war and the slaughter of Ravana. The bridge said to have been constructed for the passage of Rama's army to Ceylon is the Adam's Bridge of English maps. It touches the Island of Rameswaram, where, on his return from Ceylon, Rama established a shrine to Siva, perhaps the most frequented of all the sacred spots in India, and over which and Adam's Bridge a railway will at no distant date run, linking India and Ceylon in closer bonds. At Munissaram, in the Chilaw District, already an ancient (*mun*) shrine of Siva (*Isvara*) as its name implies, Rama is said to have worshipped on his way to battle with Rawana. The purity of Sita's character and her devotion to her husband have made her the national heroine, as he is the national hero, of India, and thousands still pass in reverent pilgrimage over their route to Ceylon. Sita's name lives in Ceylon in Sita-tàlawa (Sita's plain) and Sita-ela (Sita's stream) and Sita-kunt (Sita's pond) between Nuwara Eliya and Hakgala, where she is said to have been confined by Ravana, and in Sitawaka (Avisawella). Both the *Skanda Purana* and the *Ramayana* represent Ceylon as a huge Continent, a tradition not unsupported by science. The geology and fauna of the Island point clearly to a time when Ceylon was part of an Oriental Continent, which stretched in unbroken land from Madagascar to the Malay Archipelago and northwards to the present valley of the Ganges. The valley was then occupied by a spreading westward across Persia,.Arabia and the Sahara Desert and forming the southern limit of the Palæarctic Continent which embraced Europe, North Africa and North Asia. In the course of ages the greater part of the Oriental Continent was submerged in the sea, leaving Ceylon as a fragment in the centre, with, on one side, the Maldives, Laccadives, Seychelles, Mauritius, and Madagascar, themselves separated from one another by hundreds of miles of sea, and, on the other, the Malay Islands; while the Ganges valley was upheaved, making North and South India one land, and, later, Ceylon itself was separated from South India by a narrow sea. The greater part of Ceylon is said in the *Rámayana* to have been submerged in the sea in punishment of Ravana's misdeeds, and the Great Basses lighthouse, which stands on a solitary rock in the south-east sea of Ceylon, is still called Rawana's fort. The meridian of Lanka of the Indian astronomers which was reputed to pass through Ravana's capital passes through the Maldive Islands at 75° 53' 15 East Greenwich, quite four hundred miles from the present western limit of Ceylon. On this coast the Sinhalese chronicles record extensive submersion by the sea in the reigns of Panduwasa (*circa* 500 B.C.) and Kelani Tissa (200 B.C.). At this latter period Kelaniya is said to have been at a distance of "seven gows" (28 miles) from the sea. "The guardian deities of Lanka having become indignant with Tissa, king of Kelaniya (for the unjust execution of a Buddhist Elder), the sea began to encroach. 100,000 sea-port towns (Patunugam), 970 fishers' villages and 470 villages of pearl fisheries, making altogether eleven-twelfths of Lanka, were submerged by the great sea. Mannar escaped destruction of sea-port towns Katupiti Madampe."

The first historical event recorded in the chronicles is the landing of Wijeya, the discarded scion of a royal race in Northern India and the founder of the first known dynasty in Ceylon. It is commonly supposed that Wijeya and his followers arrived in Ceylon from Bengal, but there is no warrant for such a supposition except in the fact that his grandmother, Suppadevi, was a daughter of the King of Bengal. She, being of an adventurous temperament, is said to have secretly fled from her father's house and accompanied a caravan bound for Magdha which was waylaid by a "lion"—most probably a bandit nicknamed "lion"—who carried her off and lived with her in a cavern in the Lala country, the modern Guzerat, where she gave birth to two children—a boy and a girl. At the age of sixteen the boy ran away with his mother and sister to Wango (Bengal), where they were followed by the bandit who terrorised the inhabitants of the villages in his search for them, till finally he was slain by his own son, who, on that account, was named Singhala, the lion slayer. After he had slain his father Singhala, also called Singhebahu, returned to the country of his nativity, Guzerat, where he established a kingdom and founded a city named Singhapura. He had many sons, of whom the eldest was Wijeya.

When Wijeya came of age, Singhebabu installed him in the office of sub-king. In this office Wijeya, together with his retinue, showed himself to be so violent and despotic that the people of the country were greatly incensed and made representations to the king. Vainly did the king censure Wijeya's retinue and severely reprimand Wijeya himself. They were determined to continue in their wicked ways until the king, having thought for the safety of his throne, decided to banish Wijeya and his followers.

Wijeya, 543-505 B.C.

The first place at which **Wijeya** landed was a place by the name of Supparaka (the modern Surat, in the Bombay Presidency), where he was compelled to put back to sea owing to the hostile attitude of the natives of the district. The next place of landing was at a spot named Tambapanni by him on account of the copper colour of the earth which attached itself to the hands of his followers, who, exhausted by their long voyage, stretched themselves on the ground for rest no sooner they landed. Some say that the spot where he landed was near Puttalam, others say it was at the mouth of the Kirinde Oya on the south coast, while the Dutch his-

Mahawansa, ch. vii.

torian Valentyn asserts that it was in the Trincomalie District. Wijeya here profited by the state-craft he must have learned during the period he was sub-king of Guzerat. He conducted himself with moderation and craftiness. He formed an alliance with a native princess named "Kuweni" and by this means insinuated himself into the favour of the reigning kings and petty governors. By her influence he and his followers obtained an introduction to the marriage feast of one of the yakka kings, Kalasena by name, the capital of whose dominion was Sirivattha, at which city was being celebrated his marriage with the daughter of another yakka king, the capital of whose dominion was Lankapura. Here with his followers Wijeya suddenly turned upon his host and his party, consisting probably of all the nobility in the two kingdoms, and treacherously murdered them. Thereafter he had no difficulty in spreading his authority throughout that district. The part played by Kuweni in aiding and abetting her husband to commit this outrage had by no means raised her in the estimation of the latter. This was brought home to her when Wijeya, having sent an embassy to King Pandawa of Madura requesting his daughter in marriage, informed her that a gentler being than herself was coming over to take her place, and that it was his wish that she should take her departure from his palace. The request had to be complied with, though it nearly broke her heart to find herself so treated by the man whom she had treated so well. Although Wijeya had asked her to betake herself to any place within his dominions she pleased, promising to maintain her there with a thousand bali offerings, Kuweni's offended pride would not allow her to avail herself of his offer. Accordingly, she wandered into the yakka city of Lankapura, where she was soon recognised and killed, lest any further act of treachery be committed by her.

Kuweni Asna, which relates the story of her love and sorrow, says that when she was asked by Wijeya to take her departure, in agonising shrieks she wailed: "When shipwrecked and forlorn, I found thee and thy men food and home; I helped thee to rout the yakkas and raised thee to be king. Pledging me thy troth thou madest me thy spouse. Didst not thou know then that I was of the yakka race? Loving thee with unquenchable love and living in such love I bore thee children.

How canst thou leave me and love another? The gentle rays of the rising full moon are now to me the blaze of a red hot ball of iron, the cool spicy breezes of the sandal groves are hot and unwelcome, the cuckoo's sweet song pierces my ear as with a spear. Alas, how can I soothe my aching heart!"

Wijeya's embassy to King Pandawa proved successful. The latter's daughter, whose name too happened to be Wijeya, was sent over to Lanka decorated with every description of gold ornaments befitting her sex and exalted rank and accompanied by seven hundred daughters of his nobility and eighteen officers of State, with elephants, horses, chariots, and slaves, attended on by seventy-five menial servants, as dowry.

On their arrival all the nobles of Lanka assembled together, accepted the sovereignty of Wijeya in due form, and the occasion was solemnised by a great festival. Thereafter Wijeya invested with great pomp the daughter of King Pandawa with the dignity of queen-consort. He gave the eighteen nobles who accompanied his wife valuable presents. He made an annual present of chanks and pearls to the value of two lakhs to King Pandawa.

He reigned with perfect justice for thirty-eight years, the greater part of which period was devoted to the consolidation of his newly-acquired power. The seat of government was a city called Tammana (or Tammana Nuwara), which he founded in the district in which he first landed.

As Wijeya advanced in years he thought it fit to provide a successor to the throne of his kingdom, as he had had no children from the daughter of King Pandawa. Accordingly he consulted his ministers about the matter and sent a letter of invitation to Summitta, his brother. Before Summitta received the letter Wijeya died; but the country was governed wisely by the ministers under **Upatissa**, their chief, for one year until Panduwasa, the younger son of Summitta, arrived. Summitta himself was not able to accept the sovereignty of Lanka, as he had succeeded his father Singhebabu, King of Guzerat. **Panduwasa** arrived in Lanka at Gónagámaka-tittha at the mouth of the Mahakandara River (Mahaweliganga) accompanied by thirty-two noble youths disguised in the character of devotees. As such

Upatissa, 505-504 B.C.

Panduwasa, 504-474 B.C.

they were afforded every assistance by the inhabitants in finding their way to their destination, the town of Upatissa, where the Prime Minister was administering the government. On the arrival of the devotees the regents made due inquiries, and, having identified them, invested Panduwasa with the sovereignty of Lanka, but Panduwasa abstained from solemnising his inauguration until he had provided himself with a royal consort.

Beyond the Ganges there reigned a king by the name of Pandu—a cousin of Buddha—who had a daughter named Bhuddakacchana. Her complexion had the tint of gold and her person was endowed with female charms of irresistible fascination, and she had seven royal suitors. Panduwasa thought it fit to be the eighth and was rewarded with success. The princess embarked in a vessel, accompanied by thirty-two attendant females, which bore them swiftly down the Ganges, foiling every attempt made by the rival suitors to capture her on her way, and reached the Port of Gónagámaka in twelve days. Thence, disguised as devotees, they made their way to "Wijita," where they were met by the ministers, identified, and presented to the king at Upatissa. The king elevated Bhuddakacchana to the station of queen-consort, and gave her thirty-two attendants in marriage to his followers. A few years after the arrival of the queen, six of her brothers followed her to Lanka, and were allowed by Panduwasa to settle down and take part in the administration of any part of Lanka they pleased, with a view to accelerating colonisation and to extending the knowledge of agriculture. The place where (the prince) Rama dwelt was called Rámagona, so also were those of Uruwela, and Anuradha, named after the princes that settled there: likewise the settlements of Wijita, Dighayo and Rhona were severally called Vijitigama (remarkable for a seige during the war of Ellala and Duttu Gamunu), Dhigayo and Rohana (where was raised a city and castle long the seat of tumult and outrage). The founding of these principalities led in after years to dissensions, civil war and disaster. These principalities were later resolved into three great geographical divisions. The portion to the north of the Mahaweliganga was called Pihitti-Ratta, or, Raja-Ratta, from its containing the ancient capital and the residence of royalty. The south of this was

Rohana, bounded on the east and south by the sea and by the Mahaweliganga and Kaluganga on the north and west; a portion of this division near Tangalla still retains the name of Roona. The third was Maya-Ratta, which was bounded on the north by the Deduru Oya, on the south by the Kaluganga, on the west by the sea, and on the east by the mountains.

In a low and level country such as the North of Ceylon, where the chief subsistence of the people is rice, a grain which can only be successfully cultivated under water, the first requisites of society are reservoirs and canals. The first of such reservoirs, the "Abeya-wewa," was built during this reign in the year 505 B.C. by Anuradha, the king's brother-in-law, who afterwards built a palace and dwelt there. According to the Engineer, Parker, this tank is what is now known at Anuradhapura as Basawakkulam. It had an embankment $1\frac{1}{8}$ miles long, 28 feet high and 8 feet broad at the top. Its original area was 330 acres, and it had a capacity of 133 million cubic feet. Parker has also discovered a large deserted tank called Pandá-wewa, situated 16 miles east of Chilaw, near a small village, Hettipola, in the North-Western Province, which was built by King Panduwasa. Its embankment is $1\frac{3}{4}$ miles long, 22 feet high, and 8 feet wide at the top. It covers an area of 1,050 acres and has a capacity of 311 million cubic feet.

Parker's Ancient Ceylon, pp. 360-362.

Parker's Ancient Ceylon, pp. 353-360.

King Panduwasa had ten sons, of whom the eldest was Abaya, and one daughter, Ummada-citta by name.

The destruction of his uncles and dethronement of Abaya, by the son to be born of this princess, having been predicted by the Brahmins, all the brothers but one were anxious to sacrifice Ummada-citta to their fears. Abaya could not bring himself to approve of so extreme a step, but to prevent the fulfilment of the prophecy, he, with the consent of Panduwasa, ordered her to be placed in solitary confinement. In this state being beheld by a nephew of King Panduwasa, the princess, who is said to have been possessed of great attractions, engaged in secret correspondence with him, which being brought to the ears of Abaya and his brothers, they determined on giving their consent to the marriage, intending the immediate destruction of any male offspring that might be born. The princess having learnt their resolution obtained a female infant, and substituting it for her son, Pandukabhayo, saved his life.

In the year 474 B.C.—the same year that Pandukabhayo was born—King Panduwasa died after a peaceful and prosperous reign of thirty-five years. The seat of government during his reign was Wijitapura.

Abhaya 474-454 B.C.

On the death of the king his ten sons assembled together and chose Abaya, the eldest amongst them, to be the Sovereign of Lanka. Ummada-citta's stratagem did not remain long concealed from her brothers, but every attempt of theirs to procure the destruction of their nephew was destined to prove abortive.

At the age of sixteen (16) Ummada-citta entrusted the education of her son to a learned and wealthy Brahmin by the name of Pandula. This the Brahmin did, making his own son Canda the fellow-student of Pandukabhayo. On the completion of his education the Brahmin provided him with money wherewith to procure fighting men, asked him to have Canda as his "purohita" (chief minister) and sent him forth to fight out his destiny.

During this period the chief attention of the Indian conquerors was devoted to the introduction and extension of agriculture for the purpose of providing food for their followers. This is clearly shown by what is incidentally recorded of the circumstances under which Pandukabhayo procured himself a bride. It is said that whilst he was on his journey of conquest, accompanied by one thousand two hundred men, he came across a lovely princess, Pali by name, attended by a great retinue, and reclining in a palanquin, on her way taking a prepared repast for her father and the reapers, her father being Girikandasiva, an uncle of his who was governing that territory, and was at that moment engaged in superintending the reaping of a harvest of one hundred karisas of land (four hundred acres). It is further said that when Pandukabhayo begged of the princess for some of the prepared feast, he was offered it in a *golden* dish, thus indicating that at this period a high stage of civilisation had been reached. Pandukabhayo carried her off, with the result that two battles were forced on him: one at a place subsequently called Kalahanagara (the town of conflict), where Girikandasiva's forces were defeated and Girikandasiva himself

Numismata, Orientalia, sect. 31.

was captured ; the other at a place subsequently called Lohitavahakhanda (the field of bloodshed), where Pali's five brothers were defeated and slain by Canda, the Brahmin's son. Pandukabhayo next took up an almost impenetrable position near the Mahaweliganga on the Dola mountain. He kept his position there for four years until, at length, he was roused into exertion by his uncles, who, leaving the king at his capital—Upatissa—to manage the affairs of State, had started throwing up fortifications near the Dhammarakkha mountain, probably identical with the modern Dumbara, with the object of attacking him. The uncles, commanding the king's forces, attacked him in his stronghold, but failed to dislodge him ; whereat he suddenly abandoned his camp, made for that of his uncles, and after a stubborn encounter succeeded in capturing their fortifications and driving the enemy in confusion across the river. Pandukbhayo, uncertain as to what further forces the enemy might have at his command, preferred not to follow up his success by crossing the river and marching upon the capital. Instead, he remained for two years in the captured entrenchments.

The uncles repairing to Upatissa reported the result of their campaign to King Abaya. Thereupon the monarch secretly sent a letter to Pandukabhayo saying : "Rule over the country beyond the river ; advance not beyond the opposite bank." This step, though highly politic and likely to have been successful, was defeated by the unyielding character of the king's brothers, who, indignant at an embassy having been sent without their knowledge of it, deposed their brother Abaya and unanimously set up Tissa, one of their own members, to rule in his stead.

Tissa, 454-437 B.C.

Tissa's advancement to the sovereignty by no means benefited their cause, for Pandukabhayo, after a lapse of four years, having determined to carry the fight into his enemy's country, and having contracted an alliance with a Yakkinni by the name of Cetiya, widow of a great yakka warrior, who was a great strategist herself, possessing great influence in the district of the Dhammarakka mountain, whereby he obtained a great accession of strength for his army, marched with his forces to Arittha, where he remained seven years preparing still further for the impending war. Here he was attacked by all his uncles (with the exception of Abaya and

Girikanda), who had thrown up fortifications at Nagaraka. They attacked him from all sides of the mountain where he had taken up his position with the yakkini and her forces. Pandukabhayo, in conformity with the advice of the yakkini, sent forward a strong party (in the character of a deputation), placing in their charge his insignia of royalty as well as the usual offerings, made as tribute, and his martial accoutrements. Thereupon the enemy were lulled to security, imagining that they would soon be in a position to seize Pandukabhayo when he entered the camp. As soon as the deputation had reached the enemy's camp, Pandukabhayo, leading his army in person together with the yakkini, made a sudden onslaught on the enemy, who found themselves attacked from within by those composing the deputation, and from without by Pandukabhayo's forces, and were cut to pieces. All the uncles were slain in this battle, and the scene of the battle was from that day forward known as Labugama.

Pandukabhayo, 437-367 B.C.

Pandukabhayo next proceeded to the capital of his maternal great uncle Anuradha, which, but for the palace there existing, was a mere village. On his arrival, Anuradha, giving up his palace to him, constructed another residence for himself and dwelt therein. At this spot Pandukabhayo having consulted a fortuneteller and also an expert in the science of sites, founded a city which he called Anuradhapura, whose ruins remain to the present day to strike the traveller with wonder at the height to which civilisation had attained in this country twenty-three and a half centuries ago. The seat of government was shifted to the new city from Upatissa. Causing his uncle's canopy of dominion to be brought from Upatissa, and washed in a natural lake that existed in the new city, he caused himself to be anointed king with the water of that very lake, which, as he had been anointed as a conqueror, received the name of Jayawewa. This lake was subsequently deepened and greatly improved by this king. It is at the present day known as Nuwara-wewa (the city tank).

Burrow's Buried Cities of Ceylon, p. 87.

Unlike most adventurers who have no sooner succeeded in the object of their ambition than the agents to whom they are in great measure indebted for their elevation, are forgotten, Pandukabhayo appointed Canda, the son of the Brahmin from whom he received his education and supplies of men and money, to the office of Purohita (adigar). He appointed his uncle Abaya, Nagaraguttika (mayor of the city). To his father-in-law, Girikandasiva, was restored the territory Girikandaka.

The yakkas or aborigines of Lanka were at this period so important and powerful an element in the country that he thought it impolitic to ignore them. Accordingly, he established the yakka Kalavela in the eastern quarter of the city, and the chief of the yakkas, Citta, he established on the lower side of the Abaya tank. A slave born of a yakkini whose tribe had formerly rendered him great service, he established at the southern gate of the city. He established within the garden of the palace the yakkini with whom he entered upon his offensive alliance as against his uncles, and provided these as well as other yakkas in the city annually with demon offerings. On days of public festivity, seated on a throne of equal eminence with the yakka Chief Citta—so great was the respect of the king for the yakkas—Pandukabhayo caused joyous spectacles, representing the actions of the *devas* as well as of mortals, to be exhibited and gave himself up to satisfying his sexual appetites.

In the year 425 B.C. the sovereign had the boundaries of all the villages in Lanka clearly demarcated for the purpose of better administration, in accordance with the Village Community system of Government, which prevails up to the present day in a slightly modified form; also the whole Island was divided into fields and gardens. *425 B.C.*

Pandukabhayo devoted a good deal of attention to the adornment and civil government of the new capital. He formed four suburbs of the city and improved the Abaya tank which had been built by his predecessor King Panduwasa; he also built the Western Rajini (palace), the great cemetery and the place of execution and torture. An idea of the dimensions assumed by the city during this reign and the number of the people that dwelt therein can be formed when reliable historical records tell us that there were five hundred chandalas (low-caste people) employed as scavengers of the city, two hundred as night men, one hundred and fifty as carriers of corpses, and the same number as watchers at the cemetery. A village was formed for these low-caste men on the north-west of the cemetery. To the north-east of this Chandala village was established a separate cemetery, called Nica-susana, for their use. To the north of the cemetery was built a range of buildings for huntsmen. Magnificent was the tolerance and encouragement of all religious systems during this period of Lanka's history. At the expense of the State, residences, temples and preaching halls were, during this reign, built for the benefit of various foreign religious bodies coming into the country.

Agriculture, too, received its due share of attention from this monarch. We find that besides the repair of Abayawewa, which was built by his predecessor King Panduwasa, two new tanks—the Jaya-wewa and Gamini-wewa—were constructed during this reign.

Pandukabhayo reigned over the kingdom very wisely, with the co-operation of the two yakkas, Kalawella and Citta, befriending the interests of the yakkas and enjoying his prosperity conjointly with them, and died in the year 367 B.C. having reigned seventy years.

Mutasiwa, 367-307 B.C.

On the death of Pandukabhayo, **Mutasiwa,** his son, ascended the throne, but having been brought up in the lap of luxury he had not the same rough energy as his father. The æsthetic taste he had developed was given effect to by the formation of a delightful royal park, provided with every requisite and adorned with fruit and flower-bearing trees to the utmost perfection. The park was called Mahamega, as an unseasonable heavy fall of rain took place at the time it was being laid out. He had twelve sons and two daughters. His seat of government was Anuradhapura. His second son Dewanampiyatissa (Tissa the delight of Dewas), who excelled all the others in virtue and wisdom, was installed king on his death after a peaceful reign of sixty years.

307 B.C.

The long period of peace that prevailed in the country during the reigns of Pandukabhayo and Mutasiwa enabled the inhabitants to devote their attention to industrial pursuits, tapping the latent resources of the country in various directions. It is interesting to note that at this period the existence of the pearl oysters off the coast of Ceylon was known to the people of the country, and that they had sufficient knowledge of the pearls as to divide them into eight varieties. It is also interesting to find that the gemming industry, too, had developed.

Not only had the people developed a civilisation along the lines of materialism, but they had developed it at such a rate that they were prepared in this reign to welcome a change of civilisation in the direction of spiritualism.

One of the first acts of **Dewanampiyatissa** after ascending the throne was to send an embassy, composed of his maternal nephew Mahaaritha, (chief of the mission), the Brahaman of the Hali mountain, Malla (the Minister of State) and Tissa, the accountant, with a present consisting of sapphires, lapis-lazuli, rubies, eight varieties of pearls, three royal chariot poles and a chank with the whorls to the right—to which the Sinhalese attach a superstitious value, professing that a shell so formed is worth its weight in gold—attended by a powerful retinue, to Dhammasoka, King of Dambadiwa, or Maghada, for whom he had developed a great admiration, having heard of him by fame. The embassy embarked at Jambukola (a spot near the modern Jaffna) and reached Patiliputta in fourteen days, and presented the gifts to King Dhammasoka, who, being delighted with them, conferred high offices on the four people composing the embassy, loaded them personally with presents, and, after consulting his ministers as to the presents proper for the King of Lanka, sent him the following in return, viz., a chowrie (the royal fly flapper), a diadem, a sword of State, a royal parasol, (golden) slippers, a head ornament, a golden anointing vase, sandalwood of the Hari mountain, a crore of cloth that requires no washing, ointments for the body and clay of a bright red colour (aruna) resembling the streaks of light at sunrise, water from the Anotatta Lake, a chank with the whorls to the right containing water from the Ganges, a royal maiden of great personal charms, golden vessels, a costly howda, the medicinal fruits "haritaka" and "amalaka," exceedingly precious medicinal drugs, and one hundred and sixty loads of hill paddy, being the articles requisite for his inauguration, and a complete suite of royal attendants.

Dewanampiyatissa, 307-267 B.C.

Mahawansa, ch. xi., p. 45.

The Sinhalese embassy, after having spent five months at Pataliputta, started on their homeward journey, accompanied by the embassy from the King of Maghada to the King of Lanka, to find on their arrival that Dewanampiyatissa had already gone through the ceremony of solemnising his inauguration as king.

However, the gifts were presented to him by the Indian ambassadors, together with a message from the King of Maghada to the effect that he had adopted the Buddhist religion and hoped that the King of Lanka would do the same. The ceremony of solemnising the inauguration having been carried out a second time, King Dewanampiyatissa conferred great favours on the members of the Indian embassy.

This was a period of great Buddhist propagandist activity in India, Maghada being the headquarters.

Mahinda, son of Dhammasoka, was sent over to Lanka, accompanied by four priests (*theras*), his nephew Sumana (a samanera), and a cousin by the name of Bhandu, a lay disciple. They are said to have taken up their positions on the summit of the Missa mountain (Mihintale)—a solitary mountain rising abruptly from the plain eight miles east of Anuradhapura as it at present stands. It rises to a height of upwards of a thousand feet, and its summit commands a magnificent view which reaches across the Island from sea to sea. Here, King Dewanampiyatissa on a festive day when he had gone out elk hunting, having provided aquatic sports for the amusement of the inhabitants of the capitial, met them and was told the purpose for which they had arrived. Having listened to a sermon—*cula hatthi padopama sutta*—preached by Mahinda that day, the king was so much impressed by it that he had a splendid hall constructed within the precincts of the palace, so that the ladies of the palace, who from the accounts of the sermon they had heard from the king were anxious themselves to listen to his words of wisdom, might have the benefit of his teaching. The hall was canopied with white cloth, decorated with flowers, and sumptuous carpets were laid on the ground. The *theras*, having accepted the invitation of the king to the palace, arrived there, though they preferred not to make use of the king's chariot which had been sent for them. Here they were feasted and given seats covered with cloths—a custom which prevails to the present day—whence they preached to Anula, the king's sister-in-law, and her five hundred women companions, till they were converted. The fame of the priests and the effect of their preaching upon the royal household having reached the masses, they clamoured for entrance within the precincts of the palace, to listen to the doctrines that were expounded there, but were ordered by the king to prepare the royal stables, where there was more room for them than within the palace. There being insufficient space for the vast crowd even there, they were ordered to resort to the Nandana pleasure garden of the king, situated outside the southern gate of the city, which was a delightful forest, cool from its deep shade and soft green turf. Here, Mahinda, from a pulpit which had been erected for him, preached to the populace, composed both of the nobility and the rabble, men and women.

The freedom of women and the respect men had for their rights during this period of Lanka's history is illustrated by the following occurrence during this reign :—

Anula and her five hundred companions were so greatly affected by Mahinda's sermon that they determined to enter the order of priesthood, but as Mahinda declared that he was not allowed to ordain females, on his recommendation, King Dewanampiyatissa sent his minister Arittha, with a letter, to King Dhammasoka requesting that he should send over to Lanka, his daughter Sanghamitta for the purpose of ordaining King Dewanampiyatissa's consort and other women, and the right branch of the great Bo-tree under which Gautama Buddha attained Buddhahood.

(The leaves of the Bo-tree are supposed by the Buddhists to exhibit a tremulous veneration associated with the sacred scene of which they were the witnesses.)

Sanghamitta, on learning the message that had been sent, determined to leave her native land, as she was a noble-minded woman intent on doing the most she could for humanity at large.

King Dhammasoka, depressed at the idea of separation from his children, had unwillingly to yield to the persuasions of his daughter.

Accordingly, Sanghamitta, the high priestess, embarked for Lanka with her eleven priestesses and the Bo-branch planted in a huge golden vase, attended on by eighteen personages of royal blood, eighteen members of noble families, eight each of the Brahmin, Vaisya, herdsmen, workers in precious metal, weavers, potters, and of all the other castes with the Sinhalese Ambassador Arittha at the head of the mission.

The ambassador arrived safely at the port of Jambukola—the present Colombogam in the north of Ceylon—with Sanghamitta and the Bo-branch, and was received at the place of landing by King Dewanampiyatissa in person, who accompanied the Bo-branch to Anuradhapura, the journey taking him fourteen days. It is recorded that the road along which the journey was made was sprinkled with white sand and decorated with every variety of flowers and lined with banners and garlands of flowers. The Bo-tree was taken into the city at the northern gate and planted, on the spot where the sacred trees of former Buddhas had stood, by the king, himself, assisted by representatives of the sixteen castes at that period existing in the country, in the presence of Mahinda, Sanghamitta, the princes from Kataragama and Kandanaggama, the Brahman Tiwakka, and the whole population there assembled. The planting of the Bo-tree (which is the oldest historical tree in the world, being at the present day 2,217 years old) forms the grandest episode in the sacred annals of Ceylon. It is alive and healthy at the present day, and has been an object of solicitude to successive dynasties.

Anula with a host of women from the king's household had been awaiting the arrival of Sanghamitta, devoting her time to the pious observances of the "dassasila" order, clad in yellow garments. By the king's orders the fine residence of one of the king's ministers (Dona by name) had been converted to a nunnery for her and her companions. Here, Sanghamitta on her arrival took up her residence and admitted Anula and her retinue into the order of priesthood. This is the first recorded nunnery in Lanka. It was known as Upasika Vihara. Subsequently a second vihara, Hatthalhaka Vihara, was built for Sanghamitta and her priestesses who were desirous of a more retired place for the purpose of leading a life of devotional seclusion for the advancement of the cause of religion.

The followers and successors of Wijeya preserved intact the institution of caste which they had brought with them from the valley of the Ganges. Although there are passages in the Buddhist scriptures in which an effort to discourage the rigid observance of caste is apparent, it was not till the year 1802 that a priest of a lower caste than the goigama was permitted to enter the higher order known as Upasampada. Till then men of the low castes had to remain in the lower order of the priesthood known as Samanera, however learned some of them may have been. In that year some adventurous priests, led by Ambagahapitiya Gnana Wimala Tissa Samawera, incensed at the refusal to admit Miripenna Dharmaratane—the greatest poet of that period—to the Upasampada order, went to Amarapura, in Burmah, and there obtained the Upasampada ordination. The Amarapura sect that exists in Ceylon at the present day owes its origin to them.

Along with food, clothing, consisting of three garments to complete the sacerdotal robes as enjoined by the Buddhist ritual, was distributed at certain seasons, and in later times a practice obtained of providing robes for the priests by causing the cotton to be picked from the tree at sunrise, cleaned, spun, woven, dyed yellow and made into garments and presented before sunset—a practice that prevails at the present day and is known as Catina Dhawana. To avoid the vanity of dress or the temptation to acquire property, no Buddhist priest is allowed to have more than one set of robes consisting of three pieces, and if an extra one be bestowed on him it must be surrendered to the chapter of his vihara within ten days. The dimensions must not exceed a specified length, and, when obtained new, the cloth must be disfigured with mud, or otherwise, before he puts it on. The condition of the priesthood was a state of absolute dependency on alms, and at the earliest period of their history the vow of poverty by which their order is bound would seem to have been rigidly observed.

Buddha had directed that if a pansala (a dwelling of leaves) be built for priests to dwell in, the internal measurement of a cell should be twelve spans in length, seven in breadth; and, in accordance with the simplicity so strongly enjoined by him, down to the present time, the houses of the priesthood are modest and humble structures.

Mahinda, desirous of establishing in Ceylon some visible, tangible, token of Buddha which should appeal to the imagination of the masses, and having obtained from King Dewanampiyatissa a promise that he would enshrine in dagobas any relics of Buddha that were brought over to Lanka, sent his nephew Sumana to his father Dhammasoka, requesting him to send over to Lanka Buddha's dish used for his meals, together with as many other of his relics as he could spare. Thence Sumana was directed to journey to King Sakka, ruler of a country situated by the Himalaya mountains, who possessed both the right canine tooth and the right collar-bone of the great Teacher, and request him to send the collar-bone over to Lanka, where numerous people were being converted.

Sumana's journey was successful. The relics were brought with the dish and collar-bone. A dagoba (from dathu, a relic, and gabbham, a shrine) was erected with bricks in front of a temple called Pamojawatthu, on the summit of which, in an excavation as deep as the knee, the collar-bone was buried.

Having completed the dagoba (Thupa) the king erected a vihara (Arama) there. From this circumstance the place was distinguished by the appellation Thuparama. This dagoba is the oldest of its kind erected in Lanka, and is the most venerated. Its height is about seventy feet from the ground. Many other viharas and dagobas, such as Insurumuniya Dagoba, were built during this reign, and the relics brought by Sumana from King Dhammasoka were enshrined in the latter. The king also caused caverns, which are to be seen at the present day to be cut in the solid rock at the sacred place of Mihintale for priests to reside in. Many colleges (pirivinas) were built in the country during this reign, the chief of them being the one built at the expense of the (Senapathi) minister for war, and called Digasanda-Senapathi-Pirivena (the College of the Commander-in-Chief Dhigasanda). It became a great seat of learning and the home of great men. It was attached to the first great vihara in Lanka—the Maha Vihara,—which was built by Dewanampiyatissa for Mahinda, where the latter was patronised by the former.

Rajawalia, p. 184.

Mahawansa, ch. xii., p. 65.

The whole town of Anuradhapura was consecrated during this reign, King Dewanampiyatissa marking the boundary of the consecrated ground with a golden plough. The number of persons who entered the priesthood during this period was no less than thirty thousand.

Mahawansa, ch. xv., p. 63.

Mahawansa, ch. xvii., p. 70.

The political events of this reign were of no moment, except for the fact that Anula, ambitious of administering the government during the minority of her son, was incessantly plotting the destruction of Mahanaga, the king's brother, who had been appointed sub-king and was much beloved by the king.

The most important of her designs was an attempt to take him off by a present of a basket of mangoes containing a poisoned one. Dewanampiyatissa's son was living with Mahanaga at the time, and, having been innocently asked by the latter to taste the fruit, ate the very one intended for his uncle and died. Mahanaga, on hearing the circumstances of the case, fearing the vengeance of the royal family, fled to the southern division of the Island, the then uncultivated district called Rohana, and set up there a local sovereignty, making Magama his capital and maintaining the religion of Buddha. The development of agriculture did not escape the king's attention in his great zeal for the furtherance of religion. The Tissa-wewa was constructed during this reign, and is up to this day largely utilised in the cultivation of the paddy fields round Anuradhapura. Its area is 396 acres, its embankment is $2\frac{1}{12}$ miles long, 25 feet high, and the breadth of the top of it (crest) varies from 12 to 18 feet.

Mahawansa, ch. xxii., p. 83.

Parker's Ancient Ceylon, pp. 364-365.

Also we find that it was whilst Mahanaga was superintending the construction of the Tarraccha tank that the basket of mangoes arrived containing the one destined to bring about the death of the king's son.

Dewanampiyatissa died in the year 267 B.C., having devoted his reign of forty years mainly to the advancement of the Buddhist religion, and having permitted the establishment of a principality at Rohana without opposition. Peace and plenty reigned throughout the Island during this reign.

Uttiya, 267-257 B.C.

Uttiya succeeded his elder brother Dewanampiyatissa to the throne, the latter having died without issue. He followed in the footsteps of his predecessor. In this reign in the year 258 B.C. Mahinda, who had renounced his father's throne for a priesthood and played such an important part in the history of the Island in this as well as in the preceding reign as a luminary little inferior to Gautama himself in dispelling the benightedness of Lanka, died at Mihintale. The sovereign as well as all the inhabitants were in mourning for him for seven days. His body was embalmed in scented oil and placed in a golden coffin, which was also filled with spices and scented oils and well closed. It was next placed in a highly ornamented golden hearse and removed, accompanied by a magnificent procession, to the capital and taken along the principal highways—the capital as well as the road along which the hearse travelled being decorated for the occasion. For seven days the coffin was deposited on the premises of the Maha Vihara, the vihara and a space of three yojanas from it being decorated with triumphal arches, banners, and the vases with fragrant flowers. During these days the monarch kept up a festival of offerings. The ceremony ended with the cremation of the body, the king in person lighting the huge funeral pile of odoriferous drugs, erected at the eastern side of the city. Half the relics of Mahinda were taken possession of by the king, who enshrined them in dagobas built at Mihintale and at numerous other viharas.

Mahawansa, p. 31.

In the year 258 B.C. Sanghamitta, sister of Mahinda, who had deserted friends and relations, comfort and luxury for the purpose of establishing her religion in a foreign land, died at Hathalhaka convent leaving behind thousands of profoundly learned priestesses to carry on her noble work. In her case, too, the monarch caused offerings and funeral obsequies to be kept up with the utmost pomp, for seven days, the whole of Lanka being decorated in veneration of the event, and he himself lighted the funeral pile erected in the vicinity of the Bo-tree.

King Uttiya died in the following year, 257 B.C. The *Mahawansa* mentions the event in the following terms:—"If mortal man would but comprehend the relentless, the all-powerful, irresistible principle of mortality, would he not be disgusted with the wearying course of renewed existence? Thus disgusted, would he not avoid that which is evil and cleave to that which is good? But even knowing the truth, still would he be led astray? How exceeding great is the strength of his ignorance and delusion!"

Mahasiva, 257-247 B.C.

Mahasiva, Uttiya's younger brother, succeeded the latter (257 B.C.) and reigned peacefully for ten years, following in the footsteps of his two predecessors.

This monarch, being a great admirer of the priest of Bhaddasala, built for him the beautiful vihara, Nagarangana, on the eastern side of the city.

Suratissa, known prior to his accession as Suwanapinda Tissa, succeeded Mahasiva, his elder brother. He, too, followed in the footsteps of his three predecessors in advancing the religious and social development of the people; built, without committing any oppresion, five hundred beautiful viharas in various parts of the Island on both sides of the river Mahaweliganga. *Suratissa, 247-237 B.C.*

The genius of the Sinhalese people was essentially adapted to agricultural pursuits. Busied with such employments and with the erection of sacred edifices and in the formation of religious communities, the early colonists had no leisure for military service. Hence arose the practice during this reign of retaining mercenaries from the Continent of India—a practice which was destined to lead to constant disturbance of the tranquillity of the country. King Suratissa took into his pay two Indian youths **Sena** and **Gottika**, "powerful in their cavalry and navy," who proved unfaithful to their trust by murdering the king and retaining the supreme power for twenty-two years. They are said to have reigned wisely during this period, at the close of which they were in their turn dethroned and slain by the adherents of Asela, brother of King Suratissa. *Sena and Gottika, 237-215 B.C.*

Asela had reigned at Anuradhapura for ten years, when he was defeated and slain by **Ellala**, an invader from Sollee (Tanjore) on the Coromandel coast, who, landing his army at the mouth of the Mahaweliganga, marched directly upon Anuradhapura, where, after a decisive battle, he soon found his authority acknowledged by the native chiefs throughout the Island, excepting those at Rohana—the southern division which was still governed by a branch of the old family. Ellala was a man of upright character and proved an excellent administrator. Though he was not a Buddhist he was loved by his subjects, as he was wont to administer justice impartially to friends and foes. He had ruled over Lanka for forty-four years, when he was slain in battle by Duttu Gamunu, great-great-grandson of Mahanaga, brother of Dewanampiyatissa. *Asela, 215-205 B.C.* *Ellala, 205-161 B.C.*

The tank situated in the Northern Province, known at the present day as Vavunik-kulam (formerly Pali-wewa), was constructed by Ellala. When full its water covered an area of 1,975 acres. The length of its embankment across the Pali river is $2\frac{1}{2}$ miles. The top of the embankment is from 10 to 12 feet wide. The *Parker's Ancient Ceylon, pp. 365-371.*

embankment has been breached in five places, and the bed of the tank is now overgrown with jungle. Its capacity was 596 million cubic feet.

Although the term Damala is always used in the Sinhalese chronicles in respect of continental invaders, it was by no means confined to the Tamils,—the inhabitants of the south-western tract of the Deccan, known in modern geography as Malabar. It was used in respect of invaders from all parts of India—as far north as Cuttack in Orissa.

Mention has been made already of Mahanaga's flight to Rohana, where he established a local sovereignty, having Magama for his capital, a place situated on the bank of the Kirindiganga, five miles from Tissa-wewa and three miles from the village called Kirinde. He, like his brothers, was devoted to religion. Among many other viharas constructed by him were the Mahanaga and the Uddhakandhara viharas. The Tissa-wewa of the Southern Province was constructed by this king. Its embankment was ¾ of a mile long, 18½ feet high, and from 15 to 20 feet wide at the top. The embankment appears always to have been used as a cart road (as at present). The area of the tank was 662 acres and its capacity 160 million cubic feet. This reservoir was of such vital necessity to the city Magama that important measures had been adopted in order to ensure it getting a proper supply of water. For this purpose a permanent stone dam had been erected across the Kirindi-oya at a distance of 2½ miles from the upper part of the tank. A short shallow channel, with a bed about 10 feet wide, had then been opened from a point immediately above it in the river, up to a spot whence the water conveyed by it could flow into the tank by gravitation, without further works, beyond the closing of a hollow which led back to the river. He was succeeded at his death by his son Yatalakatissa, who appears to have extended his rule to Bintenne on the north-east and beyond Saffragam on the north-west. He fixed his capital at Kelaniya. On his death he was succeeded by his son Gotabhaya, who went to Magama to reign at his grandfather's capital, leaving a Kshatriya, by the name of Kelanitissa, to reign at Kelaniya. In the reign of Kelanitissa a great part of the coast adjacent to Kelaniya was overflowed by the sea, reducing the distance from Kelaniya to the sea to one gow. Gotabhaya was succeeded on

Parker's Ancient Ceylon, pp. 389-390.

his death at Magama by his son Kakawanatissa, who married Viharadewi, daughter of Kelani Tissa—a princess of great beauty, purity and ability. Kakawanatissa built many edifices in different parts of his kingdom, to be devoted to the cause of religion, amongst them was the Tissamaha Vihara. The tank Digha-vapi, now known as Kandiya-kattu or Mahakandiya, at which we shall subsequently find that his son Saida Tissa was stationed, was built by King Kakawanatissa. It has been supposed to be capable of irrigating 10,000 or 20,000 rice fields. At present it is overgrown.

Parker's Ancient Ceylon, pp. 396-397.

During Kakawanatissa's life it had been one of his main desires to avoid any aggressive military operations against Ellala, who reigned supreme on the northern side of the Mahaweliganga.

It is interesting to find that seven ships laden with golden utensils and other goods arrived in Ceylon destined for King Kakawanatissa during this reign. Most probably the goods were those of Chinese or Arabian traders, who at that period carried on the trade in the East and made the south coast of Ceylon their meeting place, where they traded with each other. Probably they had to pay a regular tribute to the King of Ceylon for allowing them the privilege to land on his shores.

Mahawansa, ch. xxii., p. 86.

He had two sons by Vihara Dewi, Duttu Gamunu and Sadda Tissa, the former being two years older than the latter.

Even during their boyhood the children showed that they had inherited their mother's strength of character and acquired her hostile disposition towards foreign rule over any part of Lanka. The *Mahawansa* says that Duttu Gamunu at the age of sixteen had attained a high degree of "piety, prosperity, wisdom, strength and martial accomplishments," from which we may presume that he had been instructed in the 18 sciences prescribed for princes, viz., (1) Oratory (Surtia), (2) General Knowledge (Smurtia), (3) Grammar (Wyacarana), (4) Poetry (Chandass), (5) Languages (Nirôte), (6) Astronomy (Jaté), (7) The Art of giving Counsel (Sangshiksha), (8) The means of attaining Nirwana (Mókshaggnanaya), (9) The Discrimination of Good and Evil (Creya-Widiya), (10) Shooting with the Bow (Danurivedey), (11) Management of the Elephant (Hastisilpey), (12) The Penetrating of Thoughts (Cawmatantra), (13) Discernment of

Mahawansa, ch. xxii., p. 87.

Rajaratnacara, p. 100.

Invisible Beings (Swalateshana), (14) Etymology (Purauna), (15) History (Eitihasia), (16) Law (Neeti), (17) Logic (Tarka) and (18) Physic (Wydyaharo).

As time went on King Kakawanatissa entrusted to his sons the command of portions of his army, assigning to them varied duties. Saida Tissa was stationed with a powerful and efficient force at Digawapi (Diga-wewa) in the Batticaloa District, for the protection of his dominions against the invasion of the Malabar subjects of Ellala. Duttu Gamunu, the heir to the throne, who was skilled in elephant, horse and bow exercises, and was in addition pious and wise, was stationed at the capital of his kingdom, Mahagama, at the head of an army of over 10,000. The mode in which the men who composed this army were selected was as follows :—Ten men of proved ability and valour, viz., Nandimitta, Suranimala, Mahasena, Godimbara, Theraputtabhaya, Bharana, Velusumana, Kanjadewa, Pussadewa and Labhiyavasabha, were each of them commanded to enlist ten warriors, and each of these one hundred was ordered to enlist ten warriors, and each of the thousand men thus obtained was ordered to enlist ten, thereby making up the total eleven thousand one hundred and ten (11,110).

After a certain period had elapsed Prince Gamunu, having held a review of his army and being convinced of his efficiency for the purpose, proposed to his father that he be allowed to start on the enterprise of expelling the foreigners from the shores of Lanka. The aged king looking to his son's personal safety refused his consent saying, "within this bank of the river is sufficient." Gamunu was more ambitious than his father and was too impatient to wait till his father's death to carry out his project. He repeated his request over and over again, but met with the same reply. Exasperated at his failure to obtain his father's approval, he rashly sent the aged monarch a female trinket remarking to those who witnessed its despatch : "Friends, my father, if he be a man, would not say so, let him therefore wear this."

King Kakawanatissa, enraged at the insult offered him by his son, ordered his courtiers to have a special gold chain made wherewith to fetter him. On hearing the news of this Gamunu fled from his court to Kotta, in the Malaya District, where he remained until his father's death, which took place a few years later, during which time King Kakawanatissa constructed numerous viharas, including the Mahanugalla Cetiya. At the festival held, on the completion of this Cetiya, in the presence of the priesthood there assembled, the monarch, foreseeing that there would be a contest between his sons for his throne on his death, made all his warriors swear that they would abstain from taking part in any conflict that may arise between them—a vow which was faithfully observed.

On the death of the king, the queen conveyed his corpse in a covered hearse to the Tissamaha Vihara, which was the chief one of the sixty-four viharas made by this king, and informed the priesthood thereof. Prince **Tissa** hearing of this event hastened thither from Digawapi, performed his father's funeral obsequies with great pomp, and taking charge of his mother and the State elephant Kandula, hurried back to Dhigawapi, lest he should be attacked by his brother, who, since his departure from his father's court, was known as Duttu (Disobedient) Gamunu. *Mahawansa, ch. xxii., p. 84.*

On the receipt of a despatch regarding his father's death from the latter's ministers Prince **Duttu Gamunu** repaired to Mahagama, effected the assumption of sovereignty, and sent a despatch to his brother Tissa demanding the custody of their mother, Vihara Dewi, and the State elephant Kandula. The request was firmly refused, though thrice repeated. Whereupon King Duttu Gamunu marched his forces against his brother and fought a great battle at Chulanganiyapitthi, at which the king's forces were defeated with heavy loss of men. The king, however, mounted on his mare Dighathulika, succeeded in escaping, accompanied by his minister .Tissa to Mahagama, though for a time they were closely pursued by Prince Tissa. It was during this flight, when the king was worn out with fatigue and hungry, that he refused to partake of the small meal which his faithful minister had carried for him, until the call for refection had been sounded and a priest had arrived, who should share the meal with him—an act which, as it was performed at a time of adversity, gave him greater consolation whilst he was at death's door than any other of his mighty deeds of valour and charity whilst prosperity attended him. *Duttu Gamunu, 161-137 B.C.*

As soon as the king reached Mahagama he busily engaged himself in collecting an army wherewith to wipe off the indignity he had suffered at the hands of his younger brother. He gathered an army of sixty thousand men and hastened to the attack. A great battle ensued, in which Tissa's army was defeated with great loss of life. Kandula, the State elephant on which Tissa was mounted, got restive while the battle was raging, and ran amongst the trees causing Tissa to scramble up a tree, whence he took refuge in a neighbouring vihara. The king was loathe to violate the sanctity of the place, so he placed guards round the vihara, whereby he hoped to capture his brother in the act of escaping. But the priests of the temple, in order to save the life of Tissa, laid him on a bed, covered him with a robe, and got four young priests to carry out the bed by the four posts, as if he were the corpse of a priest. Although the king knew the game the priests were playing, through the respect he had for the office they held, he would not lay hands on his brother; allowing him to thus escape to Digawapi, a fallen man; he returned to Mahagama with his mother and the State elephant, the prizes of the battle.

Shortly afterwards a reconciliation was effected between the two brothers through the instrumentality of the priests and Vihara Dewi, resulting in Tissa being appointed superintendent of the agricultural works which were in progress in the Batticaloa District, whilst Duttu Gamunu himself attended to the agricultural development of the Rohana districts calling the people for work from their villages by beat of drum.

Evidently the king's object in pushing forward the agricultural development of the country was to provide himself and his army with the necessary supply of rice and other requisites during the mighty war he contemplated waging with Ellala.

After some time spent in so doing, King Duttu Gamunu found himself in a position to carry out his designs against Ellala. The army which the king, during the life-time of his father Kakawanatissa, had collected for that purpose, remained in a great measure intact owing to the prudent conduct of Kakawanatissa, who, foreseeing that on his death a contest for the crown between the two brothers would ensue, had bound the ten leaders who had formed the nucleus of the army before collected, under a solemn promise not to assist either of his sons in their internecine strife. This promise having been faithfully kept, on the restoration of peace they no longer hesitated to offer their services to Duttu Gamunu.

Having had a road cleared through the Malaya country (the region round Adam's Peak) for his march, and having held a review of his forces which consisted of a huge body of cavalry and infantry supported by mounted elephants and chariots, mounted on the State elephant Kandula, he started out on his enterprise. He crossed the Mahaweliganga, at the Amba ferry, after a contest which lasted for four months, with an experienced Indian chieftain named Titthamba at that post. His noble mother Vihara Dewi accompanied him throughout this war and played no small part in it. The capture of Titthamba and the crossing of the Mahaweliganga were effected by a stratagem, in which she played the most important part. Once the river was crossed he marched on to Wijitapura driving in the outposts of Ellala and distributing the riches of his plunder among his forces. Wijitapura was a strongly fortified town, founded, as we have before observed, by Wijita, the brother-in-law of Panduwasa, three hundred years before. The siege of Wijitapura, by some said to have continued four, by others six, months, was concluded by a general assault.

Mahawansa, ch. xxv., p. 96.

The assault is thus described in the *Mahawansa* :— At the southern gate there was a terrific conflict between the warriors of the two armies. At the eastern gate, the warrior Welusumana, mounted on the charger (carried away from the stables of Ellala), slew innumerable Indians. The enemy then closed the gates, and the king advanced his warriors; Kandula (the State elephant) and Nandimitta and Suranimala charged the southern gate. Mahasena, Gotha and Theraputtra, these three charged the other three gates. The tusk elephant (Kandula), placing himself on his knees and battering a stone wall which was cemented by fine lime, made his way to the iron gate. The Indians who defended that gate hurled upon him every kind of weapon, heated lumps of iron and melted resin. Thereupon, on the melted resin falling smoking on his back, the agonised Kandula rushing to water submerged himself therein. Godimbra thus addressed him: "This is no soothing drink for thee; return to the demolition of the iron* portal and batter down the gate." This noble elephant recovering his courage and roaring defiance, emerging from the water, stood up with undaunted pride.

The king detailed an elephant doctor, who dressed his wounds, after which, a covering of buffalo hides having been wrapped round him, he once more rushed against the gate, and, with a force that nothing could resist, burst it open. Meanwhile the others had been breaching the walls, and King Duttu Gamunu, entering the city with his army, dispersed or slew the whole Malabar force.

Mahawansa, ch. xxxv., p. 100.

Digajanthu, the commander-in-chief of Ellala's forces, who had in person conducted the defence of Wijitapura, succeeded in escaping to Anuradhapura, where he informed Ellala that King Duttu Gamunu was no mean warrior, and persuaded him to summon the assistance of his nephew Bhalluka with an army from India.

Meanwhile King Duttu Gamunu continued his onward progress towards Anuradhapura, capturing fort after fort which Ellala had raised for protecting the level country leading to the capital. Girilaka was captured and razed, Casaw Totta and Mahawetta surrounded, Mahéla, a fort near the capital, which was surrounded on all sides with the thorny kadamba creeper, within which was a great triple line of fortification in which there was but one gate of difficult access, resisted every assault for four months. It finally fell, after King Duttu Gamunu had got hold of the person of the Rajah of Mahéla, by diplomatic stratagem. By this time the rival sovereigns had developed a mutual respect for each other. Extreme caution characterised each step they took towards the final encounter. King Duttu Gamunu threw up a fortification at the foot of the Kasa mountain and built a tank there, wherefrom he might draw his supply of water in case of a protracted siege. He next took counsel with his mother Vihara Dewi, who, as mentioned before, was a woman of rare ability, courage and patriotism, whose one object in life was to rid the country of foreign domination. On her advice King Duttu Gamunu formed thirty-two strong ramparts, and on

---

* Abundance of iron ore can be extracted from the mountains round Adam's Peak, and this is smelted with comparative ease by the Sinhalese.

each of them displayed personifications of himself with a royal standard-bearer attending on him, while he himself defended the innermost fortification.

Ellala, on the other hand, consulted with his ministers as to what was the best course to adopt in order to resist Duttu Gamunu, and was advised to attack him without delay.

As soon as King Ellala, accoutred for battle, supported by his military array, mounted on his State elephant Mahapabbata and accompanied by Digajanthu, the chief of his officers, was seen advancing to the sound of the trumpet, King Duttu Gamunu, supported by his chiefs, sallied out of the lines and hurried forward to meet him leading on the centre of his army in person. A fierce onset was made on Duttu Gamunu's front by Digajanthu, which was no less resolutely received. Nothing, however, could resist the unyielding valour of the Malabars, and Gamunu's army was forced to retrace its steps to his fortifications and there make a stand. The valiant Malabar commander Digajanthu, with sword and shield in hand, striking terror by the fury of his attack, springing into the air and piercing the figure which represented the king, took the first rampart; in like manner, redoubt after redoubt fell a prey to the army of Ellala until it came to taking that which was defended by King Duttu Gamunu in person. Here Digajanthu, whilst slashing at the shield of Suranimala, who was standing beside his king, lost his balance and fell prostrate at his feet, thereby giving Suranimala an opportunity to slay him, which was taken full advantage of. No sooner he was slain, Pussadewa sounded his chank and Ellala's army was panic-stricken. Vainly did Ellala rally it. It had become thoroughly demoralised by the loss of its commander, and was routed with great slaughter by Duttu Gamunu's forces. Thereupon King Duttu Gamunu, proclaiming by beat of drum "No other person than myself shall assail Ellala," mounted his elephant Kandula and pursued Ellala till he met him at the southern gate of the city mounted on his elephant. Here the two monarchs entered into personal combat. Ellala hurled his spear, Duttu Gamunu evading it made Kandula charge Mahapabbata with his tusks, whilst he himself successfully hurled his javelin at Ellala. Both Ellala and his elephant fell on the spot and were slain. Here Duttu Gamunu caused Ellala's body to be cremated with much ceremony and a dagoba to be built in honour of his valiant opponent. He promulgated an ordinance to the effect that every citizen, though of royal blood, should refrain from rejoicing and dismount on passing the tomb. This ordinance was punctiliously observed by the people and kings of Lanka up to the time of the cession of the kingdom to the British.

Forbes' Eleven Years in Ceylon, vol. I., p. 233.

Tennent says that in 1818, on the suppression of an attempted rebellion against the British Government, when the defeated aspirant to the throne was making his escape by Anuradhapura, he alighted from his litter on approaching the quarter in which the monument was known to exist, and although weary and almost incapable of exertion, not knowing the precise spot, he continued on foot till assured that he had passed far beyond the ancient memorial.

Bhalluka, nephew of Ellala, whose assistance had been summoned on the fall of Vijitapura, arrived in Lanka seven days after his uncle's cremation, at the head of sixty thousand men. Undaunted by the news of his uncle's defeat and death, he advanced direct from Mahatitha to Anuradhapura with all possible haste in the hope of finding Duttu Gamunu inactively reposing on his laurels.

On receiving intimation of Bhalluka's landing Duttu Gamunu got ready his army composed of elephants, cavalry, chariots of war, and infantry, accoutred himself with his martial equipments, and mounting Kandula with Pussadewa, the most expert archer in the land, who sat on the animal behind the king, advanced to meet the invader. Bhalluka with his army rushed on with the characteristic impetuosity of his race and a great fight ensued on the northern side of the great cemetery, where Duttu Gamunu, who at the outset had been forced to beat a retreat with his army, made a stand. In the course of this fight Bhalluka hurled his spear at Duttu Gamunu, but it fell to the ground, having struck the handle of the latter's sword; before Bhalluka could throw a second javelin he was hit on the mouth by an arrow shot by Pussadewa, who followed it up by another shot which hit Bhalluka on the knee and brought him prostrate to the ground from off his elephant. The shout of victory was set up at Bhalluka's fall and his army was cut to pieces. For the part he played in this battle,

Pussadewa was rewarded with a heap of gold, which covered the top of the arrow, with which he shot Balluka as it stood on its feather end.

In the course of these wars the Malabars were in the habit of using arrows drenched with the poison of serpents. Against such weapons the Sinhalese carried shields covered with plates of the chank shell. Amongst the Sinhalese it was considered a disgrace for a soldier to run away or allow his hair to fly behind. *Rajaratnacara, p. 101.*

After he had fulfilled the dreams of his youth, Duttu Gamunu turned his attention towards furthering the cause of religion in the country. Three years were spent in the construction of the Mirisvettiya Vihara by the Tissa tank and a dagoba for it. The Lowa Maha Paya, or the Brazen Palace, was next constructed, in the celebrated Mahamega garden, by the king. The *Mahawansa* says that all the labour used for its construction was paid for with money, thus shewing that the country had at the time evolved from a state of natural economy into one of money economy. This quadrangular palace was one hundred cubits square. The apartment rested on 1,600 granite pillars placed in forty parallel lines, forty pillars in each, the relics of which at the present day evidence the reality of the native account. It had nine stories, and in each of them there were one hundred apartments for priests. Those most eminent for their piety, Arahat priests, were given the uppermost stories, the other stories being occupied by priests less learned in order of their learning; those possessing fewest claims to sanctity being lodged nearest to the earth. *Rajawalia, pp. 217-218.*

All these apartments were highly finished with silver; and the cornices thereof were embellished with gems. The flower ornaments appertaining thereto were also set with gems, and the tinkling festoons were of silver. (The use of silver at this early stage of Ceylon's history is interesting, inasmuch as silver comes into use at a far later date than gold and requires a high degree of metallurgical knowledge to work.) In the middle of the palace was constructed a magnificent gilt hall supported on golden pillars representing lions and other animals. The extremity of this hall was ornamented with festoons of pearls all round, and the cornices with beads as before described.

Exactly in the centre of this hall, which was adorned with all the seven treasures, there was an enchanting ivory throne floored with boards; on one side of it there was the emblem of the sun in gold, on another the moon in silver, and on the third the stars in pearls. From the golden corners or streaks in various places most suitable in that hall, bunches of flowers made of various gems were suspended, and between golden creepers were representations of the various Jatakas. On this magnificent throne, covered with a cloth of great value, an ivory fan of exquisite beauty was placed. On the footstool of the throne a pair of slippers ornamented with beads, and above the throne the white canopy or parasol of dominion mounted with a silver handle glittered. The eight auspicious objects (lion, bull, elephant, water jar, fan, flag, chank and lamp) represented on the canopy were made of the seven gems: at the points of the canopy were suspended a row of silver bells. The palace was suitably furnished with couches and chairs of great value, and the floors were covered with carpets of woollen fabric most probably imported from Kashmir*—a Buddhist country—with which Ceylon had intercourse from a very early period. Even the laver and its ladle (for washing the hands and feet of priests kept at the door of the temple) were made of gold. The roof of this palace was covered with brazen tiles, hence the appellation "Brazen Palace."

King Duttu Gamunu next turned his attention to the erection of the Ruwanwelisaye. He had the stone pillar which contained the prophecy that on the spot it was standing a superb dagoba would be raised by a pious and a fortunate monarch, removed, and in order that he might in every way make the thupa firm and stable, digged a foundation for it seven cubits deep. *Mahawansa, p. 109.* He next caused round stones to be brought by his soldiers and had them well beaten down with pounders. In order to ensure great durability he had them trampled by enormous elephants whose feet were protected in leather cases (from which it may be inferred that the art of tanning leather from the hide of the buffalo was understood at this early period). Over this layer of stones was spread imported clay of the very finest description called "butter clay." Over the clay was placed a layer of bricks and over them was laid a

* The Rajatarangini (Dutt's Trans. p. 19) says that as early as B.C. 735 Ceylon cloth with golden footmarks were in use in the Court of Kashmir.

coat of rough cement; over that was placed a layer of "Kuruvinda" stones, over that was placed a net-work of iron, over that was spread Narumbu (a fragrant substance brought from the Himalayas), over that a layer of Halika stones, and over that a layer of common stone. In every part of the work the clay used was the imported "butter clay." Above the layer of common stones was laid a plate of brass eight inches thick embedded in a cement made of the gum of the kapitta tree (wood-apple) diluted in the water of the king-coconut. Over this was placed a plate of silver seven inches thick cemented in vermilion paint mixed in the tala (Sessamum) oil. This is interesting, as it is the earliest testimony extant of the use of oil as a medium for painting The distinction of the discovery of oil painting must remain with the Sinhalese until a higher claimant appears. Van Eyck's claim of having invented it in the fifteenth century is untenable.

Mahawansa, ch. xxix.

There were next placed the eight festival bricks with great ceremony in the presence of a vast multitude of Buddhist priests assembled from all quarters of the Buddhist world. The monarch caused a minister of noble descent, well attired, to hold the end of a fine rod of silver that was entered into a gold pivot and trace a circle, in accordance with the directions of the eminent priest, Siddhattha by name, over the prepared spot. Eight golden and eight silver vases were placed in the centre of the circle so traced, these were surrounded with one hundred and eight fresh vases and with cloth in quantities of one hundred and eight pieces. The monarch was then handed an excellent brick marked with divers signs of prosperity by a minister. This he placed in the fine fragrant cement in the eastern quarter. The other seven bricks were severally laid by seven ministers of State at each of the remaining seven quarters. This was the foundation of the great dagoba which is said to have been 270 feet in height (now 150 feet), and to have stood on a square mass of building two thousand feet in circumference, paved with large stones of dressed granite, and surrounded by a fosse seventy feet broad, the scarp of the sides of the platform is sculptured to represent the foreparts and heads of elephants projecting and appearing to support the massive structure to which they form so appropriate an ornament. Within are contained a beautiful artificial Bo-tree made of precious substances and numerous relics of Buddha brought by the priest Sonuttara from India. For a detailed description of the magnificent ceremony attending the enshrinement of the relics the reader is referred to chap. xxx. and xxxi. of *Mahawansa.*

The labour employed for the building of this dagoba was punctiliously paid for with money, as it was not only derogatory to the sacredness of the object, but also impolitic to exact any avoidable sacrifices from a people so recently suffering from internal warfare. King Duttu Gamunu did not live to see the completion of the structure, but he had himself carried within view of it, the proudest monument of his life, and spent his last hours under its shadow.

Sinhalese historians give a minute description of the events immediately preceding his death. Suffice it here to say that on that occasion he had a memorial of his religious acts produced and read in his hearing, and at the conclusion remarked that all these acts done in the days of prosperity afford him no mental relief. Only the recollection of two offerings made during adversity regardless of his fate bring comfort to his mind, and he frequently interrogated the priests on the nature of the heaven reserved from him, and expired with the gratifying expectation of reigning with the future Buddha "Mettiya" in the heaven named Tusitapura. It is recorded that vast numbers of yakkas became converts to Buddhism during the progress of building the dagoba.

Mahawausa, ch. xxxii., p. 125.

Rajaratnacaria, p. 40.

Among other works of public utility of King Duttu Gamunu not mentioned above, was the establishment and the maintenance of hospitals, provided with suitable diet and medicines prepared by medicinal practitioners at eighteen different places in Lanka, and the appointment and maintenance at the expense of the State of a doctor, an astronomer, and a priest for every group of sixteen villages in the country. The king was not an orator, although in his youth he had received instruction in the art of oratory. On one occasion, having been told that expounding the scriptures was an act of greater merit than the bestowal of offerings, he attempted to expound the "Mangala" discourse of Buddha to the priesthood from the pulpit on the ground floor of the Lowa Maha Paya (Brazen Palace), but found that utterance failed him: from that day forward he showed his appreciation of the art of oratory by supporting the ministers of religion in all parts of the country who were gifted with the power of preaching. He provided each of them regularly with a nali (=4 handfuls) of ghee, sugar and honey, together with a piece of liquorice of the length of the four fingers of the hand; and two cloths for each. Robes with flowers and a turban of silk constituted the dress of State bestowed on men whom the king delighted to honour. *Mahawansa, p. 90.*

Pávat-kulam (situated 28 miles south of Vavunikkulam), in the Northern Province, bricks—17·36 inches long, 8·6 inches broad, 2·89 inches thick—employed in the low-level sluices indicate that it must have been constructed during the first half of the 2nd century B.C. The tank is still doing good work. The embankment is 9,700 feet long, 28 feet high, crest 1,025 feet broad, area 2,029 acres, capacity 779 million cubic feet. *Parker's Ancient Ceylon, pp. 371-383.*

At the southern end of the bank there is a flood-escape, 125 feet wide, in the line of the bank. Its floor and the ends of the embankment at it are covered with large wedged slabs of stone carefully laid, those on the floor occupying a transverse breadth of 60 feet. A road-bridge of stone slabs laid on stone pillars enabled the stream from this flood-escape to be crossed when a considerable volume of water was passing down it. The extent to which this reservoir was utilised in ancient times may be gauged by its being provided with four sluices, in addition to a high-level culvert under the flood of the southern waste-weir. The culvert at the waste-weirswas built of stone, and the well of the northern low-level luice was also lined with stone, with a substantial backing of brickwork. At the others, the well of the central sluice probably, and those of the other two sluices certainly, were built of stone at the lower part, with a backing of brickwork, but after the first two or three courses were finished in brickwork only, the side of the southern low-level sluice adjoining the central line of the embankment being, however, faced throughout with stone slabs. All the brickwork was laid in excellent mortar made with lime burnt from coral. With reference to this tank, Parker says :—" Since about the middle of last century, open wells, called 'valve-towers' when they stand clear of the embankment, and 'valve-pits' when they are in it, have been built at numerous reservoirs in Europe. Their duty is to hold the valves, and the lifting-gear for working them, by means of which the outward flow of the water is regulated or totally stopped. Such also was the function of the bisôkotuwa of the Sinhalese engineers; they were the first inventors of the valve-pit, more than 2,100 years ago."

Parker's Ancient Ceylon, p. 395.

The Yoda-kandiya tank was also constructed by this king. It is formed in a very shallow valley on the western side of the Kirinde Oya. Its embankment is 2 1/6 miles long, the top of which is from 15 to 20 feet broad. Its area was 1,407 acres. Its capacity was 380 million cubic feet. It is at present overgrown with jungle.

From what has been said it will be seen that King Duttu Gamunu in no slight degree contributed to the political, moral, and material advancement of Ceylon; his energy, bravery, and perseverance restored to the Island its old royal dynasty, and by the expulsion of the Indians removed also a source of oppression.

During the latter part of his reign the embellishment of Anuradhapura, the erection of temples, &c., must have instilled a taste for the arts and humanised the character of the people.

Duttu Gamunu died in the year 137 B.C. after having reigned twenty-four years, during which time the nation enjoyed great prosperity.

King Duttu Gamunu had a well educated and pious son, Sali by name. Unfortunately for the country he fell a victim to the charms of Asokamala, a maiden of the scavenger caste, and married her, thereby disqualifying himself for the throne occupied by the Mahawansa, (the great solar dynasty). **Saddha Tissa**, on the death of his brother Duttu Gamunu, found himself without a rival, and in the tranquil possession of a peaceful and well-ordered government. He had hitherto been occupied in furthering the agricultural development of the country. The first work that engaged his attention after he ascended the throne was the erection of a pinnacle of glass at the top of the Ruwanwelisaye and the plastering of the dagoba in accordance with the wishes of his brother. The making of the pinnacle with glass seems to indicate that the Sinhalese, so early as 137 B.C., had some idea of the electrical nature of lightning and a belief in the possibility of protecting their buildings by means of conductors.

Sadda Tissa, 137-119 B.C.

Dipawanse.

During this reign the brazen palace caught fire from a lamp and was burnt down. Saddha Tissa had it rebuilt. The new building cost less than one-third the amount spent on the original by Duttu Gamunu, and was only seven stories high.

Viharas, each at a distance of one yogana from the other, were built by this king as far as Dhigawapi (Dhiga-wewa in the Batticaloa District), at which place he built a vihara bearing the name of the town, together with a dagoba, which latter he covered with a golden net-work resplendent with divers gems suspending on the seams thereof, exquisite flowers made of gold. The Mulgerigal Vihara in the Matara District was also built by him. Agriculture, for which the king had developed a particular taste, received its due share of attention, inasmuch as eighteen tanks were formed in various parts of the country during this reign, chief of them being the Diga-wewa in the Batticaloa District. *Rajaratnacaria, p. 41.*

Parker says that the Duratissa tank, now known as the Yoda-wewa, was constructed either by this king or one before him. Its embankment is two-thirds of a mile long, about 14 feet high. The depth of water retained by it was 9 feet, at which level the area was 1,230 acres and the capacity 336 million cubic feet. The top of the bank was 15 feet wide, and was doubtless used as a cart road. The reservoir received its water supply partly from some short streams that flowed down from adjoining rocky hills, one being about 4 miles and another about 6 miles in length, but its chief and unfailing source of supply was from the flood-escape of Tissa-wewa, over which the water brought down from the Kirinda Oya flowed into Yoda-wewa. This tank has been restored by the British and is doing good work for the villagers. *Parker's Ancient Ceylon, pp. 393-394.*

Saddha Tissa died at Anuradhapura in B.C. 119, leaving four sons.

Thullathanaka (Thulna), the second son, having been at Anuradhapura at the time of his father's death, unhesitatingly had himself elected king by the officers of State, with the approval of the priesthood convened for the purpose at the Thuparama Vihara. Lajjatissa, the eldest son, on hearing of this proceeding, hastened to the capital from Digawapi, and putting Thullathanaka to death assumed possession of his rightful sovereignty. Thullathanaka's reign was of forty days' duration. He was a pious man, though ambitious. He built a vihara called Kandara, and had come *Thullathanaka, 119 B.C.*

to Anuradhapura to present it to the priesthood when his father died, and he was seized with a desire for the throne. It is said that he was stabbed to death by his brother while superintending, in person, the erection of a dagoba in the capital.

Rajawalia, p. 223.

Lajjatissa, 119-110 B.C.

Lajjatissa showed the utmost contempt for the priesthood during the first three years of his reign saying: "They cared not even for the order of seniority;" at length, thinking it politic to turn his attention to religious works, he relaxed the rigour of his treatment of the priesthood and spent the remaining six years and eight months of his reign mainly in ornamenting and extending the existing edifices. The ground between Ruwanwelisaye and Thuparama was levelled with the expenditure of a lac of money on it. He encased the Thuparama and Chetiyagiri dagobas in stone. He built a minor dagoba called Sita Thupa, several viharas, and a hall called Rajjatissa hall for the accommodation of the priesthood in front of the Thuparama. He devoted special attention to the priestesses, providing them with rice and other requisites. Itinerant priests were provided with medicinal drugs.

Kalunna, 110-104 B.C.

Kalunna (or Kallatanaga), the third son of Saddatissa, succeeded Lajjatissa and spent the six years of his reign in embellishing the brazen palace by the construction of thirty-two edifices around it, and in constructing other minor religious edifices of his own. He was murdered by his minister Maharattaka at the capital in 104 B.C.

Walagambahu, 104 B.C.

Wattagaminiabaya (Walagambahu I.), the fourth son of Saddatissa, immediately putting the perfidious minister to death assumed the sovereignty. He adopted Mahachula, the son of his predecessor in office, as his son and raised the latter's mother Anula to the dignity of queen-consort. His reign was by no means a peaceful one. Five months after the king's accession, instigated by a prediction that on him should one day devolve the duties of sovereignty, a Brahmin youth from Rohana took up arms against the king, while an army of 7,000 Indians, led by seven chieftains, having landed at Mahatitha, were demanding the surrender of the sovereignty prior to an advance upon the capital. By a politic recognition of the pretended rights of the Rohana chief the king induced him to divert the force

Rajawalia, p. 223.

intended for his own destruction against the common enemy, while he himself, in the character of a spectator, was anxiously preparing to attack the victor, weakened, as he would necessarily be, by the previous contest. He had not long to wait, the raw levies of the Rohana pretender were no match for the disciplined force of Indians. The pretender himself was taken prisoner. However much King Walagambahu might have been adapted for intrigue, he possessed no virtues of a military character. In an encounter near the capital he met with a decided repulse and was compelled to flee with the pregnant Queen Anula, Mahachula, his own natural child Mahanaga, and his (second) Queen Somadewi. As he was being closely pursued by the enemy, and as there was a possibility of his chariot being overtaken, Somadewi volunteered to get out of the chariot rather than allow her husband to be captured on account of her weight impeding the speed of the horses. Her offer was availed of by the ungallant king, who, as a token of his recognition of her noble self-sacrifice, bestowed on her his beautiful crest gem prior to parting from her. He wandered in the forests, moving from cave to cave, until he was introduced by the priest Mahatissa, who found him in the region round Adam's Peak (called the Malaya country), to Tanasiva, the chief of that district, who provided Walagambahu and his party with a refuge in his house, and ministered unto him for fourteen years, at the end of which a quarrel having taken place betwhen the queen-consort and the wife of Tanasiva, in which their husbands joined on behalf of their respective wives, Walagambahu shot Tanasiva and, proclaiming himself to be the Maharaja, rallied the population round him. He found himself at the head of the eight officers of rank (Kapisisa, Uttiya, Mulawa, Mula, Solli, Pabbata, Tissa and another), reputed to be great warriors, and a formidable army. He next proceeded to celebrate a festival of offerings unto Buddha at Acchagalla Vihara, and with the assistance of the priesthood raised additional forces wherewith to wage a religious war against the infidels who had usurped the throne of Lanka. Meanwhile the seven Indian chiefs with their army had plundered Anuradhapura of everything profitable. Two of the chiefs had quickly recrossed the ocean, one with Queen Somadewi, who had been discovered concealing herself in the Kadambapuppha forest, as his trophy; the other with Buddha's refection dish, which Walagambahu in his hurried exit from the city had left behind. The chief **Pulahattha** reigned supreme for three years, and was murdered by the chief Bahiya, whom he had appointed as his minister. **Bahiya** reigned for two years with the chief Panayamara as his prime minister. He met the same fate at the hands of his minister as he had meted out to his king when he was minister.

Pulahattha, 103-100 B.C.

Bahiya, 100-98 B.C.

Panayamara, 98-91 B.C.

Panayamara reigned for seven years and was murdered by the chief Pilayamara, who had acted as his minister.

Pilayamara, 91 B.C.

Pilayamara enjoyed the sovereignty for the short period of seven months, when he in turn was murdered by the chief Dathiya, whom he had for his minister.

Dathiya, 90-88 B.C.

Dathiya reigned two years at the capital, when he was defeated and slain by Walagambahu I., whose sovereignty over Lanka had been in abeyance for fourteen years.

As Walagambahu after his defeat was fleeing through the city gate situated by Tittharama—an edifice built during the reign of Pandukabhaya and assigned as a residence to people of foreign religions ; he had been reviled by a Nigantha (one of a sect of Hindu anchorites), by the name of Giri, who shouted at him "The great black Sinhalaya is flying."

Walagambahu I., 88-76 B.C.

One of the first acts of **Walagambahu** after regaining the sovereignty was to demolish the Tittharama and to build on the site thereof a vihara with twelve pirivenas (schools) in unbroken ranges, and a dagoba, the most stupendous of its kind in Ceylon, attached to it. By reason of the arama having belonged to Giri (the Nigantha), and by reason of the vihara having been made on that site by the King Abaya (Wattugamini Abaya), it was called Abayagiri Vihara. This vihara Walagambahu conferred on the priest Mahatissa as a token of gratitude for having befriended him during his adversity.

The dagoba was originally 405 feet high, its dome was hemispherical, and described with a radius of 180 feet, giving a circumference of 1,130 feet. Its summit was therefore fifty feet higher than St. Paul's Cathedral. The diameter at the base of the belt is about 325 feet and at the outer circle or basement 357 feet. The area of the platform on which it stands is about eight acres, and the total area enclosed by the outer boundary wall about 11 acres.

Mr. H. C. P. Bell, the Archæological Commissioner, has by recent researches identified the pansala of the Abayagiri fraternity. In the course of his report he says that the building had a frontage of hundred feet with a depth of fifty-two feet four inches, and at the back a bay forty-three feet three inches by twenty-five feet three inches. A verandah, six feet wide, ran round the building inside and cut the interior space into four rooms ....The outer wall was strengthened by sixty-four pillars, probably bricked up ; those of the inner rooms by twenty-two. The main entrances were eleven feet wide ....The proximity of the pillars and their bulk most certainly prove that the building was storeyed, probably more than once.

Five of the warrior chiefs built viharas and presented them to the renowned priest Mahatissa, who in due form established priests at all of them ; and they were maintained by the chiefs. To celebrate the recovery of Somadewi, the king constructed a huge dagoba, the Suwanaramaya (Somarama), 313 feet in height.

The king next turned his attention to embellishing the five caves at Dambulla, in which he took refuge during his flight from Anuradhapura, and making temples of them. The most important of them are: (1) The Dewa-raja-Vihara (the temple of the great god). Its stone doorway is decorated with a "Makara Torana." Its interior is very dark, so that the eye has to become accustomed to the gloom before it discerns the glory of the shrine—the gigantic recumbent figure of Buddha, which, together with the pillow and couch on which it rests, is cut out of the solid rock, and measures forty-seven feet in length. The head rests on the right-hand and that on the pillow, on which is apparent the impression supposed to be made by the head and the arm. The soles of the feet are ornamented with lotus flowers (magul-lakuna). (2) The Maha Vihara, by far the finest and largest of the five measuring one hundred and sixty feet by fifty, its height at the entrance being twenty-three feet, the roof sloping downwards towards the back of the cave, where it is only four feet high. As the doors are opened the coolness, the gloom, the circle of sedent Buddhas dimly visible, and the deathlike stillness combine

Circa, 80 B.C.

to produce a feeling of reverence in the true believer. There are in it fifty-three statues, most of which are life-size. On the centre of the roof is a painting of Buddha in glory, worshipped by gods; to the left is painted Buddha being assaulted by the powers of evil. On the left of the entrance is a dagoba surrounded by sedent Buddhas, some of which have a canopy formed by the hooded cobra. Past the dagoba to the left there is a large statue of the King Walagambahu, facing it on the roof are depicted Buddha's wars with demons. The story of his life and the worship paid him by various divinities. Opposite to the king is an upright figure of Buddha and canopy, both cut from the solid rock. At the back of the line of statues that face the entrance are painted three Hindu deities, Ganesha, Kataragama, and Wibhishana, a long procession of Rahat priests, a painting of King Duttu Gamunu and his relations, and the great combat between Duttu Gamunu and Ellala. At the eastern extremity of the cave there is a small recess covered with historical paintings, the landing of Vijeya, the planting of the Bo-tree at Anuradhapura, the dedication of the relics to the Ruwanweli dagoba, and of the Island to Buddha figured by a king guiding an elephant plough.

During this reign considerable dissensions arose among the priests at the capital, as a result of the expulsion of the renowned priest Mahatissa, by his
Mahawansa, fraternity, from the Maha Vihara, for the offence of
ch. xxxiii., having unduly associated himself with lay families,
p. 132. leading to the establishment of three separate fraternities.

The reign of King Walagambahu formed a new era in the history of Buddhism, inasmuch as during this reign, by order of the king and his adigar, five hundred learned priests from all parts of the country assembled at the Alu Vihara—then a cave situated amid a jungle of gigantic boulders near Matale—and there committed to writing in Pali as best as they could the Banapotha (or Buddhist scripture), the Pitakattaya (exhortations of
Tennent, Buddha) consisting of 592,000 stanzas, and the Attha-
vol. I., p. 515. katha (commentaries), all of which form the esoteric system of Buddhist doctrines, simple, pure, and religious, and greatly at variance with the external rites and ceremonies superimposed thereon, which are called the exoteric system, and are meant to appeal to the imagination of the uneducated masses who are unable to appreciate the pure doctrines.

Hitherto the doctrines of Buddha had been orally transmitted from one generation to another, and it was the fear of interpolation, admixture, and corruption that led to the convocation of priests.

The most popular portion of the Pittakas are the tales which profess to have been related by Gautama Buddha himself in his sutras or discourses, and were collected under the title of Pansiya Panas Jataka-potha, or the five hundred and fifty births. The series is designed to commemorate events in his own career during the states of existence through which he passed preparatory to his reception of the Buddhahood. In structure and contents it bears a striking resemblance to the Jewish Talmud, combining with aphorisms and maxims, philological explanations of the divine text, stories illustrative of its doctrines, into which, not only saints and heroes, but also animals and inanimate objects are introduced, and not a few of the fables that pass as Æsop's are to be found in the Jatakas of Ceylon.

Parker's Ancient Ceylon, pp. 400-405.

During this reign was constructed the tank which is now known as Nuwara-wewa, situated on the east side of the Kadamba river (the Malwatu Oya), ½ mile from the present town of Anuradhapura. Its embankment is 3 miles long, 37 feet high, and from 12 to 16 feet wide at the top. The main bank has never given way except at one insignificant spot, where it has been probably cut by the Indian invaders. It has two sluices. The size of the bricks used in constructing them indicates that it was built during the same period as the Abhayagiri dagoba. It had a flood-escape 136 feet wide.

Of this tank Parker says:—"With a depth of 17 feet the area was 2,160 acres, at six feet higher, the level now adopted, which appears to have been nearly the former higher level, it became 3,180 acres according to my tracing of the contours. The capacity then was about 1,500 cubic feet. Immediately after the reservoir was made, the flow off the catchment area must have failed to fill it year after year, and an additional supply of water was discovered to be necessary. This was obtained by taking levels (as we may assume) up the adjoining Malwatu Oya, until a point was reached sufficiently high to permit water to be diverted from it into the reservoir. Above this spot a ridge of rocky ground approached close to the river, and indicated the most suitable place for the dam which was required. At this site, therefore, a strong masonry dam of wedged and more or less cut stones was built across the river.

"Nearly all the stones were removed in 1873 for use in a road-bridge that was erected over the river. The remains show that the dam was at least 33 feet wide and nearly 160 feet long; it was well and solidly built. It rose about 8 feet high above the bed of the river. At the north end, an abutment 10½ feet high, of rough stones, laid in four courses, protected the end of the bank of the channel that was cut for conveying the water to Nuwara-wewa.

"From this point a channel about 40 feet wide, capable of passing a depth of four feet of water, was opened till it met with a small stream that flowed into the reservoir, at 5½ miles from the dam. The bed of the channel had a gradient of about one foot in 5,000 feet—a slope adopted in several later instances.

"At 150 feet from the dam an escape for floods was provided at a rocky site, in order to pass out surplus water when it entered the channel. This was 44 feet wide, and over it a bridge 12½ feet wide was constructed, supported by two pairs of wooden pillars, for which socket-holes were cut in the rock. The ends of the bank at each side were protected by boulders.

"At 6 miles, a bridge 154 feet long crossed the stream down which the water flowed. It was carried on three lines of stone posts, fixed in rows of three, which were 6 or 7 feet apart. Over each set of three posts a stone beam about 12 inches square cut 10 feet long was placed; on these longitidunal wooden beams must have been laid for carrying the planking of the bridge.

"The bricks found at the dam are a proof of its age. They are 9·05 inches broad and 3·25 inches thick; Bt. is 30·9, and the length 18 or 19 inches. It is evident that they belong to the period when the larger types of bricks were burnt, that is, that they must belong to the early part of the first century B.C., since they cannot be of earlier date than Nuwara-wewa."

Walagambahu died in the year 76 B.C., twelve years after he had regained the throne. The state of Ceylon during this period of its history, judging from the devotion paid to architectural embellishments and other improvements, must have been very prosperous.

Maha Chula (Mahadailitissa), nephew as well as adopted son of Walagambahu, succeeded him. A certain degree of originality characterised his gifts to the priesthood. Having heard that it was an act of great merit to confer an alms-offering earned by the donor's personal exertion, in the very first year of his reign, he bestowed an offering on a priest in the shape of his earnings as a result of reaping, *incognito*, a crop of hill paddy. *Maha Chula, 76-62 B.C.*

Subsequently he spent three years working in a sugar factory in the Seven Korales (where fifteen centuries later a Dutch Governor made an attempt to restore the cultivation of sugar), and presented the sugar, which he obtained as the hire of his labour, to the priesthood at Anuradhapura. As it was a matter of doubt whether the priesthood would continue to be pleased if his offerings to them were to be limited to his personal earnings, the king decided to follow the procedure of his predecessors and bestowed presents on them lavishly. He is said to have bestowed during his reign sacerdotal robes (consisting of three garments for each) on ninety thousand priests and twelve thousand priestesses. *Tennent, vol. I., p. 455.* *Mahawansa, ch. xxxiv., p. 133.*

During this reign the internal tranquillity of the country was constantly disturbed by the depredations and incursions of Naga (Coranaga), the natural son of Walagambahu I., and his band of robbers.

Maha Chula died in 62 B.C. after having reigned for fourteen years.

Chora Naga succeeded his cousin and gave the priesthood in general, and in particular the priests at the eighteen pansalas that refused to give him an asylum during his marauding career, whom he expelled from their abodes, which in turn he razed to the ground—a very bad time of it for twelve years. The Sinhalese historian priests wreak upon his memory the vengeance they were powerless to accomplish during his life-time. The depths of a lower hell (Lohantarika) than is reserved for ordinary mortals wherein he will for ever remain, they say, was reserved for him. *Chora Naga, 62-50 B.C.* *Mahawansa, p. 133.*

Lanka is said to have been visited by a famine in this reign.

Chora Naga was murdered after a reign of twelve years by one of his subjects. *Rajaratnacara, p. 44.*

Kudatissa, 50-47 B.C.

Kudatissa, son of Maha Chula, succeeded him, but was poisoned after an uneventful reign of three years by his Queen Anula, who was a licentious woman, and had developed a passion for Siva, the senior gate porter at the king's palace.

Anula, 47-41 B.C.

Anula next ascended the throne as the first Queen of Lanka and associated Siva with her rule over the Island for one year and two months, at the end of which period, growing tired of Siva, she poisoned him and caused Vatuka, an Indian carpenter of the town, to take his place in respect of her. Vatuka met with a similar fate to that of his predecessor after a period of one year and two months. His place was filled by Tissa, a firewood carrier serving in the palace. He was associated with her rule over Lanka for the space of one year and one month, during which period there was constructed a reservoir in the park (Mahamega garden) at the capital. Tissa, too, was poisoned in order that the queen may have in his place the Adigar, a Brahman by the name of Neeliya, who in turn was poisoned after a period of six months. Four months after the murder of Neeliya, during which period the queen governed the country unassisted and continued to live an infamous life, she was burnt alive by Kalakannie Tissa (Makalan Tissa), second son of Maha Chula, who had found that the whole people of Lanka were prepared to join him in ridding the country of such an ignominious sovereign.

Mahawansa, ch. xxxiv., p. 134.

Kalakannie Tissa, 41-19 B.C.

Kalakannie Tissa reigned for twenty years. He built a great Uposathasala—a hall attached to a vihara built on a specially consecrated spot and devoted to the use solely of priests of the higher order (Upasampada)—on Mihintale and constructed a dagoba (Ambastalla dagoba) in front of it, which is still to be seen at the top of the third flight of steps that lead to the top of the mountain. It is built of stone instead of brick, the terrace round it being circled with octagonal pillars, the capitals of which are ornamented with figures of the sacred goose. He also planted a Bo-tree on the same mountain. A great canal called Vannakanna, as well as two great tanks named Amadugga and Bhayoluppa, were constructed during this reign, so that agriculture received its due share of attention. For the better defence of the capital, the king had a wall seven cubits high ($10\frac{1}{2}$ feet) built and a ditch dug round the capital, enclosing an area of two hundred and forty-four square miles, the terrace of the wall are still to be seen near Aliaparte, a place seven miles from Anuradhapura, confirming the account given as to the extent of the wall, Mihintale being about the east face.

Kalakanni Tissa would not reside in the palace in which his predecessors had taken up their abode, as he considered it to have been polluted by the burning of Anula therein. He had a new palace constructed, not far from the old one, and resided there. Being an æsthete Kalakanni Tissa formed the Padumassara park within the capital. He also had a convent named Dantageha built close to his palace for his mother, who had become a nun.

Bathikabeya (Bhattika Raja), son of Kalakanni Tissa, next ascended the throne. He too was an æsthete, but carried it to the extreme of childishness, giving effect to all his fancies regardless of cost. Remitting the taxes due to himself he caused the country round Anuradhapura, within a space of one yojana (rather less than eight miles), to be planted with the small and large jessamine plants. He devoted a good deal of his time to the acquirement of sacred learning, and bestowed gifts, consisting of oil, beverage, and cloths, on the priesthood, especially those of them (1,000 in number) resident at Mihintale. He dedicated villages, fields, and gardens to various temples, especially to the Ruwanweli, for the purpose of keeping them in repair with the income thereof. He built an "Uposatha" hall at the Thuparama dagoba, repaired the Brazen Palace, and also constructed two basement cornice-ledges at the Ruwanweli dagoba (Mahathupa). He also built four temples.

Bathikabeya, 19 B.C.—9 A.C.

Rhys David's, sect. 28, p. 16.

Rajaratnacara, p. 51.

The rites and ceremonies observed by this king at the Ruwanweli dagoba, for which he had a special veneration, being the only person recorded in history as having been permitted by the priests to enter the subterranean chamber beneath it and behold the glorious treasurers hidden within, are extremely interesting. On one occasion, in the fervour of his devotion, he is said to have buried the dagoba from the step at its enclosure to the top of the pinnacle, by heaping the space up with flowers, and then by raising the water of the Abaya tank (Tissa-wewa) by means of machinery, celebrated a festival of water offering by pouring the water on the flowers thus heaped up. Many other, but more costly, ceremonies were observed at this dagoba by this king, for which the reader is referred to *Mahawansa* xxxiv. and *Rajaratnacara*, pp. 48-51. The use of machinery wherewith to raise water 120 cubits high is interesting, as it shows that the Sinhalese over two thousand years ago had hydraulic machines of great power. He died after a reign of twenty-eight years.

Dathika, 9-21 A.C.

Mahadithaka Mahanaga (Maha Dalia Mana or Dathika) succeeded his brother Batikaraja. He was no less devoted to religion and a slave to the priesthood than his brother. He made offerings of preaching pulpits to all the viharas in the Island. He built a dagoba called Sigiriya (Cetiyapabatta) on the summit of Mihintale, reached by 1,840 stone steps partly hewn out of the rock, but generally formed of slabs of granite fifteen feet wide. This dagoba (now known as Etwehera or Mahaseiya) enshrines a single hair from between Buddha's eyebrows. It is hundred feet high, made of brick, and commands a magnificent view. At the four entrances to it the king caused four artificial flower trees to be fixed resplendent with divers gems, the workmanship whereof was executed by the most skilful artificers in the land. Having enveloped the dagoba with a jewelled covering he caused balls of gold and festoons of flowers to be suspended thereon. In order that pilgrims might make their way to the above mentioned dagoba from the river (*i.e.*, one of the outlets from the Tissawewa) with unsoiled washed feet, he had a foot carpet spread for them all the way a distance of about more than seven miles, and alongside thereof choruses were kept up by dancers and musicians instrumental as well as vocal. Rows of shops were built alongside each of the streets and trade flourished. To celebrate the completion of this dagoba the king caused the whole Island and sea around it (causing dhonies or ships to be placed at a distance of one league from the shore) to be illuminated and alms to be lavishly given at the four gates of the city. On one occasion he presented six robes each to as many as 24,000 priests at eight different places in the country, simultaneously summoning them by the beat of eight golden drums. On another occasion, allowing his zeal for religion to get the better of his discretion, he ordered the release of all the imprisoned convicts. Barbers were stationed constantly at the four gates of the capital by orders of this king in order that his subjects

Mahawansa, p. 136.

Rajaratnacara, p. 52.

may have the convenience of being shaved free of charge. Three viharas were built by this king, one of them in Rohana. Gifts, both pudgalika (clothes, medicines, &c.) and sanghika (lands) were lavishly bestowed on the priesthood by this monarch, who died after a reign of twelve years, during which peace and prosperity prevailed.

Amanda Gamunu, 21-30 A.C.

Addagamunu or **Amanda Gamunu**, son of Dathika, reigned for eight years. He was remarkable only for his piety. He issued positive orders against killing any animal whatsoever, prohibited all people from committing sin, and enjoined them to do works of charity. He built a wall round the Ruwanweli dagoba and caused a chatta (in imitation of the white umbrella which is emblematic of royalty) to be fixed on the spire thereof. To serve the place of meat he had a great number of fruit trees and creepers planted throughout the country, and developed his favourite habit of filling the bowls of priests with melons (ámanda), which, when presenting, he called "melon-flesh."

Rajaratnacara, p. 52.

The *Rajatarángini*—a history of Kashmir—gives King Meghavahana of Kashmir, who visited Ceylon during this reign and was a guest of the King of Lanka, the credit of having induced the latter to forbid the slaughter of animals as the former had done in his own kingdom.

Dutt's Trans. bk. III., p. 37.

Such a king could not long hope to retain possession of a throne whose tenure depended on the possession of something in the shape of manly virtues. He was murdered by his brother Kanijanu Tissa.

Kanijanu Tissa, 30-33 A.C.

Kanijanu Tissa (**Kinihiridaila**) decided a controversy which for a long time had suspended the performance of religious ceremonies in the "Uposatha" hall of the Cetiya Giri Vihara (Mihintale), and forcibly seizing sixty wicked priests who were engaged in a conspiracy against him imprisoned them in the Kanira cave at Mihintale. He died after a reign of three years.

Culabhaya, 33-34 A.C.

Culabhaya, son of Amanda Gamini Abaya, ascended the throne and built a vihara on the banks of the river on the south of the capital. He died after a reign of one year.

Sivali, 34 A.C.

Sivali, sister of Culabhaya, reigned for four months, when she was deposed.

Elluna, 34-44 A.C.

Illa Naga (Elluna) in the first year of his reign visited the Tissa tank, when a great number of Lambakannas (who had accompanied him as attendants) left him behind and returned to the city. The king, missing his men, was wroth and, as a punishment, laid on them the task of trampling down heaps of earth by the side of the tank in preparation for a great thupa (dagoba) which he intended to build; and he set overseers of the Chandala (scavenger) caste over them. This act of indignity incensed them to such an extent that they rose in a body against the king, supported by the populace in general who held caste to be a sacred institution, and imprisoned him in his own palace, whence, with the assistance of his consort, he succeeded in escaping on his elephant to Mahatitha-Mantotte, a port on the North-Western coast. From here he fled to India in a boat. Three years later Illa Naga returned to Ceylon with an army, collected in the land of his sojourn over seas, and landed at Sakarasobba (a port not far from Hambantota). Having enlisted a large force from the district in addition to the force he had brought with him, and having secured his faithful elephant who had during his absence from the country been roaming in the forests, and having devoted some time to securing a hold of the affections of the people by means of repairing and enlarging the Naga Maha Vihara (Tissamaharama) to the extent of 600 feet,—of which all to be seen at the present day are a few squared upright pillars which formed part of the walls,—and the Tissa and Dura tanks, he finally found himself in a position to start out on his campaign against the Lambakannas. The latter, on hearing the news of Elluna's advance, made every preparation to meet him. A series of indecisive conflicts ensued, in the last of which the king's army was on the verge of defeat, when he, by boldly stepping out of the line and charging with fury on his elephant, changed the tide of victory. A fearful carnage followed, and it was not long before Elluna entered his capital in triumph with a host of captive Lambakannas bound in pairs. As he entered the garden of his palace elated at having recovered his kingdom, the recollection of the fact that the Lambakannas had been the destroyers of his former prosperity made him give the order to his officers to decapitate them; but yielding to the intercession of his mother on their behalf, he moderated his punishment of them to the extent of only having their noses and toes cut off. This was done with a view to preserving living examples of what would happen to those who might venture to follow in their footsteps.

The king showed his gratitude to his elephant by devoting the revenue of the whole province in which the animal had taken refuge, during his three years' absence from the country, towards his upkeep. Elluna died at Anuradhapura, the capital, six years after he had regained the throne.

Candamukha Siva (Sanda Muhuna) succeeded his father. He signalised his reign by constructing a tank and dedicating it to Isurumunni Vihara. It is said that his wife Damiladewi dedicated the profits accruing from the village Manikara to the same vihara, thereby raising the presumption that the Sinhalese, like the Persians, had the custom of appointing a particular town or towns as a specific part of a prince's revenue. We learn from Pliny (lib. vi., chap. 34) that four ambassadors, the principal of whom was an aratchi, were sent during this reign to the Emperor Claudius at Rome. From information conveyed by the ambassadors to the king we learn particulars as to the conditions which then prevailed in Ceylon, which we are unable to get from the *Mahawansa* :— *Sanda Muhuna, 44-52 A.C.*

There were at the time five hundred towns in Lanka, of which the chief was Anuradhapura (called Palaesimunda by Pliny), where the sovereign resided, with a population of 200,000 souls. Coral abounded in the Gulf of Mannar, where also existed tortoise-shell-coloured marble, pearls and precious stones. Vegetation was luxuriant. There was profusion of all kinds of fruits except the grape, the people had everything they required, the government was mild, and there was an absence of vexatious laws. The inhabitants were long-lived, a large percentage living longer than a hundred years. Commerce had been carried on with China overland by way of India and Tartary by the Sinhalese for ages past, long before ships had attempted the voyage by sea.

After a reign of eight years and seven months, Candamukha Siva was murdered by his younger brother Yasalaka Tissa at an aquatic festival held at the Tissa tank.

Yasalaka Tissa's (Yasa Silo's) reign of seven years and eight months was uneventful. He was a jovial youth lacking in the dignity that befits sovereignty. Decking his hall porter Subha, who greatly resembled *Yasalaka Tissa, 52-60 A.C.*

him, in his regal vestments and seating the porter on the throne, himself donning the heavy bonnet of the porter and standing at the palace gate with the porter's staff in hand, the king was in the habit of enjoying the fun of watching his ministers of State as they bowed low to him who occupied the throne. On one occasion, whilst this farce was being repeated, the porter who occupied the throne, pointing to the king, exclaimed: "How does that balatha (porter) dare to laugh in my presence," and succeeded in getting the king put to death and usurping the sovereignty.

Subha, 60-66 A.C. **Subha** reigned for six years under the title of Suba Raja. He constructed two viharas, each with a range of fine buildings attached to it, for the purpose of being used as pirivenas (schools). These were called Suba Raja pirivenas. There were four other viharas made by this king. The innate jealousy of Subha, which won him the throne, was also the cause of his death. A prediction by his predecessor on the throne to the effect that "a person by the name of Vasabha will become king" worked in his mind to such an extent that he issued orders to the dissawas of the various districts that all those who possessed that name should be brought to him to be executed. The nephew of the commander-in-chief of the forces in the North of Lanka happened to possess this name, and his sorrowful uncle, having consulted his wife Metha one night, decided to take the boy to the king the following day. Metha, having revolved a plan during the course of the night of rescuing the boy from his impending fate, handed the betel to be used by her husband (the minister) during his journey to the capital to the youth Vasabha who accompanied him, deliberately omitting the chunam. While well on his way, discovering that the chunam for his betel had been forgotten, he sent the lad back for it to his wife. The wife revealing the secret to Vasabha and providing him with funds enabled him to escape. At first Vasabha took refuge at the Maha Vihara, where the priests gave him shelter and clothed him. At a subsequent stage of his flight, encouraged by the words of a leper, who was also a fortune-teller, that he would some day attain sovereignty, he turned into a marauder, and having secured a following of a number of fearless enterprising men he made his way to Rohana,—the focus of every outbreak,—and there, in the course of ten years, secured a sufficiently powerful and organised force to start for the capital, carrying everything before him in the course of his march till he reached it. Here, after a stubborn engagement, in the course of which his uncle was slain, the king was put to death in his palace, where he had taken refuge. Thus, by a curious coincidence of circumstances were fulfilled the prophecies of both King Yasasila and the leper, viz., that Vasábha would ascend the throne of Lanka.

Tennent, vol. I., p. 113.

The allusion in this reign to the habit of chewing betel is interesting, inasmuch as it indicates the antiquity of the custom which still prevails almost universally amongst the Sinhalese people. This, like all customs, takes its origin in necessity. Being practically forbidden by the Buddhist religion to eat meat, the non-azotised elements which abound in every article the villager consumes, with the exception of the breadfruit, the jak and some varieties of bean, are likely to degenerate into flatulent and acrid products, but for the adoption of a simple prophylactic. No medical prescription could be more judiciously compounded to effect the desired object than betel, as it is customarily consumed (*i.e.*, accompanied by areca-nut, chunam and cloves)—a practical combination of antacid, the tonic, and the carminative.

Vasabha, 66-110 A.C.

One of the first acts of **Vasabha** (Wahapp) after ascending the throne was to raise his uncle's wife Metha to the dignity of queen-consort in recognition of the great services she had rendered him in saving his life. Partly in recognition of the services rendered to him by the priesthood when fleeing from place to place for his life, and partly with the idea of prolonging his reign for a longer period than twelve years (which was the limit fixed by a horoscopist when he had consulted), the king devoted a great deal of his attention to the construction of fresh religious edifices (*e.g.*, the Anura Vihara in Rohana, where he raised the greater part of his army, on which he bestowed eight thousand karisas—equals 32,000 acres extent of land,—the Mucela Vihara, on which he conferred half the water of the Alisara canal, a range of pirivenas (schools) at the Maha Vihara, which was the first place at which he sought shelter and was most hospitably treated, and to the repair of many dilapidated ones.

Numismata Orientalia, sect. 31.

Once in every three years King Vasabha is said to have conferred the three sacerdotal garments on all priests throughout the Island, at the four gates of Anuradhapura alms were constantly given to mendicants and medicinal drugs to priests afflicted with diseases

For the extension of cultivation the king constructed eleven tanks—the Mayetti, Rajuppala, Kolambágama, Mehanikavitti, two called Mahagama, Kehela, Kelivasa, Canbutthi, Vatamangana, Abhivaddhamana—in various parts of the country with twelve irrigation canals. He employed civil engineers and had a tunnel (ummaga) constructed for the purpose of supplying Anuradhapura with water, as, on account of the density of the population, the water within the town was not safe for human consumption.

Dipawansa, Tennent vol. I., p. 469.

With a view to further protecting the capital King Vasabha raised the rampart round it, which had hitherto been seven cubits high (constructed by Kalakannitissa in B.C .44), to eighteen cubits. His favourite pastime was the laying out of the park, where he had many ponds dug in which he kept swans. Vasabha died after a peaceful reign of forty-four years, leaving his son Wankaanasika in tranquil possession of the throne.

Wankaanasika, 110-113 A.C.

Wankaanasika (Waknais), during his father's reign, had married Mahamatta, the only daughter of Subha Raja, a maiden of great beauty, who had been brought up *incognito* in the humble home of a mason, to whose safe-keeping she had been entrusted by her father just before the sovereignty was wrested from him. Mahamatta's identity was later discovered by the production of the royal robe of her father and the ornaments suited to her rank, by the mason to whom they had been handed together with the child. Wankaanasika had a son by her named Gajabahu (= strong arm).

During this reign Ceylon was invaded successfully by a Tamil force from Tanjore led by their king in person. They landed in the north-west part of the Island, ravaged that part of the country, and penetrating to within sight of Anuradhapura retired with an immense quantity of plunder, and no less than 12,000 prisoners of war.

Gajabahu I., 113-125 A.C.

Wankaanasika died after a reign of three years, having built the Mahamangala Vihara in the neighbourhood of Anuradhapura. **Gajabahu I.** (Gamani) succeeded his father. He was a man of great personal valour, hence his name (Gaja = strong ; bahu = arm). One of the first acts of his reign was to build a vihara, in deference to the wishes of his mother, on a land purchased by her in a forest in the neighbourhood of the capital, at a spot where, when a maiden, an aged priest had prophesied she would be raised to the dignity of a queen, with funds supplied by her for the purpose, himself causing a stone dagoba to be erected there. The king next, with a view to ingratiating himself into the favour of his people, built a tank and bestowed the benefits of it on the Abhayagiri Vihara, and further ornamented the Mirisvetiya Vihara dedicating to it land pruchased at a hundred thousand pieces of money (massa). Gajabahu next proceeded to avenge the insult offered to the Sinhalese people by the Tamils during the reign of his father. He marched over Adam's Bridge with a large force under the command of Nela-Yodhaya, devastated the country, and threatened to raze the city of Tanjore to the level of the ground, unless the King of Tanjore consented to return the 12,000 Sinhalese, and in addition double that number of Tamils to be taken to Lanka as hostages. The request was complied with, and Gajabahu returned to Lanka bringing with him, besides the hostages and the Sinhalese who had been carried off, the refection dish of Buddha which had been carried away from Anuradhapura by one of the seven Tamil chiefs who had invaded the Island successfully in the reign of Walagambahu I., and various other valuables, *e.g.*, the foot ornaments of Patiny Dewy and the arms of the four gods which his forces had plundered.

Mahawansa, ch. xxxv., p. 142.

Rajawalia, pp. 229-232.

Ratnacara, pp. 57-58.

The annual perahera of the Maha Devala in Kandy still commemorates his victory. It is said that the tooth-relic which now heads the procession was not connected with it before the time of Kirti Sri. At this festival a high place has always been assigned to the goddess Patiny, whose "Halamba" or golden anklets Gajabahu had brought with him to Ceylon, and with it introduced her worship into the country. Bronze copies of the anklet are kept in Patiny Devalas, and an oath taken on them is particularly binding. The national game of "Ankeliya" established in her honour is still resorted to in times of sickness.

Coomaraswamy's Mediæval, Sinhalese Art, p. 6.

On his return the king restored to their ancient possessions all those who had been carried away captive and allowed the rest to reside in the country then called Cooroo Rata (*i.e.*, the country for taking elephants), since known as Alut Cooroo Corle, a little to the northward of Colombo. The inhabitants of this district to this day retain many marks of their continental origin. (Some of these families are said to have been placed in other provinces, and various places are said to derive their names from this circumstance, thus: Hewahetta is expressive of sixty, Toompane of one hundred and fifty, Haraseapattu of four hundred, Panceapattu of five hundred, and Matale of many—a multitude.) The last few years of Gajabahu's reign was devoted to the building of the Ramaka Vihara and the Maha Asana hall at Anuradhapura. He died A.D. 125 after a reign of twelve years.

Mahallaka Naga, 125-131 A.C.

Mahallaka Naga (Mahalumaana), father-in-law of Gajabahu, ascended the throne as an old man, hence his name—Mahallaka (= old), and devoted the six years of his reign as might well be expected to the erection of sacred edifices. Seven viharas did he build in various parts of the Island: the Pejalaka in the east, the Kotipabhata in the south, the Udakapásána in the west, the Salipabbata in the extreme north, the Tenavéli in a village called Bijagama, the Tobbalanagapabbata in the Rohana district, and the Girihálik in the interior country.

Bhatika Tissa, 131-155 A.C.

Bhatika Tissa (Batiya Tissa II.) succeeded his father to the throne of Lanka. He was a very kind-hearted man and had a profound respect for the priesthood of both sexes, which was shown by the great offerings bestowed on them. He built a wall round the Maha Vihara. He built two viharas and dedicated the Mahagama tank to one of them. He also constructed an "Uposatha" hall at the Thuparama and constructed the Ekavapi tank for the benefit of the inhabitants of the Vanni country. He had a peaceful and prosperous reign of twenty-four years.

Kanittha Tissa, 155-183 A.C.

Kanittha Tissa, younger brother of Bhatika Tissa, reigned over Lanka for twenty-eight years and devoted a good deal of his revenue to erecting pirivenas (schools) at the viharas in the capital and its neighbourhood. Pleased with a priest by the name of Mahanaga, the king constructed the Ratana-pasada for him at the Abhayagiri Vihara. Twelve spacious and magnificent square edifices were erected at the Maha Vihara. A portion of the wall built during the previous reign round the Maha Vihara was pulled down and a road leading from it to the Dakkina Vihara was constructed. A refection hall was erected within the Mahamega park; seven new viharas and "Uposatha" halls at three viharas—viz., Kelaniya, Mandalagiri and Dubbalavapitissa—were erected during this reign.

Chulanaga succeeded his father and had an uneventful reign of two years, when he was murdered by his younger brother Kudanaga. *Chulanaga, 183-185 A.C.*

Kudanaga reigned but one year, when his brother-in-law Sirinaga, whom he had as minister at the head of the military, raising a rebellion, marched on the capital, and having defeated the forces there which had remained faithful to their sovereign, himself assumed the sovereignty of the kingdom. The rebellion probably was rendered easy, as there was a famine in the country in A.D. 185, and the king had found himself able only to alleviate the condition of the priesthood in the city. *Kudanaga, 185-186 A.C.*

Siri Naga (Kuda Sirina) caused a beautiful gilt chatta to be fixed on the Ruwanweli dagoba in place of the one erected in A.D. 20 by King Amanda. He re-built the Lohapasada (Brazen Palace) five stories high and had a fresh flight of steps made at each of the four entrances to the enclosure round the sacred Bo-tree. He also released persons of good families in the Island from royal services and died after a reign of ninteen years. *Siri Naga, 186-205 A.C.*

Tissa (Vohoraka Tissa or **Waira Tissa),** son of Siri Naga I., commenced his reign by having two halls constructed at the two great viharas and two metallic images placed on the eastern side of the Bo-tree, and the chattas (parasols surmounting the spires) of the dagobas at the eight most important temples (except the Ruwanweli) repaired. One of the king's ministers, Mukanaga, had walls built round five viharas, including the Tissa Vihara, situated on a small island in the extreme north of Lanka. *Waira Tissa, 205-227 A.C.*

It appears to have been the practice during this reign for priests to read in public the recorded lives of great men on stated occasions and at fixed places, and the king spent no less than three hundred thousand pieces of money (massa) in maintaining such priests and relieving of their indebtedness those of them who were in debt. *Mahawansa, ch. xxxvi., p. 145.*

The most interesting event of this reign was an attempt made by a Brahman by the name of Wytulya, whilst posing as a Buddhist, to establish his own religion by putting an independent interpretation on points of the Buddhist religion.

Buddhism, although tolerant of heresy, has ever been vehement in its persecution of schism. Boldly confident in its own superiority, it bears without impatience the glaring errors of antagonists and seems to exult in the contiguity of competing systems as if deriving strength by comparison. To the assaults of open opponents the Buddhist displays the calmest indifference, convinced that in its undiminished strength his faith is firm and inexpugnable, his vigilance is only excited by the alarm of internal dissent. All his passions are aroused to stifle the symptoms of schism. Various kings of Ceylon had hitherto made State provision for maintaining offerings to demons, and built dwellings at the capital to accommodate the ministers of foreign religions, but when it came to an attempt to establish a new sect with new "Buddhist doctrines" (Wytulian), the king thought it his duty to use the resources of State for its suppression; accordingly, the minister Kapila, who was entrusted with the work, burnt all the books relating to the Wytulian system and degraded the priests who had embraced the new doctrines.

Rajaratnacara, p. 600.

Mahawansa, ch. xxxiv., p 144.

King Waira Tissa is said to have been thoroughly conversant with the principles of justice and equity, and to have abolished the practice of inflicting torture in the course of administering the law, which had been the recognised method up to that period in the country. Waira Tissa's domestic life was not free from troubles. His younger brother Abhaya having developed an affection for his queen, which was reciprocated by the latter, the king grew very indignant on its discovery, so much so that Abhaya sought a refuge on the adjoining continent accompanied by some of his faithful friends, leaving Subha Dewa, the queen's father, at the Royal Court, having entrusted to him the task of preparing the country for a revolution. As soon as Subha Dewa had notified Abhaya of the ripeness of the scheme, the latter hurried across the sea with a large force of Indians and marched straight on the capital; Wairatissa, on discovering the conspiracy, found no other course open to him but flight. This he did on horse back together with his wife, who was a good horsewoman, and for a time sought refuge in the mountainous country round Adam's Peak (Malaya country), but was ultimately deprived of his queen and murdered by Abhaya after he had ruled over Lanka for twenty-two years.

Abhaya Naga ruled over Lanka for eight years, during the course of which he built a stone ledge round the Bo-tree as well as a hall in the square of the Lohapasada (Brazen Palace), and is said to have spent no less than 200,000 massa in the purchase of robes for the priests of the country. *Abhaya Naga, 227-235 A.C.*

Sirinaga II., son of Wairatissa, reigned for two years, and in the course of it repaired the wall round the Bo-tree and built a magnificent hall, not far from the hall by the Bo-tree, called Hansewatta hall. *Sirinaga II., 235-237 A.C.*

Wijaya II. succeeded his father Sirinaga, but was murdered by three Lambakannas (people of a race who wear large ear ornaments). Sangatissa, Sanghabodi and Gothakabhaya, residents of Bintenne, who had been given high offices of State and established at his court by the king, who had taken a fancy for them, as they presented themselves to him at his court one day, having journeyed all the way from Bintenne for the purpose. *Wijaya II., 237-238 A.C.* *Mahawansa, p. 145.*

Sangha Tissa, by common consent amongst the three murderers, ascended the throne. He had been holding the office of commander-in-chief of the army during the previous reign. With a view to gaining popularity amongst his subjects, he caused the "chatta" fixed on the Ruwanweli dagoba by the King Sirinaga I. to be renovated, and set four gems, each of which cost a lac of massa (pieces of money), in the centre of the four emblems of the sun and placed an invaluable adamantine or diamond ring on the top of the thupa, to serve as a protection against lightning, and bestowed two sets of garments on each of forty thousand priests at a festival held in honour of this chatta. He also caused rice broth to be supplied to the priests daily at the four gates of the city. *Sangha Tissa, 238-242 A.C.* *Tennent, vol. I., p. 509.* *Mahawansa, p. 145.* *Rajaratnacara, p. 62.*

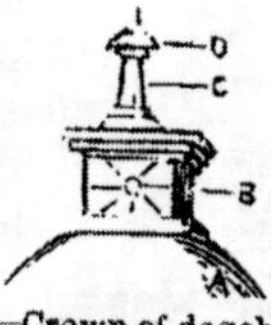

A=Crown of dagoba.
B=The capital with the sun on each of the four sides.
C=The spire.
D=The umbrella or chatta gilt and surrounded by "chumbatam," a diamond circlet.

He was poisoned by the inhabitants of the little island named Paenina, who had grown tired of his visits with the ladies of his palace and his ministers for the purpose of indulging in eating jambu fruit which they cultivated there. He reigned over Lanka for four years.

The Lambakanna, **Sanghabodi (Sirisanghabodi I.)**, who had held the office of commander-in-chief during the previous reign, was installed king on the recommendation of the minister Abhaya. In this reign *Siri Sanghabo I., 242-244 A.C.*

a great famine, with its seldom failing attendant pestilence, thinned the population of Lanka. This dire misfortune was attributed to the working of a demon with red eyes, Dala Raksa, to mollify whose wrath the king caused bali (rice, etc.) to be offered to him at the entrance of every village. By a strange coincidence it had the desired effect. The practice of devil-dancing which prevails at the present day is said to trace its origin to the ceremonies that were performed during this reign to appease the evil spirits.

Siri Sanghabo was a rigid devotee and had taken the vows of the order Atta Sil, the ordinances of which, along with observance of many rules of devotion and self-denial, prohibited the destruction of animal life. Crimes of the greatest enormity committed with impunity rapidly increased in all parts of the kingdom. After malefactors had been tried, convicted, and brought to the prison of the capital, as the king's vows prohibited their execution, they were secretly released at night with an admonition against such practices in hopes of their reformation ; and in order to satisfy the righteous indignation of his people as against such malefactors, the corpses furnished by the usual casualties of a populous city were exhibited at the place of execution, on impaling poles and gibbets as the victims of the violated law. A government administered by such a monarch soon led to anarchy. In the midst of such anarchy Gothakabhaya, the Lambakanna, who held the office of State Treasurer, deciding to wrest the sovereignty from Siri Sangbaho marched on the capital. Siri Sangbaho, as might be expected, refusing to be the cause of the death of others by fighting for his throne, fled unattended from Anuradhapura, taking with him a perankada (water strainer) used by devotees to prevent the destruction of animalculæ, which they would otherwise swallow in drinking unstrained water.

Rajaratnacara, p. 93.

Gothabhaya, 244-257 A.C.

Gothabhaya (Meghavannabhaya or **Goluamba)** not satisfied with the permanence of his power, so long as a holy man such as Siri Sanghabo was alive, caused proclamation to be made throughout the whole of his dominions by beat of tom-tom, that whosoever will bring the head of Siri Sanghabo should receive a great reward. Many heads were presented, but not one was acknowledged as genuine. A very poor man, who knew the place of Siri Sanghabo's concealment, started out, at the instigation of his wife, tempted by the promised reward, with the intention of murdering him. In the Siyane Korale he met with Siri Sanghabo, and ignorant of his identity entered into conversation with him as he walked along, and when questioned freely confessed the nature of his mission. On reaching Attanagalla (the place of Siri Sanghabo's residence) they stopped, and the poor man insisted on Siri Sanghabo sharing his meal consisting of rice and haal-massas (a small variety of fish) which he had been carrying with him. Siri Sanghabo is said to have taken a handful of it and thrown it down saying: "If I am destined to become Buddha, this rice will immediately spring up," and it is said to have instantly vegetated and continued to reproduce its species season after season, and year after year, and even at the present day the visitor to the Attanagalla Vihara is shown the plants alleged to be descended from the original handful of rice cast there by Siri Sanghabo. After having partaken of the repast, Siri Sanghabo is said to have disclosed his identity to this poor man and said to him "Do what you intended—carry my head to my brother; and should he be incredulous, as he probably will be, many attempts having been made to deceive him, put my head on a white cloth, on a chair, and it will answer for itself;" as the poor man had now repented and refused for all the riches in the world to be guilty of the deed he had originally contemplated, Siri Sanghabo is said to have laid hold of his own head and said, "If I am to become Buddha let my head separate from my body, and it is said to have come off, and his body is said not to have lost its life and powers till the hands had given the head to the poor man, who carried it to Anuradhapura, where, in accordance with the directions he had received, he requested that it might be put on a white cloth on a chair, whereupon the lips are said to have opened and cried aloud three times: "I am the King Siri Sanghabo." This miracle is said to have been taken by King Gothabhaya as conclusive proof of Siri Sanghabo's identity, and the poor man returned to his wife a rich one.

Rajawalia.

Attanagalu-wansa.

King Gothabhaya next devoted his attention to appeasing the priesthood, as they possessed immense influence over the masses, and it was necessary for the security of this throne that he should possess their good-will. He constructed nine viharas, one of which was

Rajaratnacara, pp. 64-67.

built upon the rock Attanagalla, the place of Siri Sanghabo's hermitage, the house was five stories high and fenced round about. Many fields and villages were dedicated to it and 1,000 servants were appointed to attend to it. At the bottom of the said rock the king caused to be erected several hundred small lodging places and accommodated the same with large halls and agreeable walks, he also made places for lodging in at night, for staying in by day, and places of preaching and performing the exercises of religion, and enclosed the same with a wall. He rearranged the pillars at the Brazen Palace (Lohapasada) with a view to reconstructing it. He constructed a fine hall of stones and a square for peripatetic meditation at the Maha Vihara. He added a stone ledge or cornice to the parapet wall round the great Bo-tree, a porch at the northern entrance, altars at the southern entrance, and placed hexagonal stone pillars at the four corners. Also three stone images of Buddha were placed at the three entrances. Many religious edifices erected by his predecessors were repaired, and on one occasion sacerdotal garments were bestowed on 30,000 priests. He formed a park with a hall at its gate, where numerous priests were daily served with rice broth, confectionery, all sorts of sweet things and robes.

During this reign Wytulian heresy again reared its head, acting on the advice of five high-priests summoned for the purpose from the greatest temples in the country; the king had sixty priests of the fraternity at the Abhayagiriya temple, who had adopted the Wytulian tenets, seized, excommunicated and banished to the opposite coast. Their books were burnt to ashes.

A priest named Sanghamitta from Chola—a country on the south-east of India—having succeeded in winning the confidence and admiration of the king, as the result of a discussion between him and the priest of the Sanghapala pirivena in the presence of numerous other priests assembled at the Thuparama, was entrusted with the education of the king's two sons Jetthatissa and Mahasena. Mahasena, the younger, being the brighter of the two princes, special attention was paid to his education by the tutor, so much so that Jetthatissa, the elder of the princes, developed an intense hatred for him and his teachings, which were later on proved to be Wytulian in character.

Jetthatissa succeeded to the throne on the death of his father, after a reign of thirteen years. Gothabhaya had never been much loved by his ministers, and some of them showed a reluctance to attend to his funeral obsequies. When, finally, they arrived, King Jetthatissa caused them, eight in number, to be impaled on poles around his father's funeral pile. Having witnessed this act of ferocity Sanghamitta thought it wise to flee from the country ere he met with a like fate. Accordingly he did so, but continued a correspondence with his favourite pupil Mahasena in the hope of keeping alive in the latter's mind the Wytulian doctrines that he —Sanghamitta—had carefully instilled into it, and finally introducing them throughout the country when Mahasena became king.

Jettha-tissa I., 257-269 A.C.

Rajawalia, p. 236.

Jetthatissa devoted a good deal of his attention to the agricultural development of the country, inasmuch as he caused six tanks to be constructed, one of which was at the village called Elugama and another at Alambagama. The construction and repair of religious edifices were not neglected during this reign. The Brazen Palace, the construction of which had been left unfinished by his father, was built seven stories high at a cost of 10,000,000 (koti) massa. He built a hall named Mani Hall, three portal arches at the great Bo-tree, and a vihara at the Pannatissa mountain.

Rajaratna-cara, p. 67.

Mahawansa, ch. xxxvii., p. 149.

Rajawalia, p. 237.

Mahasena succeeded to the throne on the death of his brother Jetthatissa after a reign of twelve years. One of his first acts was to recall his tutor and the sixty priests who had been expelled from the country during the previous reign. On the advice of Sanghamitta he determined that the new sect should change places with the establishment, and forbade the bestowal of offerings on the recusant priests, its adherents, a penalty of one hundred massa being prescribed for those who violated this order. Thus, deprived of sustenance, the Maha Vihara fraternity, in great distress, took their departure for the orthodox province of Rohana, where they remained for a period of nine years. Enraged at their obstinate adherence to the old religion, the king went so far as to order the demolition of their houses and temples. The Brazen Palace, together with 374 temples, was razed to the ground, and their sites ploughed up and sown with grain, and their materials were used, on the advice of the minister Sona, for the purpose of erecting edifices at the Abhayagiri Vihara, where the new sect established themselves and flourished for a time.

Mahasena, 269-296 A.C.

Rajaratna-cara, p. 67.

The minister named Megavannabhaya, profoundly versed in all affairs of State, who had enjoyed the confidence of the king, being averse to the change in the religion, determined on an appeal to arms in its defence. With this view he betook himself, with a small band, to the mountainous district round Adam's Peak, where, after due preparation, he resolved to march against his sovereign. Mahasena, conscious of the fact that he could not rely on the support of the masses—whose sympathies were entirely with the Maha Vihara fraternity—deemed a sacrifice of Sanghamitta and Sona and a change of his religion preferable to the loss of the crown. Accordingly Sanghamitta, his quondam tutor, and Sona, the adigar, were beheaded for having misdirected his energies. Megavannabhaya was made adigar and the old religion was restored, and, to complete his repentance, the king rebuilt the temples he had destroyed, recalled the priests that had taken refuge at Rohana, re-erected their pansalas, and, in a word, made every effort to establish those doctrines which a short time before he had striven to uproot.

278 A.C. In his infatuated partiality for the Thera Tissa of the Dakkhina fraternity, King Mahasena constructed Jetawanarama Vihara and dagoba (which originally was 316 feet and is still 269 feet high and 360 feet in diameter, and is, to this day, the most picturesque and massive ruin in Anuradhapura) within the consecrated limits of the garden called Joti, belonging to the Maha Vihara, in spite of the protests of the Maha Vihara fraternity. Maha Vihara was again deserted for nine months by the priesthood (who, however, left seven of their number hidden on the premises so as to prevent the interloper's attempted consecration being made valid) as a protest against the arbitrary conduct of the king, at the end of which period a charge involving excommunication was brought against the priest who accepted the vihara. The plaint having been entertained, it was duly investigated by a certain minister surnamed the Just, who, albeit against the wishes of the king, caused him—the Thera Tissa—to be expelled and disrobed, thereby indicating the independence of the judiciary during this period of the country's history. *Mahawansa, ch. xxxvii., p. 151.*

With regard to the Jetawanarama dagoba, Tennent says that the cubic contents of the dome or brickwork and the platform on which it stands exceeded twenty millions of cubic feet. The same author remarks with reference to this dagoba :—"Even with the facilities which modern invention supplies for economising labour, the building of such a mass would at present (1859) occupy five hundred brick layers from six to seven years and would involve an expenditure of at least a million sterling. The materials are sufficient to raise eight thousand houses, each with twenty feet frontage, and these would form thirty streets half a mile in length. They would construct a town the size of Ipswich or Coventry, they would line an ordinary railway tunnel twenty miles long or form a wall one foot thick and ten feet high reaching from London to Edinburgh." But only the glory of outline is left to Jetawanarama, its four chapels have crumbled away almost beyond recognition, enormous trees have eaten into the brickwork to the very summit, and troops of the large grey "wanderoo" monkeys are the only devotees who frequent the holy place. This dagoba is said to enshrine a portion of the girdle of Buddha. During this reign the adigar (chief minister) constructed numerous schools (pirivenas) at the Maha Vihara. The king had numbers of new viharas, and two nunneries, built in various parts of the Island, besides repairing most of those he had broken down. Special attention was devoted during this reign to the extension of paddy cultivation. No less than sixteen tanks were constructed in different parts of the country. Their names were Jallura, Khánú, Mahámani, Kóka-váta, Móraka, Paraka, Kumbálaka, Váhata, Rattamála-kandaka, Tissava, Velangawitthi, Mahágallaka, Círavápi, Mahadáragalla, Kálapásánavapi, and Minneriya. The last of these tanks was built at Mahagama (Bintenne) by damming the Karáganga and turning its stream into it. It is still in existence, and is about twenty miles in circumference, the artificial bund being five miles in length and sixty feet in height. The sluices are on a level with the deepest parts of the tank and are never closed. Eighty thousand* amunams (160,000 acres) of ground are said to have been brought under paddy cultivation with the aid of the water from this lake. Tallawat-tuella (Pabbata), a great canal built during this reign, connected the Minneriya tank with the large tanks of Kanthalai or Gantalawa and Kowdelly.

Burrows, p. 65.

Rajawalia, p. 238.

Rajaratnacara, p. 69. Burrows, p. 10.

Tennent, vol. II., p. 484.

Though not mentioned in the *Mahawansa*, local tradition attributes to King Mahasena the construction

Parker's Ancient Ceylon, pp. 405-408.

* Numismata Orientalia, section 31.

of the tank, now called Náccádúwa. The truth of the tradition is confirmed by the size of the bricks that have been used in constructing its sluices. This tank has been formed by raising an embankment across the valley at a spot where two ridges projected into the Kadamba river (Malwatu Oya), 3½ miles below the dam mentioned as having been constructed in the reign of King Walagambahu I. It was a bold scheme, as floods estimated to amount to 14,000 feet per second were to be expected, and there was no suitable rock over which they could be allowed to flow ; but it was carried out successfully.

"The embankment, running nearly north and south, is 5,550 feet long, or a little more than a mile. It was 36 feet high above the sill of the sluice, and 55 feet above the bed of the river ; its top was about 50 feet wide, and both the sides sloped at the rate of 2½ feet horizontal to one foot vertical. The slope facing the water was protected by a small layer of boulders."

"The crest of the flood-escape was 21 feet 6 inches below the top of the embankment, and 14 feet 2 inches below the level of the sluice. The tank had an area of 2,015 acres and a capacity of 525 million cubic feet. It has been restored so as to retain an increased depth of 8 feet 5 inches, at which the area is 3,920 acres and the capacity 1,600 million cubic feet."

296 A.C. Mahasena died after a reign of twenty-seven years, and with him end the glories of the Mahawansa—the great solar dynasty. Although his race was not extinct and two of his sons successively ascended the throne and continued the family, yet from that period the royal race of the Suriyawansa (solar race) is classed of the Sula-wansa, or lower dynasty. Various but insufficient reasons are given by Sinhalese traditions to account for this change of appellation. After Mahasena's death a series of disastrous seasons, accompanied by famine and disease, is said to have decimated the sinking population, who, in their superstition, invoked the deceased king as an incarnation of Kartikeya or Kataragama-déyio (the Indian Mars), one of whose names is also Mahasena. They thought the power of this monarch, as evinced by his great public works, supernatural—an impression that prevailed even before his death ; and a century after the termination of the great dynasty, the fevered imagination of a suffering people

Forbes, pp. 405-406.

conjured a dream, which they adopted as a revelation, and then began to make offerings to Mahasena, claiming his protection if he were a god, and deprecating his wrath if he had become an evil spirit. Pestilence at the time abated, but Mahasena remained an object of fear and worship, and Ceylon continued to decrease in wealth, power and population. Mahasena, from the situation of his principal temple, is called in Matale Minneriya-deyio.

Sirimeghawanna, 296-324 A.C.

Sirimeghawanna (Kitsiri Maiwan) succeeded his father and reigned over Lanka for twenty-eight years. He devoted the early part of his reign to the work of rebuilding all the edifices, *e.g.*, pirivenas, viharas, etc., that had been destroyed by his father and had not already been restored by him. The Lohapasada (Brazen Palace), the restoration of which had been commenced during his father's reign, was completed by him, as well as the Jetawanarama dagoba, which, too, was in the course of construction during his father's reign.

Having studied the life of Mahinda in Ceylon he developed such an admiration for him that he had a golden image of him made, summoned all the priests throughout Lanka to the capital, and celebrated a festival in honour of him (Mahinda) with a pomp of power that had not been previously attempted. So much so was the king carried away by his enthusiasm on this occasion, that he released all the prisoners who were in the jails of the city.

305 A.C.

In the ninth year of the reign of Sirimeghawanna Gautama Buddha's right eye-tooth, which for eight hundred years had been preserved at Danthapura—probably the modern Jagarnath in Kalinga, the modern Orissa, having been rescued from the flames after his cremation at Kusinara in B.C. 543,—was brought to Lanka. The circumstance under which it was brought over are as follows :—Guwaseenam Rajah, King of Kalinga, had in his possession the tooth of Buddha called Daladasamy, which he worshipped and to which he made offerings. The king of the city Sawat Nuwara, having declared war against the King of Kalinga, in order to make himself master of the tooth, the King of Kalinga asked his daughter, Ranewalenam Kumari and her husband Dantanam Kumara, to disguise themselves as pilgrims and convey the tooth to his friend. the King of Ceylon, in case he

Rajavalia, p. 240.

should suffer defeat at the hands of the enemy, which would be indicated by the hoisting of a red flag on the battle-field. Having been defeated, his instructions were duly carried out. The princess and her husband are said to have fled, with the tooth concealed in the folds of the hair of the former, to Tuticorin, whence they set sail for Ceylon, where they delivered it to King Sirimeghawanna, who is said to have provided the princess and her husband with a residence at Kerigama, in the Beligal Korale, and heaped upon them many favours. The tooth was deposited by the king in a casket made of "Phalika" stone and lodged in the edifice, called Dhammachakka, built by the Dewanampiyatissa in the royal park. Thenceforward the house received the name of Dáthádhátu-ghara. So elated was the king at receiving such a precious gift, that he spent 900,000 massa over a festival held in honour of it, and ordained that it should be taken every year to the Abhayagiri Vihara, and that a similar festival to the one he had just held be celebrated in honour thereof.

Tennent, vol. I., p. 388.

Mahawansa, ch. xxxvii., p. 154.

Rajaratnacara, p. 70.

Most probably the reason why the King of Kalinga decided to send the tooth to Ceylon was the fact that King Mahasena, during his reign, by more peaceable means, viz., by sending an embassy to him with a magnificent present of pearls, diamonds, and other precious things, attempted to get the sacred tooth whose fame had spread throughout the Buddhist world.

Sirimeghawanna is said to have constructed eighteen viharas and several tanks which should perpetually contain water, in parts of the country that suffer from want of water during the dry season.

Jetthatissa II., 324-333 A.C.

Jetthatissa, brother of Sirimeghawanna, succeeded him as ruler of Lanka. He was renowned for his skill in painting and carving, and himself taught the art to many of his subjects, who showed a taste for it. The *Mahawansa* says : "He sculptured a beautiful likeness of the Bodhisatta, so perfect that it seemed as if it had been executed by supernatural power, and also a throne, a parasol and a state-room with some beautiful works in ivory made therefor." He is also said to have made a casket (caranduwa) for the sacred tooth ; he died after a reign of nine years.

Rajawalia, p. 241.

Buddhadasa, 333-362 A.C.

Buddhadasa (Bujas Raja) succeeded his father. He was as renowned for his skill as a surgeon as his father was as an artist. From the description in the *Mahawansa* of his surgical performances it is to be gathered that such important, difficult, and comparatively modern operations as Caphalatomy and Laparatomy were performed by him. He is said to have effected several astonishing cures. He composed a work on the art of medicine—Sarátthasangha—which is still considered by vederalas to be an authority on the subject. It is a Sanscrit work, and has a paraphrase or commentary attached to it in Sinhalese. He ordained that there should be a physician appointed and maintained by government for every group of ten villages throughout the country, and presented a copy of his work to each of the physicians so appointed, and set apart one-twentieth of the produce of fields for their maintenance. He also appointed medical practitioners to attend on elephants, horses, and the army. He built asylums in various places alongside the main road for the benefit of the lame and the blind and maintained them. Being of opinion that the most effective method of regulating the conduct of citizens aright was by instilling into them, through the medium of religion, the fundamental principles of morality, he appointed to every sixteen villages throughout the Island a preacher who could expound the doctrines of the faith and himself devotedly attended to their doctrines. He provided preachers, so appointed, with the means of sustenance. He also provided every sixteen villages with an astrologer.

The most important edifice erected during this reign was the Mayura or Monara Pirivena (Peacock College), so called from the beautiful manner in which the floor, walls, and pillars thereof were painted with the colours of the peacock. It was a five-storied building, twenty-five cubits high, attached to the Maha Vihara. A circle of very fine monolithic pillars, with elaborate capitals surrounding a low mound, is all that remains of it at the present day.

During this reign a learned priest named Maha Dhammakathu, translated the sutras of the Pitakattaya from Pali (the language of Maghada) into the Sinhalese language for the benefit of priests who were unacquainted with the former language. So great a humanitarian was King Buddhadasa, that it is said of him that he was wont to carry his case of surgical instruments at his waist within the folds of his cloth and afford relief to every afflicted person he met. The *Mahawansa* says of him :

"He entertained for mankind at large the compassion that a parent feels for his children. The indigent he rendered happy by the distribution of riches among them, and he protected the rich in their property and life. This wise ruler patronised the virtuous, discountenanced the wicked, and comforted the diseased by providing medical relief."

Alwis' Introduction to the Sidat Sangarawa, p. 50.

The two semi-religious works, Mulasika and Kudusika, were written during this reign.

King Buddhadasa died in the twenty-ninth year of his reign leaving behind him no less than eighty sons.

Upatissa, 362-404 A.C.

Upatissa, eldest son of Buddhadasa, succeeded his father to the throne of Lanka and occupied it for forty-two years. Though he did not excel in the chirurgical art as did his father, he had undoubtedly inherited the latter's humanitarian disposition. He built homes for the crippled, for pregnant women, for the blind and for those suffering from incurable diseases. He constructed no less than seven tanks, the Rajuppalla, Gijjhakula, Pokkharapasaya, Valahassa, Ambutthi the Gondigama, and the Kandaraji tanks, which would contain water during the driest of seasons. Evidently the motive that prompted him to do this was a severe drought which prevailed in the Island during this reign, bringing with it indescribable disease and distress.

King Upatissa was an extremely religious man, and very frequently allowed his zeal for religion to get the better of his discretion. He constructed to the south-west of his palace an Uposatha hall (*i.e.*, a hall built upon a specially consecrated spot attached to a vihara and devoted solely to the use of priests who have attained to the highest standard of learning and sanctity, and had thus been admitted to the Upasampada order), and a hall for an image of Buddha, and a park sourrounded by an enclosing wall. Here on the fourteenth and fifteenth days of each half month and on the eighth days thereof, as well as during the extraordinary season (patihariya pakkha), he would tarry, strictly conforming himself to the eight precepts: Ata Șil = (1) Not to kill; (2) Not to steal; (3) Not to commit adultery; (4) Not to tell a lie; (5) Not to indulge in strong drink; (6) Not to eat by day; (7) Not to attend any parties of pleasure; (8) Not to dress the head with flowers, nor anoint the body with perfumes.

He led a very simple life, indulging in no more

luxurious food throughout his life than the alms prepared for the priesthood. He had a favourite habit of feeding the squirrels in his park with lumps of cooked rice.

In a good many respects Upatissa resembled Siri Sanghabo, chiefly in respect of his treatment of culprits condemned to suffer capital punishment and brought to the capital to undergo the sentence. These he was in the habit of releasing during the night, after providing them with money wherewith to flee into districts where hey were unknown. In their stead he would place in the cauldron meant for them corpses procured from the cemetery, in order that the righteous indignation of the public as against the criminals might be appeased.

Several great festivals were celebrated during this reign in honour of the dagobas. Special attention was devoted by Upatissa to the Thuparama, inasmuch as he is said to have crected a golden pinnacle on it.

Upatissa's domestic life could not have been a happy one, inasmuch as his temperament differed widely from that of his wife, so much so that his wife, having grown tired of him, induced his brother Mahanama, who was then a priest, to murder him, cast aside his yellow robes, seize the throne and take her for his consort. *Mahawansa, ch. xxxvii., p. 160.*

Mahanama, 404-426 A.C.

Mahanama, on ascending the throne, thought it prudent to devote his attention to the erection of sacred edifices and other works of charity, whereby he might neutralise the effect on the public mind of the crime, by the commission of which he ascended the throne. Accordingly he built three viharas, which he presented to the Abhayagiri fraternity and continued to provide the Mahapali alms-hall with food from the royal stores as his predecessor Upatissa had done. He also built hospitals for the sick, and a fourth vihara, which, through his queen, was bestowed on the Maha Vihara fraternity. He is said to have repaired many dilapidated viharas, and been a constant contributor towards the maintenance of religion.

During this reign Ceylon was visited by a very learned and eloquent Buddhist from India named Buddhaghosa (the voice of Buddha). Making use of the books at Anuradhapura in which the *Pittakattaya* and the *Atthakatha* were recorded, he translated the whole of the *Atthakatha*, which was only to be found written in the Sinhalese language, into proper grammatical Pali. This is the Pali version now used by the Buddhists of Ceylon.

Another important visitor to Ceylon during this reign was Fa Hian, the celebrated Chinese traveller, who arrived in the country about the year 413 A.D. His writings (Foe Koué Ki = "Description of Buddhist Kingdoms," chapters 37 and 38) are independent evidence of, and strongly corroborate the truth of, the *Mahawansa*.

He describes the flourishing state of the Island and the city of Anuradhapura which was inhabited by numerous magistrates, nobles and merchants engaged in foreign commerce. He describes accurately the geniality of the climate, whose uniform temperature rendered the seasons undistinguishable; winter and summer, he says, are alike unknown, but perpetual verdure realises the idea of spring, and periods of seed-time and harvest are regulated by the taste of the husbandman. This statement has reference to the multitude of tanks which rendered agriculture independent of the periodical rains.

Tennent, vol. I., p. 388.

Fa Hian speaks of the lofty monuments which were the memorials of Buddha, and of the gems and gold which adorned his statues at Anuradhapura. Amongst the most surprising of these was a figure, in what he calls "Blue Jasper," inlaid with jewels and other precious materials, and holding in one hand a pearl of inestimable value. He describes the Bo-tree in terms which might almost be applied to its condition at the present day, and he states that they had recently erected a building to contain the tooth of Buddha which was exhibited to the pious in the middle of the third moon with processions and ceremonies which he minutely details.

The streets of Anuradhapura he describes as broad and straight, the houses as handsome, and the public buildings as beautifully ornamented. At all the crossings of the streets were built preaching rooms, whither the people resorted to hear an exposition of the law on the eighth, fourteenth, and fifteenth days of the moon.

Fa Hian stayed in Ceylon for two years, and spent the greater part of that time in transcribing the sacred books at Anuradhapura. Hence his descriptions are confined almost exclusively to the capital. He dwells with delight on the magnificence of the Buddhist buildings, the richness of their jewelled statues, and the prodigious dimensions of the dagobas, one of which from its altitude and solidity was called the "Mountain without fear" (Woo-wei). But what most excited his admiration was his finding no less than five thousand Buddhist priests at the capital, two thousand in a single monastery on a mountain (probably Mihintale), and between fifty thousand and sixty thousand dispersed throughout the rest of the Island. Fa Hian says that two footmarks of Buddha (Foe), one on Adam's Peak and the other towards the North of the Island, were venerated by the inhabitants.

A Chinese chronicle (Leang-Shoo) states that at the beginning of the fifth century an embassy from Ceylon proceeded overland by way of India, and was ten years reaching the capital of China. It was the bearer of a Jade Stone image of Buddha, exhibiting every colour and in purity and richness, in workmanship, unique, and appearing to be beyond human art. The encyclopædia of Ma-Touan-Lin says that the statue was four feet two inches high, painted in five colours and of marvellous beauty, and that it was presented to the Chinese Emperor Nyawti, who had it placed at the Buddhist temple at Kien Kang (Nankin).

Tennent, vol. II., p. 134.

405 A.C.

Gibbon's Decline and Fall of the Roman Empire, ch. 40, vol. III., p. 55.

During the latter part of his reign another embassy was sent by Mahanama with an address to the Chinese Emperor and a model of the shrine of the tooth. The address will be found in the history of the northern Sung dynasty (Shung-Shoo, bk. 97, p. 5). An embassy was also sent to the Emperor Julian at Rome during this reign. Mahanama died in 426 A.D. after a reign of twenty-two years, leaving two children, one a son named Sothisena by an Indian woman, the other a daughter named Sangha by his queen.

Tennent, vol. I., p. 620.

Armianus Marcellinus, lib. xx., ch. 7.

426 A.C.

Sothisena succeeded to the throne of his father, but was poisoned on the very day of his accession by Sangha.

Sothisena, 426 A.C.

Jantu (Laimini Tissa II.), husband of Sangha, who held the office of Chattagahaka, was proclaimed king by beat of drums at the instance of Sangha. He lived but one year to occupy the throne of Lanka, during which he constructed the Chattagahaka tank. Jantu having died without issue, the duty of choosing a king devolved on the chief minister, who, thinking it unseemly to recommend himself to the chiefs as the fittest person to occupy the throne, thought he would be serving the interests

Jantu, 426-427 A.C.

both of the country and himself if he were to place a noted marauder on the throne and keep him in strict confinement within the palace, while personally attending to the administration of the country, which he accordingly did.

Mitta Sena, 427-428 A.C. **Mitta Sena** (also called Karalsora, from the reputation he had as a plunderer of crops) succeeded Jantu, but was never to be seen outside the precincts of his palace. It had been the custom of Sinhalese kings to identify themselves with the rejoicings of the people on days of festivity. On several occasions the people were satisfied with the excuse furnished them by the adigar for the king's absence, namely, ill-health. Finally, on one occasion, they were determined that the king should show himself to them if he were in existence. Accordingly they besieged the palace and shouted to him their wish, until the adigar was forced to yield to their clamour and advise the monarch to ride out on the State elephant through the city, from which time forward the king was allowed to enjoy a greater measure of liberty. Mitta Sena is said to have been devoted to the performance of acts of piety. He had occupied the throne *428 A.C.* for scarcely a year, when Lanka was invaded by an army of Indians commanded by Pandu, the king was slain on the field of battle, and Anuradhapura and the country on the Anuradhapura side of the Mahaweliganga subjected to their sway.

Pandu, 428-433 A.C. **Pandu,** having heard that there existed a youth of undiluted royal blood, clad in the garb of a priest, at the Gonisada Vihara in the capital, who might some day challenge his right to the throne, issued orders for his arrest. Fortunately the news reached Mahanama, the priest in charge on the temple, who was his maternal uncle, prior to the arrival of Pandu's emissaries, thereby enabling him to flee to a place of safety with the youth, crossing the Gona river, though it was overflowing its banks at the time. Finally they made their way to Rohana, where the youth's family commanded immense influence, his grandfather having taken refuge in that district and acquired vast tracts of land there, at the time Suba, the gate-keeper, usurped the throne of Lanka and was disposed to slay all those of royal blood in the kingdom. Soon after his arrival the youth, Dathusena, was hailed as king by the populace in the district, who found in him a leader fit to rid the country of foreign domination.

Pandu died after a reign of five years and was *Khudda*
succeeded by his younger brother **Khudda Parinda,** *Parinda,*
who oppressed all the people whose sympathies were with *433-449 A.C.*
Dathusena. Dathusena, however, kept up a constant war with the usurper for sixteen years until his death. He
was succeeded by **Tiritara,** against whom Dathusena *Tiritara,*
carried on a vigorous campaign for two months, when he *449 A.C.*
was defeated and slain. Tiritara was succeeded by
Dathiya, who, too, was slain in battle by Datusena *Dathiya,*
after a war lasting for three years. Dathiya was *449-452 A.C.*
succeeded by **Pithiya,** and was likewise slain by *Pithiya,*
Datusena at the end of seven months—with Pithiya *452 A.C.*
the Indian dynasty was extinguished.

Dathusena now found himself absolute ruler of *Dathusena,*
Lanka. He re-established peace and happiness in the *452-470 A.C.*
country. He restored Buddhism to its former ascendency, restoring and again adorning the statues of Buddha which the Indians had despoiled. He confiscated the lands of those nobles and landlords who joined the foreigners and made them serfs of the land over which they were lords before. With due discrimination he conferred honours and lands on all the nobility that had fled to Rohana, rather than fight for the foreign usurper. Special honours were conferred on those devoted officers who had personally shared his own adversities. He next turned his attention to agriculture. By damming the great river Mahaweliganga (Mahawaluka) he formed fields possessed of unfailing irrigation. He formed 17 small tanks in various parts of the country, and the
Kala-wewa. This gigantic tank which is still in existence *Burrows,*
is the reservoir which ultimately supplies Anuradhapura *pp. 93-94.*
with water, being connected with that place by a winding canal called the Yodha-ela, or giant's canal, fifty-four miles in length, which on its way feeds a widely extended system of village tanks. The tank itself is fed from the spurs of the northern end of the hill district, the Dambulu Oya and the Mirisgoni Oya being the two largest feeders. The tank has a total area of 4,425 acres, or about seven square miles, with a contour of thirty miles. Natural high ground runs round the greater part of it, but an enormous or artificial bank runs along the western side, measuring six miles in length, with a breadth of twenty feet at the top and an average height of sixty feet. It is formed of large blocks of stone and earthwork, and is provided with a fine spill wall two hundred feet wide and about forty feet high.

The cause of religion was not neglected by the king. He built no less than eighteen viharas and endowed them with land. Regular walks were added to the Maha Vihara, which rendered its appearance very beautiful, and the Monara Pirivena and the Brazen Palace which were in a dilapidated condition were repaired. Also, the eyes of the stone statue of Buddha—Sila Sambuddha—which had been adorned by King Buddhadasa with the cobra's gem, which was carried off by the Tamil usurpers, were reset with two valuable sapphires during this reign. The king also caused the halo, the crest and the curled hair of this image to be thickly studded with blue sapphires, and made an offering to the Datha-Dathu of a tooth-relic casket and a halo circlet thickly studded with radiant gems and golden lotuses set with a profusion of precious stones. Many other improvements were made to religious edifices in the capital, for which the reader is referred to the *Mahawansa*, chapter thirty-eight. A great festival was held in honour of Mahinda during this reign at the spot where he was cremated, and on that occasion, by the king's orders, the *Dipawansa*, the skeleton history of Ceylon on which the *Mahawansa* is based, was publicly read.

Geiger's Dipawansa and Mahawansa, Trans. by Coomaraswamy, sect. 11.

It is said that the *Mahawansa* was written by Mahanama, uncle of King Datusena, during this reign, but certain eminent authorities, of whom Geiger is one, are disposed to doubt it, although they agree that it was written by a person named Mahanama in the last quarter of the fifth century.

During this reign several hospitals for cripples and for the sick were built and maintained by the king The *Mahawansa* speaks thus of Datusena: "This king, with whom none but Dhammasoka could compare, built and dedicated temples and images both inside and outside the city. Who can describe in detail all the good works that he hath done? It is only a mere outline that has been set forth here."

Datusena's family consisted of two sons, Kassapa, from a woman of inferior rank, and Mogallana, a mighty man, whose mother was of equal rank (with his father), and a daughter of whom he was passionately fond. He gave her in marriage to his sister's son Migara, whom he appointed the commander-in-chief of his forces. Migara having behaved himself like a brute in respect of his daughter, in that he was in the habit of chastising her with no excuse whatever for so doing, the king losing the balance of his judgment subjected his sister (the mother of Migara) to torture by way of punishment to the latter. Enraged at the treatment to which his mother had been subjected, Migara conspired with Kassapa, the low-born son of the king, who was less loved than Mogallana, to dethrone him; and succeeded in making the king prisoner and placing Kassapa on the throne of Lanka. In order to have the imprisoned king subjected to torture, the son-in-law informed Kassapa that great treasures have been put away by Datusena for his favourite son Mogallana, and advised him to extract the secret as to where they were hidden. In vain did Datusena protest that he had hidden no treasure when requested repeatedly by Kassapa's emissaries to reveal the secret. Finally, exasperated by anger and despair, conscious of the fact that a violent death was in store for him, he revolved a plan by which he might see his best friend, his uncle Mahanama, and get some spiritual comfort from him before departing from the world. Accordingly, when the question as to where the royal treasures were concealed was next repeated, Kassapa's messenger was told: "Now, if he will cause me to be taken to Kalawapi (Kala-wewa), then shall I be able to find out the treasure." Delighted with the reply Kassapa sent his messenger back with a chariot, wherein his father should be conveyed to the spot where the treasures were hidden Meanwhile the news of the latest development had spread abroad and reached Mahanama, who immediately prepared a meal of beans together with the flesh of water-fowls, which was Datusena's favourite dish, and hastened to the tank, where his favourite pupil, whom he had saved from the Tamil usurpers and assisted in a great measure to mount the throne, who in return had been ever grateful to him, was due to arrive. As soon as Datusena saw his uncle priest he went up and made obeisance unto him and sat beside him, and it seemed to both as if they enjoyed the pleasures of a kingdom in each other's company. They talked much, and by so doing quenched the great sorrow that burned within them. Mahanama next persuaded his nephew to partake of the meal provided for him, after which a deal of spiritual comfort was ministered unto him. Datusena next had a bath in the Kala-wewa—one of the monuments of his reign—after which he turned to Kassapa's messengers who had driven him there, and, pointing to Mahanama and the tank, said : "Oh, friends, that is all the treasure I possess." Kassapa, furious at what had occurred, issued orders to Migara to execute his father. Thereupon, Datusena was bound with chains within the walls of his prison, and with his face to the east was, while alive, plastered up with clay. Thus ended Datusena's reign of eighteen years.

Kassapa, 470-488 A.C.

An attempt was made by **Kassapa** to take the life of his step-brother Mogallana, through the agency of the former's cook and groom, but it proved abortive, the latter having fled to India for refuge accompanied by a kinsman of his named Silakala, who there entered the priesthood. Kassapa, conscious of the fact that by his conduct towards his father he had estranged the sympathy of the people and could not rely upon their support in case an attempt were to be made by his brother to oust him from the throne, took himself to a rock, eleven and a half miles north-east of Dambulla, rising abruptly from the plain to a height of four hundred feet, surrounded it by a rampart, and built galleries in it ornamented with figures of lions, wherefore it took its name of Sihagiri (the Lion's Rock.) Here he buried his treasures and regalia in various places and built a magnificent palace. The ascent of the rock is very easy by means of the stout iron ladders and hand-rails provided since the year 1894.

Mr. Bell describes the excavations on the mountain summit as follows :—

"Directly in front looking south from the vantage ground of the east and west cross bank, stretched below as far as the central *pokuna*, is so much of the lower area as lies between the rock's north and east edges and the high ridge that occupies the western half of the summit. Most here is comparatively level—the only level portion of any extent in a citadel where a terraced arrangement was inevitable from the irregular conformation of the rock's surface. This area was seemingly allotted to courtyards, passages, and side-rooms ; half way a winding staircase of three or four flights of steps—the longest on the Rock, and pierced at its head through tall flanking walls—shows the means of direct communication with the upper area to the west. At the side of these stairs is the magnificently carved '*yal-asanaya*,' or granite throne, discovered in 1895. On the left, skirting the east edge of the Rock, was a range of minor rooms and passages doubtless communicating with an outermost corridor which almost encircled the citadel. This series of side chambers was continued to near the south end of the Rock, interrupted only at the pond where extra rooms, etc., intervene. That part of the ancient citadel lying south of the pond and east of the high level strip was laid out in a series of cross-terraces, east and west, varying in width and falling away southwards. From the *pokuna* to the foot of the last stair-case at the extreme south, are seven or eight distinct terraces. The centre is taken up with an open courtyard and on either side, passages leading to the pond and round it, by stairs and intermediate landings—all admirably planned to suit the physical conditions, and displaying great ingenuity in turning to full account the limited space and surface inequalities, of the Rock's summit. More than one of these terraces has been curtailed and hideously disfigured *by single brick-walls* of later construction 'patched up into a smoothness and smugness more tragic than uttermost ruin.' The lowest stair-case—at the south-west corner of the Rock—descends with a right angle turn to the 'watch cave' in the perpendicular crag on this side. The southernmost terrace, to the east of these stairs, was clearly dedicated to Cloacina.

"Of the higher-level half of the summit I have already spoken as containing a succession of apartments rising northwards in tiers. The backbone, as it were, of the citadel is found in the paved way, with steps descending ever and anon, that was carried along its axis from end to end, hugging the retaining wall of the upper ridge, and winding with its angles, but for the most part running straight as an arrow. From this 'spinal column' branch off east and west stair-case 'ribs,' which would render communication between all parts of the citadel easy and rapid, whilst each section was equally well served by the cunningly designed interconnection of its own component divisions through a maze of minor passages and stairs. No less perfectly planned was the *water supply*. The rock-hewn pokuna, nearly thirty yards square, centrally situated and accessible from every side, would suffice, when replenished yearly by the north-east monsoon rains, for ordinary requirements during the ensuing dry months. For drinking water resort was had, in all probability, to two, at least, of the three smaller cisterns close to the Rock's north, south-west and south-east edges.

"A word or two regarding the architectural construction of the citadel.

"The foundations were throughout the low-level area, generally, of that form of stone work known as 'irregular-horizontal' and run down to the rock core. Upon this rested brick walls vertical or in batter, plain or moulded, according to position and purpose, but all alike coated thickly with a tough plaster, white and polished, that in places has resisted the damp to this day. The massiveness of many of these walls bespeaks considerable height originally, despite the fact that the brick work was almost dry-laid and indifferently bonded crosswise. But in 'make' these ancient bricks—some a cubit in length—shame most of our modern outturn, being as well burnt as they are sharp and close. Of the system of roofing we know nothing beyond the certainty that it was timbered throughout and flat-tiled, in the style familiar among the Anuradhapura ruins. A marked feature of the ground plan is the *erratic location of steps*. As often as not, they are pushed aside from the centre of the rooms into which they lead and relegated to all sorts of odd corners. This vagary was no doubt forced upon the architects by the unconformable surface of the rock, which had to be reckoned with everywhere. But noteworthy, above all, is the *complete absence of monolith pillars and stone carved doorways*, the most salient characteristic of ancient structures in the Island. Whilst quartzose steps and flagstones were lavishly employed to enhance the beauty of this peerless citadel, not one fragment of column, door-frame, or window-sash in *stone* has come to light in *Sigiriyala*. Above the floor all was of brick or wood. As for gneiss, with the sole exception of the noble throne above mentioned—like silver in the days of Solomon—'it was nothing accounted of,' and finds no place in Kassapa's citadel."

With regard to the frescoes in the picture gallery, Mr. Bell says: "Only three pigments were used, *yellow*, *red*, and *green*, though *black* seems to have been given a trial as back-ground to one figure. The particular shades of these colours predominating the paintings may best be realised from the modern corresponding media employed by Mr. Perera in copying them, viz., chrome yellow, yellow ochre, raw sienna, burnt sienna, raw umber, light red, Indian red, sap green, terra vert, lamp-black, and flake-white. The entire omission of blue is very remarkable, and difficult to account for, as this colour enters freely into the sister paintings at Ajanta.

"The scene intended to be portrayed would seem to be *a procession of the queens and princesses* of Kassapa's court with their attendants on the way to worship at the Buddhist Vihara *Pidura-gala*, the hill lying about a mile north of Sigiriya. The figures are manifestly all moving in that direction, and the flowers held in their hands by the ladies, and carried after them by servant maids, can hardly bear any other signification. Grouping in pairs is chiefly favoured throughout, the queen or princess being usually followed by a lady-in-waiting, of the same or of kindred blood, or by a dark-skinned maid-servant of alien race. The latter are given a greenish complexion— a 'badge of servitude,' which clearly marks them off from the high-born dames, their mistresses, whether pale-yellow 'blondes' or orange-hued 'brunettes'—all three-coloured types reproduced frequently at Ajanta."

The type of features is Aryan—oval face, thick fleshy lips, but straight, almost Grecian nose and forehead. The almond-eyes of one of them betoken a slight tinge of Mongolian blood.

The *Rajaratnacara* says that unlike his predecessors Kassapa could not tolerate the sight of beggars, pilgrims, children, sick people and women. During this reign Migara, the commander-in-chief of the army, built a pirivena (school) and called it after his own name. He also built a house for one of the great statues of Buddha (Abhiseka Jina), which had been restored and adorned by Datusena, and applied to the king for permission to display in honour of it ceremonies of greater splendour than were displayed on the occasion of the setting of the eyes (= Abhiseka) in the image Sila Sanbuddha at the Abhayagiri Vihara during the reign of King Buddhadassa; this however was refused. The humiliation and resentment resulting from this refusal caused Migara to decide upon supporting the cause of Mogallana in his attempt to gain the throne of Lanka.

Meanwhile Kassapa attempted by all manner of religious acts to gain the sympathy of his people. He repaired the Issurumuniya temple which had been built during the reign of King Dewanampiyatissa, and by buying and making gifts of more lands for its support rendered it richer than it had ever been before. He also built a vihara near the Sigiri Rock. On one occasion he bestowed on numerous priests robes, and food consisting of rice boiled in milk of king-coconuts and ghee flavoured highly with sweet condiments. He observed the sacred days and practised the Appamanna—*i.e.*, friendliness, compassion, goodwill and equanimity—and the Dhutanga—the thirteen austere practices prescribed for ascetics. He assisted the cause of learning by having books written. He had many images, alms-houses, &c., made, but they were all of no avail, inasmuch as he lived in constant fear of his people and of Mogallana. At length, Mogallana returned with an army enlisted in India commanded by twelve noblemen. Kassapa, in his impatience to put an end to the suspense in which he had been living ever since he ascended the throne, descended from his stronghold at Sigiri-gala and engaged his brother in a great and decisive battle at Ambathaloko in the Seven Corles. During the course of the battle Kassapa, perceiving a swamp in front of him, turned his elephant back so that he might advance by another route, whereupon his army in alarm raised the shout: "Friends, our Lord here fleeth," and broke their ranks. Elated by the panic prevailing amongst their opponents, Mogallana's army attacked them with redoubled energy and slew vast numbers of them. On finding himself defeated Kassapa, rather than submit to the indignity of being taken a prisoner, committed suicide on the field of battle. In his great admiration of his brother's chivalry, Mogallana performed the rite of cremation over his dead body with due ceremony, and having collected together all his spoils advanced to Anuradhapura. He was welcomed at the entrance to the Mahamega park by the priesthood of the Maha Vihara, to whom he offered his royal parasol as a token of submission to the church.

Mogallana, 488-506 A.C.

After reaching the city **Mogallana** proceeded to the Abhayagiri and the Jetawana viharas, and, having saluted the priests at these establishments, took the government of the kingdom into his hands. On his accession to the throne, Mogallana thought only of revenge. More than a thousand people who held offices under Kassapa were put to death, and some had their noses and ears cut off for having condoned and sought office under his parricide brother. It is said that later he was calmed in spirit, and that his temper became serene as a result of listening to the sacred discourses of Buddha, and that he bestowed alms plentifully on the priesthood. Every year he gave alms on the full moon day of the month of Phussa (January and February)—a practice which has been ever since observed in Lanka. He permitted Migara, the commander-in-chief of Kassapa's army, to hold the feast of the dedication of the Abhiseka Jina according to his heart's desire. He converted the fortress Sigiri into a vihara and bestowed it on Mahanama, his grand-uncle. He built a convent called Rajini and gave it to the Sagilika sisterhood. He rebuilt the temple at Attanagalla—which was originally five stories high and had crumbled to the ground,—made it three stories high, and bestowed it on the priesthood in general. *Rajaratnacara, p. 76.*

For the first time in Lanka's history a national marine was established during this reign for the purpose of protecting the coast from foreign invasion. Measures were also introduced by the king whereby the observance of discipline among the priesthood might be enforced

The most important event of this reign is said to have been the arrival in Lanka of Silakala, Mogallana's companion in his flight to India, with a lock of Buddha's hair (the kesadhatu). Magnificent was the reception accorded by Mogallana to this relic, and the bearer of it, Silakala, was rewarded with the king's own sister for a bride, together with a handsome dowry. Full details as to the reception of the relic are contained in the *Kesadatuvansa.* Suffice it to say, that the Hair-relic, placed in a casket of great value, was deposited in a beautiful image-house, where great offerings were made to it, and that subsequently a casket, a parasol, a small pavilion studded with gems, statues of Sariputra and Mogallana—the two chief disciples of Buddha,—and a chowrie were made for it by the king. Mogallana died after a reign of eighteen years and was succeeded by his son **Kumara Dass** (Kumaradatusena), who, on his accession, desirous of cultivating the friendship of the Emperor of China, sent an embassy to him with presents, and an address announcing his accession to the throne of Lanka. He was a man passionately devoted to literature. He convened an assembly of the learned priests in the country and revised the sacred Buddhist writings, purging them of all alterations and additions. The celebrated Indian bard Pandita Kaalidaas (not Rishi Kaalidaas, the Shakespeare of the East) visited Lanka during this reign, and is said to have lost his life in the following manner: —One night, when the king was in the house of a

Kumara Dass, 506-515 A.C.

Tennent, vol. I., p. 620.

courtesan, he watched a bee light on a water-lily, which, on closing, confined it. In extemporising on the circumstance, the king is supposed to have compared it to his own position, entangled in the toils of the courtesan, and written the following *impromptu* lines:—

සියතඹරා සියතඹරා සියසෙවෙ නි
සියසපුරා නිදීනොලබා උන්සෙවෙ නි

which Forbes translated very freely thus:—

" By beauty's grasp, in turmoil uncomposed
He's kept a prisoner with eyes unclosed."

This riddle was written by the king on the wall of the house, accompanied by an intimation that any person who should finish the verse interpreting the riddle should be gratified in any request he might make. The Poet Kalidaas, on visiting the house and seeing the lines, wrote as follows underneath, and sought therefore the reward:—

වනබඹරා මලනොතලා රොණටව නි
මලදෙදරග පනාගලවා ගියසෙව නි

" But if all night the manel water-lily keeps the bee
The morn beholds him gay, unhurt and free."

The courtesan, unwilling that any other than herself should carry off the prize, murdered the poet, buried him beneath the house, and maintained that she had written the distich. The king, incredulous, ordered a search to be made, and the murder being discovered, the murderess was put to death. The body of Kaalidaas was exhumed, and a funeral pile was erected for its conflagration at a spot named Hath-bodiwatte at Anuradhapura; as soon, however, as the flames had reached the body, the king who was present with his whole court, being distracted with grief at so irreparable a loss, rushed into them and was himself burned to death. The same occasion witnessed the spontaneous immolation of his five queens. Kumara Dass' reign was of nine years' duration.

Alwis' Sidat Sangarawa, Intro. p. 153.

Kumara Dass was an elegant writer, and a celebrated poet; and gave to the public many a valuable work, of which the ravages of succeeding times have left behind but a solitary Sanscrit poem called the "Janakeebarana."

An interesting account of Lanka during the reign of Kumara Dass is contained in the writing of Cosmas, a Greek merchant resident in Egypt, who had derived his information regarding Lanka from a Greek trader named Sopatar, whom he had met at Adule in Ethiopia on the latter's return from Ceylon. He says:—

Tennent, vol. I., pp. 567-571.

"It is a great Island of the ocean lying in the Indian sea, called Sielendib by the Indians, but Taprobane by the Greeks. The stone, the hyacinth is found in it, it lies beyond the pepper country—Malabar or Narghyl Arabia. Around it are a multitude of exceedingly small islets (the Maldive islands), all containing fresh water and coconut palms; these (islands) lie as close as possible together. The great Island itself, according to the accounts of its inhabitants, is three hundred gaudia (a Sinhalese gow = about three miles) long, and as many in breadth. There are two kings ruling at opposite ends of the Island, one of whom possesses the hyacinth (probably the famous ruby described by Marco Polo and the Chinese pilgrim Hiouen Thsang as being a span in length and as thick as a man's arm, brilliant beyond description without a single flaw, having the appearance of a glowing fire), and the other the district in which are the port and emporium (the port and harbour of Point de Galle), for the emporium in that place is the greatest in those parts. The Island has also a community of Christians chiefly resident Persians, with a presbyter ordained in Persia, a deacon and a complete ecclesiastical ritual. The natives and their kings are of different races. The temples are numerous, and in one in particular situated on an eminence (probably that at Mihintale) is the great hyacinth, as large as a pine-cone, the colour of fire, and flashing from a distance, especially when catching the beams of the sun—a matchless sight.

"As its position is central, the Island is the resort of ships from all parts of India, Persia and Ethiopia, and in like manner many are despatched from it. From China and other emporiums it receives silk, aloes, cloves, clove-wood, sandal-wood and whatever else they produce. These it again transmits to Malabar (Malé), whence pepper comes to Bombay (Calliana), where there is brass and sesamine-wood and materials for dress, for it is also a place of great trade; and to Scinde (Sidon), where they get musk, castor, etc.; to Persia, Southern Arabia, chiefly Hadranaut, and Adule; receiving in return the exports of those emporiums. Taprobane exchanges them in the ports east of Cape Comorin, sending her own produce along with them to each."

Amongst the subjects, the introduction of which was eagerly encouraged in Ceylon, Cosmos particularises horses from Persia, the traders in which were exempted from the payment of Customs duties. The most remarkable exports from Lanka were elephants, which from their size and sagacity were found to be superior to those of India for purposes of war. Cosmos observes upon the smallness of the tusks of the Ceylon elephant as compared with the African, which is true of them at the present day.

Kirti Sena, 515 A.C.

Kirti Sena succeeded his father Kumara Dass. He, too, sent an embassy to China with presents to the Emperor of that country. He was a very religious man and lacking in the warlike qualities demanded of a king of Lanka. He was murdered and succeeded by his maternal uncle Siva.

Siwaka, 515 A.C.

Maidi Siwu or **Siwaka** began his reign by the performance of many a pious act by way of atonement for the murder of his nephew, but was not permitted to occupy the throne for longer than twenty-five days, inasmuch as he was murdered at the close of that period by Upatissa, who succeeded him.

Upatissa III. 515-517 A.C.

Upatissa III. (Laimini Upatissa) was quite an old man with his eye-sight fast failing him when he ascended the throne. He appointed Silakala, brother-in-law of Mogallana, the commander-in-chief of his forces. With the intention of ensuring the sympathy and support of Silakala, Upatissa gave him, who was at the time a widower, his daughter in marriage, together with a great dowry, which unfortunately for the king had the effect of kindling in him a desire for still greater wealth and power until at length he decided to secure the throne for himself by deposing the king. Having collected an army in the Rohana district he made eight attempts at taking the capital, but was each time successfully opposed by Kassapa, the valiant son of the aged king. Every reverse he received instead of having a demoralising effect on him, made him more determined than ever he was before to attain his object.

Silakala's ninth and successful attempt is thus described in the *Mahawansa* :—" The king's men fought hard against the enemy for seven days, but they were routed and put to flight. Kassapa then communed thus within himself : 'All the people of the city are suffering from the siege, the defenders have been reduced and the king is blind and aged; wherefore it is meet for me that I should convey my father and mother to a place of safety at Merakandaraka, and afterwards raise an army wherewith to fight the enemy.' Accordingly, Kassapa took his parents and their treasures at night and, accompanied by his friends, began his journey to the Malaya country, but his guides, not knowing their way, wandered hither and thither about the capital. When Silakala heard of it he hastened after them and surrounded them. A terrible battle ensued. When the battle was raging most fiercely, like unto a battle between the Devas and the Asuras, when his friends were falling thick around him and his noble tusker was giving way, he gave (the elephant) in charge of its rider and cut his own neck (rather than suffer the indignity of being captured alive). When Upatissa heard this he was struck down with grief, as if shot by an arrow, and died."

Ambasamanera Silaka, 517-530 A.C.

Ambasamanera Silaka, after he had attained the height of his ambition, proved himself to be a wise and humane ruler. For the benefit of the sick and infirm he increased the emoluments of the hospitals that had been built and endowed by Kings Duttu Gamunu, Buddhadasa and Datusena. He is said to have performed innumerable acts of merit to the end of his life. In the twelfth year of this reign (529 A.D.) a young Sinhalese merchant visited Benares and returned with a sacred book (*Dhamma-dhatu*), which was presented to the king. The king, ignorant of its contents, treated it with the utmost respect and reverence, and placed it in a house close to his palace, whence it was taken yearly to Jetavanarama, where a festival was held in its honour. Silakala had three sons—Mogallana, Dathapabhuti and Upatissa,—whom he associated with himself in the administration of the country. He entrusted the administration of the eastern part of the country to his eldest son, Mogallana. To his second son he entrusted the administration of the southern portion of the country and the protection of the sea-coast in that division from invasion. Upatissa, his youngest and favourite son—a very handsome youth with a strong character and lofty ideas,—he kept with him at his court. Silakala died in the thirteenth year of his reign.

Dathapabhuti, 530 A.C.

Dathapabhuti, who was administering the Rohana and Malaya regions—the districts inhabited by the most warlike and conservative people of the country,

—seized the vacant throne and slew his younger brother for having remonstrated with him for having usurped the throne to which Mogallana was entitled by right of birth. When the news of the usurpation, and especially of the murder of his younger brother Upatissa, reached Mogallana, he became very wrath and determined without delay to risk his life in attempting to avenge the cruel act of Dathapabhuti; accordingly he marched with his army on the capital, but found King Dathapabhuti with a mighty army encamped near the Karinda mountain prepared to obstruct his progress any further. Conscious of the superiority of Mogallana's army, Dathapabhuti thought it diplomatic to send him the following message: "The inhabitants of this Island have sinned neither against you nor against me. If one of us die, then will there be no occasion for the kingdom to be divided in twain. Wherefore let not others fight, but let the combat be between us, each on his elephant—before all the army, and it shall be that he who shall be victorious shall be king." Mogallana's proud and chivalrous nature would not permit him to refuse to entertain such a challange. Although aware of the sacrifice of his superior position relative to the enemy, he accepted it, and a fierce contest ensued between the two brothers mounted on enormous tuskers. The *Mahawansa* thus describes the fight:—"The huge beasts encountered each other in the fight, and lo! the sounds of their heads as they beat against each other was heard like the roaring of the thunder, while flames of fire like unto lightning went forth from their tusks as they dashed against each other. With their bodies covered with blood they appeared like two clouds in the face of the evening sky. At length the king's elephant was pierced by the tusker of Mogallana, and he began to give way. And when the king saw this he proceeded to cut off his own head. Whereupon Mogallana raised his hands in supplication and besought him saying, 'Do not so,' but he gave no heed to Mogallana's entreaty, and caring rather to obey the promptings of his pride, the king cut his own neck." Dathapabhuti's reign was of six months and six days' duration.

Mogallana II., 530-550 A.D.

Mogallana II. (Dalamagolan), on finding himself secure in possession of the throne, let the inhabitants of Lanka have experience of the finer side of his nature. He was a highly accomplished poet. He was also very learned in the doctrines of Buddhism. By giving alms and dwelling-places, food and raiment to the sick, and by affording protection to the lives and property of his subjects, and by bestowing offerings lavishly on those of the priests who were learned, he won their sympathy and goodwill. He had the habit of getting men mounted on elephants to recite sacred songs of his own composition at the end of discourses, and at the services of the church. He personally supervised the education of his children coaxing them to learn their lessons by offering them dainty food such as they loved. For the furtherance of agriculture he built three tanks: Pattapásána, Dhanavápi, and Garítara. Considerable additions were made to the religious literature of the country during this reign as a result of the encouragement offered by the king. He is said to have loved his subjects as a mother does her children; he died in the twentieth year of his reign.

On the death of Mogallana his queen, a woman with a strong character, brought about the accession to the throne of her son **Kirti Sirimegha** by having all possible rival claimants poisoned. This king was too sentimental and socialistic in his acts, and would have helped to demoralise and pauperise the inhabitants of the country by squandering the revenues of the State, but for the fact that in the ninteenth day of his reign he was slain and his government overthrown by Mahanaga, a descendant of the Moriya race, who had occupied the post of minister for war under King Dathapabhuti and had been engineering a rebellion during the reign of King Mogallana in the Rohana district. The *Mahawansa* says of Kirti Sirimegha: "He was likely unto a public hall of charity wherein all men were able to partake freely of, according to their necessities." *Kirti Sirimegha, 550 A.C.*

Mahanaga (Senewi) was an old man when he ascended the throne. He occupied it for three years, during which he repaired and adorned many existing religious edifices and presented vast tracts of land to the Jetawana Vihara and the Maha Vihara. *Mahanaga, 550-553 A.C.*

Aggabodhi I. (Akbo), who had occupied the office of sub-king during the reign of Mahanaga, his maternal cousin, succeeded him to the throne. He is described in the *Mahawansa* as "Surpassing the sun in glory, the full-orbed moon in gentleness, the mount Meru in firmness, the great ocean in depth, the earth in *Aggabodhi I., 553-587 A.C.*

stability, the breeze in serenity, the teacher of the immortals in knowledge, the autumn sky in spotless purity, the chief of the gods in the enjoyment of pleasure, the lord of wealth in riches, the holy Vasittha in righteousness, the king of beasts in courage, Vessantara in generosity, an universal monarch in the justice of his rule and the extent of his dominions." The successive deposition of monarchs and the usurpations of their thrones during the reigns immediately preceding that of Mahanaga were events which must have disturbed the tranquillity of the great majority of the inhabitants, because of their accountability to the petty chiefs with whom they were more immediately connected. The crimes which led to the rapid transfer of supreme power must have brought in their train every germ of demoralisation and disorder. Under such circumstances the country was badly in need of the services of such a monarch as Aggabodhi I.

Conscious of his superior abilities "he envied not to give power into the hands of others." Accordingly he made his mother's brother viceroy. He made over the southern country (Rohana), and all the men thereof who owed service in time of war, to his younger brother, giving him the title of King of that district; he appointed his uncle's son the Rajah of the Malaya country and gave his daughter in marriage to him, rich men and nobles were given high offices according to their deserts. It is not surprising that by such liberality and by the right exercise of the duties of his kingly office he was able to win the love and goodwill of his people and free the country of all the thorns of strife, although it took him nine years to do so. No less than twelve poets flourished during this reign. They were:—Dehemi, Temal, Bébiri, Bisódala, Anurut, Dalagot, Puravadu, Dalasala, Kumara, Kitsiri, Kasubkota, and Epá.

Pujavaliya.

The two classical works, *Pradeepikáwa* and *Amawatura*, judging from the very chaste style in which they have been written, must have been written during this period of Lanka's history. Their author was Gurulugomi.

Alwis' Sidat Sangarawa, Intro. p. 157.

Many schools (pirivenas) were built during this reign, amongst them were the Siri Sanghabodhi pirivena, which was built in the Malaya district; the Aggabodhi pirivena, which was built and presented by the king to the chief priest Maha Siva; and the Mahanaga pirivena, which was built in the hope that merit may attach to the spirit of his immediate predecessor on the throne. Many viharas were constructed and endowed by the king with a view to spreading the Buddhist religion, and several "Uposatha" halls were added to existing viharas. Golden parasols set with gems of great value were presented to the Maha, Jetawana, and the Abhayagiri viharas. The temple of the tooth-relic was repaired, and a golden casket, glittering with gems and jewels of various colours, was made, wherein the tooth was deposited. *Mahawansa, ch. 52, pp. 18-19.*

A golden canopy weighing twenty-four bháras (or loads, a load being 20,000 kalandas) was presented to the Ruwanweli dagoba. Two tanks were constructed during this reign—the Mihintale-wewa and Minimevula-wewa,—also a great channel was opened into the Minneriya tank, which had been constructed during the reign of King Mahasena (278-296 A.D.).

King Mahanaga also built a bath for the priesthood at Mihintale, watered by a continuous natural stream. It was called Nagasondi or Nagapokuna, and is to be seen at the present day. A narrow path to the right from the middle of the last flight of steps leads to it. It is formed out of the solid rock, and measures about 130 feet in length. At the back a five-headed cobra has been carved in high relief out of the rock, and is represented as rising from the water. It measures nearly 7 feet high and 6 feet across the head., and is a striking piece of realistic stone carving.

During this reign the Wytulian heresy, which had apparently been extirpated during the reign of Mahasena, again revived, as a result of the book (*Dhamma-dhatu* which had been brought into the country during the reign of Silakala (517 A.D.). Jotipala, a learned high-priest, took a prominent part in a great controversy that arose with the heretics and completely succeeded in exposing and silencing them. In recognition of the service done by Jotipala to Buddhism, the king presented him with a monastery and directed the governor of the province to pay every attention to his comfort and well-being.

King Aggabodhi I. (Akbo) died in the thirty-fourth year of his reign.

Aggabodhi II. (Kuda Akbo), nephew and son-in-law of Akbo I., who had during the previous reign held the office of rajah of the Malaya country, succeeded *Pujavalia, Aggabodhi II., 587-597 A.C.*

him. He followed the footsteps of his predecessor, inasmuch as he bestowed high offices of State on his subjects, according to their deserts. For the furtherance of religion he built many viharas and endowed them. He repaired the Thuparama dagoba, a portion of which is said to have fallen down during this reign, exposing the right collar-bone of Buddha deposited therein. His ministers, following his example, repaired many of the edifices built in the reign of King Dewanampiyatissa, which were in a dilapidated condition. He added a dormitory to the Abhayagiri Vihara and called it Dathaggabodi, after his Queen Datha and himself. He improved the Mahapali alms-hall, and provided it with a receptacle of solid granite shaped like a boat, to hold boiled rice.

For the furtherance of agriculture three tanks—Gangátata, Valáhassa, and Giritata—were built during this reign. The last of these is the only one that remains to be seen at the present day situated four miles from the Minneriya tank.

Tennent, vol. I., p. 476.

During this period of Lanka's history, the art of sculpture appears to have flourished in the Island, and the works of Sinhalese sculptors were eagerly sought after by all the surrounding nations. The Wei-shoo—a history of the Wei Tartar dynasty, written in A.C. 590, bk. 114, p. 9—says that one peculiarity in their execution consisted in so treating their features that "on standing at about three paces distant they appeared truly brilliant, but the lineaments gradually disappeared on a nearer approach."

During this reign the King of Kalinga (the modern Orissa), resolving to lead the life of a recluse, arrived in Lanka and joined the brotherhood under the great high-priest Jothipala. He was accompanied by his queen and chief minister, who, too, followed his example, the one entering the Ratana Convent, where she was affectionately ministered to by Queen Datha, and the other the Vettavasa Vihara.

Aggabodhi II., or Kuda Akbo, died in the tenth year of his reign.

Sanghatissa, 597 A.C.

Sanghatissa, the brother and sword-bearer of Kuda Akbo, succeeded him on the throne, but occupied it for a period no longer than two months, although during that short period he gave promise of ruling the country with justice, following the footsteps of his two immediate predecessors.

As soon as the news of his accession reached Mogallana, the commander-in-chief during the reign of Kuda Akbo, who was at the time stationed in the Rohana district, the latter, deciding to fight for the throne, advanced on the capital with a large army, but was met by the king's forces at Kadalládi-Niváta and forced to retreat. Undaunted by this reverse he made a second attempt, after having entered upon an understanding with the commander of the king's forces that the latter should attack the king from the rear whilst the battle was in progress. In the second attempt the king in person and his eldest son commanded the royal forces (as his general, feigning illness, kept to his bed in the city), and engaged the enemy at the eastern Tissa mountain, but, in accordance with prior arrangements, was attacked from the rear by his treacherous general whom he had visited and spoken kind words to, and to whose custody he had entrusted his younger son prior to starting out for battle. Although hemmed in by two armies, the valiant prince and his father, the king fought hard until all chance of success had vanished. Whereupon they dismounted from their elephants, and taking advantage of the general chaos that prevailed fled into the Merumajjara forest, which was close by, accompanied by their faithful minister. Thence they betook themselves into a vihara, whence they started out for the Rohana district clad in the yellow robes with which the priests had presented them.

Mogallana, 597 A.C.

Meanwhile **Mogallana** had established himself on the throne; had rewarded the treacherous general with the office of Malaya Raja and his son with the office of sword-bearer to the king; had ordered the hands and feet of the boy prince that had been left behind at the capital to be cut off; and had offered rewards for the heads of the fugitive king and his son. Unfortunately for Sanghatissa his identity was discovered, and he, his son, and his minister were taken captives.

Mogallana, overjoyed at the news of their capture, ordered Sanghatissa and his son to be executed at Sihagiri, and the minister to be brought alive to the capital, but as the latter was determined that he should die with his master, all three of them were executed. Mogallana next decided to enlist the sympathy of the priesthood, as the security of his throne depended largely, if not entirely, on his possessing their sympathy and goodwill, so great was their influence over the masses. Accordingly, he gave robes to all the priests dwelling in the Island and issued orders that new images should be made and that old buildings should be repaired. He built five viharas in various parts of the country and endowed many viharas with land for their support. He held festivals according to the rites that were in custom and purged the whole religion of Buddha by means of a disciplinary act which appears to have consisted in the promulgation by the king of a decree enjoining the observance of discipline amongst the priesthood, and, in the case of certain offences, empowering one or more of its members, sitting as an Ecclesiastical Court, to give effect to the decree.

Mahawansa, Note by Wijeyasinha, p. 25.

He caused the three Pitakas to be rehearsed with great pomp and bestowed great presents on all the learned monks in the Island.

Sanghatissa's treacherous general, who, as we have seen, had been elevated to the office of Malaya Raja, did not remain long before he was found guilty of entertaining similar designs in respect of Mogallana. As a punishment his hands and feet were cut off by order of the king; whereupon his son, the sword-bearer, fled to Rohana taking with him his own son. Here he was welcomed by the inhabitants, and soon found himself in a position to avenge the treatment meted out to his father, in conjunction with Jetthatissa, a son of the late King Sanghatisssa, who had taken refuge in the Malaya district on hearing the fate that had befallen his father and brothers, and had remained in concealment there.

Mogallana, on hearing that an army, commanded by the sword-bearer and Jetthatissa, had encamped at the Dolha-pabbata, marched out with all possible haste at the head of his army and entrenched himself near the enemy. Here, a fever having broken out among the king's forces, the greater portion of his army was incapacitated for warfare. On the receipt of news as to the state of affairs in the enemy's camp, the joint forces of Jetthatissa and the sword-bearer made a sudden attack and routed the royal forces. The king himself, who was following his men in their flight, was overtaken and slain at Sihagiri.

Silameghavama, 603-612 A.C.

On the death of Mogallana, the sword-bearer ascended the throne under the little of **Silamegha-**

vama, and extended his rule over the whole Island, having Anuradhapura for his capital.

During this reign the chief, Sirinaga, uncle of Jetthatissa, made an attempt at gaining the sovereignty with the assistance of an army which he had enlisted in India. He effected a landing in the North, but was soon after defeated and slain by King Silameghavama. Those of his army that did not fall in battle were taken prisoners and distributed amongst the viharas in the Island, for the purpose of being used as slaves. Considering the difference in the figure and height of the Rodiya as compared with the Sinhalese of other castes, it is probable that the Rodiyas of Ceylon of the present day are descendants of the Indian captives who were degraded during this reign. There are several other local traditions regarding the origin of Rodiyas: one of which is that they are the descendants of the royal huntsmen who were degraded for having provided the royal table with human meat one day, as a result of their failure to obtain any game; another is that they are the descendants of people of this country who had been tried for treason or murder and condemned to death, but whose sentences had been commuted by the king to perpetual degradation; amongst them being families of royal blood, to which fact the Rodiyas of the present day owe their fine physical appearance. They had been in by-gone ages deprived of every form of facility for advancement and had led nomadic lives, their chief source of livelihood being the making of rope with the skins of wild animals and tanning monkey's skins (used for the construction of musical instruments of the drum species), which they exchange with villagers for cooked rice. At the present day, through the instrumentality of the British Government and the missionaries who have established schools specially for them in the districts where they exist, there is facility afforded them for advancement, of which they have availed themselves to such an extent that some of them have begun to acquire land, ownership of which had hitherto been unknown to them.

The remainder of the reign of Silameghavama was spent in attempting to reform the priests of the Abhayagiriya fraternity, who had developed certain undesirable practices. In the course of this attempt he outraged the feelings of the Maha Vihara fraternity by subjecting them to severe abuse on their refusal, at the instance of the king, to observe the Uposatha ceremony in common with the monks of the Abhayagiriya fraternity. Refusing to apologise to them for the insult thus offered, the king betook himself to Rohana, where he fell ill and died in the ninth year of his reign.

During the early part of this reign the Island was visited by a famine, and while it was at its height, the king is said to have devoted himself unsparingly to the alleviation of the sufferings of the poor.

Tennent, vol. I., p. 441. In the Suy-shoo, a Chinese history of the Suy dynasty, it is stated that in 607 A.C. the King of Lanka "sent the Brahman Kew-mo-lo, with thirty vessels, to meet the approaching ships which conveyed an embassy from China;" thereby indicating that the national marine established by King Mogallana I. in 488 A.C. continued to be maintained by subsequent kings of Lanka. The *Tennent, vol. I., p. 607, n. 3.* same history says that in the same year—607 A.C.—an embassy from China to Ceylon was entrusted to Chang Tsuen, "Director of the Military Lands."

Aggabodhi III., 612-628 A.C. **Aggabodhi III. (Sirisanghabodi II.)** succeeded his father Silameghavarna and commenced his reign by appointing his brother Mána, governor of Rohana. Aggabodhi had not been long in the possession of the throne before his right to it was challanged by Jetthatissa—son of the late King Sanghatissa—who had at his command a large army drawn from the Eastern portion of the Island, where his influence was great. A portion of Jetthatissa's army, which was sent under the command of his general Dáthásíva to reduce the Western Province, was repulsed by Mana, the king's brother, who had been ordered there by the king for the purpose. During his retreat Dáthásíva, together with his army, was surprised and captured, at the village Máyetti, by the king himself at the head of the royal forces. Elated by this victory, the king pushed on by forced marches in the hope of gaining a similar triumph over Jetthatissa unawares, but found the latter fully prepared to meet him with a force superior in every respect to his. A battle ensued, in which the king's forces were overwhelmed and routed. The king, however, succeeded in escaping from the scene in disguise; whence he took refuge in India.

613 A.C. **Jetthatissa,** thereupon, ascended the throne and reigned at Anuradhapura for five months, during which he, for the most part, occupied himself with enlisting the sympathy of the priesthood by bestowing presents, in the from of land, on various viharas scattered throughout the country. Finally, the fugitive King Aggabodhi returned at the head of a large force enlisted in India and fought a great battle by the Kala-wewa with Jetthatissa, who, when he found his army was being defeated, said to his minister, who was riding an elephant alongside the king, as follows: "Take this, my message, first to my queen and do after it as it pleaseth you. Say unto her 'Take thyself into a convent, great queen; learn there the doctrines of religion, and, having preached the Abhidhamma, give the merit thereof unto the king.'" So saying, the monarch rode forward on his elephant slaying every Indian that ventured to assail him, until, exhausted by fatigue, he saw an Indian by the name of Veluppa coming forward to the combat; whereupon, rather than be slain by other hands, he committed suicide. On seeing his master fall, the minister rushed off the battlefield to convey the message to the queen. After having delivered it, on being questioned by the queen as to the particulars attending her husband's death, the minister is said to have illustrated it by drawing out a knife and cutting his own throat. The advice of her husband was faithfully observed by the noble woman.

Aggabodhi III., on regaining the throne, took up his abode at Anuradhapura and restored the country to its former state of tranquillity. *613 A.C.*

In 624 A.C. Mana, the king's brother, who had occupied the office of sub-king, was found guilty of misconduct in respect of the queen and executed. Kassapa, another of the king's brothers, was elected to the office which thus fell vacant. Dáthásíva, the general of Jetthatissa, on hearing of the death of Mana—the only man in the kingdom whose ability he respected as a result of the defeat sustained at his hands,—rose in rebellion and defeated the royal forces, commanded by the king in person, at a village named Tintini. The king, however, succeeded in escaping to India, leaving everything behind except the royal necklace, which was carried off for the purpose of proving his identity.

Dathopatissa I., 624-636 A.C.

Dáthásíva, on ascending the throne, assumed the name of **Dathopatissa I.**, and, instead of observing the usual practice of paying his respects to the priesthood, proceeded to despoil all the temples at the capital of all their wealth, including the golden pinnacle of the Thuparama and the golden canopy studded with gems of immense value which covered the top of the Ruwanweli dagobà. He is said to have melted all the golden images and appropriated the gold for his own use. His Indian soldiers are said to have carried off the vessels, for holding rice, that were in the Mahapali alms-hall, and also to have carried away a deal of booty obtained from the royal palaces.

Tennent, vol. I., p. 621.

Dathopatissa is said to have at length repented of his crimes in respect of temple property, and to have started to make good the damage done, when Aggabodhi returned with an army from India and deposed him. During his reign an embassy was despatched by King Dathopatissa to the Emperor of China with a memorial and present of the products of Lanka.

The third time **Aggabodhi III.** ascended the throne, he pillaged the temples of what little there was left to them. The dagoba at the Thuparama is said to have been levelled with the ground by Kings Devanampiyatissa and Kuda Aggabodhi and deprived of all the rich offerings which it contained. The same treatment was meted out to the dagoba of the Dakkhina Vihara, from which much substance of great value is said to have been taken. It is said that Kassapa, the sub-king, was mainly responsible for the sacrilege then committed, and that King Aggabodhi, who was unable to restrain him, spent 1,000 massa in rebuilding the Thuparama dagoba. Before he was able to reconstruct the dagoba at the Dakkhina Vihara, Aggabodi III. was again defeated by Dathopatissa and compelled to seek refuge in the Rohana district, where he contracted a malady which caused his death in 628 A.C.

Thereupon **Kassapa**, the sub-king, having defeated Dathopatissa and driven him to India, took the reins of government into his hands and occupied himself busily making good what damage he had done to the temples, as he had learnt from experience that the security of his government largely depended on the possession of the confidence of the priesthood. He also laid out gardens of flowers and fruit and built many tanks. He is said to have made great offerings to the Ruwanweli, Abhayagiriya, Jetavana and Thuparama dagobas, and caused religion to be preached by learned and holy monks who lived not among the habitations of men.

Whilst he was thus engaged, Dathopatissa, who had taken refuge in India, returned with a large army which he had enlisted there, but was defeated and slain in 636 A.C.

Chinese chronicles dealing with this period describe the dress and customs of the Sinhalese people in great detail. They appear to have worn comboys, and had their hair tied in knots at the back of their necks as at the present day. Women did not sit down to meals with husbands, but " retired into some private apartment to eat their food," as is the practice at the present day in the Kandyan districts. *Tennent, vol. I., p. 617, n. 7.*

Kassapa II. now ascended the throne and continued his religious benefactions. He patronised the learned priest Maha Dhammakathi and bestowed on him a special habitation and the income of the village Maha-Nitthila. He presented the first three of the dagobas mentioned in the preceding reign with crest jewels glittering with divers gems for their pinnacles, and made gifts of land in divers parts of the country to the priesthood. He had many children, of whom the eldest was Mánaka ; but as they were all very young and he was at death's door from illness, he summoned a nephew of his by the name of Mána—a man reputed to possess remarkable administrative ability—from Rohana, and entrusting his kingdom and the guardianship of his children to him, he died in the ninth year of his reign. *Kassapa II., 636-645 A.C.*

During this reign a great many temples, schools, and hospitals were constructed in the Rohana district by Aggabodhi, the wise and wealthy chief of that portion of the country.

The regent, Mána, being of opinion that the disturbed state of the country was mainly attributable to Indian intrigue and restlessness, deprived them of all office and power in the country. As a result they, being an influential element at the capital, raised a rebellion at a time when Mána was away in the Rohana district. They seized and held it until, dissensions having arisen amongst them, Mána, with the assistance of his father Dappula who had succeeded Aggabodhi, his (Dappula's) brother, as chief of Rohana, was enabled to regain it and reduce them to subjection. Thereafter Dappula was crowned King of Lanka.

Dappula II., 645-648 A.C. After **Dappula II.'s** accession, tranquillity prevailed in the country, but for a brief period. The Tamils, having again conspired to overthrow the existing dynasty, invited to their aid Hattha-datha, a nephew of Dathopatissa I., who had been a refugee in India ever since his uncle was slain in battle. They rose in rebellion the moment Hattha-datha landed with his auxiliaries and seized the capital unopposed, Mána and King Dappula having sought refuge with all their treasure in the eastern and southern portions of the Rohana district respectively, in the hope of some day retrieving the disaster they were about to sustain.

After three years of incessant labour Mána succeeded in raising an army in his district, with which he felt confident of gaining a victory over Hattha-datha's forces. Accordingly he started out on his enterprise—his army having been reinforced by troops sent by his father Dappula II.—and took up a position at Tipucullasa, where he was attacked by Hattha-datha, who had been crowned at Anuradhapura and had assumed the name of **Dathopatissa II.** Fiercely was the battle contested for a time, when at length, by sheer superiority in the number of his men, Dathopatissa II. succeeded in defeating the army of Mána, who was slain in the course of the struggle.

Dathopatissa II., 645-654 A.C.

The news of the defeat and death of Mána broke the heart of his proud and aged father Dapula II., who thus died having reigned seven days at Anuradhapura and three years in Rohana. For a detailed account of the ancestry and works of King Dapula II. the reader is referred to the *Mahawansa*, chapter 45, pp. 35-38. King Dapula II.'s wife was a daughter of King Silamegha, and his ancestors had been chiefs of great power in the Rohana district.

Dathopatissa II. was not allowed to remain in peaceful possession of the throne of Lanka, inasmuch as his title to it was again challenged by one Manavamma—a son of King Kassapa I., who had married Sangha, daughter of the wealthy and powerful chief of the Malaya district (the region round Adam's Peak),—who had enlisted an army in India and was greatly assisted by an Indian king named Narasingha. King Dathopatissa was at first compelled by the invaders to retire with his army from the capital; but at length, Manavamma, finding that the

Mahawansa, ch. 47.

greater portion of his army had deserted him, was compelled to give up the pursuit of King Dathopatissa, and to beat a hasty retreat across the sea to India, where he remained for 27 years at the court of his friend Narasingha.

During the remaining portion of his reign of nine years the king devoted himself, on the one hand, to appeasing the priesthood by endowing their temples, building schools for them, observing all the sacred days, and listening to discourses by priests of learning; and, on the other hand, to bestowing offices, according to their deserts, on all those who had served him faithfully.

He appears to have been unpopular with the Theriya brethren (priests belonging to the Maha Vihara), as a result of his having built a temple for the Dhammaruchi fraternity (priests belonging to the Abhayagiriya Vihara) on land claimed by the former. It is recorded that priests of the former fraternity inverted their bowls as they passed the royal palace, thereby indicating that they were not prepared to accept hospitality from him.

Aggabodhi IV., 654-670 A.C.

Aggabodhi IV. (Siri Sanghabodi III.), younger of Dathopatissa, succeeded him. Like Aggabodhi I. he was not ambitious of keeping all power in his hands alone. He bestowed offices on men according to their capacity, and conferred honours according to their attainments or their rank. He devoted special attention to the Maha Vihara fraternity, repairing those of their viharas and pirivenas that were in a dilapidated condition, and endowing their monasteries with gifts of land of great value. Being a man of culture he took a great delight in listening to the Budhhist scriptures propounded by priests of learning, his special favourite being Dathasiva, the elder of the Nagasala Monastery, for whom he built a house of devotion, which he endowed with the income of the eleven villages. So great was this king's zeal for the furtherance of Buddhism, that he is said to have "bestowed on all the three fraternities one thousand villages of great plenty, whereof no man disputeth the title" The officers of State as well as men of wealth in the country, following the example set by the king, vied with each other in their religious benefactions. A wealthy Tamil officer, by the name of Pottha-kuttha, is said to have built a wonderful house of devotion, which he named Mátambiya, and endowed with four villages and their tenements. A wise Sinhalese commander in the king's army built a college attached to the Jetavana Vihara and called it by the king's name. The sub-king Sangatissa built the Séhala Uparaja pirivena (college). Likewise the Makanda and Cullapantha colleges and numerous viharas were built by various people in all parts of the kingdom. Álso the convent Jettharama for the use of the sisterhood was built by the king's loving and virtuous spouse Jetthá.

It is interesting to note that Polonnaruwa, which was destined in later years to become the capital of the Island, was the place where the king spent the evening of his life. He died there in the 16th year of his reign. The *Mahawansa* describes his illness and death as follows:—"And while he dwelt there (at Polonnaruwa) he was attacked by an incurable disease. And as he knew that death was drawing nigh unto him, he called all the people together and exhorted them to live according to the law, and thus departed this life. And the people were all stricken with great grief at his death, and bewailed and lamented accordingly, and failed not in one single ceremony at his cremation. Even the ashes of the pyre they collected and kept for their use as medicine."

Datta, 670-672 A.C.

On the death of King Aggabodhi IV. (Siri Sanghabodi III.) the Tamil officer Pottha-kuttha took the government into his hands and cast into prison those who were disposed to oppose him. Finding that the people were not disposed to accept him as their sovereign, he had a chief of royal blood, by the name of **Datta** (Walpiti Wasidata or Dantanama), annointed king, but continued to administer the government himself. Datta died after a reign of two years, and the only event recorded during this period is the building of a vihara which was called after the king's name.

Hattha-datha, 672 A.C.

Hattha-datha II. (Hununaru Riandalu), a youth, was next placed on the throne by Pottha-kuttha.

In the sixth month of this reign the kingdom was again invaded by Manavamma with a powerful Indian army, which, having conquered the northern portion of the country, was marching on the capital, when it was met outside the city walls by an army led by Pottha-kuttha and King Hattha-datha in person. A great battle was fought, in which the king was defeated and slain. Pottha-kuttha, who had fled from the field of battle, committed suicide on finding that he was a source of danger to the friends in whose houses he sought refuge.

Manavamma (Mahalepa) ruled the country very wisely for thirty-five years. Special attention was devoted by him to education. The following pirivenas (colleges) were built during this reign: Uturalamula, Vádúmula, Kapugam, Dematahal, Alagiri, Satveliya, and Uturu. During this reign were also built a terraced house called Kappagáma, the Sepanni, and Siriat Padhánarakkha viharas, a beautiful terraced house at Siri Sanghabodhi Vihara; also a terraced house at the Thuparama, which he presented to the Pansukulika fraternity (a sect that wore robes made of cast off clothes). The king also caused considerable repairs to be made to existing religious edifices, for which the reader is referred to *Mahawansa*, chapter xlvii. The *Lankawistariyaye*—a Sinhalese work written during this period—speaks thus of Anuradhapura: "Temples and palaces whose golden pinnacles glitter in the sky, the streets spanned by arches bearing flags, the sideways strewn with black sand, and the middle sprinkled with white, and on either side vessels containing flowers and niches with statues holding lamps. There are multitudes of men armed with swords and bows and arrows, elephants, horses, carts, and myriads of people pass and repass, jugglers, dancers, and musicians of all nations with chank-shells and other instruments ornamented with gold. The distance from the principal gate to the south gate is four gows (16 miles), and the same from the north to the south gate. The principal streets are Moon Street, Great King Street, Hinguruwak and Mahawelli Streets—the first containing eleven thousand houses, many of two stories in height. The smaller streets are innumerable. The palace has large ranges of buildings, some of them two and three stories high, and its subterranean apartments of great extent." On his death he was succeeded by his son Aggabodhi.

Manavamma, 672-707 A.C.

Pujavaliya.

Aggabodhi V. was a very wise and pious monarch. The *Mahawansa* (ch. xlviii.) records details as to the numerous religious edifices errected by him and presented to the Dhammaruchi and Pansukulika fraternities. The king also made new additions to the Sanghamitta Vihara and to many others in different parts of the country. He spent twenty-six suvannas* (a weight or coin of gold = 175 grains troy) in repairing the dilapidated structures at the Cetiya-pabbata (= Ruwanweli

Pujavaliya, Agabodhi V., 707-713 A.C.

* Wilson.

dagoba). For the furtherance of agriculture he restored to its former condition the Gondigama tank, which had fallen into disrepair.

King Aggabodhi is also said to have punctiliously observed the Uposatha days, together with all the inhabitants of the Island, and preached to them the doctrines of the Buddhist religion. The *Mahawansa* speaks thus of this monarch :—" Hence the King Aggabodhi, diligent in good works both by day and by night, left no act undone that tended to the welfare of beings in this world and in the world to come. Even the fine garment that he wore he gave away to the Pansukulika monks to be made into robes. The love of impropriety, the injurious exercise of patronage, the enjoyment of unlawfully acquired property, these were not at all of his nature. On the contrary, whatever food animals lived upon, that he gave to them; by whatever means living things could be made happy, by these means he secured their happiness. In this manner this chief of men, who spread peace on earth, after a course of good deeds extending over six years, departed this life to join the king of the gods."

Kassapa III., 713-720 A.C.

Khattiya Kassapa (Kasubu) III., younger brother of Aggabodhi V., succeeded the latter and proved himself to be an ideal monarch. He caused to be built three pirivenas (schools), one of which was the Helagam pirivena, three viharas, and a beautiful house of devotion. He is described in the *Mahawansa* as "a man able to bear the weight of the kingdom and to govern it as in days of old. He loved his people with the love of a father, and won their affections by his liberality, his courtesy, and his beneficent rule. He bestowed offices only on those who deserved them, and freed from all the cares (of State), took his share of the pleasures of life." He died in the eleventh year of his reign and was succeeded by his younger brother, Midel.

Pujavaliya, Mahinda I., 720-723 A.C.

Midel (Mahinda I.) was a very sentimental and altruistic person, who attached special sanctity to friendship. As his old and faithful friend Nila had died a short time before his accession to the throne, "he wore not the crown, although he assumed the kingly office." He bestowed not a thought on the pleasures of the kingly office of this Island, because his friend was no more. He governed the kingdom under the title of Adipáda (governor), as if the object of his life was simply to protect the people of the Island. He raised Aggabodhi, the son of his brother Kassapa, to the office of sub-king, and, having enriched him with much wealth, entrusted the administration of the eastern portion of the country to him. His own son was entrusted with the administration of the Rohana district. He caused ten cart-loads of food to be given daily, in alms, at the Mahapali alms-hall. He built a vihara and also a convent, which latter was called after his own name, and endowed it with the income of two villages. He died in the third year of his government, and was succeeded on the throne by his nephew Aggabodhi.

Prince Aggabodhi (the son of Mahinda), who was governor of the Rohana district, was in the capital on some business when his father died. The reins of government having thus fallen into his hands, he undertook the administration of the Island, but sent to Aggabodhi, the sub-king, the nephew of Mahinda, asking him to hasten and take possession of the kingdom. He, accordingly, came up and ascended the throne under the name of **Silamegha (Aggabodhi VI.)** and appointed Prince Aggabodhi, the son of Mahinda, to the office of sub-king. The latter, who was an able administrator, took upon himself the administration of the entire country, telling his cousin: "Banish from your mind all thoughts of the cares and anxieties of State and enjoy the pleasures of the kingly office (while I look after the affairs of the kingdom)." The sub-king, by showing favour or disfavour to people, according to their deserts, soon turned into order all the lawlessness that was rife in the land. *723 A.C* *Aggabodhi VI., 723-763 A.C.*

Unfortunately for the country, those who had suffered under the rigorous administration of the sub-king succeeded in exciting the jealousy and suspicion of King Silamegha, by telling the latter: "Your Majesty is only king in name, but another is king in reality, and doubtless this sub-king, after he has gained favour in the eyes of the people, will soon take possession of the kingdom.'

The sub-king, on finding a change in the attitude of King Silamegha towards him, fled to the Rohana district, and there, having determined to give the king justification for his suspicions, collected a large army, wherewith he waged a civil war until he received a crushing defeat at Kadalinivata, after which he took himself to the Malaya district (the hill-country round Adam's Peak).

Ere long, King Silamegha, who was by nature a grateful man, having pondered over the service done him by his cousin, who in the past had made over to him the kingdom when he might easily have kept it for himself, decided to make friends with him. Accordingly, he set out unattended into the Malaya district, and there, having effected a reconciliation, brought him back to the capital, where he gave his own daughter Sangha in marriage to him.

The first years of Sangha's married life were so unhappy, that she forsook her husband and entered a convent, whence, some time later, she fled with a male cousin of hers to the Rohana country. Enraged at the conduct of his nephew, King Silamegha, together with the sub-king, Sangha's husband, marched with a large army to Rohana, where Sangha's husband, having assumed the command, subjected the whole territory and recovered his bride. Thenceforth the king, the sub-king, and his wife lived together "in peace and happiness with much loving confidence in one another, enjoying themselves as it pleased them most."

Rajatarangini, bk. iv., sect. 502.

So far had the renown of the excellence and expertness of Sinhalese engineers with regard to the construction of tanks reached during this period of Lanka's history, that we find it recorded in the *Rajatarangini* (a history of Kashmir) that "in A.C. 745 King Djaya-pida of Kashmir sent to Ceylon for engineers to form a lake."

Tennent, vol. I., p. 621.

Although the Sinhalese chronicles make no mention of them, the Chinese chronicle Tsih-foo Yuen-kwei (b. dccc clxxi., p. 17) says that there were no less than four embassies sent from Ceylon to China during this reign—one in the year 742 A.C., one in 746 A.C., another in 750 A.C., and the last in A.C. 762. With regard to the one in 742 A.C. the Chinese chronicle says that King "Chi-lo-mi-kia" sent to the Chinese Emperor presents consisting of pearls, golden flowers, precious stones, ivory and pieces of fine cotton cloth. With regard to the embassy of 746 A.C., the king, who despatched the embassy, is described as sending as his envoy a "Brahman priest, the anointed graduate of the three-fold repository, bearing as offerings head ornaments of gold, precious neck pendants, a copy of the great *Paraina Sutra*, and forty webs of fine cotton cloth."

Tennent, vol. I., p. 387.

King Silamegha died in the fortieth year of his reign, during which, in addition to what has already been mentioned, extensive repairs were made in the buildings at the Abhayagiri Vihara, and also in those at the Thuparama, where the pillars were set up in a different order. Repairs were also made in the terraced houses of four other viharas.

Prince Aggabodhi, who had during the preceding reign occupied the office of sub-king, succeeded his cousin Silamegha to the throne of Lanka and assumed the title of **Aggabodhi III.** As he was well advanced in years at the time he ascended the throne, it is not surprising that he should have devoted his sole attention during the six years of his reign to the furtherance of religion. The *Mahawansa* says: "He repaired and strengthened all that had decayed of the old house of the Bodhi-tree and restored it. He also built two viharas—Kollanda and Molla-vátaka. By means of decrees issued to enforce discipline among the priesthood, he thoroughly purged the Buddhist religion, and stopped the way of those who set up false cases by deciding the latter according to the law. He also supervised everything that was done in the Island, even the distribution of food and medicines for the sick, and prescribed the form and manner of holding festivities and funerals. He caused ticket-rice to be issued to the dwellers within all the three fraternities (*i.e.*, those dwelling at the Jetavana, Maha, and Abhayagiri viharas, known as the Ságali, Theriya, and Dhammaruchi sects, respectively). He also caused richer victuals, such as were fit for the king's table, to be issued to the Pansukulika monks. This man, so full of self-control, died in the sixth year of his reign during his stay at the city of Pulathi" (Pollonnaruwa), which was, during this period, rising in importance from the fact that, since the time of Aggabodhi IV., royalty had been in the habit of occasionally residing there.

Mahinda, son of King Silamegha,—who had had a military career and had occupied the office of general during the reign of his father,—on hearing the news of King Aggabodi's death hastened to Anuradhapura from Mahatittha (Mantotta, a port at the extreme north of the Island), where he was stationed. On his arrival at the capital he received the news of restlessness prevailing among the chieftains and landlords of the northern districts, who had decided to withhold their dues towards the *769 A.C.*

State. Without any delay he pushed forward against them with a large army and subdued them. He next proceeded to Pollonnaruwa, where he met the widowed queen and wept with her in his attempt to console her. And in his anxiety not to let her undergo any sense of degradation, as a result of her husband's death, he thus addressed her: "Noble queen, be not sorrowful at the death of your husband. I will take upon myself the burden of administering the Island, while you reign as queen." To this she made no reply. So Mahinda left her quietly and proceeded to administer the country. Ere long news reached him of a conspiracy on the part of the ambitious queen to put an end to his life. He thereupon, having defeated the queen's adherents, took her, a prisoner, to Anuradhapura, where he had himself crowned King as **Mahinda II.** Dappula, a chief possessed of great wealth, and who had the command of a large army, challenged the title to the throne of his cousin Mahinda II. He advanced with his forces on Kala-wewa (Kalawapi), and having seized it pushed forward to a spot named Sanghagama, where he was met by King Mahinda II. and the captive queen at the head of a well-equipped army, and after a fiercely contested and sanguinary battle compelled to retire. Mahinda was prevented from following up this victory, by the fact that news reached him that during his absence from the capital the chieftains of the northern portion of the country had seized it, finding it unprotected, which made him hasten back with his army and retake it after a prolonged struggle. Thereafter a few years of peace prevailed in the Island, during which King Mahinda ruled the country with justice, doing "all that was meet to be done for the order of monks, his subjects, the lower animals—birds, beasts, and fishes—and his kinsfolk and the army." During these years Dappula, having recovered from the effects of his defeat, determined to make another attempt to capture the throne. Accordingly, he started, with an army enlisted in the Rohana district, together with two of his nephews, also from the same district, and, having subdued the people of the Malaya country (the hilly region round Adam's Peak), surrounded the capital (Anuradhapura) at night with a great host. "His men encompassed the city all around, shouting on all sides, so that with the neighing of horses, the trumpeting of elephants, the sound of gongs and cymbals, the blare of trumpets and the tumult of soldiers, the heavens were like to rend asunder on that day."

Mahinda II., 769-789 A.C.

King Mahinda, thus situated, hastily summoned his ministers of State and the leading officers of his army for consultation, and is said to have received the following reply from the latter :—"From the day that your servants entered your service, their lives have they given unto you. If therefore they should, in this hour of their danger, draw back, regardful of their lives, what advantage is it to their lord that he should have maintained them so long a time in comfort?"

The king and his ministers, on finding that the spirits of the fighting men were high, determined upon holding the city. Accordingly, every preparation having been made during the course of the night, "in the morning, at sunrise, the king mounted on his elephant, went forth from one of the gates, and fell upon the enemy suddenly like a thunderbolt, with his thousands of warriors and made a terrible slaughter among them. He broke altogether, and scattered on all sides, the hosts of Dappula, and having stopped his men from pursuing the enemy, he arrayed his army in order, and shared with them the joy of victory." In this battle Dappula's two nephews were taken prisoners, but Dappula himself, with the remnant of his army, retreated to the Rohana country. The king next turned his attention to the eastern and northern portions of the country, where the loyalty of the inhabitants was in doubt. After having reduced them to subjection and compulsorily enlisted a great number of warriors from those regions, and brought them to the capital, he reigned supreme for some years in the Island. During this period he married the captive queen, who, though she was his uncle's wife, was probably not related to him by blood. She proved to be a devoted and loving wife and bore him a son. This son was made sub-king as soon as he attained the age of discretion. Thereupon, Dappula, together with two brothers who were chiefs in the eastern portion of the country, having secured a large supply of men and money, determined to make yet another bid for the throne. Accordingly the three chieftains, with their great hosts, advanced and encamped on one of the banks of the Mahaweliganga. No sooner the news reached the king, he summoned a meeting of the chiefs in his district, and, having enlisted their sympathy and support, set out with a large army and his queen to meet the enemy. In order to prevent a repetition of his former experience, when the city was taken by the inhabitants of the north whilst he was absent from it with his whole army, he left a garrison behind and had those residents in it, who were known to be disloyal to him, executed prior to his departure. When the three chieftains received the news of the king's advance, they shifted their camp to a spot in front of a place named Kovilára, where they were attacked and routed by the royal forces. In this great battle both the brothers of Dappula were slain, but Dappula himself succeeded in escaping to Rohana, where he levied yet another army wherewith he might oppose any progress of the king into this region.

So sturdy, warlike, and independent were the people of Rohana, that the king "summoned together at the Thuparama all the monks and wise men available," and laid before them his proposal to advance into Rohana prior to embarking upon the herculean task. After he had secured their approval, he gathered together his four hosts with all the material of war, and by forced marches reached the hill Márapabbata (in Rohana), on the summit of which he took up his position. When Dappula and the inhabitants of the district found that the position was impregnable, they made overtures to negotiate a treaty —which were availed of by the king—for the purpose of exacting a tribute of horses, elephants, and gems from Dappula, and also of fixing Kaluganga as the future western boundary of the province Rohana. Thereafter peace prevailed in the land for the remainder of the reign, and King Mahinda was enabled to devote his attention to the furtherance of religion and the welfare of his subjects. He built the Dama Vihara and another called Sannira-tittha at Pollonnaruwa (Pulatthi). He built a monastery called Maháleka attached to the Abhayagiriya temple. He built a magnificent terraced and many storeyed palace named Ratanapásáda, at a total cost of 300,000 pieces (coins) of gold and placed in it an image of Buddha made of gold obtained from 60,000 pieces of pure gold given by him for the purpose. He also made a silver image of Buddha, which he presented to a convent named Silamegha..

He made a cover of gold circled with bands of silver for the dagoba at the Thuparama temple and repaired the dilapidated palace that stood there. He repaired many old déválayas (temples of Hindoo origin, where images of the Hindoo gods, etc., are kept and reverenced by Buddhists who have no god of their own) and caused very valuable images of the gods to be made for them. He gave the Brahmans the best of such food as was meet for kings, and made them drink their milk and sugar out of golden vessels. He provided the lame with oxen as well as the means of subsistence. In the case of lame Tamils who had scruples about using oxen, he provided them with horses. He provided the poor belonging to respectable families who were ashamed to beg publicly, with the means of subsistence. His charities were not limited to human beings, for, "having considered the manner in which it was most fit that food should be given to cattle in charity, he set apart for their use 100 rice fields of standing corn, with the ears thereof, full of milky juice, whereon they might graze."

That King Mahinda took an interest in agriculture is indicated by the fact that the flood-gate of the Kalawewa (Kalavapi tank) was strengthened during this reign.

The king's son by the queen whom he had captured having predeceased him, another of his sons, who was born of another wife prior to his ascending the throne, had been appointed sub-king.

On the king's death in the 20th year of his reign this sub-king, who had proved himself to be a mighty man of valour during the wars waged by his father against the chieftain Dappula, succeeded to the throne under the name of Dappula III.

Dappula III., 789-794 A.C.

Dappula III. (Uda) had Pollonnaruwa for his seat of government. At the commencement of this reign there was a revolt against his authority of the chiefs of the north-eastern portion of the Island, and he sent his eldest son and the commander-in-chief of his forces with an army to subdue them, whereas he remained at Mineriya, where he happened to be at the time the news of the revolt reached him. On finding that his son as well as the commander-in-chief had joined the rebels as against him, he proceeded forthwith at the head of the main body of his army and subjected them to a crushing defeat at Duratissa, in which his son, the commander-in-chief, and their confederates were all slain and their treasures captured. Thereafter the king returned to Pollonnaruwa, where he resided for the remainder of his reign. During this time Mahinda, the son of one of the chiefs of Rohana, named Datasiva, arrived at his court to seek the king's assistance against his father. The king being much impressed by the noble demeanour of the young man, and desirous of being on good terms with the turbulent chief of Rohana, gave him his daughter Deva in marriage, and, having supplied him with men and money, let him set out upon his enterprise, in which he defeated his father and compelled him to seek refuge in India.

Two general hospitals were built during this reign, one at Pollonnaruwa and the other at a town named Pandáviya. Hospitals were also built for the lame and the blind in various parts of the country.

It is interesting to note that during this reign all the important judgments delivered in the courts of law in the country were by the king's order recorded in books, and kept in an office in the king's palace, "for fear that they may be perverted by corrupt means."

Mahawansa, ch. xliv., vv. 18-20.

Numerous viharas were either built or repaired and endowed by the king, and in particular by his queen named Sená, for which the reader is referred to the *Mahawansa*, ch. 59, vv. 21-33. The *Mahawansa* concludes its description of this reign as follows:—"He (Dappula III.) was a man of great learning, he caused the doctrines to be preached at the three houses of the priesthood, and compelled the priests to accept his offering of alms-bowls well-strung and wrought in iron. Yea, he left nought undone that pertained unto charity. To such poor women as were of good repute he gave jewels, and to them that were in need of food he sent it unto them, and generally at night. He set apart fields of grain that cattle might graze on them, and gave food that had been cooked to crows and other birds, and fried rice mixed with sugar and honey to children. In this wise did this chief of men.........perform many acts of great merit and enjoy the good things of the earth, and leave it at the end of five years."

Mahinda III., 794-798 A.C.

Mahinda III. (Dhammika Silamegha) succeeded his father Dappula III. to the throne of Lanka. He was a very handsome as well as religious monarch. The *Mahawansa* says of him that "he neglected not to perform all those things that were in keeping with the commandments of religion, as they had been done by former kings. But evil he abhorred utterly." He died in the fourth year of his reign, during the course of which many dilapidated religious edifices were renovated and a water-course was presented to the Ratanapasada. He was succeeded by his brother Aggabodhi.

Aggabodhi VIII., 798-809 A.C.

Aggabodhi VIII. was a very religious monarch with a profound reverence for his aged mother. He held two great feasts during his reign, one in honour of the Tooth-relic, and the other in honour of the golden image of Buddha, which had been made during his grandfather Mahinda II.'s reign. He had two pirivenas (colleges) built, one of which was meant to perpetuate the memory of his father as well as himself, and was accordingly named Udayaggabodi; the other was dedicated to his teacher Búta and three hundred other priests. In order to ensure the fact that people worshipped with all due reverence on Upósatha (Sabbath) days, he decreed that on such days no flesh, fish, or spirituous drinks be brought into the inner city (= that portion of the capital where the three great temples are situated). This king had the peculiar habit of washing his feet prior to leaving the precincts of any temple, lest any sand be lost by cleaving to the soles of his feet.

With regard to his mother, it is recorded that he used daily himself to anoint her head with oil, wash her and dress her in clean and soft clothing. He would also daily make her offerings of flowers and perfumes as at a shrine, bowing three times before her and walking round her with great reverence. He also "fed her from his own hands with dainty food, and himself ate of the remnants." Before his mother retired to bed, he used daily to wash her feet and anoint them with sweet smelling oil; and after she had got into bed he used daily to massage her until she fell asleep, after which he would walk with great reverence thrice round the bed and withdraw himself from the appartment, stepping noiselessly backwards to the door, where he would bow thrice again to his sleeping mother before leaving her.

The king died in the eleventh year of his reign and was succeeded by his younger brother Dappula.

Dappula IV., 809-825 A.C.

Dappula IV. had not occupied the throne for any great length of time before two of his nephews (his sister's sons), who had been banished from the Rọhana district by their father Mahinda, the chieftain of that portion of the country, sought refuge at his court. Having determined to help them against their father he placed an army at their disposal, with which the two youths advanced into Rohana against the experienced chieftain. Finding their father's forces more than a match for theirs, the youths, deeming discretion to be the better part of valour, fled from the field of battle leaving the royal forces in charge of a captain, at the mercy of the enemy. Thereafter, the sons lived in the service of King Dappula until the news reached them of their father Mahinda's death in battle whilst quelling a rebellion in his own province. Whereupon King Dappula gave his daughter Deva to Kittaggabodhi, the elder of the two refugees, in marriage, and sent him out with a great army fully equipped, wherewith he might establish his (Kittaggabodhi's) lordship over Rohana in succession to his father. In this enterprise Kittaggabodhi was successful, and he proved to be a wise and popular administrator. The remainder of King Dappula's reign was devoted mainly to furthering the cause of religion in the country. He rebuilt the old house at the Bo-tree and ornamented it with works inlaid with gold and held a great feast in connection with it. He converted the rock at Vahadipa into a vihara, which he named Láváráma. He had a golden image made at the Jetavana Vihara, which he conveyed to the Bo-tree-house and held a festival in that connection "with such great splendour that the mind of man could not imagine it." He ordered gifts, equal to his weight in precious things, to be given to the poor. He repaired old buildings and punctiliously maintained the customs of ancient kings.

During this reign Vajira, one of the king's generals, built the Kacchavála Vihara for the Pansukulika fraternity and covered the house at the Thuparama with tiles of gold, and also fixed doors of gold to it. King Dappula IV. died in the 16th year of his reign and was succeeded by his son Aggabodhi.

Aggabodhi IX., 825-827 A.C.

Aggabodhi IX., on ascending the throne, had his title to it challenged by his cousin Mahinda (a son of King Aggabodhi VIII.), who during the preceding reign, finding that he was not given the governorship of a province, as was the custom in respect of princes of royal blood, by his uncle Dappula IV., lest the latter should by so doing increase the influence in this country of the rivals of his own son in the claim to the throne, had left Lanka for India in the hope of there enlisting an army wherewith to assert his claims. No sooner did King Aggabodhi hear of Mahinda's landing in Lanka with a foreign army than he sent an adequate force to meet them, and in the battle which ensued Mahinda's army was routed, and Mahinda himself, together with those of his relatives who had joined him, were executed. Thereafter the king devoted his attention to religious benefactions. Having heard that the priests of the less important viharas in the capital were wont to take their morning gruel at the Maha Vihara, he granted these viharas the three villages—Kantha-pitthi, Yábála, and Telagáma—as well as a water-course, and ordained that those priests should take their gruel henceforth each one at his vihara. It is recorded that on one occasion the king had money distributed among the beggars throughout the country in accordance with their needs, summoning them by beat of drum.

King Aggabodhi IX. died in the third year of his reign and was succeeded by his younger brother Sena.

Sena I., 827-847 A.C.

Sena I. (Silamegha II.), as soon as he ascended the throne ordered his nephew Mahinda (Aggabodhi IXth's son), who had crossed over to the continent with a view to enlisting an army wherewith to challenge his uncle's right to the throne, to be killed. He next proceeded to use his great wealth for the purpose of winning the goodwill of the priesthood and the people. He is said to have made exceeding great presents to the poor and needy, and to have given priests and Brahmans the best of his table.

The king had three brothers younger than himself, of whom the eldest was Mahinda, the next was Kassapa, and the youngest was Udaya. Of these Mahinda occupied the office of sub-king, while the other two were given offices as provincial governors.

During this reign the country was invaded by the King of Pandu with a large and well-trained Indian army, who, taking advantage of the discord that existed among King Sena's ministers, seized and fortified the Northern Province, and later, defeating the Sinhalese forces which were sent out under the command of Mahinda at Mahape Uagama, occupied the capital (Anuradhapura), which they sacked. They than took possession of the king's treasury, the golden images of Buddha, and every other valuable which they could get at in the viharas, so much so, that the *Mahawansa* says: "The beautiful city he (King of Pandu) left desolate, even as if it had been laid waste by evil spirits; and made Lanka of no value whatsoever."

During the course of this war the king's brothers, Mahinda and Kassapa, perished, the former having committed suicide on the field of battle at Mahapellagama rather than be taken a prisoner, the latter having been killed in battle at Pollonnaruwa, where he showed conspicuous gallantry on horse back, charging the enemy ahead of his army with sword in hand. Lust of conquest and plunder appear to have been the leading objects of the King of Pandu's ambition, for it is recorded that he was willing to commute a permanent retention of the Island for a suitable ransom. This offer was eagerly grasped by King Sena, who sent his own messengers to the King of Pandu with two elephants and all the jewels he had carried away on his flight from the capital. Satisfied with this ransom, the King of Pandu is said to have placed the great city in charge of the king's messengers on the self-same day, and retired from the country with his army. Thereupon King Sena returned to the capital and raised his brother Udaya to the office of sub-king, and gave him for his maintenance the revenue of the southern portion of the country.

About this time Kittaggabodhi, the chieftain of Rohana, died leaving four sons and three beautiful daughters. Thereupon Kittaggabodhi's sister, having put the eldest of his sons, Mahinda, to death, took the administration of the whole district into her own hands. Whereupon the remaining children sought refuge at the court of King Sena, who welcomed them as if they were his own children, and when the eldest of the boys, Kassapa, had reached the age of discretion, provided him with an army, wherewith he defeated his aunt's supporters, and having put her to death administered the district in conjunction with his two younger brothers Sena and Udaya. As for his sisters who, according to the *Mahawansa*, grew up to be as "fair and beautiful as goddesses;" Sanghá, the eldest, was raised to the dignity of a queen and given in marriage with an enormous dowry to the king's nephew Sena (son of Kassapa), a strong and valiant prince, full of energy and administrative ability, who had been appointed to the office of sub-king on the death of his uncle Udaya a few years after he (Udaya) had attained that office; Tissa and Kitti, the other two sisters, were given in marriage to his nephew Mahinda, Sena's brother, a very learned and virtuous man.

The country having rapidly recovered from the effects of the Indian invasion, King Sena and his queen Sangha found themselves in a position, during the later years of their reign, to devote themselves to re-embellishing the capital. A palace of many stories was built at the Jetavana Vihara, wherein was placed an image of Buddha wrought in solid gold. The enormous dwelling-house attached to the pirivena (college) of this same vihara, which had been destroyed by fire, was rebuilt. A casket of gold was made for the Hair-relic, and a great festival was held in honour of the shrine. With the help of the great Toopa-wewa (built in the reign of Upatissa II., 362 A.C.) he built several smaller tanks at Pollonnaruwa. A hospital, too, was built on the western side of this city. The Pansukulika priests, who appear to have been in great favour with royalty during this period, were presented with a great vihara, constructed by King Sena at Aritta-pabbata. A separate kitchen was also built at Pollonnaruwa for the sole benefit of this fraternity. *Mahawansa, ch. 50, p. 66.*

Bhadda, the commander-in-chief of the royal army, and the ministers Uttara and Vajira, following the example of their royal master, built schools and monasteries attached to the more important temples in the capital (Anuradhapura).

For further details as to the various edifices erected during this reign the reader is referred to the *Mahawansa*, chapter 50.

King Sena I. died in the 20th year of his reign while residing in Pollonnaruwa, and was succeeded by his valiant nephew Sena (son of Kassapa).

Sena II., immediately he ascended the throne, raised his wife Sangha to the rank of queen-consort and conferred on her the privileges that were due to her regal position. He appointed his brother Mahinda to the office of sub-king and assigned to him the revenue from Maya-rata for his maintenance. In order to ensure the allegiance of Mahinda, the king, after a consultation with his ministers, had his son Kassapa married to Mahinda's daughter Sangha by his wife Tissá. Having thus ensured internal tranquillity, King Sena awaited an opportunity for wiping off the indignity imposed upon the Sinhalese people by the King of Pandu during the reign of his predecessor. He had not long to wait, inasmuch as a prince of the royal family of Pandu, having *Sena II., 847-882 A.C.*

been ill-treated by his king, arrived in Lanka with a design to overthrow that kingdom. Eagerly seizing the opportunity, the king, after consultation with this ministers, despatched a large force under the command of Tuttha, the foremost general in the Island, with instructions that he should take the fugitive prince along with him, depose the reigning monarch, place the prince on the throne, and bring back the plunder that had been taken away from Lanka. King Sena himself accompanied the forces to the port Mahatittha (Mantotta) in the extreme north of the Island, and there, fervently wished his general good fortune in the enterprise. The Sinhalese forces having effected a landing laid sieze to the town Madhura, where, the King of Pandu, in his attempt to raise the siege, was defeated and wounded, and subsequently perished with his queen. Madura was taken and plundered by the invading army. The treasures that had been carried off from Lanka as well as much more were found in the palace within the city. These, together with other spoil obtained in various parts of the city together with many prisoners of war, horses, and elephants, were brought back at leisure by the victorious general after he had placed the prince on the throne that had been rendered vacant. Great was the festival of triumph held at the capital (Anuradhapura) on the return of the victorious army. The *Mahawansa* says: "Having accompanied the rejoicing army to his own city, the king held a feast of triumph and drank wine in honour of his victor." He caused the golden images which had been recaptured to be kept in their proper shrines, and the image of Buddha to be refixed on the altar in their Ratana temple. Thenceforth he devoted considerable attention to strengthening the defences of the Island against foreign invasion, and also to the furtherance of agriculture in the country. With regard to the latter, the *Mahavansa* says that "he made the Island look like Uttarakuru (one of the four great continents in Buddhist mythology supposed to abound with wealth and plenty)."

880 A.C. In the year 880 A.C. Mahinda, the sub-king, died after having devoted a good portion of his life to religious benefactions, of which the most notable was the repairing and beautifying of the house that stood by the Bo-tree, and was succeeded by his younger brother Udaya. Several tanks were constructed during this reign, amongst them being the Kánavápi and Katthantanagara. There were also constructed a sluice for the Manihira (Mineriya) tank and the Manimekhalá dam. A hospital was built at Mihintale. Numerous were the religious edifices erected and benefactions made by King Sena II., for a detailed account of which reader is referred to the *Mahawansa*, chapter 51. Suffice it here to mention that the Brazen Palace was repaired, so that it looked like the Vejayanta (mansion of the gods), and a statue of Buddha inlaid with gems firmly imbedded in gold was placed therein, that a lofty house was built attached to the Uttarálha pirivena (college) as a residence for the students.

The country appears to have suffered from pestilence during this reign, inasmuch as it is recorded that "the king caused the image of Ananda to be carried in procession round about the city and the Piritta to be recited by the priesthood, and saved the people from sickness by sprinkling the holy water thereof upon them." Wesak—the birthday of Buddha—was celebrated annually by King Sena II. with great festivity, himself joining with the meaner folk in their pastimes. The king died in the thirty-fifth year of his reign (882 A.C.), and was succeeded on the throne by his brother Udaya, the sub-king.

It is interesting to note the following description of Lanka by the Arabian topographer *Soleyman* who visited it during this reign (851 A.C). He says that "in Serenedib (Lanka) his earliest attention was devoutly directed to the sacred footstep on (Adam's Peak), in his name, for which—al-rohoun—we trace the Buddhist name for the district, Rohana.........On all sides of the mountain, he adds, are the mines of rubies, hyacinths, and other gems; the interior produces aloes, and the sea the highly valued chank-shells, which served the Indian for trumpets. The Island was subject to two kings (king and sub-king); and on the death of the chief one his body was placed on a low carriage, with the head declining till the hair swept the ground, and, as it was drawn slowly along, a female, with a bunch of leaves, swept dust upon the features crying: 'Men, behold your king, whose will, but yesterday, was law! To-day he bids farewell to the world, and the angel of death has seized his spirit. Cease, any longer, to be deluded by the shadowy pleasures of life.' At the conclusion of this ceremony, which lasted for three days, the corpse was consumed on a pyre of

Tennent, vol. I., pp. 583-584

sandal, camphor, and aromatic woods, and the ashes scattered to the winds. The widow of the king was sometimes burnt along with his remains, but compliance with the custom was not held to be compulsory."

Udaya I., 882-893 A.C.

Udaya I., on ascending the throne, appointed Kassapa—son of King Sena II.—sub-king. Thereupon Kittaggabohi—son of King Udaya's brother Mahinda—raised a rebellion, devastated the Rohana country, and ill-treated the priesthood in that region. The rebellion was soon crushed by Mahinda, the valiant son of the sub-king, whom the king had deputed to do the work in conjunction with Vajiragga, the commander-in-chief of the royal forces.

The suppression of the rebellion is thus described in the *Mahawansa* :—" Mahinda shone at the head of his army with great splendour even as Mahinda (the chief of the gods, the great Indra), as he proceeded at the head of his celestial hosts to the great battle of the gods and the giants. Soon he reached Guttasála. All the country folk as well as the chiefs of the provinces and districts whom the wicked rebel had maltreated joined him saying: 'Now have we received our rightful lord and master.' The rebel, while he yet tarried at Girimandala, felt that his fall was at hand. So he seized all the royal costly treasures and fled to the mountains, taking all his elephants and horses with him. Mahinda's host crushed the enemy on every side, and pursued the fugitive step by step, even to the foot of the mountain, where they came upon his elephants and horses and captured them. Saying to themselves, 'Here must he be also,' they ascended the mountain, treading under foot the whole forest, and making the rivers and marshy places look like highways. The foolish man, seeing that Mahinda's men were following hard after him, waxed exceeding wroth, and throwing all the jewels that he had into ponds and rivers and other such places, hid himself alone in a cave in the rock. There he was captured and brought straightway with great joy to Mahinda, who was at Guttasálaka. When Mahinda saw him, he laughed him to scorn saying to him: 'Has thou then possessed the Rohana?' He next gave the captive in charge of Vajiragga to be taken to the king, and himself proceeded at the head of the army to Mahágama and made himself lord of Rohana—the reward which had been promised him by King Udaya prior to sending him out on the enterprise. As chief of

Rohana Mahinda is said to have planted orchards and gardens of flower trees in various places, and built a dam across the great river and formed tanks for the furtherance of agriculture and the well-being of the inhabitants. As for the rebel, by the king's orders he was kept in prison under strict confinement at Anuradhapura, the capital."

King Udaya appears to have devoted a deal of attention to the furtherance of agriculture. He is said to have "made a waterfall with a strong dam on the Kadamba river (Malwatu-oya, the stream that flows by Anuradhapura) and enlarged the bounds of the tank at Mayetti, and every year made therein an outlet for water."

King Udaya is said to have built a great temple—the Tumbarup Vihara—in the Rohana district and covered it with gold and silver plates. Famine appears to have visited the Island during this reign, inasmuch as it is recorded that the king, in years of famine, caused dining halls to be built and gave abundantly in charity. *Rajawalia Rajaratnacara, and Pujavaliya.*

The sum spent on "good works" by King Udaya during his reign of eleven years is estimated at three hundred thousand pieces of gold. *Mahawansa, ch. LI.*

Kassapa IV., of whose relationship to his predecessor, King Udaya, Sinhalese historians tell us nothing, on ascending the throne had his right to occupy it challenged by Mahinda, the chief of Rohana. The king's forces were routed by those of Mahinda, and it was only by seeking the good offices of Mahinda's father, the sub-king Kassapa, that Kassapa IV. succeeded in retaining the throne. *Kassapa IV.; 893-910 A.C.*

The most important personage in the country during this reign was Ilanga Sena, the commander-in-chief of the royal forces—a prince of royal blood. He erected handsome buildings on the premises of Thuparama, Abhayagiri, Jetavana, and Ruwanweli viharas for the use of the fraternities to which they belonged.

He also built cells in groves for the use of priests who dwelt in groves. He built a magnificent college at the Maha Vihara, which he named Samuddha-Giri, and presented it to the Pansukúlika fraternity. He built a nunnery, named Tissarama, for the sisterhood, and entrusted to them the care of the Mirisvetiya dagoba as well as the sacred Bo-tree. In the neighbourhood of the two great cities, Anuradhapura and Pollonnaruwa, he built two hospitals for those suffering from infectious diseases. "To these buildings he granted fruitful lands and gardens, with keepers, and furnished them also with means for the support of images." In various parts of the capital he established dispensaries (Bhesajja-gehan).

Many other good works of less importance are said to have been done by this noble man.

The chief Rakkhasa, the chief scribe Sena, the king's minister Colaraja are also said each of them to have built noble edifices for the furtherance of religion and learning.

As for the king, he is said to have presented halo-ornaments of gold, a parasol and a jewel for the crest, to each of the stone images at the three great viharas in the capital. He also had three magnificent halls ornamented with superb paintings constructed at the three great temples and died in the seventeenth year of his reign.

Kassapa V., 910-920 A.C.

Kassapa V., son of Kassapa IV. by Tissa, sister of Mahinda, the rebellious chief of Rohana, during the preceding reign, occupied the throne of Lanka for ten years. He appears to have been a man of remarkable administrative ability as well as a man of great learning. The Elu work—Dampiya Getapada, or a Glossary on the Dhammapada—was written by him. Many colleges were built during this reign, among the more important of them were the Ganthakara pirivena built in the Mahamegha park in the capital, the Bhandiká pirivena attached to the Abhayagiri temple, the Sakka Senapati pirivena built by the commander-in-chief, and the Vijira pirivena built by Vajira, his wife.

The king purged the Buddhist religion by rigidly enforcing the rules of discipline (Dhamma Kamma) in respect of the priesthood, disrobing many dissolute monks and appointing others in their place. He restored the Mirisvetiya Vihara, which had been built by King Duttu Gamunu, but was in ruins, and presented it to the Maha Vihara fraternity. In the preaching hall of this richly decorated vihara the king expounded the Abhidhamma to a crowd of nobility as well as priests, and astonished them by the depth of his learning.

The king was fond of pageantry, inasmuch as every year "he caused the city to be decorated throughout, and adorning himself all over with jewels, so that he shone like the king of the gods, he marched through the streets of the city seated on an elephant, surrounded by a well clad host," carrying in his hands a book with a jewelled cover called the *Dhammasanyani*, which he would finally deposit in the relic-house at the Mirisvetiya Vihara. A hospital was built in the capital during this reign.

About this time a war having broken out between the two South Indian kingdoms of Chola and Pandu, the king of the latter country sought the assistance of King Kassapa. Accordingly a Sinhalese force, commanded by Kassapa V.'s valiant son—Sakka Senapati—was sent over, the king himself accompanying them as far as Mantotta, a port in the extreme north of Ceylon, where, prior to their embarking, he addressed them in a powerful speech appealing to their patriotism and recalling to their minds the victories of former kings of Lanka. Although the King of Pandu was filled with courage at the sight of the Sinhalese force and decided to push forward for the fight, at the sight of the enemy his courage failed him, and he fled from the field of battle with the Pandian forces, leaving the Sinhalese army behind to give battle to the enemy. Gallantly did the Sinhalese force maintain the fight, which lasted for days. Meanwhile pestilence broke out in their ranks and carried off many of them, including the valiant commander. Finally the news of their fate having reached Kassapa, the survivors were ordered to return to the capital, where the ceremony called Piritta was held with a view to driving out the fear of pestilence from the people. The *Mahawansa* gives the following description of the king :—"Although he sat upon the throne of Lanka, he was yet well read in the three Pitakas. Like unto a lamp did he give light to the length and breadth of knowledge. He wrote books, and was of ready speech, and a poet. He had a clear memory and clearness of purpose. He was both a preacher of the law and a doer of the same. Wise, faithful, and merciful, always seeking the good of others, he was bountiful and versed in the ways of the world. May the kings of the earth, yea, even all, be like unto him in the purity of virtue."

It is interesting to note what the Arabian topographer Abon-zeyd, on the authority of Ibn Wahab, an Arab who had visited Lanka during this reign (911 A.C.), says of her. He speaks of the pearls of Lanka, and adds regarding her precious stones, that they were obtained in

Tennent, vol. I., pp. 584-586.

part from the soil, but chiefly from those points of the beach at which the rivers flowed into the sea, and to which the gems are carried down by the torrents from the hills. He describes the frequent conventions of the heads of the national religion and the attendance of scribes to write down from their dictation the doctrines of Buddhism, the legends of its prophets, and the precepts of its law. He adverts to the richness of the temples of the Sinhalese, and to the colossal dimensions of their statues, and dwells with particularity on their toleration of all religious sects, as attested by the existence there of a sect of Manichæans and a community of Jews. Ibn Wahab, his informant, appears to have looked back with singular pleasure to the delightful voyages which he had made through the remarkable still-water channels which form so peculiar a feature in the sea-board of Ceylon. Here months were consumed by the mariners, amidst flowers and over-hanging woods, with the enjoyments of abundant food and exhilarating draughts of arrack flavoured with honey. The Sinhalese were devoted to pleasure, and their days were spent in cock-fighting and games of chance, into which they entered with so much eagerness as to wager the joints of their fingers when all else was lost.

Dapula IV., 920 A.C.

Dapula IV., who had occupied the office of sub-king during the preceding reign, succeeded his father to the throne of Lanka, which he lived to occupy for seven months. The gift of a village to the Mirisvetiya Vihara is all that is recorded of him.

Dapula V., 920-922 A.C.

Dapula V. (Kuda Dapula) succeeded his brother Dapula IV., during whose reign he had occupied the office of sub-king.

During this reign the King of Pandu sought refuge in Lanka, as a result of his country having been overrun by the Cholians. He was warmly welcomed by King Dapula, and accommodation befitting his royal rank was provided him outside the city. Great preparations were made by the Sinhalese monarch for sending a military expedition against the King of Chola. Just as the expedition was about to start out on its enterprise, civil war having broken out in the Island, the idea had to be abandoned, and the King of Pandu, finding that Lanka could not afford him a safe asylum, and still less could he expect her, in her present condition, to give him any assistance to recover his kingdom, left her shores to seek an asylum at the court of the King of Kerala—the country along the S. W. coast of India. However, he left behind in Lanka, his crown and other apparel, in order, most probably, to avoid identification during his journey to Kerala.

Internal order having been restored in the Island King Dapula spent the remainder of his reign of twelve years in furthering the cause of religion, in which he was assisted by the commander-in-chief of his army—Rakkhaka Ilanga.

During this reign, Imaum Abu Abd Allah—a Mohammedan saint who died in the year of the Hajira 331—"made known the way from India to the mountain of Serenedib;" from which time forward up to the present day Mohammedan pilgrimages are made to Adam's Peak. *Tennent, vol. I., p. 603.*

King Udaya II., who had occupied the office of sub-king during the previous reign, but of whose relationship to his predecessor historians tell us nothing, occupied the throne for three years, during which there was a great conflict between the church and the State owing to certain political refugees having been captured and beheaded at the Tapovana (forest of ascetics), where they had taken shelter. *Udaya II., 922-925 A.C.*

Sena III., brother of Udaya II., reigned over Lanka for nine years and devoted himself to furthering the spiritual and material welfare of his subjects. Large sums of money were spent by him in charities to monks, to the needy, and to artificers. He had the foreground at the Abhayagiri dagoba paved with stones, at the expense of 40,000* kahápanas (square coins whose quality and value are yet uncertain). He had all the dilapidated viharas in the Island restored, and also goodly halls, fine paintings and images made for the four great viharas at the capital. He had the sluices and spills at the great tanks of the Island repaired, and also strengthened the bunds of those tanks with stone and earth. He improved the royal palace by adding to it a row of rooms of surpassing beauty. *Sena III., 925-934 A.C.*

Udaya III., who had been sub-king during the previous reign, but of whose relationship to his predecessor on the throne of Lanka historians tell us nothing, except that he was a great friend of Sena III., proved himself to *Udaya III., 934-942 A.C.*

---

* Rhys David's Numismata Orientalia, section 5.

be a great drunkard and sluggard. The King of Chola, taking advantage of the character of Lanka's king and of the consequent restlessness and disorder which prevailed in the Island, sent emissaries to him demanding the crown and apparel that belonged to the King of Pandu.

Udaya having refused to yield them, the Island was invaded, the capital was taken, and the country overrun by the forces of the King of Chola until they received a severe check at the hands of the sturdy inhabitants of the Rohana district. Thereupon the King of Chola beat a hasty retreat to this kingdom, carrying with him the crown and other things taken at the capital.

In this war the commander-in-chief of the Sinhalese forces had fallen in battle, and in his place King Udaya had appointed Viduragga, a man of remarkable ability and resource. The latter soon organised the forces in the country, and, after having settled it, crossed over to the adjoining continent with a large army, where he ravaged the frontiers of the King of Chola's dominions, and frightened the King of Chola into giving up all the plunder which he had carried away from Lanka.

Thereafter, King Udaya III., by way of a thanks-offering for the success of his forces, presented a crest jewel that shone with gems and precious stones to the image of Buddha at the Maha Vihara ; and Vidura, his wife, presented a net-work shinning with jewels for the foot of the same image.

Udaya III. died in the eighth year of his reign, whilst he was busy with the reconstruction of the palace called Mani, which had been destroyed by the Cholian forces.

Sena IV., 942-945 A.C.

King Sena IV. who had occupied the office of sub-king during the previous reign, but of whose exact relationship to Udaya III. historians leave us in doubt, was a very learned man. Peace and prosperity are said to have prevailed in the Island during his short reign of three years. He is said to have expounded the Suttanta —Buddha's sermons—in the Brazen Palace, before an Audience composed of priests of the three leading fraternities. A college at the township Sitthagama was built by this king. Divers gems were added by him to the casket containing the Tooth-relic.

945-961 A.C

King Mahinda IV., a nephew of King Udaya III., who had occupied the office of sub-king during the preceding reign, on ascending the throne found every chief in the country ready to acknowledge his sovereignty, inasmuch as he was head and shoulders above all of them in ability and strength of character. Although there were princesses of royal blood available in Lanka, he procured himself a princess of the Kalinga Cakkavatti race from India for wife.

During this reign King Vallabha of Chola sent an army to Nágadípa* (Jaffna) with a view to conquering the Island. The Cholian army was met by a Sinhalese force under the command of Sena and cut to pieces. Thereupon Vallabha and other princes, through fear of a Sinhalese invasion of their territories, made overtures to King Mahinda and entered upon a treaty with him.

The remainder of his reign was devoted by the king to good works.

He decreed that temple lands should never, in the future, contribute anything to the royal exchequer. He caused heaps of paddy to be garnered in the four great viharas (Thuparama, Ruwanweli, Abhayagiri and Jetavana) and issued the following decree : "Let the poor and helpless take thereof according to their need." On sacred days he would get priests, eminent for their learning, to expound the Buddhist scriptures. The priests he specially patronised were Dhammamitta, the priest of Sittagama, and Dáthánága, who dwelt as a recluse in the forest. *Mahawansa, ch. liv., v.28.*

On the site of the stalls of the royal elephants near the Mahamega park he had an alms-hall made, with beds and seats for the poor. He furnished all the hospitals in the Island with medicines and beds, and improved the diet of political prisoners, inasmuch as he ordered that they should be given rice.

He built the Mahámallaka Convent, which he presented to the sisterhood of the Theriya sect. He started the construction of a many-storied house—Cadana by name—at the Miriswetiya temple. He completed the construction of the house named Mani, commenced during the reign of his uncle Udaya III. For details regarding King Mahinda IV.'s various religious benefactions the reader is referred to the *Mahawansa*, chapter 54, vv. 17-48.

---

* Casie Chitty's paper in Journal of R.A.S. (C.B.) 1848, p. 71. Also Tennent, vol. I., p. 331, n. 9.

For the advancement of learning, four of the king's ministers built each of them a college (pirivena) attached to the Jetavana Vihara. Queen Kitti, a woman of considerable culture and benevolence, built another college attached to the Thuparama. She also had three baths for the use of monks built at the Thuparama, Kappagáma and the Civara temples; and presented a flag of gold lace, twelve cubits in length, to the Ruwanweli Cetiya.

Two large hospitals were built during this reign. One was built within the city, by the king's son by his Queen Kitti, for the use of the general public; the other was built outside the city for the use of priests, by Sakka, the minister for war. Mahinda IV. died in the 15th year of his reign, and was succeeded on the throne by his son Sena, a lad twelve years old, born of the queen imported from Kalinga.

Sena V., 961-971 A.C.

Sena V. appointed his younger brother Udaya to the high office of sub-king and retained the services of the experienced general Sena as commander-in-chief of the royal forces. The young king was a self-willed, hot-headed youth, who would not tolerate any one at his court who did not show him servile obedience. On one occassion, for disobeying his orders, the king slew the younger brother of the commander-in-chief, who had been left at his court to act as his adviser, whilst the commander was out on an expedition to quell a rebellion. On hearing the news of the fate that had befallen his brother, the commander hurried to the capital with his army to wreak vengeance. Thereupon the king fled to the Rohana district, leaving his mother, the sub-king, and his queen behind in the capital, and taking with him as his companion and adviser Mahamalla Udaya, whose only qualification for the post was his servile obedience to the king.

On his arrival at the capital, the queen-mother sent for the commander-in-chief and spoke to him in such a quiet, calm, and dignified manner that he decided to leave them unmolested. However, he summoned a meeting of the influential Indians resident in the capital, and entrusting to them the administration of the country he took up his abode at Pollonnaruwa.

Here he was attacked by forces sent against him by the king; but successfully resisted them.

When the king discovered that the country was being ravaged in all quarters by Indians, and that the people looked to him for deliverance, he dismissed his adviser Udaya, made overtures and established a reconciliation with Sena, the commander-in-chief, whose daughter he married; and through his instrumentality regained the kingdom. Not many years did King Sena live to occupy the throne, inasmuch as he drank himself to death, having chosen for himself councillors who encouraged him in his habit. The *Mahawansa* describes him as "a drunkard who was like unto a mad tiger."

It is interesting to note that the Chinese traveller Kénëé, in his book Seyih King-Ching (= Travels in the Western Kingdoms in the 10th century), written in A.C. 964, mentions having seen a monastery of Sinhalese on the Continent of India. *Tennent, vol. I., p. 616, n. 5.*

Mahinda V., younger brother of Sena V., was a very slothful monarch. He allowed affairs of State to drift during the first twelve years of his reign, not even to collect the revenues due to him from the provinces did he trouble himself. At length, his exchequer having run empty, he was brought to his senses by a revolt on the part of the Malabar mercenaries who composed his standing army, they having laid siege to his palace, swords in hand, saying: "The king shall not eat of his meat until our wages be first given to us." From this awkward situation King Mahinda escaped with all his jewelry and his household by an underground passage, and took refuge in the Rohana district, where he built a stronghold at a village named Sidu-pabbata and lived with King Sena V.'s queen and daughter. After a time he left the fortress and built a city in the village Kappagallaka and ruled there over the Rohana district for years. The rest of the country was during this time under the rule of people of various races, viz., the Malabars (Keralas), the Sinhalese, and men of the Carnatic (Kannátas). *971-1007 A.C.*

The King of Chola, having learnt from a dealer in horses, who traded with Lanka, of the state of affairs in the Island, immediately sent over a large army, which devastated the country, plundering everything they could get hold of, "like demons who suck up the blood." They broke into the relic-houses of temples and carried off all the golden images and other valuables which they contained. They captured the queen with all the royal jewels and ornaments, amongst them being the crown that was the inheritance of the kings, a priceless diamond bracelet, a sword that could not be broken, and the sacred *1007 A.C.*

band worn over the forehead (chinna pattika dhátu). Next they captured the king himself in the fastnesses of the forest by means of an act of treachery in which they made a false show of peace. They then sent him and the plunder to the King of Chola and established themselves at Pollonnaruwa, from which city they proceeded to administer the country.

After a time, news having reached the King of Chola to the effect that Kassapa, the son of the captive king Mahinda V., a boy of twelve, dwelt in the Rohana district, and that the people of the Island showed him marked respect and affection, orders were issued by him to his chief officers to set out for Lanka with an army to capture the boy prince. Accordingly an army of 95,000 Cholians invaded the Island and overran Rohana searching for the prince. Exasperated by the excesses of the Cholians, two gallant and valiant Sinhalese noblemen named Kitti and Buddha, natives of the two villages Makkhakudrúsa and Maragalla (in Atakalan Korale) respectively, summoned the assistance of the inhabitants, and having built themselves a stronghold at Palutupána (Paluttha-giri) waged a determined war against the Indians for six months, in the course of which the greater portion of the invading army perished. Finally, the demoralised remnant of the Cholian army, abandoning the idea of capturing the prince, hastily retired to Pollonnaruwa. King Mahinda V. died a captive in Chola in the 12th year after his capture. It is interesting to note what Chinese historians, writing during this period, have said of Ceylon. The *Tae-ping*, written in A.C. 983, says that "the Emperors of China were accustomed from time to time to solicit transcripts of theological works from the Buddhist priests of Lanka; and their envoys, returning from such missions, brought glowing accounts of the Sinhalese temples, the costly shrines for relics, and the fervid devotion of the people to the national worship." The *Tsih-foo Yaen-kwei*, written in A.C. 1012, says: "At daybreak every morning the people are summoned, and exhorted to repeat the passages of Buddha, in order to remove ignorance and open the minds of the multitude. Discourses are delivered upon the principles of vacancy (nirwana?) and abstraction from material objects, in order that truth may be studied in solitude and silence, and the unfathomable point of principle attained free from the distracting influences of sound or smell." The same book tells us

Tennent, vol. I., p. 616.

that the palace of the king at Anuradhapura was sufficiently splendid to excite the admiration of every Chinese visitor, "the precious articles with which it was decorated being reflected in the thoroughfares." The Chinese authors, like the Greeks and the Arabians, are warm in their praises of the patriotism of the Sinhalese sovereigns and their active exertions for the improvement of the country and the prosperity of the people.

Although these histories were written during the reign of Mahinda V., there is no doubt about the fact that they dealt with conditions in Lanka prior to his accession to the throne.

Throughout all the Chinese accounts from the very earliest period, there are notices of the manners of the Sinhalese, and even minute particulars of their domestic habits showing an intimate familiarity between the people of the two countries. They describe our dress, mode of tying the hair, treatment of infants and children, and mention the fact that Sinhalese men and women were addicted to chewing betel, and that the women did not sit down to meals with their husbands.

Vikkrama Bahu, 1019-1031 A.C.

On the news of Mahinda V.'s death reaching Lanka, the people of Rohana named Kassapa, the boy prince, **Vikkrama Bahu,** and upheld his authority faithfully. The prince, on the other hand, assiduously made every preparation to rid the Island of foreign domination and establish his authority over it. He gathered together vast sums of money as well as an army of 100,000 men. He caused royal jewels to be made, as well as the crown, canopy, and the throne, but refused to yield to the request of the nobles that he should be anointed king, saying that that would be permitted after he had accomplished the object he had in view. Unfortunately for the country, Vikkrama Bahu was struck down with an illness, from which he never recovered, on the eve of his starting out on his gigantic enterprise. He died in the 12th year of his reign over Rohana.

Kirti, 1031 A.C.

Kirti, the nobleman who played such an important part in ridding Rohana of Indian domination, succeeded Vikkrama Bahu, but his authority was challenged by an influential chief by the name of Mahálána Kirti, and he was killed in battle in the seventh day of his reign.

Mahálána Kirti, 1031 A.C.

Mahalana Kirti had himself crowned King of Rohana and occupied the throne for three years, at the end of which period he was defeated in battle by the

Cholians, and committed suicide on the battle-field rather than allow himself to be taken alive. On this occasion the Cholians, for the second time, captured the crown, jewels and other treasure of the Sinhalese monarch and sent them to India to their king.

Vikkrama Pandu, 1034-1035 A.C.

Soon after the death of Mahálána Kirti, a Sinhalese prince of the royal blood named **Vikkrama Pandu,** who had been a refugee in India (Dulu), arrived in Rohana and established himself at Kalutara (Kalatittha). He was acknowledged by the inhabitants of Rohana as their supreme chief and ruled over the district for one year, when his supremacy was successfully challenged by **Jagatipala,** a native of Ayoddhya, who, soon after his landing in Rohana, was joined by a large number of the inhabitants of the district, who were dissatisfied with Vikkrama Pandu's administration. Jagatipala was slain in battle by the Cholians in the fourth year of his reign, and his queen, daughter, and all their substance were sent to the King of Chola as trophies of the war.

Jagatipala, 1035-1039 A.C.

Lokeswara, 1039-1045 A.C.

There soon arose from among the inhabitants of Rohana a brave and honest leader **Loka (Lokeswara)** by name, who, having defeated the Cholian army sent against him, established himself at Kataragama, whence he proceeded to administer the country. His right to the sovereignty was ere long challenged by Kirti, a valiant prince of the royal blood descended on his father Mogallana's side from King Mahinda V., and on his mother Lokita's side from King Dathopatissa. Several battles were fought between the forces of the rivals, one at a village named Bodivále and several at Cunnasála, in each of which the attacking forces of Loka were repulsed. At length Kirti's forces received a considerable accession of strength, inasmuch as a mighty warrior, Devamalla, with his entire following joined his ranks. Devamalla was the son of Kirti, the nobleman of Makkha-Kudrusa, who years ago had rid the Rohana district of Cholian domination. Feeling himself strong enough to join battle with Loka, Kirti emerged from his stronghold at Cunnasála and encamped with his forces at Remunusela in the Hiraññamalaya (Ratnapura) country. Here Loka made a final attempt to crush him, but Kirti, who had gained wisdom by experience, acted as usual on the defensive, thereby counteracting the superiority Loka possessed over him in the number of his forces. Finding that he met with no success, Loka retired to his capital at Kataragama, and there awaited the arrival of the enemy until he fell ill and died in the sixth year of his reign.

It is interesting to note that although Sinhalese historians make frequent mention of coins named Kahapamas and Massa (the former of which Turnour says was a gold coin worth ten of the latter) as having been in use in the country from the time of King Duttu Gamunu downwards, the oldest coins in existence at the present day are two gold ones of Loka (Lokesvara) to be found in the British Museum. *Numismatic Chronicle, 16th vol., p. 121.* *Tennent, vol. I., p. 461.*

Kassapa VI., 1045 A.C.

On the death of Loka, **Kassapa,** the chief who held the office of guardian of the Hair-relic, seized the reins of government and proceeded to administer the Rohana district. When the Cholians heard of it, they invaded the district and were marching on their way to Kataragama, when they were met and routed by Kassapa leading his army in person. Kassapa pursued them up to Rakkhapásána (Rakwana?), and there stationing a force to guard the boundary, returned with great pomp to his capital. Here he was not long allowed to rest on his laurels, for, news having reached him of Prince Kirti's preparations to challenge his right to administer the kingdom, he hastened forward with his army to Sippatthalaka, where he found Kirti with a large army, which he had enlisted in the Pañcayojana (Pasdun Korle). Kassapa, finding that the inhabitants in the surrounding districts were hostile towards him, ordered his forces to retreat, remarking "It is difficult to give battle here."

Thereupon Prince Kirti pursued them cautiously until they reached Kataragama, where proud Kassapa, enraged at finding the enemy close behind him at his capital, ordered his forces immediately to march out and attack him. A great stubbornly contested battle ensued outside the city gates, in which Kassapa was slain, and the valiant Prince Kirti, who had started his military career at the age of thirteen and was now seventeen years of age, was proclaimed king under the name of Vijaya Bahu. Rohana had been under the administration of Kassapa for six months.

Vijaya Bahu I., 1045-1095 A.C.

Vijaya Bahu, who was no less great an administrator than he was a general of consummate skill, appointed his nobles to offices suited to their capacity, and caused his authority to be proclaimed throughout Rohana by beat of drum. He next devoted his attention to the attainment of the great object of his life, viz., ridding the entire country of foreign domination. For this purpose he employed with great dexterity four recognised stratagems of war, viz., sowing dissension, sudden attack, negociation and bribery.

The King of Chola, on hearing the news of developments in Lanka, where for nearly half a century his rule over the richest portion of the Island—the Pihiti-rata—had been maintained without any serious hindrance,—sent orders to his general, stationed at Pollonnaruwa, to capture the King of Rohana and annex his kingdom. Accordingly Rohana was invaded by the Cholians, who advanced straight on to the capital, Kataragama, where they expected to inflict a crushing defeat on Vijaya Bahu. Vijaya Bahu, having received timely information as to the strength of the invading army, abandoned his capital and took refuge in a fortress on the hills. The Cholian general, deeming it unsafe to attempt to follow him to the hills, contented himself with plundering the city of what was left of any value in it, and returning hastily to Pollonnaruwa. Thereupon Vijaya Bahu descended from the hills and stationed himself at his former stronghold at Sippatthalaka. From here he sent an embassy, with presents of great value, to the King of Ramanna (the provinces situated between Araccan and Siam) asking him for assistance in the war he contemplated waging. His people, being an unwarlike race, devoted to their religion, it was not surprising to find that their king returned the compliment paid him by the King of Robana, by sending the latter ships laden with cloths of many kinds, camphor, sandal-wood and other things which King Vijaya Bahu with great tact and sagacity used for making gifts to his warriors.

The motive that prompted Vijaya Bahu to seek succour from Ramanna must have been the community of religion that prevailed in the two countries and his desire to make the struggle a religious one. As a result of the non-arrival of reinforements from Ramanna, Vijaya Bahu, for a time, abandoned the idea of invading Pihiti-rata and fixed his abode at Tammalagáma. Meanwhile, the failure of the Cholian general to capture Vijaya Bahu had shaken the confidence of the inhabitants of Pihiti-rata in the power of the Cholians. This was finally indicated by the refusal of the Sinhalese chiefs, and minor headmen, to pay any taxes to the Cholian Government. So widespread was the unrest amongst the Sinhalese inhabitants of Pihiti-rata, that the Cholian forces in Lanka were considered insufficient to assert the authority of their king. Accordingly assistance was summoned from Chola, and the King of Chola speedily despatched a large army under the leadership of the foremost general in his land. The reinforcement landed at the Mahatittha (Mantotta, a port in the north opposite the Island of Mannar), and pushed their way down south crushing the opposition of the turbulent inhabitants with great slaughter. Finally, elated with the success that attended his arms in the Pihiti-rata, the experienced Cholian general decided upon rooting out of the Island the cause of all the unrest, viz., Vijaya Bahu. Accordingly, he led his army with great caution into the Rohana country. All this while Vijaya Bahu had been evolving a plan by which he should overcome the enemy in case his kingdom was invaded ; and now arrived the opportunity to execute it. Accordingly, two of his most trusty and valiant officers—Ravideva and Chala—with a large force marched forward as deserters from his ranks and joined the Cholian general, who, delighted with the enormous accession of strength he had thus received, pushed forward against the King of Rohana, who had fortified himself at Pulutupána (Polluttha-pabbata). Here a terrible battle was fought, in the course of which Ravideva and Chala turned their forces against the Cholians, who, finding themselves attacked from within and without the fortress, broke their ranks and fled. The Sinhalese hotly pursued them, giving them no quarter until they had captured the Cholian general with all his chariots, carriages, and treasures at the village Tambavitthi. Elated by this victory and yielding to the desire of his ministers, Vijaya Bahu pushed forward with his forces and occupied the city of Pollonnaruwa. Meanwhile the news of the disaster that had befallen his general having reached the King of Chola, another army, more powerful than the last, was speedily sent to Lanka to retrieve the credit of the Cholian nation, the Cholian King himself accompanying it to the port of embarkation, and wishing his men good fortune in their enterprise, whilst recalling to their minds the valorous deeds of their ancestors whose traditions they should maintain.

When King Vijaya Bahu received the news of the landing of a Cholian army he speedily despatched a large force, under one of his generals, to meet it. A great battle was fought between the rival armies near Anuradhapura, in which the Sinhalese were defeated. Thereupon, Vijaya Bahu abandoned Pollonnaruwa and took refuge in a village named Villikábána, where he busily engaged himself in concentrating his scattered forces, while the Cholians busied themselves with settling all the disturbances in Pihiti-rata. At length, news having reached him to the effect that the Cholian army had started out in his direction, he marched his forces, with all the necessary provisions, to a rock called Vátagiri, where he threw up fortifications and withstood a siege for three months, at the end of which the Sinhalese sallied forth and routed the besiegers.

King Vijaya Bahu was not allowed any respite after his prolonged trial, inasmuch as a younger brother of Kassapa—the chief who held the office of guardian of the Hair-relic, from whom Vijaya Bahu had wrested the administration of Rohana—thought this to be his opportunity to avenge the treatment Kassapa had received at the hands of Vijaya Bahu, whom, together with his forces, he thought would be worn out by fatigue and utterly unfit for continued effort. Accordingly, he raised a rebellion, in which he was supported by the inhabitants of the Guttahálaka district. Vijaya Bahu, having determined to nip the rebellion in the bud, by forced marches reached his stronghold at Khadirangani, where he was defeated; but escaped to offer battle at Kubulagalla, where he was again defeated and compelled to seek refuge in Pihiti-rata, leaving behind his wife, children, army, and much treasure as spoil. With all this spoil Vijaya Bahu made his way to his old fortress at Tambalagama, which he renovated. Thence he moved to a city called Mahanagakula, where he made every preparation for ridding the country of Cholian domination. He next sent two strong forces, one northwards through the interior of the country and the other along the eastern coast into Pihiti-rata. The former succeeded in capturing fortification after fortification of the Cholians—whom it found thoroughly demoralised after the capture of their leading general—all along the line until it reached Mantotta. Amongst the fortifications captured were those at Mahanarugama, Badalat-thala, Vapinagara, Buddhagama, Tilagulla, Mahágalla, Mandagalla and Anuradhapura.

The force that had been sent along the sea-board was not less successful, inasmuch as it razed to the ground the fortresses at Chagama and stormed divers other encapments, until it approached the neighbourhood of Pollonnaruwa, where it halted till the arrival of King Vijaya Bahu with reinforcements, for the purpose of storming the city. Meanwhile Cholians from all parts of the country, learning of the danger which threatened their capital, hurried to defend it. Vijaya Bahu, on learning the news of the gigantic success that had attended the efforts of the detachments he had sent out, and also of the necessity of his presence at the storming of Pollonnaruwa, hurried forward with all his available forces, halting on his way for a brief rest at Mahiyangana (Alutnuwera in the Bintenne district). Soon after he had joined forces, he marched right up to the city and encamped himself strongly outside its walls. The Cholians sallied out and fought a terrific battle, but were repulsed and sought refuge in the city whose gates they closed. For six weeks they continued to defend it desperately from the walls and towers, until finally it was carried by storm, the detachments under the command of Ravideva and Chala being the first to scale the *1060. A.C.* walls. Great was the slaughter of Cholians within the city.

For two years after the capture of Pollonnaruwa Vijaya Bahu busily engaged himself with settling the administration of the country, which was in a state of chaos, as a result of half a century of incessant warfare. During these two years one small rebellion was raised against his authority by an officer of his army named Adimalaya, but it was speedily crushed.

Thereafter Vijaya Bahu—who until then had been *1062 A.C.* crowned only as King of Rohana—had himself crowned as King of Lanka with great pomp and ceremony at Anuradhapura, and was thenceforth known throughout the land by the name of Siri Sanghabo.

He next proceeded to Pollonnaruwa, which for a time he made his seat of government. He appointed his nobles to all the more important posts in the Island in accordance with their merits, and had as his prime minister his brother Vira Bahu—a man of great valour and administrative ability,—while the governorship of Rohana was conferred on his other younger brother Jaya Bahu.

He decreed that taxes should be levied by his officers equitably. He further established proper courts of justice throughout the country, where cases were determined after full enquiry, according to law.

The chief bearer of the canopy (chattagáhaka-nátha), the chief justice (dhammagehaka-náyaka), and the minister of commerce (setthi-nátha), who, having in-
1064 A.C. curred the king's displeasure, had fled from the country, returned in 1064 A.C. and raised a great rebellion in the Rohana, Malaya, and western portions of Lanka. Vijaya Bahu, with characteristic energy, pushed forward into the Rohana and Malaya districts, and crushing his enemies there, flushed by his victories, marched with his forces to the west, and there rooted out the remnant of his enemies in a bloody battle, those who were taken alive being impaled on the battle-field to serve as a deterrent to possible traitors in the future.

During this reign the queen of Jagátipála (King of Rohana), who had been carried off with her daughter Lilavati by the Cholians, escaped and returned to Lanka. After proof of their identity had been fully established Vijaya Bahu married Lilavati, who bore him one daughter (Yasodhara). Being anxious to perpetuate his family he entered upon a second marriage with one Lilokasundari, a princess, of great beauty and of delicate form, from Kálinga. She bore him five daughters—Subhaddhá, Summitta, Lokanáthá, Ratanávali, and Rupavati—and one son, Vikkrama Bahu.

Vijaya Bahu's sister Mittá was given in marriage to a prince of Pandu, in preference to the King of Chola, although the latter begged of King Vijaya Bahu that she should be allowed to marry him.

In accordance with ancient custom among kings of Lanka, Vijaya Bahu chose men from all the great families in the Island and set them to guard his person.

He fortified Pollonnaruwa by building a strong lofty wall around it, ornamented with plaster work and protected by towers built thereon. He also caused a deep and broad moat to be dug round the wall as an additional bulwark.

Finding that the result of half a century of Cholian domination was the well-nigh entire disappearance of Buddhism in the Island, Vijaya Bahu, for the purpose of reviving it—inasmuch as religion was the only medium by which the masses could be made to regulate their conduct aright,—sent for learned priests from the Ramanna country (a portion of the present Burma) and caused monks to be ordained in great numbers, so that, after a few years, Buddhism, "which had been darkened throughout Lanka, began to shine forth." *Mahawansa, ch. lx., vi 4-8.*

The *Rajaratnacara* thus describes it :—"On account of the long war in which the country had been engaged, there were not five good teroonansays to be found in the whole Island; wherefore, the king, being greatly distressed in mind, sent splendid presents of pearls and precious stones to the king of the country called Aramana, requesting that twenty-nine well learned teroonansays, with their books, might be sent to Lanka; and these having come many thousands more were ordered out, and throughout the Island, especially at Anuradhapura, the Buddhist temples were rebuilt and repaired."

The king is said to have built a good many viharas at Pollonnaruwa, and one in particular—the Lanka Tilaka—is specially mentioned by Sinhalese historians for its magnificence. The *Mahawansa* says :—"He embellished it with a gate of pillars and a wall and a moat, and adorned it with a noble house of five stories. He varied it with fine rows of dwellings round about it, of great beauty, and an excellent spacious shining gate, which was always full of people. He caused many hundreds of monks of the three fraternities to dwell there, and provided them with all that was needful for a monastic life."

In his great zeal for the furtherance of the national religion, the king found time, amidst his many other duties, to devote himself to literature. The *Mahawansa* says :—"He shut himself every morning against his people, and made a translation of the *Dhamma Sangani* within the beautiful preaching-hall."

In 1075 A.C. the peace and tranquillity that had been brought about in the Island was rudely disturbed. In this year two embassies arrived, both at the same time, at Pollonnaruwa bearing rich gifts to King Vijaya Bahu from the kings of Kannáta (a kingdom in the Deccan) and Chola. Vijaya Bahu being very pleased at it, entertained the members of the embassies, and returned the compliments by sending them back accompanied by his own men carrying gifts of great value. The petty-minded King of Chola, taking offence at the fact that the embassy from Kannáta was attended to first, inasmuch as they departed from Pollonnaruwa prior to the members of his embassy, ordered the ears and noses of the Sinhalese, who arrived with his messengers at his court, to be cut off and sent them back to their king. Enraged at the cruel and cowardly insult offered him, Vijaya Bahu summoned his ministers and, after a consultation with them, procured some Cholians, whom he caused to be clad in women's apparel, and despatched to the King of Chola with the following message: " Set we apart our armies, in either land, and make a trial of the strength of our arms in single combat between us in the midst of the ocean, or, if it please thee better, let us array our armies in battle, either in my kingdom or thine, according as it pleaseth thee, and let the strife be there." Every preparation for war having been made, and no reply to this message having been received, Vijaya Bahu set out with a force and encamped at Anuradhapura, and ordered two of his officers with a large army to embark at Mantotta and invade Chola. A serious mutiny of the regiment composed of foreign mercenaries having taken place at the port of embarkation, resulting in the two officers being killed and Pollonnaruwa being taken by the rebels, the contemplated invasion of Chola had to be abandoned. So serious was this mutiny that Vijaya Bahu was compelled to retreat to Rohana with his treasures. After he had deposited them there, in conjunction with his valiant brother Vira Bahu, he advanced with his forces on Pollonnaruwa and completely subdued the rebels. Their leaders were taken to the spot where lay the bones of the two officers that were slain, and there tied to posts with their hands behind their backs and burnt alive.

For the remaining twenty-five years of his reign peace prevailed in the land, and Vijaya Bahu was enabled to devote his attention to furthering the material and spiritual welfare of his subjects.

For the furtherance of agriculture he repaired the bunds of numerous tanks scattered throughout the Island, amongst them being the Maháheli, Sareheru, Mahádatika, Katunnaru, Pandavapi, Kallagallika, Erandagalla, Dígha-vatthuka, Mandavátaka, Kitta, Aggabodhipabhata, Valáhassa, Mahádáragalla, Kumbhíla-sobbha, Pattapásána, Kána. He also built the bund of the channel Tila-vatthuka which had been breached, and thus filled the Mineriya (Manihéra) tank with water.

For the furtherance of religion he repaired numerous viharas, for which the reader is referred to the *Mahawansa*, chapter lx., vv. 58-63. He built dagobas at Mahagama in Rohana. He caused the village Gilimalaya, that abounded in rice fields and other land, to be granted for the purpose of supplying pilgrims to the sacred foot-print on Adam's Peak, (Samanta-kuta) with free food. He built resting-places along the Kadaligama highway, and also along the Uva pathway and endowed them. He provided priests with cloaks, fire-pans, and various drugs for use during the cold season (December and January). In his great compassion for the suffering, he provided pauper cripples with bulls. To well-born helpless widows he gave lands and food and raiment according to their necessities. He gave lands to the lame and blind.

He was a great poet and was recognised as the chief of the bards among the Sinhalese.

For the purpose of encouraging literary taste in others he made rich gifts of money and land, to be held in perpetuity to those who composed fine songs.

The example set by the king was closely followed by the chiefs of the country according to their capacity; in particular, the prime minister Vira Bahu is mentioned by Sinhalese historians as having spent vast sums of money in charity.

Vira Bahu died towards the latter portion of this reign, and was succeeded in office by his brother Jaya Bahu, the king's son, Vikkrama Bahu, filling up the office of governor of Rohana, vacated by Jaya Bahu.

King Vijaya Bahu—one of the greatest of Lanka's kings—died peacefully in the fifty-fifth year of his reign after having rid the country of Cholian domination and produced order, peace, and prosperity out of the chaos and misery that prevailed when he ascended the throne. *1095 A.C.*

On the death of King Vijaya Bahu, at his capital Pollonnaruwa, his sister Mitta, conspiring with her three sons, the chief officers of State, and the monks of the chief viharas, had **Jaya Bahu** anointed king over Lanka, and in violation of ancient custom had her eldest son Mánábharana appointed sub-king. When Vikkrama Bahu, who was residing in Rohana, received the news of his father's death and of the subsequent developments, in particular, that the conspirators, after seizing his *Jaya Bahu, 1095 A.C.*

father's jewels of great value, his vehicles, elephants, and such like, were advancing into his district, with a great army, he made every preparation for war. Having defeated them in six successive battles Vikkrama Bahu reached his father's capital, where he took up his residence after he had paid his respects to his dead father, by visiting the spot where the latter had been cremated.

Meanwhile Manabharana and his brothers, having brought the Rohana and Maya (the western portion of the Island situated between the Kaluganga and Dedru-oya) districts under their yoke, divided these amongst themselves. Manabharana took upon himself the administration of Maya-rata and established his residence at Punkhagama; Kirti Sirimegha undertook the administration of Giruwapattu and established himself at the city Mahanagakula; Siri Vallabha undertook the administration of Atthasahassa (Attakalan and Kolonna Korles). King Jaya Bahu and Mitta resided with Kirti Sirimegha.

In 1096 A.C. news having reached Vikkrama Bahu of preparations being made by his three cousins to wrest from him the administration of Pihiti-rata, he advanced with his army into Maya-rata and routed their conjoint army at Bodhisena-pabbata, whence they sought refuge in Pasdun Korle (Panca-yojana). Whilst Vikkrama Bahu was on his way there, he received information at Kelaniya of the invasion of the Island by an Indian army, led by an experienced chieftain, Viradeva of Palandipa, which had already effected a landing at Mantotta. Abandoning the advance against his cousins, he hurried north with his army and gave battle to the enemy not far from their port of landing. In it, Kirti, the commander-in-chief of the Sinhalese army, two of Vikkrama Bahu's sons and many nobles were slain, and Vikkrama Bahu was compelled to beat a hasty retreat to Pollonnaruwa, whence with his treasures he took refuge in a fortress surrounded by a great marsh at the village Antaravitthika, which was well stocked with stores of grain. The invaders, having entered Pollonnaruwa without opposition and taken a rest there for a few days, proceeded against Vikkrama Bahu in his stronghold, but received a crushing defeat at his hands.

Vikkrama Bahu I., 1096 A.C. 1117 A.C.

Thereafter **Vikkrama Bahu I.** was left undisturbed in the administration of Pihiti-rata, and his cousins remained content with the administration of the districts they had taken charge of.

The *Mahawansa* speaks thus of these four administrators :—" These foolish men gave no heed to religion, neither cared they ought for their subjects, whom the King Vijaya Bahu had prospered in divers ways. They forcibly took the possessions of honourable men away, though there was no fault to find in them. And, for their avarice and covetousness, they oppressed their subjects and levied grievous taxes from them, yea, even as the mill extracts juice from the sugar-cane."

For the priesthood residing in Pollonnaruwa, Vikkrama Bahu had supreme contempt, inasmuch as they had conspired with Mitta to deprive him of his legitimate right to the office of sub-king. To such an extent did the king show his contempt for them and their religion, that they left the city in a body carrying away with them, to Rohana, the sacred Tooth-relic and Alms-bowl.

The *Mahawansa* further says :—" The chiefs who had been set to guard the boundaries, by the kings of both parties, fell out among themselves and made war on each other continually. They burnt down many rich villages and made cuttings in tanks full of water, and in divers other ways destroyed all the conduits and dams and hewed down cocoanut and other serviceable trees......... The inhabitants of Samanta-kuta (the region round Adam's Peak) and many other strongholds refused all payment of taxes and lived in open defiance of royal authority."

Mahawansa, ch. 62, vv. 64-72.

Jaya Bahu, as well as Mitta, died a few years after they had taken up their abode in Giruwapattu. A few years later Ratanavali, sister of Vikkrama Bahu and wife of Manabharana, gave birth to a son, who was named Parakrama Bahu in accordance with a prophesy made by the household Brahmans to the effect that the child would grow up to be a mighty warrior capable of conquering the whole of India.

Manabharana died a few years after the birth of his son, whereupon his brother Kirti Sirimegha took upon himself the administration of Maya-rata, letting his brother Siri Vallabha administer the whole of the Rohana district. Ratanavali, her two daughters, and son Parakrama Bahu, resided with Siri Vallabha.

Vikkrama Bahu died in the twenty-first year of his administration of Pihiti-rata, and was succeeded by his *1117 A.C.*

Gaja Bahu II., 1117-1138 A.C. son **Gaja Bahu.** Thereupon his uncles Kirti Sirimegha and Siri Vallabha decided upon making a second attempt to gain Pihiti-rata, which was considered to be the richest portion of the Island. They succeeded, by bribery, in getting a portion of Gaja Bahu's army, which consisted of foreign mercenaries (Velakkaras), to rebel; but in spite of it, Gaja Bahu found himself strong enough to inflict crushing defeats on the two armies of his uncles that invaded his territory from two sides. Gaja Bahu himself led that portion of his army which defeated Siri Vallabha after a stubborn encounter, lasting from morn till night; and his general Gokanna led the other, which defeated Kirti Sirimegha.

Soon after Parakrama Bahu had attained the years of discretion he left the court of his uncle, Siri Vallabha, and journeyed to that of his uncle Kirti Sirimegha—the place of his birth. Kirti Sirimegha extended the youth a hearty welcome, adorning the city with arches, etc., in honour of his arrival, and after a time grew passionately fond of him, as he was a respectful and obedient youth. Furthermore Kirti Sirimegha, having no male issue of his own, thought Parakrama Bahu, of whom the soothsayers had prophesied such great things, would make an excellent successor. Accordingly, every care was taken with regard to his education. The
ch. 64, vv. 2-5 *Mahawansa* says:—"In religion, in the various systems of laws such as kocalla and the like, in the science of words, in poetry, including collections of synonyms and the art of planning stories, in dancing and music and riding, in the use of the sword and the bow, and in such other arts did he perfect himself exceedingly, because he had been thoroughly instructed therein."

In addition to this, Kirti Sirimegha closely associated his nephew with himself in the course of administering the country, so that he might learn the art of governing. At length, Parakrama Bahu having come of age, by order of Kirti Sirimegha the rite of investiture (Upanayana = the investitures with the sacred thread of the Brahmana, Kshatriya, and Vaisya classes, which take place respectively from eight to sixteen, from eleven to twenty-two, and from twelve to twenty-four years of age) was performed with great pomp and ceremony. Soon after this event news reached Kirti Sirimegha of his brother Siri Vallabha's death, and of the succession of the latter's son Manabharana to the administration of Rohana, whereupon he hastened to Rohana with Parakrama Bahu and spent a year there at the court of Manabharana.

After his return to Maya-rata, Parakrama Bahu's restless and ambitious spirit began to assert itself. Inspired by the great deeds of valour performed by characters in the *Ramayana*, which he had studied, he set out secretly from Kirti Sirimegha's palace, accompanied by a handful of daring and reckless spirits, with the intention of personally acquainting himself with the exact conditions that prevailed in Pihiti-rata—which had a reputation of being possessed of great material and military resource.

On his way to Pihiti-rata he halted at Badalatthali, a village on the borders of Kirti Sirimegha's province (Maya-rata), where was stationed his foremost general Sangha Senadhipati with a large force for the purpose of guarding the frontiers. The general, suspecting that Parakrama Bahu was travelling without the cognisance of Kirti Sirimegha, detained him with his following until he could learn the wishes of his master. Enraged at the insult thus offered Parakrama slew the general, and seizing hold of all his treasures, etc., fought his way into Pihiti-rata, defeating the forces sent by Kirti Sirimegha to prevent his progress, in four successive battles at the villages Buddhagama, Saraggama, Khiravapi, and Navagiri. When Gaja Bahu received the news of Parakrama Bahu's presence at the village Janapada situated within his dominions, he hastily summoned a meeting of his ministers and consulted them as to the manner in which he should act. It having been decided that the wisest course to adopt would be to extend Parakrama a hearty welcome, an invitation was sent to him together with presents of rich garments, jewels, etc. As Parakrama was approaching Pollonnaruwa in accordance with this invitation, Gaja Bahu went forth to meet him surrounded by his army, and was received with great respect. Thereupon, in the fulness of his joy, he made Parakrama mount the elephant on which he himself rode, and together they rode to the palace after Parakrama had been shown all the beautiful sights of the city. After he had spent some time as Gaja Bahu's guest in his palace, Parakrama set about accomplishing the object of his mission. The manner in which he did it is thus described in the *Mahawansa*:—"So that he may know to a certainty those who were faithful from those who were unfaithful among the subjects of Gaja Bahu, he chose faithful

Mahawansa, ch. 66, pp. 139-140.

men of his own, who were skilled in all expedients and were familiar with the languages of many countries. From among them he, who was skilled in planning devices, appointed some who were experts in the science of poison to go hither and thither in the disguise of snake-dancers, and some of physiognomists, and some of musicians, wearing the garments of Chadálas and Brahmans. From among the Tamils and other foreigners he chose such as were skilled in singing and dancing, and induced them to assume the guise of such as wander about displaying puppet shows and other sports. Some also he appointed to walk about disguised as pedlars, taking with them as merchandise rings and bangles and other ornaments made of glass. He made some to carry umbrellas, staves, and other things needful to hermits, and causing them to take the guise of devout ascetics, sent them forth to wander from village to village, as if they made pilgrimages to shrines. He commanded others who were skilled in healing diseases to go about the villages and towns practising as physicians. Likewise also he commanded those who were versed in teaching the young the knowledge of letters and arms, and those who were versed in alchemy, those also who were sorcerers, and many who were cunning in working in gold and other metals, to betake themselves to their trades and to wander about the country. As he himself desired to know the true feeling of them that dwelt without the city, he feigned himself to be fond of talk, and spoke to all men whom he met with; and when he happened to be in the company of those who constantly found fault with Gaja Bahu, he pretended to be uninterested. Thus did he find out from among the chief ministers and soldiers those who were puffed out with pride and those who were kindled with anger and resentment, those who lacked courage, and those who were greedy of gain.

"And the spies, who were well versed in the folklore of the divers systems of religion that are contained in the *Itihasa*, the *Purana*, and the other books, and who were skilled in devising proper means to lead the minds of their companions, took themselves the guise of samanas (mendicant monks) and repaired to the houses of people, and, having gained their entire confidence and obtained their favour and regard, took to themselves the office of household counsellors, and undermined the fealty of the people, and themselves acted in such a manner and gave such counsel as made them to be one with them."

In order to allay all possible suspicions in Gaja Bahu and thereby ensure all possible freedom of locomotion for himself, Parakrama Bahu sent for his sister Bhaddavati with a great quantity of wealth from Rohana.

He gave her in marriage to Gaja Bahu, while he kept for his own use the wealth she had brought with her. Having gained the entire confidence of Gaja Bahu he began to go about the streets, as if for pleasure, accompanied by a spirited elephant of noble breed, and feigning to be pursued by the beast he would run a distance and take refuge in the houses of those whose goodwill he thought it needful to obtain by making suitable gifts to them of ornaments of great value and other treasure; and in this manner he secretly brought them all under his influence, "so that all the traders, and townsfolk, even to the lowest of people, everyone, regarded him only as his sole benefactor." "Thereafter this clever prince (Parakrama) set his own writers to work, commanding them according to their several branches, to take account of the king's treasures of the number of his stores of grain and of his fighting men, and of the quantity of his material of war."

He next "ascertained from the hunters the secret way by which the army would enter the city (in time of war) to make ready (for a siege), the way by which they would depart from the city, in secret, when it was needful to leave it, and also the secret way by which spies are sent out. He himself wandered about the forest in the neighbourhood of the city, seeming to hunt the deer, and set various signs there, and thereby became familiar with the ways and by-ways thereof."

Gaja Bahu having begun to grow jealous of the extreme popularity of Parakrama amongst the people of his capital, and having by several of his acts indicated his feeling to Parakrama; the latter, deeming it ungallant to use the influence he had gained at the capital at a time he was enjoying Gaja Bahu's hospitality, for the purpose of overthrowing his authority on the spot—a feat which could have been accomplished with ease—preferred to hasten to the land of his birth and win glory and renown by the pastime of an open war. *Mahawansa, ch. 67, p. 141.*

Accordingly, having instructed his soldiers and followers to make their way to Janapada, where he would meet them, he stealthily left the capital (Pollonnaruwa) one night, and after a perilous journey through the forests, where he was attacked in turn by a she-boar and a wild-boar, he arrived at his destination. Here with his followers he spent a few days beguiling the time with deer-stalking and other forms of sport; until at length, news having reached Kirti Sirimegha of his arrival on the borders of his territory, the aged chieftain sent him a letter, together with presents by the reputed heads of the five trades (carpenter, weaver, washerman, barber, and shoemaker) imploring him to come and comfort him in his old age by his presence at his court. Thereupon Parakrama crossed the border, and whilst on his way to his uncle's palace was met by his mother Ratanavali, Kuthara, together with the chiefs of the various district assemblies, and Deva the general stationed at Badalatthali to guard the frontier. Escorted by them, he arrived at Punkhagama, where he was lovingly received by Kirti Sirimegha, who, having entrusted the entire administration of Maya-rata to him and appointed him his successor, lived in peace and happiness until his death, which took place not long afterwards. Thereupon Parakrama, having sent messengers to Gaja Bahu and Manabharana—the rulers of Pihiti-rata and Rohana respectively—informing them of the death of Kirti Sirimegha and his having succeeded him, proceeded to devote his undivided attention towards the attainment of *the* object of his life, viz., to bring Lanka under the dominion of one canopy and to advance the welfare of the country and its religion.

He conferred on those officers that had been brought up with him offices in accordance with their capacity to fill them, and gained their affection by giving them wealth and power. He placed his soldiers in divers places in the borders of Maya-rata from Adam's Peak as far as the sea-board. With a view of securing an abundance of provisions for the war he contemplated waging, he summoned a meeting of his ministers and thus addressed them :—" In the kingdom that belongeth to me there are many paddy lands that are watered chiefly by the water from rain clouds; but the fields that depend on a perpetual supply of water from the rivers and tanks are verily few in number. The land is studded thickly with numerous rocks and forests and great marshes. In a country like unto this not even the least quantity of water that is obtained by rain should be allowed to flow into the ocean without profiting man. Therefore save the mines of gems and gold and other precious things, the rest of the land should be turned into rice fields. Remember also, that it is not in the least meet that men like me should live and enjoy what has come into our hands and care not for the people. And all of you who have a hard work to do, slacken not your energy because of the difficulty of your task, nor take any account thereof, but fail not in the least to perform all that I have commanded you according to the command that I have given unto you. To men of perseverance, what is there in this world that cannot be accomplished." He built a causeway across the Deduru-oya (Jajjira). The *Mahawansa* says :—" Before beginning to build the causeway this prudent ruler of the land caused a great channel to be cut of great breadth and strength, the depth whereof was equal to the height of several men holding their hands aloft, and extending from (the site of) the head of the causeway up to the country of Ratta-karavha (probably it is the present Ratkerauwa in Atakalan Korle of Sabaragamuwa, where extensive remains of stupendous irrigation works are still to be seen).

Mahawansa, ch. 68, p.p. 148-149.

" This great and renowned ruler assembled a multitude of stone-cutters from among the dwellers of the country, and a great many workers in brass and copper and iron and gold, and employed them in the work of cutting stones, and caused them to build a causeway of exceeding strength and firmness, with stones so closely knit together that the joints thereof were difficult to be seen, like unto a single slab of stone, having the plaster work beautifully finished.........In such a manner did this prudent ruler finish the work that the whole stream of water flowed to the sea through this channel. And when he had caused the forest on both sides of the stream to be cut down, he formed fields of several thousand waggons of paddy seed in extent ; and because this portion of the country was full of granaries, filled with a perpetual supply of paddy, they called it Kotthabaddha, which signifieth ' the perpetual granary.'

" Afterwards at the confluence of the two rivers Sankhavaddhamána and Kumbhilavanaka he caused the place Sukara-nijjhara to be dammed up, and there also he built a channel in the manner aforesaid, and caused the water of this channel to fall into the tank Mahagallaka, after he had completely repaired the breaches thereof. And then he enlarged the gates of the sluices and enlarged the flow of water through them. From that place (Mahagallaka) up to Sukara-nijjhara he formed paddy-fields, and collected heaps of grain there also.

"And in the middle of the Jajjira river (Deduru-oya), at the place Doradattika, he built a waterfall, and a large channel also to convey the water thereof, and from thence to Sukara-nijjhara he formed paddy fields, and there also he collected stores of grain in the same manner.

"The tank Panda-vapi, which was aforetime of very small size, he rebuilt with embankments greatly enlarged in height and length and breadth, and with sluices, to convey a body of water of great and exceeding height and gave to it the name of 'The Sea of Parakrama.' In the centre thereof, on an islet, he built a royal palace of surpassing beauty, three stories high—a palace fit (to draw unto it) the multitude of joys in this world." The engineer Parker, in his monumental work entitled *Ancient Ceylon*, says that the great abandoned tank now called Pandik-kulam, situated in the southern part of the Uva Province, is most probably the ancient "Sea of Parakrama." The *Mahawansa* gives the names of thirty-eight other tanks which were restored to proper working order by this king.

Parker's Ancient Ceylon, p. 410.

In Pasdun Korle (Panca-yojana) Parakrama "drained great marshes and bays, and made the water thereof discharge itself into rivers, and formed paddy-fields, and gathered together a store of grain. In the forest of that part and in many other places he set boundaries to all forest land; and when he had assembled all the village chiefs of the people together to set the inhabitants of the country to work in making paddy-fields. Thus did this wise ruler make the revenue that was obtained from the new paddy-fields alone to be greater than the revenue which had been derived from the old paddy-fields in the kingdom; and when he had accomplished this he made the country so prosperous that the inhabitants thereof should never know the evils of famine."

The cultivation of paddy was not the only branch of agriculture that received Parakrama's attention, for it is recorded that "He caused delightful gardens to be planted in every place, and many fine groves, thickly covered with all manner of running plants and trees, famous for their divers fruits and flowers, and fit for the use of man."

Thereafter Parakrama Bahu began to make more direct and active preparations for war. He summoned all the chiefs of Maya-rata and commanded them to have all their forces trained in readiness for the campaign. He chose for himself many thousands of men of great strength and stature and formed them into a regiment armed with maces and all the requirements of warfare. Of foreigners, consisting of natives of Kerala and other Indian kingdoms, he formed a body of thousands of trained warriors. He formed a body of a thousand moonlight archers, skilled in fighting at night, and provided them with dresses made of furs and the like. He trained many thousands of hunters (veddas) and gave them suitable swords, black clothes, and such like things. For the purpose of providing the levies of the chieftains with proper implements of warfare he chose from divers artificers a thousand of each kind and commanded them that they should devote themselves each man to his own labour, *e.g.*, making swords, lances, darts, and other weapons, as well as ships.

In order to provide himself with a good supply of administrators for the districts he contemplated conquering, he brought up in his own palace many youths of noble descent saying: "Let them grow up and become familiar with the service of kings and be skilled in managing horses and elephants and fencing, in the knowledge of foreign languages and in music and dancing."

Having taken an account of the amount of money in the State exchequer, and found it insufficient for the purposes of a prolonged campaign, he divided the army and the revenue into two separate departments of his administration, with an able officer at the head of each. From the country on the sea-board, from the country of gem quarries (the Ratnapura district), from the country of the great Malay (the district round Adam's Peak), he separated all the land of great value for the purpose of taxation, and gave the charge thereof to a third officer, for whom he created the office of Antarangadhura (= Minister of the Interior). He exported gems in great number; and by this and other means soon found himself possessed of sufficient means to start upon the campaign.

Prior to embarking upon his enterprise, he held a review of his forces, making them engage in sham fights. Those who showed themselves unable to stand the stress and strain of battle, he sent away to their homes, commanding them to devote themselves to husbandry and other labour during the absence of their comrades.

It happened that at this time there had arrived at Gaja Bahu's court certain foreign princes who gained his favour and dwelt there as if they were members of his own household. As there was a possibility of Gaja Bahu, who had no issue of his own, appointing one of them as as his successor; and as they professed faiths other than Buddhism, Parakrama Bhau made it a pretext for declaring war, knowing full well that he could make his Sinhalese soldiers fight as they never otherwise would, if the war were made a religious one.

That it was Parakrama's mind that guided and controled the whole course of the operations during this mighty campaign is indicated in the *Mahawansa* in the following words :—" As he had diligently studied the books that related to the business of war, viz., the *Kocallasattha*, the *Yudhannava* and others, and had used his own judgment in those matters, he knew well how to carry on the war according to the times and places, and wrote down the plan of carrying on the war, and caused it to be delivered to the chief officers that were in command of districts, and enjoined them strictly not to turn aside from his commands, even unto a hair's breadth. And they all received the king's command with great submission, and began the attack with great force on all points both by sea and land. The valiant commander Malaya Rayar led a fleet to the pearl banks and captured them after fighting a great naval battle with Dandanatha, the commander of Gaja Bahu's fleet. He next landed his forces in that region of Phiti-rata and engaged the forces of the enemy sent against him, while Parakrama's other generals, with Lankánátha as commander-in-chief, pushed their way in all directions by land towards Pollonnaruwa."

After his forces had received several defeats at the hands of those of Parakrama, Gaja Bahu attempted to win over the enemy's forces by bribery. It is thus described in the *Mahawansa* :—" But King Gaja Bahu sent a host of men that was called the Catasso Parisa (the four companies) that were in the Alisára country to fight again ; and Lankánátha advanced and fought with them, and some of them he took alive, and subdued the Taláthala country. Whereupon Gaja Bahu, wishing to subdue them by favour and kindness, sent him numerous presents of jewels and ornaments of great value, and divers garments of silk and linen. And the chief of the army (Lankanatha) received the presents, and after he had disfigured the messengers, he sent them with the bribes to his own master (Parakrama). Parakrama was much pleased on seeing them, and sent back all the wealth and the valuable presents to him (the chief of the army)."

Thereafter the fighting was continued all along the line, Gaja Bahau's forces, under their commander-in-chief Siká, contesting every inch of ground in a most determined fashion. Too numerous are the battles fought, and the names of the generals that took part in each of them, for the author to include them in this book. For such details the reader is referred to the *Mahawansa*, chapters 70 to 72. Suffice it to give one sample of the nature of the fighting indulged in : "Lankánátha left the Talathaliya fortress and took possession of the fortress at Aligáma, which is by the side of the river. Thereupon Gaja Bahu sent Siká, the chief of his army, and other valiant and mighty men of war against him. They all set out with an abundant supply of men and waggons, and besieged the fortress and poured showers of arrows into it. Some of Lankánátha's mighty men, armed with weapons, stood at the gates and carried on a fierce fight. Archers and other strong men also, who stood on the battlements, killed many of the enemy with their arrows, lances, and javelins. In this manner did all the warriors exert themselves to the utmost and carry on the great struggle for three days. At last the mighty men of Gaja Bahu, who were determined to destroy the enemy, essayed to break the great gate of the fortress. Whereupon, Lankánátha and his strong men sallied forth, and after a hard struggle drove back the enemy, killing so many of them all along unto the river that he made the water of the river mingle with the blood of the slain; and at the same time he took captive many of the chief officers of the enemy's army. Thereafter the victorious general Lankánátha enjoyed the pleasure of a feast of triumph in his own fortress, and sent to his master Parakrama the heads of the chiefs of the enemy that he had slain, with their umbrellas, waggons, weapons, and also those whom he had taken alive."

Finally all of Parakrama's forces joined in storming Pollonnaruwa, where Gaja Bahu was taken prisoner, and the city pillaged by the soldiery, in spite of Parakrama's orders that no unnecessary damage should be done.

Those of the chiefs of Pihiti-rata, who, through the friendly regard they had for Parakrama, had not opposed the progress of his army to their capital, were so disgusted with the excesses committed by his soldiery after their entry into the city, that they invited Manabharana from Rohana, promising him their support in any effort he may make to rid their country of Parakrama's domination and rescue Gaja Bahu, who had been taken a prisoner. Accordingly Manabharana arrived with a large army and utterly defeated Parakrama's forces at Pollonnaruwa, who by the dissolute lives they had led since their entry there had rendered themselves totally unfit for war.

Manabharana, after he had established himself at Pollonnaruwa, determined upon putting an end to the existence of Gaja Bahu, whom he in turn held a prisoner. Deeming it impolitic to have him publicly executed, and conscious of the fact that so long as Gaja Bahu was alive his dominion over Pihiti-rata was insecure, Manabharana resorted to the device of bringing about his death by a slow and steady process of torture.

Under these circumstances Gaja Bahu secretly addressed a pitiful appeal to Parakrama begging him to deliver him from his affliction. Thereupon Parakrama gathered together as large an army as he could and sent them under his general Kesadatu-Nayaka and others who, having defeated Manabharana's general Kanta Disanayaka, succeeded in recapturing Pollonnaruwa, setting Gaja Bahu at liberty, and compelling Manabharana to seek safety in Rohana, together with Buddha's Tooth-relic and Alms-bowl-relic.

Gaja Bahu, ungrateful for the service done him by Parakrama, set about asserting his right to Pihiti-rata by force. After having been defeated in several battles, when he was on the point of being captured a second time by Parakrama Bahu's forces, he sent the priests of the leading temples at Pollonnaruwa to intercede on his behalf. Thereupon Parakrama Bahu conceded him his right to rule over Pihiti-rata and retired with his forces to Maya-rata.

In gratitude for the magnificent magnanimity of Parakrama, Gaja Bahu, no sooner he arrived at Pollonnaruwa, caused this solemn declaration to be inscribed on a rock at the vihara Mandalagiri : "I have given Phitirata to King Parakrama." It is to be seen there even at the present day.

Gaja Bahu died a few years after he had resumed the administration of his province. Thereafter a prolonged struggle took place between Parakrama and Manabharana for the dominion of Pihiti-rata : no less than fifty-eight pitched battles were fought between the contending forces. At one stage of this war it looked very much as if Parakama's trained but mixed army of foreigners and Sinhalese was no match for the army of Manabharana, which was composed solely of the sturdy inhabitants of Rohana. For details as to the places where the battles were fought, the commanders on either side, and the result of each battle the reader is referred to chapter 72 of the *Mahawansa.* When almost all hope of success had been lost to his generals, Parakrama's personal courage and tenacity of purpose asserted itself and turned the tide of victory in his favour. The conclusion of this war is thus described in the *Mahawansa :* —"Thereupon the mighty and terrible King Parakrama Bahu gathered together his armies that were set at different places. That he might drive the King Manabharana out of Pihiti-rata he placed Rakkha, the great secretary, and Anjana, the chief of works at Kyánagáma, and sent forward Kitti Potthaki and Rakkha Adhikari to the village Mángalaba. And he sent companies of hunters and robbers, and such as were accustomed to the fastnesses of the forest and the mountain, and to roaming at night, and caused them to destroy the enemy by day and night, wheresoever they found them. So greatly did they disquiet the King Manabharana and harass the city, that the inhabitants of Pulatthi (Pollonnaruwa), like unto birds that were made captive in a cage, feared to come out of their houses, even in the daytime ; neither were they who had been for a long time in want of fuel and water able to do the works that were needful, because that all the grass and the plants had been rooted out. Yea, everything that was in each man's house was destroyed; even all the divers stuffs in the markets on the borders of the city were cut off, and, by reason of the constant tumult that was raised by this war of kings in the streets that led to the town, the whole city trembled with fear, even to the court of the king's palace."

Then the King Manabharana, being sorely vexed, and filled with anxious thoughts, communed with himself in this wise: "Alas! if we flee into Rohana the people of Pihiti-rata who dwell there, seeing that we are weakened and in flight, will not permit us to remain there, that so they might show their fealty to King Parakrama. On the other hand, it is difficult for us to remain here, by reason of the distress we endure by day and night. It is therefore meet for us that we should engage in a fierce battle with the enemy, and partake of the pleasure of victory or suffer the misery of defeat." And when he had thus resolved he stirred himself for the fight, and put his four-fold army in battle array and proceeded to Pallavavalaka. Here he was met by Parakrama's generals Lankapura and Lokagalla, who kept his forces engaged in daily encounters for the space of one month. Thereafter Manabharana secretly made his way through his enemy's ranks and reached the village Konduruva. In the neighbourhood of this village, in a village named Mihirana-Bibbila, Rakkha Adhikari, in accordance with Parakrama's injunctions, had raised up a fortification. He had put up posts, pointed like unto arrow-heads, and fixed them firmly in the ground, joining the one with the other, that so they might not be shaken even by elephants. On the outside thereof he had put up huge posts, greater in size than the rest, and placed them close together on the ground, that so there might not be any fissures, and bound them crosswise with poles. Moreover, he had caused a moat to be dug between the two stockades, twenty or thirty cubits in breadth, the circumference whereof was equal to the measure of one hundred men with their hands raised, and he had laid sharp spikes and thorns therein. On the ground outside thereof he had also fixed rows of spikes, and made a fence of thorns along it without gap or opening; and between them also he had made a trench as before, and in it also he had planted rows of spikes and thorns, and had caused the ground outside the fence to be dug, and had thus formed a trench so deep that it reached the water. He had covered the bottom of it with spikes and thorns. At the same time he had caused the forest beyond the trench to be cleared to a distance of two or three bow shots ; and outside this space, where there were secret paths, he had dug pits, and spread the bottoms thereof thickly with sharp throns, and covered them all over with dry leaves and sand that so they might appear passable. In order that he might utterly destroy the enemy who ventured to come from that side, he had caused secret paths to be made round about it, and placed sharp shooting bowmen therein. He had built a tower of four stories in the middle of the fortress. In it he set archers in divers places.

In order that he might tempt the enemy's hosts to draw near the fortress, he sent forth two or three thousand skilled archers. And they cunningly feigned that they were driven back by a shower of arrows which the enemy had poured out on them on all sides as they came forth to meet them, pursuing them as they stood still (and turning round and fleeing from them when they pursued after them). When the enemy had come sufficiently nigh unto the fortifications many thousands of good and valiant men, skilled in warfare, armed themselves quickly, and rushed forth on the enemy like unto so many elephants, and fought like the hosts of the king of death that had appeared against them. Then the showers of arrows began to pour down on all sides ; and they that were placed on the top of the tower began to shoot their arrows on those that were on the ground. The battle waxed hot, and stones without number were seen hurled from engines that flew about on every side. The heat of the fire of the reeds that were lighted and thrown among the enemy could not be endured, nor the many burning javelins bound with chains with which they harassed them. This cruel work lasted for seven days, at the end of which time Manabharana, taking advantage of a dark and stormy night, effected an escape, though he was closely pursued till the Mahaweliganga was reached. Here his son Sirivallabha and many other of his great officers were taken alive, together with much treasures, elephants, horses, armour and weapons. Thereafter Parakrama Bahu arrayed with all the ornaments of kingly office, surrounded by his army and followed by the captive prince Sirivallabha, entered the beautiful city of Pulatthi, filling the whole heaven with shouts of

Parakrama Bahu I., 1140-1173 A.C.

victory. Not many days later news reached Parakrama to the effect that Manabharana had died of a broken heart, and that he had, on his deathbed, enjoined his ministers, as well as his son Kirti Sirimegha, to swear allegiance to Parakrama. Thereupon, Parakrama, after he had ordered Kirti Sirimegha to be brought to Pollonnaruwa, had himself crowned as King of Lanka. The ceremony is thus described in the *Mahawansa* :—
"Parakrama Bahu, being now freed from his enemies, held the great feast of the coronation under a good star and a prosperous hour. On that day the deafening sound of divers drums was terrible, even as the rolling of the ocean when it is shaken to and fro by the tempest at the end of the world. The elephants, decked with coverings of gold, made the street before the palace to look as if clouds had descended thereon with flashes of lightning; with the prancing of the steeds of war, the whole city on that day seemed to wave even like the sea. The sky was wholly shut out of sight with rows of umbrellas of divers colours and with lines of flags of gold. There was the waving of garments and the clapping of hands. The inhabitants of the city shouted saying, 'Live! O live! Great King.' There was feasting over the whole land, which was filled with arches of plantains intermingled with rows of flower pots. Hundreds of minstrels chanted songs of praise, and the air was filled with the smoke of sweet incense. Many persons also arrayed themselves in cloths of divers colours and decked themselves in ornaments of various kinds. The great experienced warriors, armed with divers kinds of weapons, with the countenances of graceful heroes, moved about hither and thither like unto elephants that had broken asunder their bonds.

"By reason of the many archers who walked about with their bows in their hands, it seemed as if an army of gods had visited the land; and the city with its multitude of palaces, gorgeously decorated with gold and gems and pearls, appeared like unto the firmament that is studded with stars.

"Parakrama Bahu, with eyes that were long like the lily, caused many wonderful and marvellous things to be displayed, adorned himself with divers ornaments, and ascended a golden stage supported on the backs of two elephants that were covered with cloth of gold. He bore on his head a crown that shone with the rays of gems, like as the eastern mountain beareth the glorious and rising sun. Casting into the shade the beauty of spring by the strength of his own beauty, he drew tears of joy from the eyes of the beautiful women of the city. He marched round the city beaming with the signs of happiness and, like unto the god with the thousand eyes, entered the beauteous palace of the king."

He then caused men of great families who had been utterly ruined by the war to be restored to their position and defended according to custom.

King Parakrama Bahu next devoted his energies to the herculean task of establishing Buddhism, which had been almost totally neglected during the preceding forty-four years, on a firm foundation by bringing about a unity of doctrines preached by the various fraternities and by purging the priesthood of undesirables. For this purpose he established an Ecclesiastical Court (or Council of Elders) composed of the leading priests summoned from divers parts of the country, and appointed Maha Kassapa, who was recognised to be the most learned of them, to preside over their deliberations. After prolonged deliberations, in which the king himself exerted his influence to the uttermost, his object was attained. The *Mahawansa* thus describes the work done by the king and his Council of Elders:—" Verily, it seemed as if the endeavour to accomplish this unity was like unto the endeavour to raise the Mount Meru. But the king was a just man and partial to none and resolute withal. He encouraged the priests, and with much labour prevailed on them to consent. When questions arose for their judgment, he caused the priests, over whom Maha Kassapa was chief, to solve them. In order that these judgments may be accepted (by those whom they concerned) he joined unto himself the great doctors learned in the three Pitakas, and caused the priests, whose causes could be remedied, to be restored to their purity according to the provisions of the law, thus did he bring to pass the unity of the priests of the Maha Vihara fraternity. He caused the robes to be taken off those priests that were reputed evil, and gave them high lay offices, saying: 'Let them not destroy religion for the sake of lucre.' In this manner did he purify the Maha Vihara fraternity. And the Abhayagiri fraternity who had started a separate existence during the reign of King (Vattagamani) Abhaya, and the Jetavana

Mahawansa, ch. 78, pp. 255-256.

fraternity who came into existence during the reign of King Mahasena and taught the Wytulian heresy as Buddhism, setting their faces against order and discipline —these fraternities did King Parakrama attempt to reconcile to the Maha Vihara fraternity, who abounded in all virtue. But the Jetavana brethren, devoid of piety or other stable virtue, even then cared not to regard the commandments of Buddha, notwithstanding the majesty of the great priesthood and the king. Nevertheless the righteous king caused inquisition to be made by them, who had knowledge of the laws, and not even one priest was found who preserved the State in which he had been ordained. Many of these priests did he cause to return to the life of novices, others he caused to be disrobed and given offices of much profit. Thus did the king, after spending much time and labour, bring about the purity and unity of the church and restore the priesthood to the place they held in the days of Buddha."

The king next had a square hall of great size built in the centre of Pollonnaruwa, so that hundreds of monks might be fed there daily. He also had four alms-halls built in the four quarters of the city, and furnished them with many vessels made of metal, pillows, cushions mats, coverlets, beds, and thousands of cows that yielded rich milk. Near these halls he laid out parks of great beauty with fountains of pure water and rows of trees bearing divers flowers and fruits. He also had store-houses built near them, and kept them filled with much grain for the use of monks, Brahmans, begging minstrels and other paupers.

He built a large hospital provided with hundreds of beds in the city. "To every sick person he allowed a male and a female servant, that they may minister to him by day and night, and furnish him with the physic that was necessary, and with divers kinds of food. Many store-houses also did he build, attached to this hospital, filled with grain and all things needful for medicine. He made provision for the maintenance of wise and learned physicians who were versed in all knowledge and skilled in searching out the nature of diseases. It was his habit on the four Uposatha (Sabbath) days of every month to visit the patients at this hospital and discuss the nature of their diseases, etc., with the doctors in charge of them."

After the king by his acts had gained the love of his people, he began with vigour to adorn and enlarge the famous city (Pollonnaruwa). Outside the belt of the city-wall of former kings he caused a great chain of ramparts to be built, exceeding high, and greatly embellished it with plaster work, so that it was as white as an autumn cloud. Thence he built three lesser walls, one behind another. He surrounded his own palace, and the chambers of the women of his household, with a circle of lesser walls.

The king next caused a palace of great splendour, called Vejayanta, to be built. "It had seven stories, and contained one thousand chambers supported by many hundreds of beautiful pillars. It was surrounded with hundreds of pinnacles and adorned with networks of divers leaves and flowers. Its gates and doors and windows were made of gold, and its walls and stair-cases were so ordered, that they were a pleasure to behold, at all times of the year. It was always well supplied with thousands of beds of divers kinds covered with carpets of great value, made of gold and ivory, and other substances. The splendour thereof was increased by the addition of a bed-chamber for the king, which sent forth at all times a perfume of flowers and incense, which was made beautiful by rows of large lamps of gold, and exceedingly so, by reason of the garlands of pearls of great size, which were hung at the four corners thereof. The network of tinkling bells of gold that hanged here and there in the palace, and sent forth sounds like unto those of the five instruments of music, seemed to proclaim the unlimited glory of the king."

Thereafter King Parakrama caused several buildings of a semi-religious character to be constructed.

He next caused a theatre hall named Sarassati Mandapa to be built close to his palace, "so that he might listen to the sweet and melodious singing of divers singers and witness the delightful dance. It glittered with golden pillars all around, and pleased the mind with paintings that described the events of his own life. It was adorned with an imitation of the 'wish-conferring tree of heaven' (Kappa-rukkha). The trunk and the branches thereof glittered with gold and were ornamented with a multitude of divers kinds of birds of beautiful workmanship. It shone also with divers ornaments, such as earrings and bracelets and garlands of pearls and the like, and with beautiful garments made of linen and china silk, silk, and the like."

He also caused a very pleasant open hall of recreation named Rájavesi Bhujanga to be erected. "It was a three-storied building (probably the stories corresponded to the galleries in the leading theatres and music halls of London), ornamented with beautiful pictures, and surrounded by rows of seats arranged with much beauty. It was also ornamented with a throne of great price (the royal box)."

A magnificent park named Nandana was laid out close by the royal palace during this reign. It had trees entwined with creepers of jasmine.

The air was filled with swarms of bees attracted by the flowers in it.

Mahawansa, ch. 73, v. 102, p. 202. The Campaka (Sin. Sapu), Asoka (Sin. (Moona-mal), Tilaka (doubtful), Naga (Sin. Na), Punnága (Sin. Dhomba), Ketaka (Sin. Kéla), Sála (Sin. Hal), Pátali (Bignonia Suaveolens), Nípa (Nauclea Cadamba), Amba (Mango), Jambu, Kadambaka (a species of Asoka), Vakula (Sin. Moona-mal), Nalikera (Cocoanut), Kutaja (Sin. Kelinda), Bimbijálaka (Momordica Monodelpha), Málati (a species of Jasmine), Mallika (a species of Jasmine), Támala (Valernana Jatamansi), Nava-mallika (Jasmine), these and divers charming fruit and flower-bearing trees were found there. It was rendered more delightful by the tones of peacocks, kokilas (the Indian cuckoos), and other birds. It was interspersed with sheets of water ornamented with fine banks, and made pleasant by the abundant growth of the lotus and the lily, and the musical tones of the saras (wild duck). It was railed also with pillars, decorated with rows of images made of ivory. It had a bathing-hall that dazzled the eyes of the beholder, from which issued sprays of water conducted through pipes by means of machines, making the place look as if the clouds poured down rain without ceasing. It (the park) also had situated within it, a mansion of great splendour with gracefully carved pillars of sandalwood, a hall shaped like an octagon, and a special stone-bath for the use of the king.

Another park named Dipuyegána (= Park of the Island), because two streams flowed on either side of it, was constructed by King Parakrama. In it was built a white house, "wholly of plaster work," which had one hall named Vijja-mandapa, where was displayed various branches of knowledge as well as the arts (vijjá), and another hall named Kílá-mandapa (=Hall of Pleasure), to which the king at times resorted with the gay and witty attendants of his court. There were various other beautiful edifices built in this park, such as the Mora-mandapa (=Hall of Mirrors), and a four-storied palace ornamented with divers paintings, and baths, one of which named Citta-pokkharani, with paintings of divers colours, was reserved for the use of the king.

Thereafter the king caused broad roads to be laid out within the city, many thousands of two and three-storied edifices were built on the borders thereof. They abounded on all sides with shops, filled with goods of all kinds. Elephants, horses, and carriages passed without ceasing along these roads, and they were crowded every day with people devoted to pleasure.

A temple of great splendour was built within the city, by one of the king's ministers named Mahinda. Queen Rupavati caused the Rankot (golden spire) dagoba to be built in the middle of the city. It is to be seen at the present day. It is 200 feet high and has a diameter of 108 feet. The king himself had three temples—Veluvana, Isipatana, and Kusinárá—built in the suburbs of Polonnaruwa.

Parakrama Bahu next turned his attention to restoring the sacred city of Anuradhapura which the Cholians had ruined. This task was well-nigh completed when his attention was diverted by two simultaneous rebellions, one of the inhabitants of Rohana instigated by Sugalá, the mother of the deceased ruler of Rohana, who possessed in her custody Buddha's Alms-bowl as well as Tooth-relic; the other of the foreigners—natives of Kerala—who resided in the central portion of the country and had been joined by some Sinhalese partisans of Manabharana, who had after his death lost office and been reduced to misery. The insurrection of the foreigners was put down without much difficulty and their lands confiscated; but it was by no means with ease that the rebels of Rohana were subdued. Sugala, it is recorded, "gave up all the jewels and pearls and such like treasures that she had, also a great quantity of precious things that belonged to the Tooth- and Bowl-relics, and expended them on the revolutionaries as if she had thrown them into a fire." All the inhabitants of Rohana were animated with a similar spirit of self-sacrifice for the sake of preserving their independence, and, considering the nature of the country, the task of subjugating them was a herculean one. The generals of Parakrama Bahu engaged in this campaign were Rakkha (the commander-in-chief), Bhútádhikári' and Kirti ; Sukarabhatu, an old general of Manabharana, led the insurgents. No less than fourteen pitched battles were fought before Parakrama's forces were able to secure possession of the Tooth- and Bowl-relics. These were seized in the. fifteenth battle of this war fought at Uruvela Mandala. Rakkha (the commander-in-chief) did not long survive this victory, inasmuch as he was laid low by dysentery.

The rebels were far from demoralised as a result of the loss of the two relics. They continued to attack Parakrama's forces with redoubled energy, so much so that the king, thinking it wise to have the relics brought forthwith to the capital lest they be recaptured, sent a general named Manju from Polonnaruwa with a force for that purpose. At twelve different places did the enemy force Manju to give them battle on his way to and back with the relics, but Manju, in conjunction with Kirti and Bhútádhikári, succeeded in beating them off and conveyed the relics to Polonnaruwa, where they were received with great reverence and ceremony by the king. For a minute description of the magnificent ceremony, the reader is referred to the *Mahawansa*, chapter 74, pp. 213-216.

Thereafter, Parakrama sent his generals, together with their forces, to conquer Rohana, commencing operations in the Baticaloa district (Dighavapi), In order that there might be no unnecessary slaughter of men, and in order to bring about a thorough subjugation of the people, one of Parakrama's generals—Kancuki-nayaka—conceived the idea of sending messages to the chief men of the district to inform them that those who surrendered themselves without opposition would receive protection both in their persons and property, but that those who did not would receive no quarter. Accordingly, the inhabitants of Válukagama (Veligama, between Galle and Matara) and many other districts gave in, and sought the protection of Parakrama's forces ; but the majority of the inhabitants were as determined as ever to fight for their independence, although at the cost of their lives. No less than fifty-two battles were fought before the country was finally subdued, and Sugalá, the leading spirit among the rebels, was captured. She was captured at Vanagáma after a fiercely contested battle and brought prisoner to Pollonnaruwa, after the whole of Rohana had been placed under the administration of one of Parakrama's most experienced officers named Bhútádhikari.

The entry into the city of the victorious generals, with their armies, is thus described in the *Mahawansa* :—"They were followed by the inhabitants of the city, with singing and music and clapping of hands and the waving of thousands of cloths on every side and with shouts of triumph. When they came to the magnificent palace of the king they saw the gracious king of kings seated with great majesty on his throne of State, and cleansed their heads with the dust of his lotus-feet."

The cessation of hostilities, subsequent to the capture *1147 A.C.* of Sugalá, the spirit that inspired as well as in large measure guided and controled the operations on the side of the rebels, was of short duration. It is recorded that in 1147 A.C. a rebellion broke out again in Rohana, necessitating military operations in that district on as large a scale as on the previous occasion, with the result that the country was completely subjugated.

In the year 1155 A.C. the tranquillity of the country was again disturbed by a rebellion of the inhabitants of Mahátittha (Mantotta) and the country round about it; but Parakrama's forces succeeded with little difficulty in completely subduing them.

There next arose complications with a kingdom—Ramanna (a portion of Burma)—with which Lanka had from ages past been on very friendly terms owing to the community of religion that prevailed in the two countries, as well as trade and other common interests. For some unknown reason King Arimaddana of Ramanna decided upon severing all connection with Lanka and her king. "He ceased to furnish the ambassadors of Parakrama Bahu, who were at his court, with the expenses that were given to them aforetime, according to custom. He decreed that his subjects should no longer sell elephants to be exported to Lanka. He put an end to the ancient custom of giving an elephant by way of gift to every ship that bore presents to him. Notwithstanding the fact that he knew that every kindness and consideration was shown to his ambassador Tapassi by King Parakrama Bahu, he deprived the messengers of King Parakrama of their wealth, their elephants, their ships, and all that pertained to them, and caused the soles of their feet to be beaten with sticks—the Mongolian fashion of inflicting corporal punishment on prisoners—and employed them to draw water in prisons. He next forced the two Sinhalese ambassadors accredited to his court —Vagissara and Dhammakirti—to give him a document in their own handwriting to the effect that they had been told by the King of Ramanna that no Sinhalese or presents from Sinhalese chiefs should land in future on his shores, and had them sent on the open sea in a ship that leaked."

The climax was reached when King Arimaddana seized a Sinhalese princess who was on her way to Cambodia (Kamboja) to be married to the king of that country.

Enraged at the insult thus offered "Parakrama Bahu commanded that a fleet of hundreds of ships of various kinds should be got ready without delay. All the country round about the coast seemed like one great workshop busied with the constant building of ships. The construction of all those ships was completed in five months. He gathered them together at the port Pallavanka and filled them with all things necessary for the enterprise, *e.g.* rice and other provisions that would last for one year, armour, weapons, thousands of coats wrought of iron and skins of deer wherewith to ward off arrows, divers kinds of medicines filled in the horns of bullocks to serve as a balm to wounds caused by poisoned arrows, drugs of various kinds to serve as antidotes to the poisoned waters of streams which the soldiers might happen to drink, pincers of iron for drawing out arrows that have sunk deep into the flesh; physicians of great skill and nurses. Finally the king sent on board a mighty army, numbering many thousands, and the fleet appeared like an island moving in the midst of the sea whilst it was on its way to Ramanna."

That portion of the fleet commanded by Kirti and Nacaragiri reached the port, Kusumi, in Ramanna, and there the valiant soldiers, after they had effected a landing, like furious elephants, destroyed a great number of cocoanut and other trees, burned numerous villages and devastated the country. That portion of Parakrama's fleet which was under the command of Adicca, the Indian, cast anchor at the port Papphala in Ramanna and began a fierce and bloody war, in which many inhabitants were taken as prisoners. Finally, "the mighty and terrible

Sinhalese entered the capital of the country and spared not their weapons. They slew the King of Ramanna who had disregarded the law of nations, and after they had completely subdued the country, the great warriors rode on the noble white elephant and marched round the city without fear, and thereafter by beat of drums proclaimed the supreme authority of the King of Lanka."

At length, Parakrama Bahu's forces left the country, after representatives of the inhabitants had entered upon a solemn covenant to acknowledge the suzerainty of Lanka; and to pay her a yearly tribute in elephants.

Shortly after the conquest of Ramanna had been completed, conditions developed on the neighbouring Continent of India, which brought about an invasion and conquest of the two kingdoms of Pandu and Chola by the Sinhalese. The King of Pandu who was besieged in his capital, Madhura, by King Kulasekhara of Chola, summoned the assistance of King Parakrama Bahu. Although news of the capture of Madhura and the killing of the King of Pandu reached Parakrama before he had time to despatch a force, yet he sent a powerful army across, commanded by generals Lankapura (commander-in-chief), Dandanáyaka, Loka Kesadhatu, and Gokanna, with instructions that they should seize the kingdom and place one of the deceased king's offspring on the throne; many battles were fought commencing with one at Ramesvaram, in all of which the Sinhalese were victorious.

When King Kulasekhara saw that his army was discomfited in every battle he went forth from the camp and himself led it into battle. Then Lankápura caused all the gates of the fortress he had constructed for himself at Kundukala and named Parakrama Pura to be opened, and led his army in battle array. He engaged the enemy and gained the victory. He slew many Tamils, captured their horses, and pursued after them till he reached Kurumbandankali, and there commenced to make himself a fortress. Thereupon Kulasekhara, who hitherto was a terror to his enemies, gathered together his great host that was broken and discomfited in battle, and choosing himself the flower of his army went up himself and offered battle. And their swords flashed like thousands of fishes, the horses were like waves in number, the footmen like an expansion of water, their parasols also were like seas of foam, their arrows flew about like streams, and the sound of their drums was like the roaring of the tempest; yea, with all this, the field of battle was on that day as terrible as the mighty ocean itself. As the battle waxed fiercer and fiercer, the Sinhalese, with their valour and might, satisfied the itching of their fingers for the fight. And they slew Villava Rayar and Cola Konára and the Yadhava Rayars and a certain exceeding powerful chieftain, and many hundred soldiers and officers of the king. The horse on which Kulasekhara rode was shot under him. Then Kulasekhara and his army turned their backs and fled, as if to give the Sinhalese a better opportunity to slaughter them with their swords. As he fled from the field of battle, he left behind him his valour; and his throne, his canopy, his ornaments, and divers other things. Then Lankápura proceeded to the stronghold Erikkávúr, which Kulasekhara, his enemy, had held, burnt it to the ground, and built himself another fortress and tarried there awhile. Very many battles were fought subsequent to this by the Sinhalese against King Kulasekhara and the allies he had summoned to his assistance; but the Sinhalese forces which had been reinforced from home by the distinguished general Jagad Vijaya Náyaka and his army, were invariably victorious. Not only Pandu did they completely rid of Cholian domination, but they carried the war into Chola itself, and after they had devastated a large portion of that country and crippled the enemy's power of aggression they returned to Madura, where they placed Prince Vira Pandu on his father's throne. Prior to the return of the Sinhalese forces to Lanka, Lankápura ordered that the kahapana coins (which are still found), bearing the superscription of King Parakrama Bahu, should be struck and circulated through the kingdom of Pandu, probably as a token of the suzerainty of Lanka over that country. These coins, like all other coins of Sinhalese kings, have a rude standing figure of the Raja holding the *trisula* in his left hand and a flower in the right. His dress is a flowing robe, the folds of which are indicated rather than imitated by the artist; and on the reverse the same figure is seated, the name in Nagari characters being placed beside the face. Many prisoners of war were brought over to Lanka during the course of this war, and were made use of by King Parakrama Bahu for completing the reconstruction of the edifices at Anuradhapura, which had been interrupted by the rebellion in Rohàna raised by Sugalá. It was considered by Parakrama appropriate to have those edifices restored by the very men who had destroyed them, viz., the Cholians,

Thereafter Parakrama Bahu, satisfied, in his desire for military glory, turned his attention to furthering the spiritual and material welfare of his subjects.

For the purposes of administration he created the following chief offices:—1, Adhikara (Justiciar); 2, Senevirat (Commander-in-Chief of the Army); 3, Epá (Heir-apparent and Aide-de-camp to the King, and virtually First Viceroy); 4, Mápá (Heir Presumptive and Second Viceroy); 5, Mahaléna (Secretary of State); 6, Maharetina (Minister of the Interior); 7, Anuná (Second Minister of the Interior); 8, Sabhápatiná (President of the Council); 9, Situná (Director of Commerce); 10, Siritléná (Chief Legal Adviser); 11, Duléná (Under Secretary and Keeper of the Rolls); 12, Viyatná (Chief Intelligencer); 13, Mahavedaná (Chief Medical Officer); 14, Mahaneketná (Chief Officer of the Calendar); 15, Dahampasakná (Minister of Education). He also established eight departments of record, eight departments of transport, four departments of the treasury, eight departments of the elephant industry, and eighteen thousand villages not included in the services to be rendered in the above departments (*i.e.* villages that had to serve the State by the mere payment of taxes). *Fernando's Trans. of Nikiya Sangrahawa, p. 20.*

He caused numerous colleges and other religious edifices to be built at Pollonnaruwa, chief among them being the Jetavana Vihara, the remains of which are still to be seen there. It is oblong in shape and about 150 feet in length; and is divided into two large chambers, the inner one being broader than the outer. The decoration of the interior of the side walls, which are nearly 80 feet high, is very elaborate. The main entrance is to the east: opposite to it are some decorated pillars, which are locally said to mark the sight of the Gansabhawa, or tribunal where minor offences were tried; but this is improbable. The entrance to the shrine is flanked by two polygonal turrets, and was originally guarded by two figures in high relief. The flight of stone steps, each 20 feet long, is elaborately carved, and there is an inscription on the near side of one of the janitors. There was evidently a gateway between the outer and inner shrines; and at the western end of the latter stands a gigantic brickwork figure of Buddha, nearly 60 feet high, which was originally coated with chunam. A small row of windows, low down in the wall, appears to have been the only means of admitting light into this shrine; and Tennent conjectures, with some probability, that, by means of a window situated above the entrance to the inner shrines, and invisible from below, a ray of light was thrown full upon the face of the statue, giving it a mysterious halo amid the surrounding gloom.

For detailed information regarding the various religious edifices raised by this monarch which has rendered Pollonnaruwa famous even to the present day and the 128 libraries which he established the reader is referred to the *Mahawansa*, chapter 78.

For information as to the numerous tanks—no less than 1,470 in number—constructed by this monarch, and the twenty-eight parks laid out by him in various parts of the Island, where numerous varieties of sweet-smelling flowers, and edible fruit-bearing trees, were grown, the reader is referred to the *Mahawansa*, chapter 79.

Tennent, vol. I., pp. 448-449. The Moor geographer Edrisi, writing in 1154 A.C., says of Lanka (Serenedib):—"In the mountains around Adam's Peak they collect precious stones of every description, and in the valleys they find those diamonds, by means of which they engrave the setting of stones on rings.

"The same mountains produce aromatic drugs, per fumes, and aloes-wood, and there, too, they find the animal, the civet, which yields musk. The islanders cultivate rice, cocoanuts and sugar-cane; in the rivers is found rock crystal remarkable both for brilliancy and size; and the sea has a fishery of magnificent and priceless pearls. Throughout India there is no prince whose wealth can compare with that of the King of Serenedib; his immense riches, his pearls and his jewels being the produce of his own dominions and seas; and thither, ships of China and of every neighbouring country resort, bringing the wines of Irak and Fars, which the king buys for sale to his subjects; for he drinks wine and prohibits debauchery; whilst other princes of India encourage debauchery and prohibit the use of wine. The exports from Serenedib consist of silk, precious stones, crystals, diamonds and perfumes."

Tennent, vol. I., p. 598. He says that the sovereign, who was celebrated for the mildness of his rule, was assisted by a council of sixteen ministers, of whom four were of the national religion, four Christians, four Mussulmans, and four Jews;

and one of the chief cares of the government was given to keeping up the historical records of the reigns of their kings, the lives of their prophets, and the sacred book of their law.

Edrisi also says that natives of Oman and Yemen resorted to Lanka for the purpose of making cordage from the fibre of the cocoanut (Edrisi, t. i., p. 74).

Tennent, vol. II., pp. 604, 605

Tennent, during his travels through the Island, came across " a figure of Buddha, nearly fifty feet high, carved from the face of a granite cliff, and so detached that only two slender ties had been left unhewn at the back to support the colossus by maintaining its attachment with living stone." This figure is to be seen at the Ankana Vihara, which is situated close to the Kala-wewa. The priest at the vihara informed Tennent that the statue was one that had been made by order of King Parakrama Bahu; of the Gal-vihara at Pollonnaruwa, which was built by this king, Tennent says: " It is a rock temple hollowed in the face of a cliff of granitic stone, which overhangs the level plain at the north of the city. So far as I am aware, it is the only example in Ceylon of an attempt to fashion an architectural design out of the rock, after the manner of the cave temples of Ajunta and Ellora. The temple itself is a little cell, with entrances between columns; and an altar at the rear on which is a sedent statue of Buddha, admirably carved, all forming undetached parts of the living rock. Outside, to the left, is a second sedent figure, of more colossal dimensions, and still more richly decorated; and to the right are two statues likewise of Buddha, in the usual attitudes of exhortation and repose. The length of the reclining figure to the right is forty-five feet, the upright one is twenty-three, and the sitting statue to the left sixteen feet from the pedestal to the crown of the head."

Alwis' Intro. to the Sidath Sangarawa, p. 165.

About this period of Lanka's history Sanscrit became mixed up with the Sinhalese language. Not that the pure Elu became obsolete, but it became the fashion of the time to interweave the one with the other, or to adapt a variety of Sanscrit expressions to the Elu. This possibly arose from the successful wars of Parakrama Bahu, who made two of the Indian States tributary to him, a circumstance which necessarily led the Hindu Brahmins to resort to this Island, perhaps more freely than before, and to bring along with them almost the greater part of their literature in Sanscrit and Pali. The *Winayartha Sanuchchaya* was written by a priest of the name of Médankara during this reign. It is a paraphrase upon the *Vinaya Pitaka.* Much literature, other than the book above named, must have been produced under the encouragement of this enlightened monarch; but this is the only work that has escaped from destruction at the hands of the South Indian invaders.

Parakrama Bahu I. died in 1173 A.C., and such was the internal tranquillity which, during the last portion of his reign, pervaded Lanka, that an inscription, engraved by one of his successors, on the rock of Dambool, after describing the great peace and "security which he established, as well in the wilderness as in the inhabited places," records that, "even a woman might traverse the Island with a precious jewel and not be asked what it was."

Vijaya Bahu II., 1173-1174 A.C.

Vijaya Bahu II., son of Parakrama Bahu's sister, marked his accession to the throne by extending a free pardon to the numerous political prisoners that filled the jails in the country, and by restoring to them all their lands which had been confiscated by his uncle. He was a devout Buddhist, endowed with great tenderness of heart and purity. He always preserved a gentle and cheerful disposition. He also showed himself to be a man possessed of great energy and strength of character. In deciding questions that came before him in the course of his administration of the affairs of State "he yielded not to the four evil influences that pervert justice, viz., love, hatred, fear, and ignorance; but encouraged the good and discouraged the wicked."

The king was a man of considerable literary attainments and a poet of great renown. Most histories call him Pandita Vijaya Bahu. The code of law in accordance with which justice was administered in Lanka during this reign was that of Manu.

Beloved though this king was by his subjects, he was not destined to occupy the throne for longer than a year, having been foully murdered at the instance of a treacherous friend of his—a native of Kalinga named Mahinda.

Mahinda VI. was not allowed to occupy the throne for a longer space of time than five days, inasmuch as he was put to death by Kirti Nissangha, who had occupied the office of sub-king during the reign of Vijaya Bahu II. *Mahinda VI., 1174 A.C.*

Kirti Nissangha ascended the throne with the unanimous approval of the chiefs of Lanka and occupied it for nine years. During this period he formed gardens of fruit trees and flower trees throughout the Island to be devoted to the public benefit. He also built many beautiful mansions. He built of stone a beautiful temple for the Tooth-relic at Pollonnaruwa, a description of which is contained in the inscription which is to be seen at the present day on the Gal-potha, situated opposite the Sat-mahal-prasada. It says that "it had a covered terrace around it, and an open hall decorated with wreaths and festoons, and likewise gateways and walls." This description closely corresponds to the ground-plan of the ruin to be seen there at the present day. *Kirti Nissangha, 174-1183 A.C.*

The king also rebuilt two viharas which the Indians had destroyed, one of them was the temple at Damboola. This he caused to have polished walls and pillars dazzling with gold and silver. Its floor was painted with vermillion and its roof covered with gilded tiles; and seventy-three gilded images of Buddha were placed in it.

The inscription to be seen at the present day in the courtyard of this temple speaks of this king's munificence in its restoration and embellishment.

Certain improvements were made by this king to the Rankot dagoba, by building round it a number of profusely ornamented chapels. The enormous stone slab called the Gal-potha (or stone book, from its resemblance to a volume of olas), to which we have alluded above, is a monolith 26 feet in length over 4 feet in breadth and 2 feet in thickness. It bears an inscription, one passage of which records that "this engraved stone is the one which the strong men of the King Nissangha brought from the mountain of Mihintale at Anuradhapura—a distance of over 80 miles. The edges of the slab are richly carved with ornamental borders representing rows of the hanza, sacred goose of the Buddhists. *Appendix to Turnour's Epitome, p. 94.*

King Nissangha had a peculiar idea as to the method by which robbery could be ended in the Island,—an idea which, if carried out for any great length of time, would certainly have induced many who were not by nature disposed that way to make robbery a profession. In the great tablet at Pollonnaruwa, inscribed with his exploits, it is recorded that under the belief that "robbers commit their crimes through hunger for wealth, he gave them whatever riches they required, thus relieving the country from the alarm of their depredations."

So fervent a Buddhist was this king that he, together with four divisions of his army, ascended Adam's Peak and worshipped at the shrine there.

Vira Bahu, 1183 A.C.

Pujavaliya.

Vira Bahu, son of King Nissangha, succeeded his father to the throne and was crowned king at night, but was slain at dawn by Tavuru Senevirat (the commander-in-chief of the army), on the ground that he was a son not equal to his father.

Vikkarama Bahu, 1183 A.C.

Vikkarama Bahu, younger brother of King Nissangha, succeeded Vira Bahu and occupied the throne for three months, after which time he was murdered and succeeded by Codaganga, King Nissangha's nephew.

Codaganga, 1183-1184 A.C.

Codaganga ruled over Lanka for nine months and was deposed and deprived of his eyes by the general Kirti Senevirat, who placed Lilavati, one of the queens of King Parakrama Bahu the Great, there.

Lilavati, 1184-1187 A.C.

Lilavati had ruled over Lanka wisely and well for three years, when she was deposed.

Sahasa Malla, 1187-1189 A.C.

Sahasa Malla, "the lion-hearted king," succeeded Lilavati and ruled the kingdom for two years, when he was deposed by Ayasmanta, the chief of the army, who placed Kalyanavati, queen of the late King Kirti Nissanga, on the throne in his stead and administered the affairs of State for her.

Kalyanavati, 1189-1195 A.C.

Kalyanavati's reign of six years was a peaceful one and devoted to the cause of religion. She built a vihara at a village called Pannasalaka and called it after her name. Ayasmanta built a vihara and a college named Sarajakula-vaddhana at Weligama. He also caused a treatise called Dhammâdhikarana ("Rules of Practice") to be written dealing with the question of caste, with a view to arresting the tendency of the different castes to commingle, by drawing strict lines of demarcation between them. Perhaps this step was taken by him through a recognition of the scientific principle that children inherit the qualities of their parents, and are capable of developing them to a greater extent than they were to be found in the parents, and a desire to produce special aptitude and skill in individuals belonging to the various trades and professions.

History does not tell us what brought about the end of Kalyanavati's reign. So we may assume that she was deposed.

Dhammasoka, an infant three months old, succeeded Kalyánavati and occupied the throne for the space of one year, during which time Ayasmanta acted as regent. He and the regent were put to death by Anikanga, the governor of Maya-rata, after the royal forces had been defeated at Polonnaruwa. *Dhamma-soka, 1195-1196 A.C.*

The *Pujavaliya* tells us that Dhammásoka was the son of Anikanga, and that the latter arrived in Lanka with an army enlisted in Chola, so it is very probable that the cause of war was the fact that Anikanga's right, as the chief governor of the land (the governor of Maya-rata was considered such), to succeed to the throne on the death or deposition of Queen Kalyánavati, had been overlooked by Ayasmanta, who was commander-in-chief of the army, as well as the real ruler of the land, in his desire to have a puppet on the throne.

Anikanga had occupied the throne for seventeen days, when he was assassinated by his own valiant but treacherous general Camúnakka, who placed the deposed Queen Lilavati, widow of Parakrama Bahu I., on the throne and himself administered the country. *Anikanga, 1196 A.C.*

Lilavati reigned once more for one year, but was again deposed by Lokissara, an experienced old warrior, who arrived in Lanka, with an army enlisted abroad, and defeated the royal forces at the capital Polonnaruwa. *Lilaviti, 1196-1197 A.C.*

Lokissara had occupied the throne for nine months, when, through the agency of Parakrama, the commander-in-chief of the Sinhalese army, Lilavati ascended the throne for the third time. *Lokissara, 1197 A.C.*

Lilavati is described in the *Mahawansa* as "sprung from the race of the Sun and Moon, in whose form was to be seen the majesty of kings," from which it may be inferred that she was of undiluted royal blood and a woman of dignity who commanded the respect and admiration of those with whom she came in contact. In the seventh month of her reign King Parakrama of Pandu invaded Lanka and, having deposed her and Parakrama, *Lilavati, 1197-1198 A.C.*

the chief of her army, ascended the throne. During this reign two poets of great merit produced the well-known works *Sasadawa* and *Muwadewdawa* in blank verse.

Parakrama Pandu, 1198-1201 A.C.

Parakrama Pandu proved himself to be a wise and capable monarch who administered justice strictly in accordance with the laws laid down in the code of Manu. Lanka was invaded by Mágha, a prince of Kalinga, with a force of 20,000 men enlisted in Kerala, in the third year of Pandu's reign. The ferocity, cruelty, and barbarism of these invaders were such as Lanka had never before experienced, in spite of the numerous wars waged on her soil. Of them the *Mahawansa* says: "They robbed the inhabitants of their garments and their jewels and everything that they had and violated the chastity of families. They cut off the hands and feet of people and despoiled their dwellings. Their oxen, buffaloes, and other animals they carried off forcibly. The rich men they tied up with cords and tortured and took possession of all their wealth. They broke down the image-houses, and dagobas, in their search for treasure. They took up their abode in viharas and beat the pious laymen therein. They flogged children and ill-treated the priests. They compelled the people to carry burdens and made them labour heavily. Many books of great excellence did they loose from the cords that bound them and scatter about the place and otherwise destroy. They spared not even the most sacred of dagobas—the Ruanweli—which stood like the embodiment of the glory of all the pious kings of old. From it they carried off the sacred relics of Buddha and other treasures that had been enshrined, which were as dear unto the Sinhalese as their lives Alas! Alas!

They next surrounded the city Pollonnaruwa on every side and took Parakrama Pandu captive, and plucked out his eyes and robbed all the treasures that were therein with all the pearls and precious stones."

Kalinga Magha, 1201-1222 A.C.

Thereafter **Kalinga Magha** had himself crowned king, and having bestowed on his followers, pastures, houses, gardens, servants, oxen and buffaloes that belonged to private individuals and to the priesthood, he tyrannised over the inhabitants of Pihiti-rata for twenty-one years. As for the Rohana district, every attempt made by the invaders to overrun it, was frustrated by the bravery of the sturdy inhabitants that dwelt therein and their governor Bhuvaneka Bahu.

As for the Maya district, although the invaders were successful at first in effecting an entrance into it, they were, ere long, compelled to retire into Pihiti-rata, by the forces of Vijaya Bahu, a prince of Sinhalese royal blood, round whom the inhabitants had rallied in their distress.

Vijaya Bahu III.

After the expulsion of the invaders from Maya-rata Vijaya Bahu reigned as king of that district for four years, having built himself a fortified and beautiful city at Jambudoni (Dambedeniya, 50 miles to the north of the present Colombo). During these years he afforded protection within his kingdom to the numerous priests that fled from Pihiti-rata seeking refuge from the barbarian invaders.

The high-priest Vácissara had succeeded in saving the sacred Tooth- and Bowl-relics from the hands of the invader by bringing them to Maya-rata, where he had buried them on a hill named Kotmale. Having heard of it, King Vijaya Bahu had the relics placed beyond all possible reach of the invaders by getting the rock at Beligala fortified, and a temple built on the top of it, where they were deposited. Great were the ceremonies and rejoicings over this event.

In order to save the national religion from decay, as a result of the destruction of the libraries at the great temples, King Vijaya Bahu "gathered together pious men of great learning and many scribes also—men who were not given up to sloth, but were gifted with good manners and wrote skilfully and with great speed—and set them the work of transcribing the sacred book of the law, which consisted of eighty-four thousand divisions. To them he paid as many gold kahapanas as there were divisions in the book of the law."

Thereafter Vijaya Bahu built two viharas and repaired all the temples in his little kingdom that had been damaged by the invaders in the course of their search for plunder, amongst them was the Kelaniya Vihara, whose dagoba had been destroyed.

Rajaratnacara, p. 99.

Vijaya Bahu was a sedulous patron of learning, and established a *free* school in every village in his kingdom.

Vijaya Bahu had two sons named Parakrama Bahu and Bhuvaneka Bahu respectively. The astrologers having predicted great things of Parakrama Bahu, the elder of the two, special attention was devoted to his education. The renowned priest Sangha Rakkhita and others were entrusted with the education of the prince. The Dambadeni Asna, a small pamphlet, mentions sixty-four arts and sciences, in which the prince became proficient. Some of these arts and sciences are unknown to us at the present day, and their names signify nothing; but the following are some of his studies, for which we can ascertain their equivalent English names:—(1) Sinhalese or Elu, including Wiacarana or Grammar, (2) Maghada or Pali, Kach'chano and Magallano Grammars, (3) Sanscrit, (4) Grantha, (5) Tamil, (6) Neeti (Jurisprudence), (7) Bana or Divinity, including the three Pitakas, (8) Nigandu (Botany), (9) Chandas (Prosody), (10) Tarka (Logic), (11) Lakara (Rhetoric), (12) Niruth'thi (Derivation or Philology), (13) Shruti (the Vedas, including Rajur, Yajur, and Sáma), (14) Puranas (Hindu Mythology), (15) Nakshastra (Astronomy), (16) Samud'drika (Phrenology or Physiognomy), (17) Játaka (Astrological Calculations of Nativity), (18) Whydhia (Physic), (19) Siritha (Customs and Traditions), (20) Parakatha (Biography and History), (21) Kadu-Saramba (the Art of Fencing with Swords, also Palanga-Saramba or Fencing with Shields), (22) Danub'bedha (Archery), (23) Ratnapariksha (Mineralogy or the Knowledge of Gems), (24) Chittra (Drawing), (25) Súpa Sestra (the Art of Cookery), (26) Gandarwa (Dancing Music, etc.).

As mentioned before, King Vijaya Bahu of Mayarata died in the fourth year of his reign. He was cremated, with much ceremony, on the premises of the vihara at Attanagalla, and was succeeded on the throne by his son Parakrama Bahu, who, on account of his great learning, was known as Pandita Parakrama Bahu. One of the first acts of this king was to build a temple at his capital, Jambudoni, for the Tooth-relic and deposit it there after bringing it from Beligala with great pomp and ceremony. He placed it in a magnificent jewelled casket and held a feast in honour of it, for seven days prior to depositing it in the edifice he had built for it. Thereby he won the esteem and affection of the priesthood and the people, and soon felt himself strong enough to enter upon the enterprise of expelling the foreigners from the richest portion of the country, of which they had been in occupation for no less than twenty-four years.

When King Magha and Jaya Bahu, who shared the sovereignty of Pihiti-rata with him, found that their forces were being defeated in every encounter they were having with the invading Sinhalese army of King Parakrama, they hastily summoned a meeting of their councillors at Pollonnaruwa and decided upon evacuating the country with all the treasures they had accumulated, rather than allow themselves to be taken captives, together with their plunder. Accordingly, they were hastening to get to Mantotta, when they were surprised at Kala-wewa by a Sinhalese army and mercilessly slaughtered. Thus did the Sinhalese regain much of the plunder that was being carried away from their palaces, temples, and houses

Thereafter **Panditha Parakrama Bahu** reigned as king over the whole of Lanka for thirty-five years. *Parakrama Bahu II., 1222-1257 A.C.*

One of the first acts of his reign was to restore to private individuals, as well as to the priesthood, the lands, houses and fields of which they had been dispossessed by the invaders; after satisfactory proof had been produced of such dispossession. "In like manner he ascertained, and established each in their place, the five orders of menials and the ten orders of menials that belonged to the royal households. The lord of the land so ordained the affairs of the kingdom that all the inhabitants of Lanka prospered and became exceeding rich, and the whole country abounded with food." *Mahawansa, ch. 84.*

He next turned his attention to the furtherance of religion. He caused a great vihara to be built on the top of the mountain Palábatgala, which was covered with forest, and gave it to priests who lived lonely lives in the forest practicing austerities. Having discovered "that the elders who were learned in the scriptures were but thinly scattered in the Island, he procured learned priests from India, and the books also that were necessary, and caused the priests of Lanka to be taught in all the branches of religion, and logic and grammar and all the other sciences, and made learned men of many priests." This importation of priests and books from India must have considerably increased the tendency of the Sanscrit and Sinhalese languages to become intermixed as already noticed, during the reign of Parakrama I.

He caused a great vihara named Maha Vihara to be built in his native city of Siṛivaddhanapura (Kandy), and caused a road to be made to it from the city of Jambudoni (Dambadeniya) and conveyed the Tooth- and Bowl-relics there with great pomp and ceremony. He next built two colleges (pirivenas), one of which was called after him, Parakrama Bahu pirivena, the other, which was built at Beligala (Billa), was called Bhuvaneka Bahu pirivena, after the name of his brother who was sub-king, and supervised its construction. He made further repairs in the Kelaniya Vihara (built in the reign of Yatthalatissa), than those he had made while he ruled as King of Maya-rata. He also repaired the house wherein the sleeping image of Buddha lay, in Kelaniya, and the image-house called the Sivanka. Furthermore, he presented the Kelaniya Vihara with a land adjoining it, which he had planted with cocoanuts, "that so a feast of lamps might be held there daily."

"Again, at the Attanagalla Vihara (Hathavanagalla), where King Sirisangha Bo sacrificed himself, in order to help a begger to attain wealth, where Gothabhaya had built a circular relic-house of two stories, yea even that relic-house did King Pandita Parakrama Bahu turn into one of three stories adorned with a pinnacle of gold. At this self-same vihara, on the spot where his father was cremated, did the king build a beautiful dagoba and an image-house with eight sides, in which he fixed a stone statue of the Supreme Buddha. As he was extremely anxious to behold a beautiful picture of the Blessed One—a perfect likeness of Buddha as he was in his life-time,—he employed many skilled painters to paint on a beautiful cloth a surpassing likeness of Him as He walked on the great bridge of gold and gems at Kapilavastu, his birth-place."

These and many other things, such as worshipping the foot-print at the top of Adam's Peak, did this king do in his zeal for the furtherance of religion.

Parakrama Bahu's reign is of special interest to the student, inasmuch as the *Mahawansa* records the construction of many roads and bridges throughout the country during it. It is recorded that, in accordance with royal instructions, the minister Devapatiraja journeyed to Adam's Peak, starting from Gampola (Gangasiripura), that he built a bridge about 95 cubits in length near the mouth of the Kado-oya (Kajjota), and another about 30 cubits in length across the same river. At Ulapana (Ullapanagama) he built one 36 cubits in length, and at Ambagamuwa (Ambagama), a great, strong and beautiful bridge 34 cubits in length, one over which elephants, horses, buffaloes and oxen could pass in perfect safety. "On the causeways of these great bridges he caused to be built houses large and beautiful and adorned with high pillars and such like." "He caused a great forest to be hewn down and a public path to be made, along which he ascended Adam's Peak (Samantakúta) and worshipped the foot-print there and set up the image of the God, Sumana, adorned beautifully with ornaments of gold and jewels, on the ground within the courtyard of the shrine, and built an open hall over the sacred foot."

It is further recorded that this minister proceeded to the port of Bentota (Bhúnatittha) and there built a bridge 86 cubits' span, at the mouth of the Kalu-ganga (Kadalísena), one of about forty yatthis' span (a yathi = 7 cubits of two spans to the cubit) over the Salagamu-ganga, and one of fifty cubits' span over the Salruk (Sálapádapa river).

With regard to the length of the ancient cubit there is a certain degree of uncertainty. Dr. Davy (1816-1820) remarked that "carpenters and some other artists have measures of their own. The carpenters' *angula* (inch) is equal to the space between the second and third joint of the forefinger; and his *wadu riyana* (carpenters' cubit) is composed of twenty-four *angulas* and is divided into four parts." In this case the carpenters' cubit would be about two feet long. Major Forbes stated that the carpenters' cubit was two feet three inches in length. Capt. Knox, writing of the measures used in the middle of the seventh century, said: "A *Rian* is a cubit, which is with them (*i.e.* the Sinhalese) from the bone on the inside of the Elbow to the tip of the fourth Finger. A *Waddo rian* is the carpenters' Rule. It is as much as will reach from one Elbow to the other, the Thumbs touching one the other at the tops and so stretching out both Elbows." At the present day Sinhalese artizans make these measures agree with the English scale by using a *riyana* of eighteen inches, subdivided into inches, and *nul*, which are again divided into fourths; and a *wadu riyana* of three feet, that is, two *riyanas*.

Davy's Account of the Interior of Ceylon, p. 244.

Forbes' Eleven Years in Ceylon, p. 223.

Knox On Historical Relation of the Island of Ceylon, p. 98.

As a result of the education which he received during his boyhood, the king was a very learned person and devoted a deal of his attention to literary pursuits. His writings prove that, to a vigorous and brilliant imagination he added a wonderful ease in composition and a rich stock of useful knowledge. In the department of poetry, as in that of prose, few writers, if any, have ever surpassed him. His *Kawsilumina* and *Wisudhi Marga Sanna* are both first-rate performances. The style of the first, though somewhat difficult to be understood at the present day, is, nevertheless, rendered intelligible by a commentary from the pen of a subsequent writer; and the second is the celebrated paraphrase or commentary upon the *Wisudhamagan*.

This reign is famous not only for the labours of the king in the cause of religion, education, and the literature of his country, but also for those of other eminent men in the field of literature. Amongst them we find Darmakirti, whose works (a portion of the *Mahawansa*, from the reign of Mahasen down to the period we are now writing upon, excepted) are entirely lost; and Myrupáda, also a priest of eminent talents, the celebrated author of the *Pujávalia* and the medical work titled *Yóg-aarnawa*. Another medical work was produced during this reign, to which a Sinhalese paraphrase was added in the year 1760.

The minister Dàvapatiraja, after he had constructed the roads and bridges, planted with cocoanuts the tract of land, in extent about a yojana, situated between the Bentota Vihara and the bridge over the Kaluganga. He also had the great forest Mádelgasvanaya (Mahalabujagaccha) cleared; and he planted up the land with a large grove of jak trees to be devoted to the public use.

1233 A.C. In the 11th year of this reign the peace and tranquillity of the Island was disturbed by its invasion by an Indian (Malay) army led by a prince named Chandabhanu (Moon-Beam). These fierce invaders landed in divers ports in the south of the Island and shot poisoned arrows out of quick-firing engines, and struck terror into the peaceable inhabitants who resided along the coasts. Thereupon the king sent his valiant nephew, Vira Bahu, at the head of a strong force to give them battle. "And he (Vira Bahu) placed valiant men from among the Sinhalese in divers places, and began the fight with the strong men of the Malays. In the battle that ensued, the arrows tipped with poison, that were shot quickly, from engines by the Malays, fell in plenty amongst them. But the mighty men of the Sinhalese, who were skilful marksmen, brake them in pieces with their sharp broad arrows. Like as Rámá slew the Rakkhasas, even so did Vira Bahu slay in battle the strong men of the Malays in great numbers. In his great fury, again and again did Vira Bahu lay low the forces of the Malays, even as the tempest layeth low the forest." After he had thus delivered Lanka from the enemy Vira Bahu went to Dondra Head (Devapura) and worshipped "the lily-coloured god" (Vishnu), the remains of whose temple are still to be seen there. During this reign Chinese soldiers took service in the army of the King of Lanka, and quantities of Chinese swords and musical instruments were imported for the use of the army.

Kawia-sakara.

As King Pandita Parakrama Bahu advanced in years, thinking it fit to entrust the administration of the country to his five sons and his nephew Vira Bahu during his life-time, he summoned a meeting of his ministers as well as the high-priests in the Island and left to them the choice of his successor from among his sons Vijaya Bahu, Bhuvenaka Bahu, Tilokamalla, Parakrama Bahu, Jaya Bahu, and his nephew Vira Bahu. They having unanimously recommended the appointment of his eldest son Vijaya Bahu as his successor to the throne, on account of his kindly disposition and knowledge of the art of governing, the king entrusted him with the entire administration of the country.

The *Rajavaliya* says that during this reign there were 250,000 villages in Maya-rata, 450,000 in Phiti-rata, and 770,000 in Rohana,—a total of 1,470,000 villages in Lanka. Taking only a million villages, and allowing two houses to a village and five persons to a house, the population would be 10 millions, as against a little over 3½ millions at the present day.

Accordingly Vijaya Bahu appointed his cousin Vira Bahu to be his chief minister, his brother Tilokamalla to the command of the Sinhalese army which protected the southern portion of the country from foreign invasion, his brother Bhuvenaka Bahu to the command of the army which guarded the northern portion of the country, and his brothers Parakrama Bahu and Jaya Bahu to attend on his aged father, the king, in his capital Dambadeniya, while he himself with Vira Bahu journeyed throughout the country. The first place he visited was a high rocky stronghold called Vatagiri (Vagiri-gala). Here he buried all the jewels and other treasures that had been given him by his father after he had built a palace, and further fortified it with a very high wall. He next visited Adam's Peak, and after he had worshipped at the sacred foot-print arrived at Gampola (Ganga-siri-pura), where he restored the ancient vihara Niyangampaya. He later visited "the noble city of Hatthigiri" (Kurunegala), where, at the Maha Vihara built by Bhuvenaka Bahu, his paternal uncle who was dead, he built an image-house three stories high, in which he placed an image of Buddha as well as of his uncle. He next journeyed to a city named Subhagiri, where he received the news of an invasion of the Island by an Indian army led by Chandabhanu, who had previously made an unsuccessful attempt to conquer Lanka.

Chandabhanu had on this occassion landed in the north, and, having defeated in several battles the Sinhalese forces that guarded the frontier, he sent an ultimatum to Vijaya Bahu, who was at Subha-pabbata (Yapauwa), demanding the delivery of the sacred Alms-bowl and Tooth-relic, and expressing his determination to conquer the Island if it were not voluntarily ceded to him.

"Thereupon Vijaya Bahu, after having consulted Vira Bahu, set their great army in battle array, and proceeded, both of them together, saying, 'Oh, that we may this day behold the strength of each other's arms!' and they surrounded the great army of Chandabhanu and fought a fierce battle, like unto the battle of Rámá. And that day the enemy's strong men were utterly defeated and put to confusion in the field of battle. And they threw down their arms, and bowed themselves down with fear, and spoke flattering words. And some moved not, but stood like pillars and prayed for help, and others trembled and wept sore. On that day also the enemy's soldiers fled with fear on every side, some towards the woods, others towards the sea, and others again towards the hills. Thus did he (Vijaya Bahu) fight the battle and put Chandabhanu to flight, weaponless, after he had slain many of his soldiers. He took his chief women and all his horses and elephants, his sword and numerous other weapons, his great treasure, his royal chank and umbrella, the royal drum and the royal banners. All these, however, he sent unto his father."

Thereafter Vijaya Bahu repaired to the sacred city of Anuradhapura which was overgrown with dense jungle, and had it cleared of the superabundance of vegetation. He also had the sacred edifices, in particular the Ruanweli dagoba, repaired, employing for the purpose a great number of skilled artificers. Whilst he tarried in this great city, the Vannian princes presented themselves before him with gifts in acknowledgment of their vassalage. To them he showed great kindness and consideration, presenting to them in return litters (andoli), white umbrellas, chowries, and also the emblems of the princes of the Maha Vanni. By this means he won their affection and secured their loyalty to the throne.

Vijaya Bahu next proceeded to the royal city of Pollonnaruwa and found it in a state of utter ruin, so much so that he had to address a pitiful appeal to his royal father for help. The nature of the help given by King Parakrama Bahu and the work done at the city could best be indicated by quoting the words of the historian as recorded in the *Mahawansa* :—"The king called all his great ministers together and bade them command all the inhabitants of Lanka that they should each betake himself to his trade or occupation. Then he gathered together smelters, turners, basket-makers, blacksmiths, potters, goldsmiths, painters, posters, labourers, slaves, outcasts, skilful bricklayers, masons, carpenters, and divers kinds of workers in stone. Again, he gathered together all sorts of blacksmiths' tools, such as bellows, sledges, pinchers and anvils; also numerous sharp saws, adzes, axes, wood-cleavers, stone-cutters' chisels, knives, hammers, spades, mats, baskets, etc.;—all these tools and materials and much treasure, consisting of pearls, cat's-eyes, and other precious things, together with a great host of people, did he send unto his son." "Then the prince Vijaya Báhu was much pleased thereat. And in that country which had been lying desolate and in ruins for a long time, he caused the tanks, ponds, dykes, pools, and such like stores of water that had their great embankments breached and broken to be built up as before, so that they were filled with water and covered with divers kinds of lotuses and full of all manner of fish.

"He next restored many fertile fields which had aforetime produced divers kinds of grain; and he caused the crops everywhere to flourish, and the whole of that beautiful country to abound with plenty.

"He next caused the noble city of Pulatthi (Pollonnaruwa) to be restored to its former state, and surrounded it with a deep moat, like unto the sea, and with a circular rampart like unto the Cakkavála rock; and spread abroad over it divers gardens, divers pond, many viharas and cetiyas, numerous bird-shaped buildings, many palaces and mansions of divers kinds of work, many open halls, numerous temples of gods, divers kinds of towers, many rows of beautiful houses, numerous streets, well arranged gates on the four sides thereof, and beautiful squares and courtyards."

Thereafter King Pandita Parakrama Bahu set out for Pollonnaruwa and held the feast of his coronation at the celebrated city, although it was at the latter end of his reign. He next conveyed the sacred relics—the Bowl and Tooth placed "on a stately chariot, gorgeous and beautiful as a chariot of heaven," and accompanied by procession of numerous gaily caparisoned elephants, horses, dancers, musicians and companies of mighty men of valour, etc.—from Jambudoni (Dambadeniya) to Pollonnaruwa, where they were placed "on the great throne adorned with divers gems in the ancient temple of relics."

The town of Pollonnaruwa was a scene of great feasting and rejoicing for no less than three months, in honour of the relics.

Not long after this event, King Pandita Parakrama Bahu died, and was succeeded on the throne by this illustrious eldest son, Vijaya Bahu.

Vijaya Bahu IV., 1257-1259 A.C.

Vijaya Bahu IV. reigned for two years, having Jambudoni (Dambadeniya) for his capital, and was treacherously murdered by a servant, who had been bribed for the purpose by one of his generals named Mitta, who was desirous of ascending the throne.

Mitta, 1259 A.C.

Mitta was unsuccessful in his attempt to seize Bhuvenaka Bahu, the brother of the deceased king, who getting into a litter succeeded in escaping from Dambadeniya and taking refuge in the fortress at Yapauwa (Subha-pabbata). Not many days was Mitta spared to occupy the throne of Lanka, inasmuch as he was slain in the royal palace at Dambadeniya by the loyal Aryan officer Thakuraka and his 700 Aryan men who were in the pay of Vijaya Bahu IV., and had determined on his death to have Bhuvenaka Bahu as his successor.

Bhuvenaka Bahu, 1259-1270 A.C.

Bhuvenaka Bahu I. was a beneficent monarch. During the early, part of his reign Lanka was repeatedly, unsuccessfully invaded by Indian forces under Kálinga Ráyar, Codaganga, and others. The Sinhalese Vannian princes, Kadalivata, Mápána, Tipa, and Himiyánaka, who had proved themselves disloyal, were deposed during this reign. After the king had spent a few years in the city of Dambadeniya he shifted his capital to Yápauwa (Subhapabbata), which city he greatly enlarged and beautified. For the furtherance of religion he had a large number of copies of the three pitakas made and presented a copy to each of a large number of temples, thus spreading a knowledge of the Pali scriptures throughout the land. He died at Yapauwa in the eleventh year of his reign and was succeeded by his nephew Parakrama Bahu.

During the reign of **Parakrama Bahu III.** the Island was invaded by a Pandian army, led by one Chakravatti. The invaders succeeded in capturing the fortress of Yapauwa and carrying off the sacred Tooth-relic. However, King Parakrama succeeded in bringing it back to Lanka, having himself visited the King of Pandu and asked for its return in a very conciliatory manner. On its arrival in the Island the Tooth was placed in the ancient temple of the Tooth-relic, at the noble city of Pollonnaruwa, where Parakrama reigned for the rest of his life, regulating the affairs of State strictly in accordance with the laws of Manu. *Parakrama Bahu III., 1270-1275 A.C.*

Bhuvenaka Bahu II. was the son of Bhuvenaka Bahu I. He reigned for two years having Kurunegala (Hatthiselapura) for his capital. He was a staunch supporter of the Buddhist faith, and devoted himself "to works of charity and other good deeds." During each of the two years of his reign he celebrated the feast of his coronation in a manner worthy of the dignity of a king, and followed it up by holding a festival of ordination of priests amidst great rejoicings, thus shedding light on the national religion. *Bhuvenaka Bahu II., 1275-1277 A.C.*

Parakrama Bahu IV. was the son of his predecessor on the throne, and was a very scholarly as well as mighty monarch. He caused a three-storied temple of the Tooth-relic to be built within the courtyard of the royal palace at Kurunegala, with beautiful walls, pillars and paintings, surmounted with spires of gold and adorned with door panels, also of gold. The ceiling thereof was covered with cloths of silk and the like, of divers colours, which was adorned with beautiful chains of gold, of silver and of pearls hung on every side. After a beautiful curtain-wall of silk had been fixed, a splendid throne overlaid with exquisite coverings was raised. This covering was adorned all round with rows of vases of gold and silver and rows of ornamented candlesticks of *Parakrama Bahu IV., 1277 A.C.*

gold and silver. Thereafter the king, with great reverence, placed thereon the two caskets containing the Bowl- and Tooth-relics. This was followed by great festivities in their honour.

A number of other religious edifices were built during this reign at the instance of the king. At Dondra Head (Devapura) he caused a long two-storied image-house, containing an image of Buddha in a sleeping posture, to be built, and endowed it with the surrounding land as well as with the revenue of the village Getamánna (Gantimana). At Weligama he caused a two-storied temple to be built named Parakrama Vihara, and dedicated the village Elgiriya (Sáligiri) to it for its maintenance. He caused a temple named Sirighanánanda, with a school (pirivena) attached to it, to be built near the town Ratgama (Rájaggáma), and dedicated it to a learned priest from Chola, who had been brought over to Lanka to help him in the course of his literary labours. He rebuilt the vihara at Totagamuwa which had fallen into decay. The new building was a two-storied one thirty cubits in length. It had tall spires, and was rendered very beautiful by reason of the divers paintings. To this vihara was attached a school (pirivena) managed by a great and venerable priest named Káyasatthi. For the benefit of this pirivena the king gifted a land in Totagamuwa containing 1,000 cocoanut trees, as well as the village Sálaggáma situated on the bank of the Gin-ganga (Gimha).

With the assistance of the priest imported from Chola, King Parakrama, together with his prime minister Weerasingha Pathiraja, translated the *Pansiapanas Jataka* (the 550 birth-stories of Buddha) from the Pali language into Sinhalese, and caused copies of the translation to be sent to temples throughout the Island.

The *Sidat Sangarawa*—a grammar of the Sinhalese language—was written during this reign at the instance of Pathiraja, who was prime minister, and as such held the office of Governor of Maya-rata.

The *Datuwansa* (*Daladawansa*), an elaborate work containing the history of the Tooth-relic, was also written during this reign. The date of Parakrama Bahu IV.'s death is not specified in the histories of Lanka.

Bhuvenaka Bahu III.

Bhuvenaka Bahu III., of whose relationship to Parakrama Bahu IV. historians tell us nothing, succeeded him. He was known as Vanni Bhuvenaka Bahu. No further information is available in the Sinhalese histories of Lanka regarding his reign. Perhaps the silence is attributable to the great calamity which befel the national religion during this period, which is described by Marco Polo as well as Chinese historians. We have already noted that the employment of Indian soldiers by Sinhalese kings was followed by an invasion of the country by Indian princes in search of wealth and power. So also the employment of Chinese soldiers in the Sinhalese army during the reign of Parakrama Bahu III. was followed by Chinese aggression.

Marco Polo, who left Venice as a youth in the year 1271 and resided seventeen years at the court of the Chinese Emperor, Kublai Khan, says that in the year 1281 A.C. the Great Khan Kublai demanded of the king of Lanka one of Buddha's teeth "and obtained from the king two large black teeth, together with some of his hair and a handsome vessel of porphyry."

1281 A.C. Tennent, vol. i., p. 636 and p. 200. Marco Polo's Travels, etc., bk. 3, ch. 23, p. 671.

The Sinhalese, when dealing with foreigners, never seem to have been scrupulous about multiplying Buddha's teeth.

Marco Polo further says that "the Grand Kahn Kublai sent ambassadors to Lanka with a request that the king would yield to him possession of "the great ruby" in return for the "value of a city." He still further says that after three separate envoys had been sent "the Alms-dish of Buddha was at length yielded by the King of Ceylon as a gift to Kublai Khan and carried with signal honour to China in the year 1284 A.C."

1284 A.C. Marco Polo's Travels, ch. 19. (Latin version to be found in the Imperial Library of Paris.)

A description of the Alms-bowl is contained in the Chinese "Account of Island Foreigners" (Taou-e che-leo). It says: "In front of the image of Buddha there is a sacred bowl, which is neither made of jade, nor copper, nor iron; it is of a purple colour and glossy, and when struck it sounds like glass. At the commencement of the Yuen dynasty, three separate envoys were sent to obtain it."

"It was about this time that a princess of Ceylon became the heroine of one of the most stirring tales of Indian History. Her name Padmavati has been transmitted with renown to posterity by tradition and the bards of Rajasthan. She was married to Ratan Sen, the overlord of the Rajput confederacy and Rana or

Arunachalam's Sketches of Ceylon History, sect. 12.

Sovereign of Chittore, a prince held in reverence throughout India as the lineal descendent of the hero of the Ramayana, and whose modern representative at Udaipur is still accorded the highest place among the chiefs of India. The fame of Padmavati's beauty and accomplishments reached the years of Alla-ud-din, the Mohammedan Emperor of Delhi, who, longing to make her his Empress, invaded Chittore. The Rajputs resisted the imperial arms with their wonted heroism. After a long and fruitless siege Alla-ud-din restricted his desire to a mere sight of this extraordinary beauty reflected through the medium of mirrors. Relying on the faith of the Rajput, he entered Chittore slightly guarded and, having gratified his wish, returned. The Rajput chief, unwilling to be outdone in confidence, accompnied Alla-ud-din to the foot of the fortress, amid many complimentary excuses from his guest at the trouble thus occasioned. It was for this he had risked his own safety, relying on the superior faith of the Hindu. Here an ambush was ready, and the Hindu King was made prisoner and his liberty made dependent on the surrender of Padmavati.

Despair reigned in Chittore, and it was anxiously debated whether she should be resigned as ransom. She expressed her acquiescence, and, having provided the wherewithal to secure herself from dishonour, she devised with two chiefs of her Ceylon clan a plan in pursuance of which intimation was given to Alla-ud-din that on the day he withdrew from the trenches, she would arrive, but in a manner befitting her station, attended by her ladies-in-waiting and by others who would accompany her to Delhi to pay her this last mark of respect, and strict orders were to be issued to prevent the decorum and privacy of the Rajput ladies from being violated by curiosity. 700 covered litters proceeded to the imperial camp, borne by armed soldiers disguised as porters. The imperial tents were enclosed with tapestry, the litters were deposited, and half an hour was granted for a parting interview between the Rana and his bride. They then placed him in a litter and bore him away leaving the greater number of the supposed damsels behind to accompany the Queen to Delhi. Alla-ud-din had no intention to permit the Rana's return, and was becoming impatient of the length of the interview, when, instead of the Rana and his queen, the devoted band issued from their litters. Alla-ud-din was however well guarded. Pursuit was ordered, but the Rajputs covered the retreat till they perished to a man. A fleet horse was in reserve for the Rana, and carried him safely to the fort, at the gate of which Alla-ud-din's host was encountered by the heroes of Chittore. Animated by enthusiasm for their king and the honour of their queen, they devoted themselves to destruction. Few survived this slaughter of the flower of Rajput chivalry. The havoc made in Alla-ud-din's rank by their heroism and the dread of their determined resistance obliged him to raise the siege.

Recruiting his strength, he returned to the siege with renewed vigour. The defence had not recovered from the loss of so many brave men, but was maintained with incredible valour. It was in vain. Eleven out of twelve sons of the king fell in succession, leading the fight, and then he called his chiefs around him and said: "Now I devote myself for Chittore." But another awful sacrifice was to precede this act of self-devotion; the terrible rite of *Johur* was to be performed. The funeral pyre was lighted within the great subterranean retreat, and the defenders of Chittore saw pass in procession their wives and daughters to the number of several thousands. The fair Padmavati with her attendants closed the throng. They entered the cavern and there found security from dishonour and captivity in the devouring element.

A generous contest now arose between the Rana and his sorrowing son as to which should lead the fatal charge. The father prevailed, and in obedience to his commands, the son with a small band passed through the enemy's lines and reached the outward world in safety. Satisfied now that his line was not extinct, the Rana called around him his devoted clans for whom life had no longer any charms. They threw open the gates, and with reckless despair carried death or met it in the hosts of Alla-ud-din's army.

The conqueror took possession of an inaminate capital, strewn with the bodies of the brave defenders. The smoke yet issued from the recesses where lay consumed the object of his desire. Since that awful day in A.C. 1303 the cavern has been sacred; no eye has penetrated its gloom, and superstition has placed as its guardian a huge serpent whose venemous breath extinguishes the light which might guide intruders to "the place of sacrifice." Alla-ud-din remained in Chittore some days, admiring the grandeur of his conquest, and committing every act of barbarity and wanton destruction which a bigoted zeal could suggest against the magnificent temples, palaces and other monuments of art. He spared, however, the beautiful palace of Padmawati, which still stands in silent beauty, a sad memorial of her chequered life and of the woes innumerable, of which she was the innocent cause.

A Mohammedan saint, Malik Muhammed, who lived 250 years afterwards, has made the life of this princess of Ceylon the theme of a great philosophical work called after her. It tells in vivid language the story of Ratan Sen's quest for her, of Alla-ud-din's ruthless siege, of Ratan Sen's valour, of Padmavati's wifely devotion, culminating in the terrible sacrifice of all in the cavern of fire. The poet-saint makes of these events an allegory describing the search of the soul for true wisdom and the trials and temptations which beset it in its course."

Jaya Bahu I. succeeded Bhuvenaka Bahu III. Historians give us no information regarding his relationship to his predecessor, the date of his accession, or the date of his death or deposition. We are simply told that he was "a very powerful king." Perhaps this was by comparison with his predecessor, who tamely yielded up the priceless relics to the Chinese Emperor.

Bhuvenaka Bahu IV., 1347 A.C.

Bhuvenaka Bahu IV. succeeded Jaya Bahu I. He is described in the *Mahawansa* as "a man of great wisdom and faith, and a mine of excellent virtues." He had Gampola (Ganga-siri-pura) for his capital.

The first authentic notice we have of cinnamon in Lanka occurs in the voyages of Ibu Batuta, the Moor, who, impelled by religious enthusiasm, set out from his native city of Tangiers, in the year 1324 A.C., and devoted twenty years to a pilgrimage, the record of which has entitled him to rank amongst the most remarkable travellers of any age or country. When steering for the coast of India, from the Maldives, Ibu Batuta was carried by the South-West monsoon towards the northern portion of Lanka, which was then (1347 A.C.) in the hands of the Malabars. The Hindu chief of Jaffna was at this time in possession of a fleet, in "which he occasionally transported his troops against the Mohammedans on the other parts of the coasts." Evidently the Mohammedans had settlements along the coast for purposes of trade with the interior.

Ibu Batuta was permitted to land at Battala (Putlam) and found the shore covered with "cinnamon wood," which "the merchants of Malabar transport without any further price than a few articles of clothing which are given as presents to the king. This may be attributable to the circumstance that it is brought down by the mountain torrents, and left in great heaps upon the shore." The Tamil chieftain exhibited to him his wealth in "pearls" and furnished him with an escort for climbing Adam's Peak. On the first day of his journey he crossed a river on a boat made of reeds, and entered the city of Mannar Maṇdali (probably the site of the present Minneri Mundal). This was the "extremity of the territory of the infidel king," whence Ibu Batuta proceeded to the port of Salawat (Chilaw), and thence turning inland he reached the city of the Sinhalese sovereign at Gampola (Ganga-siri-pura), which he contracts into Kankar or Ganga. He says that the Sinhalese king, on feast days, rode a white elephant, his head adorned with very large rubies found in the Island, embedded in "a white stone abounding in fissures, from which they cut it out and give it to the polishers." He enumerates three varieties: "the red, the yellow, and the cornelian." In describing the decorations of the head of the white elephant, he speaks of "seven rubies, each of which was larger than a hen's egg," and a saucer made of a ruby as broad as the palm of the hand. In the ascent from Gampola to Adam's Peak, he speaks of the monkeys with beards like a man (the wanduras), and of the "fierce leech" which lurks in the trees and damp grass, and springs on the passers by. He describes the trees with leaves that never fall, and the "red roses" of the rhododendrons which still characterise that lofty region. At the foot of the last pinnacle, which crowns the summit of the peak, he found a minaret named after Alexander the Great; steps hewn out of the rock, and "iron pins to which chains are appended" to assist the pilgrims in their ascent; a well filled with fish; and last of all, on the loftiest point of the mountain, the sacred foot-print of the First Man, into the hollow of which the pilgrims drop their offerings of gems and gold. In descending the mountain, he passed through the village of Kalanga, near which was a tomb said to be that of Abu Abd Allah (the first to lead Mohammedan pilgrims to Lanka). He next visited the temple of Dinaur (Dondra Head) and returned to Putlam by way of Kale (Galle) and Kolambu (Colombo), "the finest and largest city in Serendib."

1351 A.C

We are told in the *Mahawansa* that the fourth year of this king's reign was 1894 A.B., which works out to be 1351 A.C., from which we get an idea of its commencement. During this reign was produced the historical work named *Nikaya Sangaraha*, also the work *Dahamgete.*

Parakrama Bahu V. succeeded Bhuvenaka Bahu IV. and reigned at Gampola. Historians, however, give us no particulars as to the events which occurred during this reign.

Wickerama Bahu III. succeeded Parakrama Bahu. He too reigned at Gampola, and of him too historians tell us nothing beyond the fact that he was a wise monarch. In the year 1382 Sanga Raja (= Archbishop) Durandara composed the *Attanagaluwansa*, a work written in an exceedingly elegant style, embodying a great portion of the history of the times of King Siri Sanghabo. During his reign a prince "of great majesty, faith and such like virtues," dwelt at Peradeniya (Perádoni). His name was Alagakkonára. He succeeded Wickerama Bahu III. and took the name of Bhuvenaka Bahu on ascending the throne.

Bhuvenaka Bahu V., 1388-1408 A.C.

Bhuvenaka Bahu V. built himself a city at Cotta (Jayawardhna-Cotta), which he fortified with rows of great ramparts, gates, and towers. He was a staunch Buddhist, and devoted the greater part of his time to the furtherance of religion. He caused a casket to be made of seven thousand pieces of silver for the Tooth-relic and made offerings thereto with great devotion. The *Mahawansa* says that "when he had reigned twenty years his days were numbered." Chinese historians explain to us this ambiguous reference to the termination of his reign.

The *Se-yih-ke-foo-choo* or "Description of Western Countries," says that in 1405 A.C. the reigning king, A-lee-koo-nae-wurh (= Alagakkonára) maltreated foreigners resorting to the Island, and plundered their vessels, "so that the envoys from other lands, in passing to and fro, were much annoyed by him."

In that year a mission from China, sent with incense and offerings to the shrine of the tooth, was insulted and waylaid, and with difficulty effected an escape from Lanka. According to the *Ming-she*, or history of the Ming dynasty, "the Emperor *Ching-tsoo*, indignant at this outrage on his people, and apprehensive lest the influence of China in other countries besides Lanka had declined during the reign of his predecessors, sent *Ching-Ho*, a soldier of distinction, with a fleet of 62 ships and a large military escort, on an expedition to visit the western kingdoms, furnished with proper credentials and rich presents of silks and gold. Ching-Ho touched at Cochin-China, Sumatra, Java, Cambodia, Siam and other places, "proclaiming at each the Imperial edict and conferring Imperial gifts." If any of the princes refused submission, they were subdued by force; and the expedition returned to China in 1407 A.C., accompanied by envoys from the several nations, who came to pay court to the Emperor. In the following year Ching-Ho, having been despatched on a similar mission, the king, A-lee-ko-nae-wurh (= Alagakkonára Bhuvenaka Bahu V.), decoyed his party into the interior, threw up stockades with a view to their capture, in the hope of a ransom, and ordered soldiers to the coast to plunder the Chinese junks. But Ching-Ho, by a dexterous movement, avoided the attack, and invested the capital, made a prisoner of the king, succeeded in conveying him on board his fleet, and carried him captive to China, together with his queen, his children, his officers of State, and his attendants. He brought away with him spoils which were long afterwards exhibited in the Tsing-hae monastery at Nankin. "In the sixth month of the year 1411 A.C.," says the author of the *Ming-she*, "the prisoners were presented at court. The Chinese ministers pressed for their execution, but the Emperor, in pity for their ignorance, set them at liberty, but commanded them to select a virtuous man from the same family to occupy the throne. All the captives declared in favour of Seay-pa-nea-na, whereupon an envoy was sent with a seal to invest him with the royal dignity as a vassal of the Empire."

It is stated in the Chinese chronicle *Woo-heo-peen* or Record of the Ming dynasty that Seay-pa-nea-na was afterwards named Pu-la-ko-ma Ba-zae La-cha (= Parakrama Bahu Raja).

Vira Bahu, 1408-1410 A.C.

Vira Bahu, brother of King Bahuvenaka Bahu V., occupied the throne of Lanka during the period of time that elapsed between the capture of Bhuvenaka Bahu V. and the appointment of Parakrama Bahu to the throne.

Parakrama Bahu VI., 1410-1462 A.C.

Parakrama Bahu VI. is said in the *Mahawansa* to have ascended the throne in the year 1953 A.B., which works out to be 1410 A.C. Although the Chinese chronicles, as we have already seen, fix upon 1411 A.C., as the year of his accession, we prefer to be guided by the *Mahawansa*. King Parakrama VI. had Cotta for his capital and proved himself to be an exemplary monarch.

The king had two adopted sons named Sapumal Cumara and Ambulugala Kuda Cumara. Great attention was devoted to their education. When these princes had attained their manhood, the king, desirous of bringing the whole of Lanka—the northern portion of which had fallen into the hands of a South Indian King—under his sway, entrusted the task of expelling the invader and subjugating the district to his eldest son Sapumal Cumara.

The *Rajavaliya* thus describes the expedition :—" The prince fell upon many villages belonging to Jaffna, and took them together with many prisoners of war, whom he brought to Cotta and delivered to his royal father.

The king sent his son out for the second time with another army ; and this time the prince entered the city of Jaffna itself, and made himself master of the ports thereof. When the prince entered Jaffna he rode upon a black horse ; the Malabars lay in ambush hoping to kill the animal and take the prince a prisoner ; but the prince's steed sprang amongst them, like a tiger on his prey, and put them to flight. The prince, at the head of his forces, charged into the midst of the enemy and wrought such carnage that the streets of Jaffna ran with blood that day as if it had been a river. Moreover, the prince took the King Aria Chacrawarti a prisoner, and putting him to death brought his wife and children to Cotta, where he presented them to his father.

Journ R.A.S. (C.B.) vol. xx., p. 69.

De Coute says that Sapumal Cumara was a man of great size, prodigious strength, majestic appearance and a clever horseman.

Jaffna at the time of its conquest was a populous city with wide streets, storied houses, fine gardens, palaces and Hindu temples. Various races, *e.g.*, Tamils and Mallalas, composed its army, which included the brave regiment of the Doluwara, the special guard of the King of Jaffna—*Kowul Sandese.*

The king, highly pleased with the exploits of his son, conferred on him many presents and also the administration of Jaffna.

Later the king loaded a vessel with goods, and, sending the same to Jaffna, started to trade with his son who resided there. The said vessel, loaded with the king's commerce, was seized by a petty chief named Wira Rama, who resided in the neighbourhood of Jaffna.

King Parakrama Bahu, on hearing this news, ordered hundreds of ships to be manned and sent out. Accordingly the flotilla sailed, took and put to death the said Wira Rama, made a descent on Soly-rata and fell upon and plundered several towns and villages. Thereafter a yearly tribute was paid from the four towns called Makudam Cottah.

About the year 1459 A.C. the king, feeling himself strong enough to do so, refused to pay any longer the annual tribute to the Chinese Emperor, which he had regularly paid since his accession to the throne.

This king levied a tax upon the produce of the whole country, and also farmed the ferries throughout the Island. *Rajaratnacara.*

He built at his capital "a beautiful three-storied temple delightful to behold in the form of a crown, constructed of stone with finely carved granite pillars, surmounted by a pinnacle of solid gold, for the Tooth-relic, which he enshrined in four caskets, the innermost one being a casket of gold inlaid with the nine precious gems (*i.e.* the pearl, ruby, topaz, diamond, emerald, lapis-lazuli, coral, sapphire and *gomeda* (a variety of agate), the next also a casket of gold inlaid with precious stones shining with divers rays, the next was a casket of plain gold, and the outermost was "a great and excellent casket gilt with gold of the first and most beautiful kind." At the village Pepiliyána (Pappatakanana) near Cotta he built a temple with a school attached named Sunetrá-devi, after his mother, so that merit may accrue to her, and granted the services and income of great many villages, fields, and gardens for its maintenance. He caused copies to be made of the three Pitakas, their Atthakatha (commentary) and Tíká (glosssary), and granted lands, etc., to the scribes, so that they may devote their sole attention to the writing of such sacred books. He caused repairs to be made to the dagobas at Mahiyángana and other places. During the course of fifty-two years of his reign he presented to the priesthood in general no less than 26,142 suits of robes and other necessaries. He also presented 3,432 suits of robes made of cotton plucked from the tree and manufactured within the space of twenty-four hours (= Kathina Dhwana).

Rajaratnacara.

Nicola de Conti's "De variatate fortunæ."

The first European writer in whose pages mention is made of Lanka's cinnamon is Nicola de Conti (1444 A.C.), a Venetian trader.

Rajavalia.

In the last year of King Parakrama's reign, the tributary raja of the Kandyan district, named Sojawna Sewo, neglected to pay his annual tribute, and also to send the people for service as was usual. Thereupon King Parakrama sent his younger son Ambulugala Cumara at the head of a great army against him. The expedition was successful, the rajah's capital, Gampola, was taken, together with the rajah and many of his relatives. The relatives were brought as prisoners to Cotta, but the rajah was deposed and allowed to remain in his principality, his adigar having undertaken to pay the tribute regularly in future.

King Parakrama Bahu VI. was a great patron of literature. During his reign *Tottagamuwa*, the great luminary of science, wrote his masterly works and amazed all Lanka with the versatility of his talents. He became master of every kind of learning he chose to profess. An easy and copious style, a lively wit and a fine imagination, did not fail to establish that literary renown for which his memory is now distinguished.

He was generally named after his native country in the Southern Province, *Tottagamuwa ;* although his proper appellation was *Sri Rahulastha Wirayo.* He is said to have been the grand-pupil of Uttra'moola. Beyond this nothing is correctly known of either his parentage or early history. He possessed a correct acquaintance with several Oriental languages besides the Elu. The foreign languages of which this distinguished scholar was a proficient are enumerated in the paraphrase to his *Selalihini Sandese.* They were six in number, viz., Sanscrit, Maghadi (Pali), Apabbransa, Paisachi, Surasena, and Tamil. For this reason he was called "Shadbahasha-parameshwara" (= chief linguist, acquainted with six languages).

Tottagamuwa was a great favourite of King Parakrama, and it is believed that as he was fostered in the king's household previous to his taking holy orders, so he continued after that event to benefit by the patronage of his royal master. Nor was he ungrateful to his benefactor. Of his devotion to Parakrama and the royal family, the writings of this scholar contain many tokens. The king has inspired some of his best and most melodious strains. He gave to him the most invaluable token of his regard, the use of his pen; and besides dedicating his *Kaviasekara* to the Princess-Royal, Ulakuda Dewi, at whose request it was composed, he addressed to the king several stanzas of great beauty. His *Kaviasekara*, "a garland of flowers on the crown of poetry," has been scarcely surpassed by any other in respect of originality and depth of thought, of elegance and correctness of expression. He was master of his language in its full extent, and has used the melodious words with such diligence, that from his book alone the art of Sinhalese poetry might be learned. No Sinhalese scholar reads it, much less hears the name of *Kaviasekara* (our author's first work, a poetical version of one of the incarnations of Buddha), without mingled feelings of esteem and veneration. Its style is elaborate and energetic; and its versification correct, smooth, and elegant. It is a work which consists of 885 stanzas. According to its author, it took him no less than 29 years to write it. He says he commenced it in 1415 A.C. and finished it in 1444 A.C.

Tottagamuwa next wrote the celebrated *Selalihini Sandese*. The writer's thoughts, brilliant and original, sparkle as we go along his elegant and flowing rhymes. Both the ear and the mind are at once satisfied. Its language is free and possesses a fascination which words cannot describe. Its illustrations are original and lively, and its versification unexceptionable. Tottagamuwa undertook this work with grateful affection for the king and his country, He felt interested in the welfare of the young family of Parakrama Bahu VI., and sympathised with the Princess Ulakuda, who mournfully longed for a child. The argument of the poem is well conceived. It is an epistle addressed to Wibushana, the presiding diety of the Kelaniya temple, invoking the blessing of a grandson to the king (or rather a son to the princess), and as if intended to be conveyed by means of a bird of the name of Selalihini (Gracula Religiosa) from Cotta, the seat of government. No precise date is given in this work, although from other data it could be gathered that it was written a year after the last. It contains 100 stanzas.

This poet next gave to the world his *Parawisandese.* It is a poem of great merit, and generally of a piece with the last in style, although perhaps in many parts inferior to it in imagery. It was an epistle addressed to Krishna, invoking blessings upon the army, the king's government at Jaffna (Mayadunu), and upon Chandrawati, the grand-daughter of the king. Even in this poem there are tender allusions to the royal family. That Chandrawati might soon enter the bonds of matrimony, and that, allied to a noble prince, she might soon be the mother of a virtuous son, are amongst the warmest aspirations of the author and the topics of his song.

Of the many writings of this eminent scholar, the only other work which is handed down to us with the sanction of his name is *Moggalayana Pathipanchika*, a commentary on a Pali grammar by Moggaláyana. It contains allusions to almost the whole circle of the Hindu arts and sciences, and many of the literary men of Lanka whose works are now lost to us.

The work titled *Perakumbasiritha*, "a history of Parakrama Bahu," furnishes us with sufficient internal evidence to justify the conclusion consistent with a tradition on the subject, that it was written by Tottagamuwa.

Many a sentiment in praise of Parakrama Bahu VI., whose character and virtues the poet has delineated in this work, is indicative of the affection he entertained towards his patron and sovereign, and the knowledge he possessed generally of his country's history. This poem is by no means inferior to the rest of the writer's works, but for the admixture of foreign words which appear to have been intentionally introduced with a view to adorn his language with the glittering ornaments of the Sanscrit.

During this reign was also written the work titled *Kowul Sandese* by Irrugalchula Pariwénadipati, a priest of Mulgirigala. The writer in this poem seeks a blessing from Krishna, "the deity presiding over the temple at Dondra Head," upon Prince Singhapperumal, or Sapumal, the son of King Parakrama; and also prays that the war in which the prince was then engaged at Jaffna against Ariachakkrawarti, the King of Karnatá, might prove victorious. No date is to be found in this work. Mention, however, is made of the prince, and the war is spoken of in terms which clearly indicate that his success was uncertain at the time the poet wrote. But the *Selalihini Sandese*, to which we have above referred, alludes to the same war; and the poet joins in the general shout of joy, amidst which the prince was then returning to his father at Cotta. Therefore this work must have been written a few months before the *Selalihini Sandese*.

Another reputable and confessedly beautiful poem, the *Guttille*, was written at this period by a priest of Wettéwe, who is said to have been a pupil of Totagamuwa.

The prose of this age sustains a like character as the poetry which we have reviewed. The brilliant scholar James Alwis quotes as an illustration of the prose of this period an inscription which he found at Pepiliana, the village at which King Parakrama built a temple in honour of his mother, and translates it as follows: "Whereas with a view to its stability and prosperity, the following things, to wit, ramparts, towers, image-houses, halls, Bó-trees, dagaps (pagodas or monuments), pansils (or houses for priests), outer temples or déwálas, buildings or repositories for books, flower gardens, and orchards or parks have been offered for (the use of) the temple, which was founded or built at an expense of 25,000 (current coins of the highest value), at Pepiliána in the district of Pánabunu (Panadura), and in pursuance of the orders (unto Sikuru Mudal, one of the chiefs of the king's household, directing him to erect a new temple with a view to impart merit to the queen, the king's mother, who had gone to heaven), given on the 15th day of the lunar month of Medin'dinna (March-April), when the moon had attained her fullness, in the 1958th year of the renowned Budhistical era, and in the 39th of the reign of the Emperor Sree Sangabódhí, Sree Parakrama Bahu, born of the Solar Race, and a descendant of the King Maha'Sammata; orders given by the king himself, whilst he presenting his noble appearance, attired in his four and sixty ornaments, crowned with his crown, and

Alwis' Sidat Sangarawa, Intro., p. 199.

surrounded by kings, governors, sub-kings and ministers, sat like Indra, giving orders in respect of the affairs of the whole State, on his throne which was erected on the adorned hall opposite to the square (palace) called Sumangala in the chief city of Jayawardene (Cotta)."

The Age of Sri Parakrama Bahu VI. by E. W. Perera. Journal No. 63, vol. xxii. of the R. A. S. (C. B.) 1910.

Great educational progress was made during this reign. "Ecclesiastical colleges or pirivenas flourished throughout the country, and were presided over by abbots, distinguished alike for their knowledge of theology as for their piety and devotion to the faith; the great Padmavati pirivena at Kéragala, under the presidency of the Rajaguru Vanaratana Sanharája, the Aranyaka ("woodland cloister") at Palábatgala under the rule of the scholarly Srí Dharmakírti Sangharája, the Vijaya Báhu pirivena at Totagamuwa under the control of Srí Ráhula Sangharája, the Srí Ganánanda pirivena at Rayigama under the warden of the Maha Nétra temple, the High-Priest Maittreya Mahá Stavíra, the Sunétra Mahá Dévi pirivena at Pepiliyána under the direction of Tipitaka Mangala Sangharája, the Master of the Tripitaka. These abbots were great scholars, skilled in all the arts, sciences, and secular learning of the time."

Parakrama Bahu VI. died a peaceful death in the 52nd year of his reign, and was succeeded on the throne by Jaya Bahu, the son of his natural daughter Ulakuda Dewi, who on his accession assumed the name Vira Parakrama Bahu.

Parakrama Bahu VII., 1462 A.C. Rajavalia.

Vira Parakrama Bahu (Parakrama Bahu VII.) was not allowed to occupy the throne for many days, inasmuch as his uncle Sapumal Cumara hastened to Cotta from Jaffna, and putting the king to death ascended the throne under the title of Sree Bhuvenaka Bahu.

Bhuvenaka Bahu VI., 1462-1469 A.C. Rajaratnacara.

Bhuvenaka Bahu VI. was a staunch Buddhist. He caused a casket to be made for the Tooth-relic at a cost of 7,000 massa (coins the value of which are uncertain), and made many other offerings. He distributed alms largely, and was devoted to furthering the welfare of his people and religion.

Rajavalia.

The tranquillity of the country was but once disturbed during this reign, a chief of Pasdun Korle named Siriwardene Patty Raja having raised a rebellion in conjunction with one Cooroogama. The insurrection was speedily quelled by the king's brother Ambulugala Cumara, and the ringleaders Patty Rajah and Cooroogama, together with many of their adherents, were brought as prisoners to the capital (Cotta), where they prayed of the king that he should spare their lives and let them spend the remainder of their lives in prison, paying the penalty for the offence they had committed. The magnanimous king not only acceded to their request that they be not condemned to suffer capital punishment, but also pardoned them and set them at liberty before the termination of his reign of seven years.

During this reign there lived the poet Weedagama—named after his native village in Rygam Korle. He was a priest of great learning, deep research, and much piety. Among his works are the *Budugunalankara*, in which he has drawn a correct picture of Buddha and Buddhism; the *Lowedasangrahaya*, a work containing maxims of a moral, religious, and prudential character; and the *Tisarasandese*, a poetical epistle of considerable length.

Alwis' Sidat Sangarawa, Intro. pp. 100, 101.

On the death of Bhuvenaka Bahu VI., his adopted son ascended the throne under the title of **Pandita Parakrama Bahu** and took into his service as generals the aforementioned Patty Rajah and Cooroogama.

Pandita Parakrama Bahu VIII., 1469 A.C.

As soon as the late king's brother Ambulugala, who was at the time residing at the village named after him, Ambulugala in the Four Korles, received the news of his brother's death and of the usurpation of the throne, he hurried with his army through Seena Korle and arrived at Kelaniya, where he rested for a while, and at length met the army sent against him by the king at Inkendagama, where, after a fiercely contested battle in which both the king's generals Patty Rajah and Cooroogama were slain, he succeeded in putting to flight the royal forces and following up the victory by entering the capital (Cotta). Here he cruelly put to death, in the royal palace, the king and all the members of his family. He next had himself crowned king assuming the name **Vira Parakrama Bahu** (Parakrama Bahu IX.) He reigned for twenty years, but Sinhalese historians tell us nothing of what he did during that period beyond the fact that he had born to him four princes and a princess, and that he went to the Tosita heaven, from which last fact may be inferred that he was a devout Buddhist who spent large sums of money in the furtherance of religion.

Rajavaliya.

Parakrama Bahu IX., 1469-1489 A.C. Rajavaliya.

Parakrama Bahu X., 1489-1509 A.C. Rajavaliya.

Dharma Parakrama Bahu succeeded his father to the throne of Lanka. The *Mahawansa* makes no mention of him. The *Rajavalia* gives us an account of his reign, and tells us that he reigned for twenty years. During this period of the Island's history there existed several "kings "(rajas) ruling various parts of the country. They all paid a yearly tribute to him who ruled at Cotta and called him the "Emperor" (Maharajah). Accordingly Dharma Parakrama Bahu was known as the Emperor of Lanka, and the tributary princes, all of whom were closely related to him by blood, were known as kings ("rajas").

During this reign a force of Moors led by one Cadiraya effected a landing in Chilaw with the object of supplying themselves with pearls and elephants. At the instance of the Emperor, the rajas of Udugampola and Madampe marched their forces there and inflicted a crushing defeat on the Moors, in which "Cadiraya was slain, the pearl fishers were taken and killed, their dhoneys were broken to pieces by the elephants, and eighty-nine" brought as prisoners to Cotta.

A short time after the event, the rajah who reigned at Ambulugala, having withheld the payment of his annual tribute, an expedition was sent against him by the Emperor with his brother Rajah Singha at the head of it. Rajah Singha, in conjunction with his friend the Ralahamy of Kirawella in Galboda Korle, seized a portion of the dominion of the Rajah of Ambulugala, whereupon he sued for peace in return for "fifty-three lacs of money, two elephants, and his own daughter." Having accepted these overtures Raja Singha returned to Cotta and reported it to the Emperor. Ambulugala Raja's daughter was given in marriage to the Ralahamy of Kirawella as a reward for his services.

Not long afterwards a second attempt was made by Ambulugala Rajah to shake off his allegiance to the Emperor. This time an expedition under the Rajah of Udugampola was sent against him and his chief city Ambulugala was captured. Thereupon he sent his messengers to the Rajah of Udugampola with "an umbrella of pearls, a shield of chank, and a chain of gold" promising never again to be guilty of such conduct. The Rajah of Udugampola, having severely reprimanded him and his nobles, returned to Cotta, where he reported the result of his exploit to the Emperor.

About this period the Portuguese had started competing with the Moors for the trade in the East Indies. The profitable trade previously conducted by the Moors, in carrying the spices of Malacca and Sumatra to Cambay and Bassora, having been effectually cut off by the Portuguese cruises, the Moorish ships were compelled to take a wide course through the Maldives, and pass south of Ceylon to escape capture. Dom Francisco de Almeyda, the Viceroy of India, despatched his son, Dom Lourenço, with a fleet from Goa to intercept the Moors on their route, and wandering over unknown seas he was unexpectedly carried by the current to the harbour of Galle, where he found Moorish ships loading with cinnamon and elephants. In their alarm for the safety of their ships, the Moors attempted to deceive him by the assertion that Galle was the residence of the Emperor Dharma Parakrama Bahu, under whose protection they professed to be trading, and by whom, they further assured him, they were authorised to propose a treaty of peace and commerce with the Portuguese, and to compliment the commander, by a royal gift of four hundred bahars (loads) of cinnamon.

Ribeiro, bk. 1, ch. 5.

Meanwhile news as to the arrival of the Portuguese off Galle having reached the Emperor, a meeting of all the rajas as well as ministers of State was speedily summoned for the purpose of deciding upon the course of action to be followed in respect of these foreigners. Here it was decided to depute Chakrayuddha Rajah, invested with the powers of a plenipotentiary, to visit the Portuguese in person and deal with them as he thought best in the interests of the Island.

Accordingly, the rajah visited Galle in disguise, and arrived at the conclusion that it would be unwise to adopt a hostile attitude in respect of the strangers, armed as they were with superior weapons. He therefore took up a position in a neighbouring village and requested the Moors to bring thither the ambassador, whom the Portuguese had expressed a desire to send to the Emperor for an interview. The Portuguese historian De Barros says: "An ambassador (Payo de Souza) was next sent in charge of the Moors to wait on the king; he was led round and round about a dense forest, and after a day's walking was brought to a spot where a large number of people was collected round some wooden houses. After some delay our messenger was led before a person who was represented to be the king, and who expressed himself as being very well pleased with our coming, and intimated his desire to send ambassadors to Cochin to make a treaty with the King of Portugal. There was no doubt that this personage was some one of importance........."

The Portuguese ambassador succeeded in obtaining, at this interview, permission from the rajah for the erection of a factory at Colombo. Having obtained this concession, the Portuguese put to sea after erecting a stone cross at Colombo to record the event of their arrival.

Rajavaliya, p. 287. Upham's Translation.

Dharma Parakrama Bahu died in the twentieth year of his reign, and was succeeded on the throne by his brother Vijaya Bahu Rajah of Menick Cadawara, the Rajah of Udugampola, to whom the throne was offered by the ministers, having refused it on the ground that Vijaya Bahu had a better title to it than he.

THE PORTUGUESE PERIOD.

Vijaya Bahu V., 1509-1524 A.C.

Vijaya Bahu V. reigned for fifteen years, and is described in the *Mahawansa* as a person "adorned with many virtues."

In the year 1518 A.C. Lopo Soares d'Albergaria, the Portuguese Viceroy of India, arrived at Colombo with a powerful fleet of seventeen sail and with materials and workmen for the erection of a factory, in conformity with the promise made to Dom Lourenço de Almeyda in 1505 A.C.

During the interval between 1505 and 1518 the Portuguese had secured their ascendency in India by the capture of Ormuz, the fortification of Goa, the erection of forts at various places in Malabar, and the conquest of the spice country of Malacca. The harbours of Ceylon, situated between the extreme settlements of the Portuguese, rendered the Island a place of importance to them. Hence their determination to establish a footing in it.

1518 A.C.

On the arrival of d'Albergaria at Colombo, the apprehensions of the Sinhalese court were aroused by the discovery that 700 soldiers were carried in the merchant ships, and that the proposed factory was to be mounted with cannon. In justification of this proceeding d'Albergaria pleaded the open hostility of the Moors, and the insecurity of the new traders when exposed to their violence; but the arguments by which he succeeded in removing the king's scruples were proffers of the military services upon which the latter might rely, in case of assault from his aspiring relatives; and assurances of the riches to be derived from the trade which the Portuguese proposed to establish. Dazzled by such promises and prospects, the king gave a reluctant assent, and the first European stronghold in Ceylon began to rise on the rocky beach at Colombo.

The Moors, instinctively alive to the dangers which threatened their trade, soon succeeded in rekindling the alarms of the king at the consequences of his precipitancy. When d'Albergaria attempted to land he found the spot occupied by Sinhalese cannon and archers, who, after they had inflicted some loss on the Portuguese, turned and fled, being unable to contend against the superior implements of war possessed by the latter. Thereafter Vijaya Bahu sent one of his dissaves to open negotiations and a formal treaty was concluded, by which Vijaya Bahu undertook to provide the Portuguese annually with three hundred loads of cinnamon, twelve rings of the rubies and sapphires of Ceylon, and six elephants, on condition that they paid for the same and undertook to defend him against all his enemies.

Ribeiro's Ceilao, Pieris' Trans., p. 15.

Thereafter d'Albergaria took his departure from Ceylon, leaving his nephew Juan de Silveira in command of the new settlement.

Owing to the difficulty of finding lime or even suitable stone on the spot, the first entrenchment of the Portuguese consisted of earth-work and stockades. In 1520 A.C. Lopo de Brito arrived in Colombo with 400 soldiers, besides masons and carpenters, with orders to transport the shells of the pearl-oyster, which still form vast mounds along the sea-shore of Arippo (Kilakarai), and to burn them for cement to complete the fortifications of Colombo.

The Moors availed themselves of this undisguised attempt to convert a factory into a fortress, as an argument to rouse the indignation of the Sinhalese. Consequently they refused to supply the Portuguese with provisions, and began to harass those who ventured to go outside settlement. The Portuguese historian De Barros says: "All this compelled de Brito to have recourse to arms; accordingly one day he sallied out with 150 chosen men at a time when the inhabitants were resting unsuspiciously after their meal taking their siesta, and fell on the town of Colombo which lay close to the fort. The men taken by surprise rushed away in a panic, abandoning their women and children; we caused these no harm, but tied them to the gates of their houses and set fire to the broad straight road which formed the principal street of the place, so as to cover our return. For, indeed, the men soon recovered from their fright and hurried back prepared to die for the safety of their families, and their fury was such that in spite of the fire they inflicted considerable damage on us; and had they not been busily engaged in releasing their friends and fighting the fire, they could have forced their way within the fort along with us. All pretence was now cast aside, and they commenced to besiege us with their hatred aggravated by the loss they had sustained; a host of 20,000 men was soon assembled, two bastions were hastily erected with the help of palm trees and mounted with cannon, while more than 600 large muskets of the size of small cannon hurled against our walls wooden darts ten palms long by day and fire lances by night. The siege lasted for five months, sa the state of the weather prevented the arrival of ships from India, and all the time we suffered greatly.........At last a galley arrived from Cochin under Captain Antonio de Lemos, and a concerted attack by land and sea ended in the capture of the two bastions which had been giving so much trouble. The enemy soon concentrated all their forces, which included 120 horses and about 25 elephants. The latter carried towers on their backs filled with archers, and were led by four monsters with large swords fastened to their tusks. Our men were in great alarm, and several began to hesitate, but they were rallied by Lopo de Brito, and after a fierce struggle our muskets compelled the leading elephants to turn back on their own men and throw their ranks into confusion, whereon they gave way and fled down a broad road, being pursued by us as far as the forest."

But hostilities were merely suspended, not abandoned, and a war now commenced, which endured almost without intermission during the entire period the Portuguese held possession of the maratime provinces; a war which, as the Portuguese historian de Couto observes, rendered Ceylon to Portugal what Carthage had proved to Rome—a source of unceasing and anxious expenditure, "gradually consuming her Indian revenues, wasting her forces and her artillery, and causing a greater outlay for the government of that single Island than for all her other conquests in the East."

King Vijaya Bahu V. had had three sons—Bhuvenaka Bahu, Maha Rygan Bandara, and Maaya Dunne—by his first wife. On her death he married an Indian princess, from whom he had a son named Dewa Raja Cumara. The sons by his first wife having learnt that the king, in consultation with his ministers, had decided upon appointing their step-brother as his successor to the throne, fled from Cotta, and having secured the assistance of Jaya Wiera, the Raja of Kandy, marched on the capital (Cotta), and got their father slain in his palace. On the following day the eldest of the brothers—viz., Bhuvenaka Bahu—ascended the throne and "gave a general audience to all the people." Thereafter Rygan Bandara took up his abode at Rygama as raja of that district, and Maaya Dunne built himself a city at Sitawaka and established himself as rajah of that district.

Bhuvenaka Bahu VII. was a kind-hearted monarch, entirely dependent on the Portuguese for the purpose of maintaining his throne as against his young brother Maaya Dunne, who, exasperated by the weakness of King Bhuvenaka Bahu in his dealings with the Portuguese, devoted the whole of his life to an attempt to oust his brother and thereby preserve the independence of Lanka, which was being undermined by Portuguese intrigue.

Bhuvenaka Bahu VII., 1524-1551 A.C.

During this reign was produced the *Saddarmalankara*—a prose work containing many little apologues, explanatory of the principles of Buddhism.

In 1528 A.C. Maaya Dunne besieged Cotta assisted by a fleet sent by the Zamorin of Calicut under the command of his Captain-Major Paichi Marcar, a powerful Moor of Cochin. The siege was raised no sooner news was received that the Portuguese were on their way with help for King Bhuvenaka Bahu. The Portuguese Commander Martim Affonso de Mello, finding no traces of the enemy on his arrival at Colombo, contented himself with visiting Arippo with his fleet, and exacting from the ruler of that district a promise of an

Ribeiro, p. 17.

annual payment of a fixed sum as well as three thousand *pardaos*, on condition that the Portuguese protected the fishers during the season of the pearl fishery.

In 1536 A.C., Maaya Dunne having applied for assistance to the Zamorin of Calicut, a fleet of forty-five ships with 2,000 troops, all under the command of Ali Abrahem Marca—a bold pirate and a gallant cavalier—arrived in Colombo, and Cotta was besieged by Maaya Dunne, in conjunction with his allies, for three months, at the end of which period the siege was raised, news having reached the besiegers of the approach of Affonso de Sousa with succour for the besieged. For the service rendered de Sousa was laden with gifts by the king, who further lent him 45,000 *cruzados* wherewith to pay his troops, the greater portion of which as well as of subsequent loans was never repaid.

Ribeiro, p. 19.

In 1538 A.C. Maaya Dunne sent another embassy to the Zamorin of Calicut with valuable presents, a sum of money, and also a promise to give him some sea-ports in the Island if he would help him (Maaya Dunne) against the King of Cotta and his Portuguese allies. Thereupon a fleet of 51 ships with 8,000 men-at-arms, provided with a large quantity of muskets, bows, lances, and four hundred pieces of heavy artillery, chiefly of bronze, was sent out, but unfortunately for Maaya Dunne these forces were intercepted and destroyed by the Portuguese whilst on their way on the sea, and he was compelled to retire to his fortress at Batugedera abandoning his capital Sitawaka to the joint forces of the Portuguese and King Bhuvenaka Bahu.

In this year the Rajah of Rygama, who had made common cause with Maaya Dunne against Bhuvenaka Bahu, died. Thereupon Maaya Dunne entered Rygam Korle and, seizing his deceased brother's kingdom and treasures, sent another embassy to the Zamorin of Calicut with a large sum of money and a request for further assistance. Accordingly Paichi Marcar arrived with a fleet of sixteen ships, but on this occasion, timely notice of the approach of the Portuguese fleet commanded by Ferreira not having reached the Moors, they were taken by surprise in the harbour of Puttalam, their ships and artillery seized after a fierce struggle, and themselves compelled to seek safety at Sitawaka. King Bhuvenaka Bahu, together with the Portuguese, advanced to Sitawaka, which they found deserted, Maaya Dunne having taken

1539 A.C.

up his position in an almost inaccessible fortress at Dereniyagala in Atulugam Korle. The city at Sitawaka was razed to the ground, and great atrocities were perpetrated by the Portuguese in the surrounding country until Maaya Dunne was compelled to purchase peace, by the surrender of Paichi Marcar and seventy others of his Moorish allies to Ferreira.

King Bhuvenaka Bahu had no male issue, but he had a son by his only daughter who had married Vidiye Bandar, the eldest son of the King of Madampe. In his anxiety to secure the succession to his throne to this grandson he appealed to the Portuguese, sending an ambassador named Sallappoo Arachy, with a golden image of the grandson to the King of Portugal for the purpose *Rajavalia.* of getting him acknowledged in effigy as his successor by that monarch. The Portuguese historian De Couto describes the embassy as follows:—"There also embarked two ambassadors from the King of Cotta in Ceilaõ, who went with good credentials, and by them that king sent to beg the King Dom Joaõ to do him the favour to swear as hereditary prince a grandson of his, son of his daughter and of Vidiye Bandar (his sister's son), on account of his having no other heir; sending him the likeness of his grandson, which was of natural size, in the form of a statue of gold, placed in a large box, with a crown of gold set with many precious stones in the hand for the king to crown it therewith. These ships reached Portugal safely, and the king received these ambassadors very well; and for the act of swearing the prince the king commanded to summon all the lords of the realm, and carried it out in public assembly with the greatest solemnity and ceremony possible, crowning the prince after the manner of the kingdom, commanding great festivities and bull-fights to be held. And having passed to them his letter of confirmation, and bestowed many favours on the ambassadors, he sent them back well satisfied in the next ship."

Couto's History of Ceylon, Dec. 5, bk. 7, chap. iv., Fergusson's Trans.

1542 A.C.

During this ceremony the name of Don Juan was conferred on the young prince, in addition to his previous name of Dharmapala Bahu.

In return for what he had done, the King of Portugal, true to the policy of extending religion conterminously with his dominions, exacted a further concession from King Bhuvenaka Bahu. A party of Franciscans, with Frey Antonio do Padraõ as their chief, were directed to accompany the ambassadors on their return from Lisbon to Ceylon; license was claimed by them to preach the gospel of Christ in all parts of the Island, and Christian communities were organised by them at various places on the coast, viz., Colombo, Panadure, Maggona, Beruwela, Galle, and Weligama.

Of the priests that arrived in the Island during the preceding reign, Fr. Pascoal, with two companions, had penetrated as far as Kandy, where they were well received by King Jayaweira: so much so, that he gave them a large piece of ground, and everything needful for building a church and houses for them to dwell in. Ere long the priests gained so much influence over Jayaweira, that he professed a desire to embrace the Christian faith—a desire which, he said, he dare not gratify lest he incur the displeasure of his subjects. Accordingly, at the instigation of Pascoal, King Jayaweira sent one of the three priests, together with ambassadors, to the Portuguese Viceroy at Goa to request him to send a captain with some troops for his protection as against his subjects who may rebel against his authority when he changed his religion. The Viceroy was delighted with the opportunity presented him for extending the influence of the Portuguese in the Island. He accordingly promised to send 200 men under the command of Antonio Moniz Barreto, and at the same time forwarded a letter to King Jayaweira with some pieces of jewellery and other curiosities. Meanwhile Maaya Dunne had warned his cousin Jayaweira of the possible perils of the course he had adopted, and had completely succeeded in changing his disposition towards the Portuguese. The result was that Barreto, whilst on his way to Kandy with 120 men and a few guns, was attacked by Sinhalese archers and compelled to fly for refuge to Colombo *via* Sitawaka, where he was not molested by Maaya Dunne. Ere long there arrived at Colombo ambassadors from Jayaweira, bringing with them the guns that Barreto had left behind in the course of his flight. They said that they had been directed by their sovereign to repudiate, on his behalf, all responsibility for what had occurred and to express his regret. However, as the Portuguese had received maltreatment in his dominion, their King (Jayaweira) had sent 10,000 *pardaos* (a pardao = 4*s* 2*d*.—4*s*. 6*d*.) by way of compensation, together with the guns that had been abandoned.

In the middle of November, 1549, the King of Cotta sent ambassadors to the Viceroy of India to ask for his assistance as against Maaya Dunne, who had wrested the greater portion of his kingdom and was besieging him in his capital, promising in return 10,000 *cruzados* in cash, a shipload of pepper, ten elephants, and an increase in the annual tribute from 300 to 400 bahars of cinnamon. Accordingly, there arrived in Ceylon in January, 1550, a Portuguese force of 600 men commanded by Dom Jorge de Castro, and 10,000 *cruzados* were immediately paid them by the Sinhalese ambassadors. *1549 A.C.*

On the arrival of the Portuguese in the Island Maaya Dunne raised the siege of Cotta and retired to his capital Sitawaka, leaving a strong garrison to oppose any advance on the part of the Portuguese in conjunction with the forces of the King of Cotta. The first battle was fought at a spot situated between Mutwal and the Mulleriawa tank, where Maaya Dunne had erected a fortification. After a fierce contest, in which both sides last heavily, the allies captured it. The second battle took place at Malvana, where, too, the allies succeeded in capturing the fortress. In this battle no less than 600 of Maaya Dunne's men were slain. The third battle was fought at Hanwella, where existed a fortification "with stout walls and bastions occupied by a powerful garrison." This, too, was captured by the allies after a stubborn contest, in which both sides suffered heavily. *1550 A.C.*

The fourth battle was fought on the road from Hanwella to Avisawella at a spot where Maaya Dunne, with his forces, awaited the arrival of the allies. Here was fought a terrific battle, in which, as in the previous ones, the superior implements of warfare possessed by the Portuguese helped the allies to gain a victory. After this defeat Maaya Dunne, abandoning his capital, fled to Batugedera, while the allies busied themselves with ransacking the abandoned city (Sitawaka). De Couto thus describes the city :—"The city was a very large one, built among four mountains on the same river of Mutwal, which is also called the Kelany. On the southern bank was the palace of the King (Maaya Dunne), which resembled a fortress with strong walls, and was raised on a platform of twenty broad steps. The fortress was square with three gates on each side; half the city was on this bank, and half on the other. In this latter was the handsomest dagoba in the whole of the Island, dedicated to an idol called Paramisura (Siva). The building was of wonderful work, and it was asserted that 2,000 workmen had been continuously employed at it for over twenty years. We entered the city, the King (Bhuvenaka Bahu) occupying his brother's palace, which was full of every kind of wealth, while Dom Jorge encamped on the other side, which was sacked by our soldiers, who found in it an abundance of gold and valuable articles of merchandise. Then they passed to the other side, which was similarly plundered, though the temples were spared out of deference to the wishes of the King (Bhuvenaka Bahu of Cotta)."

At length Maaya Dunne sent ambassadors to sue for peace ; and it was established on the following terms :—(1) That Maaya Dunne surrender to the King of Cotta all the districts which he had seized. (2) That he pay Dom Jorge 100,000 pagodas to cover the expenses incurred by him, and further provide him, on payment, everything necessary for the contemplated expedition against King Jayaweira of Kandy, for which the King of Cotta had promised to contribute 3,000 men.

The King of Kandy, having received information as to the preparations that were being made for the invasion of his dominion, collected an army of 40,000 men, and when the enemy was within a league's distance from his capital marched out with his forces and put them to flight. The Portuguese historian De Couto says: "We struck our camp and retired rapidly, though in good order. The King (Jayaweira), hearing of this, seized the narrow defiles on the road and worried our men, who could not retaliate, with shot and arrows. With great difficulty we struggled through, losing seven hundred men, including four hundred Portuguese, while all the rest were badly wounded......... The King of Cotta met our men on the retreat and conducted them to his capital, where he provided them with everything that was necessary. From here Dom Jorge withdrew to Colombo, whence he departed for Cochin at the beginning of September."

In October, 1550, Dom Affonso de Noronha, the new Viceroy of India, on his way to assume office, was miscarried by the monsoon to Colombo. Here he was invited by the King of Cotta to help him in an expedition against Maaya Dunne, who had started an invasion of his territory no sooner Dom Jorge had left the Island. The Viceroy said he would gladly accept the invitation, provided the king paid him 200,000 *pardaos;* but the king, who had already spent 70,000 on Dom Jorge and his men, thought it too exorbitant a price. Thereupon the Viceroy grew very indignant and went on board his ship. In order to appease him the king sent him a present of 15,000 *pardaos* for himself, as well as the following articles to be conveyed as a present to the Queen of Portugal:—A large collar of gold set with pearls and rubies, with three crosses of precious stones pendent therefrom with a large pearl below; another collar set with rubies with a large stone in the centre; a third collar of gold set with pearls and cat's-eyes, having in the middle a large cast's-eye surrounded by rubies; three bracelets of gold set with precious stones; a large ring set with a cat's-eye surrounded with rubies and a handsome unset cat's-eye. Thereafter the Viceroy left the shores of Lanka satisfied with what he had obtained.

No sooner the North-West monsoon set in, in the *1551 A.C.* following year, when no help could be despatched from India, Maaya Dunne mustered his forces and commenced an invasion of the territory of the King of Cotta. He had come within sight of Cotta, when he was met by the joint forces of King Bhuvenaka Bahu and the Portuguese, led by the king's son-in-law Vidiye Bandar and Gaspar de Azavedo, the Captain of Colombo, respectively. After a series of skirmishes he was compelled to retire to the other bank of the Kelany river. The King of Cotta, having gone out to inspect his army to Kelaniya, was accidentally shot through the head by a Portuguese. A scene of great confusion followed. At length, Vidiye Bandar retired with his forces to Cotta, where, after celebrating the funeral rites, his son **Dharmapala** was *Dharmapala, 1551 A.C.* proclaimed king, he himself being the first to swear allegiance, followed by Gaspar de Azavedo and all the nobles within the dominion.

Maaya Dunne, hearing of his brother's death, advanced to Bollegala in Siyane Korle and sent a message to the nobles assembled at Cotta calling upon them to swear allegiance to him, and on their refusal to comply with his request advanced on Cotta, but was compelled by Vidiye Bandar to retire to Kanampella in Hewagam Korle.

News of all this having reached the Viceroy, deeming it a good opportunity for exacting money and treasure wherewith to replenish his exchequer, he arrived in Colombo towards the end of September, where he was received with every mark of respect by King Dharmapala and the Factor. In spite of it, and of the fact that the King of Portugal had in all solemnity acknowledged Dharmapala as the rightful successor of Bhuvenaka Bahu VII., he sent his son Dom Fernando de Menzes with 500 men to seize the roads leading from Cotta, and thereafter went in person to Cotta; and after arresting the mudaliyars and aged servants of the palace, began to make enquiries for the treasures of their ancient kings; and failing to obtain any information, he ordered some of the mudaliyars to be put to the torture. The people were horror-struck at such unspeakably unchristian and treacherous conduct in respect of their king and nobility, who had always cherished a warm regard for the Portuguese as their friends and allies. Within a few days 600 of the principal inhabitants of the kingdom had gone over to Maaya Dunne. De Couto says: "The royal palace was next searched, and all the gold coin, including 560 ancient *Portugueses* (a Portuguese = 10 *cruzados*), the silver, jewels, and precious stones, were seized; indeed the coin alone amounted to more than 100,000 *pardaos*." The golden spittoons that were to be found in the palace were also taken away on this occasion.

"The unfortunate king was helpless, and was compelled to enter into an agreement, by which he undertook to pay 200,000 *pardaos* to the Viceroy for the destruction of the power of Maaya Dunne, one-half of the booty to be taken at Sitawaka, being at the same time promised to the king: 80,000 *pardaos* were paid down on the spot, to raise which sum the king was obliged to sell his jewels and other private property."

"The Viceroy now took the field with 3,000 Portuguese, Vidiye Bandar was in command of 4,000 men, while Maaya Dunne waited behind his defences. The first line was carried with considerable loss. A desperate struggle took place over the second and the third, which were also carried, and we then moved on the city. Maaya Dunne, after one last effort to check our advance, fled to the fastnesses of Deraniyagala (in Atulugam Korle). The Viceroy occupied the palace, while the king took up his abode close to the pagoda. The city was now given over to plunder, the very foundations of the palace being dug up by the Viceroy in an unsuccessful search for the king's (Maaya Dunne's) treasures. The great kovil was similarly treated. An immense quantity of images of gold and silver, large and small candlesticks, basins, bells, and table utensils, all of which were made of gold, and the jewelled ornaments were seized and kept by the Viceroy, forgetful of the half that had been promised to the King of Cotta. The latter, learning that Maaya Dunne was in Deraniyagala with a few men, begged the Viceroy to send his father with 500 men to seize him ; the Viceroy replied that the plan was an excellent one, and immediately asked for 20,000 *pardaos* to make up the one-half of the sum which had been promised. The unfortunate king was unable to raise the sum ; whereupon the Viceroy declared that he had no time for this work, as he had to arrange to despatch ships to Portugal, and at once returned to Colombo."

The Viceroy, who had observed that the king's father, Vidiye Bandar was a man of conspicuous ability, deeming that so long as he remained in the kingdom he would help the king of Cotta to guide the ship of State aright as against the designs of the Portuguese, invited Vidiye Bandar to accompany him (the Viceroy) to India. Vidiye Bandar, who, on the other hand, had had sufficient experience of the arrogance, treachery, and cruelty of the Viceroy, had a shrewd suspicion as to what the invitation meant, and accordingly refused to accept it. Thereupon the Viceroy requested the King of Cotta to turn Christian, but he politely excused himself on the ground that it would furnish Maaya Dunne with a weapon to be used against him, inasmuch as he (Maaya Dunne) would inflame the minds of his subjects against him, on the ground that he had deserted the national faith. However the King of Cotta provided the Viceroy with a cousin of his to be taken to Goa and made a Christian. (This prince was with great solemnity baptized at Goa and given the name of Dom Joaõ. He was subsequently sent to Portugal, where he remained in court for several years, where he was allowed a chair in the royal presence in the same fashion as the Earls (Condes) of the country He married a Portuguese lady, the daughter of an honourable cavalier. He died in Goa and was buried in the Church of St. Francisco.)

The Viceroy still delayed in Colombo in the hope of securing his 20,000 *pardaos*, but the king's father, Vidiye Bandar, emphatically refused to pay the sum, as the Viceroy had failed to carry out his share of the compact. Thereupon the Viceroy arrested the king's Great Chamberlain, Tammita Sembahap Perumal, who was in charge of the government, sent him on board his galleon declaring that he would not be allowed to return until the money was paid. Sembahap Perumal was finally compelled to sell the golden girdle which he wore, together with some pieces of jewellery, for 5,000 *pardaos*, and hand the proceeds, together with a note promising to pay the balance before the end of the year. Whereupon he was set at liberty, and the Viceroy set sail for Goa, having instructed the Governor of Colombo to arrest the king's father.

The Portuguese Captain accordingly, by base and treacherous means, effected the arrest of Vidiye Bandar. and left him in chains in a powder tower in Colombo. Here some priests persuaded him to turn Christian and secretly baptized him. On learning what had transpired, the Governor was extremely angry with the priests for having helped to allay the suffering and the sorrow of the prisoner. He forbade the priests to have any further access to him, and took more rigorous steps to cut him off from all intercourse with the outer world. The prisoner's noble wife had not been idle all this while. She had made an appeal to the people for help as against the Portuguese tyrants, and succeeded in obtaining a considerable force of volunteers from Raigam Korle. Stationing them a short way off Colombo, she succeeded in bribing some Portuguese to open a secret passage from the orchard of the priests which adjoined the prison, and thus securing the escape of her husband. With him she hurried to the spot where the Sinhalese force lay anxiously awaiting the result of her enterprise. Vidiye Bandar was so enraged at the treatment he had received that, with the body of men that was ready for him, he took the road to Galle, destroying all the churches and killing all the Christians he came across. Finally, having destroyed a newly constructed Portuguese ship at Galle, he made his way with his wife to Pelenda in Pasdun Korle, where he built a fortified city for himself.

The King of Cotta, dismayed at the latest developments, entreated all the parties to forget their private quarrels and take joint action against Maaya Dunne. Although the Portuguese Governor of Colombo entered upon an agreement with the king and Vidiye Bandar for the purpose, which he swore on the Missal (= the Roman Catholic Mass-book) he would adhere to, it was discovered in the course of the enterprise that he was in secret communication with Maaya Dunne, and it had therefore to be abruptly abandoned.

In A.C. 1555 Vidiye Bandar, who had established himself at Bandaragama in Raigam Korle, again destroyed the Christian settlements at Panadure, Kalutara, Maggona, Beruwela, Galle, and Weligama with the churches of the Franciscans which were scattered throughout the dominions of the King of Cotta and was harassing the Christians when Affonso Pereira de Larcerda arrived as the new Governor of Colombo. He immediately entered upon an alliance with Maaya Dunne for the purpose of crippling the powers of Vidiye Bandar. Accordingly, Maaya Dunne, with his son Raja Singha, advanced *via* Kalutara and were joined by the Portuguese, who had advanced by two other routes, at a spot not far from Pelenda, Vidiye Bandar's capital, whose ruins are to be seen to the present day. Vidiye Bandar stoutly defended the city, but was at length compelled to abandon it and flee to Dondra Head (Devundera). From here he made his way to the Seven Korles, where he attempted to establish his supremacy, having slain Edirimanna Suriya, who was the rajah of the district.

The inhabitants of the principality were unwilling to acknowledge him who had treacherously slain their ruler in his palace whilst enjoying hospitality at his hands. Accordingly they armed themselves, seized all the passes and invited Maaya Dunne and the Portuguese to help them to avenge the death of their rájah. Vidiye Bandar, on finding himself hard pressed by the joint forces of the enemy, stole out one night through the enemy's lines, together with his wife, mother-in-law, and treasures, and made his way *via* Puttalam to Jaffna. Here he entered into a compact with the King of Jaffna to attack the Portuguese. Whilst this compact was being solemnised at a temple in the city an accidental explosion of some gunpowder took place, which made Vidiye Bandar imagine that he was to be the victim of an act of treachery on the part of the king. He hastily drew his sword against the king who stood beside him in the temple, and after a desperate struggle was cut down, whilst his treasures, wife, etc., fell into the hands of Jaffna's King.

The news of the death of Vidiye Bandar brought about the end of the compact between Maaya Dunne and the Portuguese. Thereupon Maaya Dunne ordered his son Raja Singha to lay siege to Cotta, and a prolonged war ensued, in which King Dharmapala of Cotta was assisted by the Portuguese, who found it to be to their interest to maintain Dharmapala's authority in his kingdom, inasmuch as they would otherwise lose all their trade in cinnamon, and most probably have been driven out of the Island altogether. De Couto says of this war: "Fights were of every day occurrence, in which both sides suffered loss.........Our sufferings were very great during this period, for our supplies of men and money had to be obtained with great difficulty from India, while the enemy had endless resources close at hand; indeed our losses were so heavy and disaster appeared imminent that we were compelled to appeal for assistance from Mannar."

1559 A.C. During this war several undecisive battles were fought at Mapitigama in Siyane Korle. The last of the battles fought at this town is thus described:—"Dom Jorge Baroche, the new Governor of Colombo, determined to attack the main body which was stationed at Mapitigama; the enemy were in a panic, for the capture of this position would have left us masters of all the roads to Sitawaka. Two wooden castles were erected on board the padda boats employed on the Kelani river; these were strongly manned for the purpose of attacking the enemy's fortifications on the river. At the appointed hour they were taken in tow by the *fustas*, and were brought close to the ramparts at Raggahawatte, when a well-aimed shot from the enemy's cannon, fired by Raja Singha in person, destroyed one of them with the loss of twenty killed; whereupon orders were immediately given to retire."

"Dom Jorge waited a few days for a favourable opportunity, and learning that Raju (= Raja Singha) was encamped in a field with three or four thousand men, he attacked him unexpectedly at dawn and compelled him to retreat, followed by our men, and seek refuge in a wood. We hastened in pursuit, when our captain was warned that our powder was exhausted; he proudly replied that he could load his gun with sand and win the day at the point of the sword; but when orders were given to advance our men hung back, whereupon Raju, who realised what had taken place, immediately charged. Dom Jorge and the cavaliers who accompanied him did what they could to rally our men. We reached a passage which had been blocked by the enemy with trees; while these were being cleared the war elephants, which had been despatched by Maaya Dunne to the assistance of his son, came up. One of these monsters was just on the point of seizing Dom Jorge, when a soldier, firing at his forehead, enabled Dom Jorge to escape. Another animal attacked the standard-bearer, who drove the spear to which the standard was attached into its forehead, but the poor man was immediately thrown into the air and dashed into pieces. Another veteran soldier of ours succeeded in turning the animal away with a blow from his halberd. Our men by this time had made their way through the passage, though with heavy loss, but some of the enemy's arachis appeared in front, and they soon found themselves between two fires. Dom Jorge now gave up everything for lost, but fortunately a soldier chanced to fire a cannon, which our men were abandoning, with such fortunate aim that the shot fell right in the midst of the enemy and caused them to hesitate. Dom Jorge at once rallied his men and got them on board the boats which were near, and escaped, leaving more than sixty dead, including some fidalgos on the field; he was so disheartened at his failure that he threw himself on the ground cursing himself for his folly. After this our men remained in their place carrying on skirmishes with the enemy, so as to prevent Raju from crossing the boundaries of Cotta, and by March, 1561, Dom Jorge returned to India on being relieved by Balthazar Guedes de Sousa." Whilst this war between Raja Singha and the Portuguese was going on in one part of the Island, Don Constantino de Braganza, the Portuguese Viceroy of India, in August, 1560, landed in Jaffnapatam, having crossed over from Goa with a fleet consisting of twelve galleys, ten galliots, and seventy rowing boats. He was opposed by the Crown Prince of Jaffna at the place of landing, with a force of 2,000 men. The Jaffnese, however, had to retire, not being able to withstand the fire of the Portuguese guns. The Portuguese advanced on the city and occupied it, the king having escaped from his palace with all his treasures during the course of the night prior to the entrance into it by the enemy, who had encamped around it the previous evening. At length peace was established on condition that the King of Jaffna was to continue in power as the vassal of Portugal paying a fixed tribute, that he should give up all the treasures which he had taken from Vidiye Bandar, as well as the latter's mother-in-law; and further that he should surrender the prince, his heir, as an hostage, which was immediately done.

Ribeiro, ch. d.

Although articles to the value of no less than 80,000 *cruzados* had been handed to him by the King of Jaffna; Braganza continued to delay his departure in the hope of obtaining 300,000 *cruzados* worth, which was the estimate he had formed of Vidiye Bandar's wealth. Meanwhile the inhabitants rose up in a body against the invaders, and it was with the utmost difficulty that Braganza succeeded in reaching his boats, together with the Crown Prince whom he carried off with him.

Pieris' Ribeiro, pp. 44, 49 & 50. Tennent's Ceylon, vol. ii., p. 30. De Couto, Dec. 5, lib. ix., ch. ii.

At the time the Portuguese entered the abandoned city of Jaffna, they discovered a tooth mounted in gold in one of the temples they had pillaged. This was considered by them to be the tooth of Buddha, which was held in reverence by the Sinhalese. Accordingly, there were great rejoicings in the Portuguese camp over what was considered to be a death-blow dealt at the Buddhist religion. As a matter of fact the tooth was that of an ape worshipped by the Hindus in honour of Hanuman.

In 1561, the King of Pegu having received, from a Portuguese merchant, news as to the capture of the sacred tooth by his countrymen, ambassadors were despatched to Goa to negotiate its purchase. The Viceroy and the officers whom he consulted were very anxious to strike a bargain, inasmuch as no less than 400,000 *cruzados*, in addition to other concessions, were offered for it by the pious King of Pegu. However the Archbishop and other prelates, supported by the Inquisitors, took a different view. "The Archbishop publicly delivered a sermon denouncing the proposal in the presence of the Viceroy and the whole of his court. The result of it all was that the Viceroy was obliged to send for the tooth from the treasury and deliver it to the Archbishop, who, in the presence of everyone, broke it to pieces with his own hand in a brazen mortar, and threw the powder into a brazier of live coal, after which the whole was cast into the sea."

1562 A.C.

Raja Singha was still carrying on a continuous and vigorous campaign against the King of Cotta and the Portuguese. In 1562 he laid siege to Colombo with about 30,000 men. De Couto says: "A terrible time followed. Assault after assault was made on the place, but were bravely repulsed by our men whose position was growing desperate. It is impossible to give details of what took place at this siege, for indeed the occurrences of one day are a history in themselves. One last and resolute attempt was made, after which Raju, in utter weariness, withdrew to Sitawaka."

The Portuguese hoped for some respite after this withdrawal, but Raja Singha soon appeared with his army reorganised and laid siege to Cotta. In describing the assault which followed this siege De Couto says: "Raju now threw the whole of his force against Preacota. The attack was led by the men of the Atapata, soldiers selected for their courage and forming the personal guard of the king. In their van came the war elephants which attacked our stockades. The king (= Dharmapala) and the captain (= Guedes de Sousa) hastened to the rescue, headed by six priests waving the Crucifix and invoking the name of Jesus. The first rampart was carried, and Preacota stormed with the loss on our side of three of the priests and over twenty Portuguese. The king and the captain rallied the men, and finally succeeded in driving back the enemy, who lost over 400 in killed. The captain himself was twice wounded, but he did not retire from the struggle, and finally Raju was compelled to withdraw to his camp."

At length Raja Singha, having learnt that Portuguese reinforcements were on their way to Colombo, retired to his father's capital, Sitawaka.

In 1564, Pedro de Ataide Inferno arrived as Governor of Colombo, together with a large Portuguese force, and Raja Singha laid siege to Cotta on the 5th of October of that year. The siege was a determined one and lasted for four months, during which the Portuguese estimate the loss sustained by Raja Singha at 2,000 men in killed. During the last forty days of this siege the Portuguese were driven to such straits, that no less than four hundred of the fattest of Raja Singha's men who were picked up dead by the walls of the city were salted for food. King Dharmapala, who had been deserted by all his forces, and the Portuguese Governor showed splendid courage during the course of this siege.

Ribeiro, ch. f.

At length reinforcements having arrived from Goa the siege was raised.

1565 A.C. At the instance of the Viceroy, Cotta was abandoned, and King Dharmapala took up his abode in a palace specially built for him in Colombo.

A period of comparative peace followed, during which time Raja Singha succeeded to the throne of his

1571-1592 A.C. father Maaya Dunne, who died in 1571 A.C. at the ripe age of eighty years. One of the first acts of **Raja Singha I.** after his accession was to put to death every one likely to dispute his claim to the throne, amongst them were his elder brothers as well as his valiant general Wickramasingha Mudaliyar. In the course of a very few years he made himself master of the interior, and drove into excile King Jayaweira of Kandy, who, with his queen and children, fled for safety to the Portuguese fort at Mannar, where he and his daughter became Christians, and were baptised, she as Donna Catherina, and he under the name of Dom Philip, in honour of Philip II., who had just acquired the crown of Portugal with that of Spain. On her father's decease, Donna Catherina was left a ward of the Portuguese.

During this period a good many Sinhalese noble families took refuge in Colombo through fear of Raja Singha.

1584 A.C. In the year 1584 Raja Singha started preparations for war with the Portuguese, whose settlements had by this time dwindled into those at Colombo and Mannar alone.

He built himself a fort at Biyagama in Siyane Korle, and was about to advance on Colombo, when, at the instance of the Viceroy, an embassy was sent to him with presents to sue for peace. This was agreed to, though not for a fixed period, the condition being that it was not to be broken without previous notice. The interval so obtained was utilised by the Portuguese for strengthening their defences in spite of the expostulations of King Raja Singha.

1587 A.C. At last, in 1587, "Raja Singha declared war and summoned all his people to assemble at Biyagama (Biagao) for a grand review.......He had fifty thousand men of war, sixty thousand workmen and camp followers, two thousand two hundred elephants, one hundred and fifty pieces of bronze artillery large and small, four thousand draught oxen, ten thousand axes, three thousand crowbars, twenty thousand bill-hooks, two thousand picks (codeli), six thousand hoes, a large quantity of spare arms, four hundred smiths to prepare arrow-heads and other implements, one thousand carpenters, four hundred gunners—Javas, Caffirs and other nationalities, the greater part of whom had deserted from the Portuguese,—a vast quantity of timber large and small, of which he made two cars resembling castles, each on nine wheels, and others of the height of a man, a great quantity of sulphur, saltpetre and gunpowder, with much lead and shot; while sixty-five *fustas* and *caturas* and four hundred smaller boats were also ordered to be got ready at some of the sea-ports."

Raja Singha next started to march on the capital, the vanguard being under the command of Wijekoon Mudaliyar and Gajanayake Arachi.

The route taken by the army was *via* Mulleriyawa, Kelaniya, and Dematagoda. On the 4th June, 1587, the whole of the Sinhalese army had encamped within a few yards of the Portuguese fort by the sea at Colombo, whilst King Raja Singha had his camp pitched on what is at the present day known as Maligakande.

The nature of the repeated assaults that were made on the Portuguese fort at first only by land, but later both by sea and land, may be judged by the following description of the first assault as given by De Couto:—"In the early morning of the 4th of August three bands, headed by elephants, attacked the bastions of St. Miguel, St. Gonçalo, and St. Francisco, their matches twinkling like fireflies in the mist, while another body advanced over the (Colombo) lake in rafts. The scaling ladders were rapidly pushed up to the walls, which were at the same time undermined by over 2,000 sappers. We (the Portuguese) replied with a tremendous shower of shot and musket balls, which covered the field with the wounded. Within and without was shouting and confusion. The captain, accompanied by the priests, was everywhere encouraging, supervising, and directing. The Arachis Manuel Gonsalves and Tanavira, who were stationed where the wall was very low, were so hard pressed that they were deserted by their lascarins. The captain's assistance was immediately summoned; he hastened to the spot and rallied the men who returned to the charge; a terrible struggle ensued, for the number of the enemy was without limit. They had started a fire on the top of the rampart, and our position was desperate at the bastion of St. Gonçalo, our men being driven back by the flames and the smoke. The enemy tried to carry our guns and a hand-to-hand fight followed; but one of our men with great courage succeeded in putting out the fire and thus enabled us to return. Again and again the enemy renewed the assault, the elephants repeatedly advancing to the walls and attempting to break them down; but the fire lances of our men, supported by the musket balls, were too much for the huge beasts which offered such a large target to our aim.........The worst fury of the assault lasted close on one hour, when their heavy losses compelled the enemy to relax their vigour.

"Raju (Raja Singha), who was posted close by, was frantic with rage at the failure of his men. He summoned all his captains, and angrily ordered them to carry the place at whatever cost, giving the signal by five beats of the drum, which was the customary signal when the whole force was to be engaged. The mudaliyars returned to the charge with renewed fury, and the personal guard of the king resolutely swarmed up the wall by a large number of ladders, the most desperate fighting being at the bastion of St. Gonçalo. The elephants were brought forward to pull down the guns, but they were beaten back. A gallant attempt was made by a small body of Sinhalese, who were anxious to win special distinction with the king to tear down the standard which floated over the bastion, but they were hurled to the bottom in confusion. The second assault lasted the same length of time as the first, and then the efforts of the enemy began to slacken. Raju was beside himself with anger; he ordered his troops back again determined to take the fort or lose everything. His men returned for the third time to the assault, prepared to throw away their lives; but after a further half hour's fighting, as the day began to dawn, Raju himself gave the signal to withdraw, and our joy at this marvellous deliverance was beyond words."

The siege of the fort was continued until February of 1588, and in the course of it two grand assaults of the nature of the one above described were made on the 20th of August, 1587, and 27th January, 1588.

During these two assaults the Portuguese were attacked, both by sea and by land.

Pieris' Trans. p. 75.

De Couto says that some of the balls fired into the fort from Sinhalese cannon weighed no less than forty-four pounds. During the periods that intervened between these grand assaults every device was adopted by both parties for the purpose of attaining their objects.

Twice Raja Singha's men tunnelled into the fort, but on each occasion the Portuguese, who had been forewarned by their spies, repulsed them with great slaughter. The wells from which the Portuguese obtained their water were poisoned on one occasion, resulting in the breaking out of a pestilence amongst them, in which a swelling would start from the feet and travel up till it reached the chest, when the patient would invariably succumb. Magicians were also employed by Raja Singha.

De Couto gives the following account of one of them :—"He was arrested and interrogated, when his suspicious replies caused him to be put to the torture, whereupon he made a confession of everything. With him was found a book containing many figures of men, animals, trees, and certain writings, which were the charms by which they invoked the devil to their assistance. In his bundle he had a skull, the dried head of a cobra, a piece of a viper, seven pieces of bark from poisonous trees, a medicinal stone which, when held near the fire, emited rays and made the air the colour of sulphur, some grains of pepper, ginger and saffron, some peacock's feathers, etc. The magician was torn to pieces and his possessions burnt."

With a view to diverting the attention of Raja Singha from the siege of Colombo the Portuguese sent out some ships to harray the coasts.

In December, 1587, Pedro Affonso made his way to Galle destroying Beruwela, Welitara, and Weligama, slaughtering a large number of Sinhalese and cutting off the hands and ears of women and children for the purpose of getting their bracelets and earrings.

In February, 1588, Thome Sousa made another similar expedition, in which Kosgoda was the first town to be destroyed. The second was Galle, where the inhabitants offered a stout resistance. Regarding it De Couto says: "We remained here three days, setting fire to the city, which was a very large one with several magazines of stores. We destroyed all the gardens and cut down all the palm trees in the neighbourhood and set fire to the ships which we found anchored there. The third was Weligama, where the Portuguese had to do some severe fighting, and were compelled to retreat to their ships in the first encounter." The same historian says of this town: "We found here three stores, one full of iron, which we cast into the sea, and the others of saltpetre and similar ammunition, which we set on fire." The fourth was Matara, regarding which Ribeiro says: "The important city of Matara, with its wealthy population of merchants, was half a league further off, and was destined to be given over to the plunder of our troops. We stormed it after some severe fighting, and set fire to it in various places, our men plundering whatever they thought best. Among the buildings that were burnt were three pagodas of great beauty, a store full of cinnamon, and a large ship which was in the harbour." The fifth was the temple at Dondra Head, regarding which the same Portuguese historian says: "The building was like a handsome city with a circuit of a full league. The temple itself was vast in size, all the roofs being domed and richly carved; round about it were several very handsome chapels, and over the principal gateway was a tall tower entirely roofed with copper; gilt in various parts. Within was a large square with verandahs and terraces with a handsome gate on each side, while all round were planted sweet-smelling flowers, which were used during their processions. There were several handsome streets, where lived all the servants attached to the temple, chief among them being the women dedicated to its service."

When the Portuguese arrived at the gates of the temple they discovered that it had been abandoned. The historian goes on to say: "We burst in the gates and proceeded to destroy the idols, of which there were more than a thousand of different figures of clay and wood and copper, mostly gilded. We destroyed the domes and colonnades and sacked the stores, where we found a vast accumulation of ivory, fine cloths, coffee, pepper, sandalwood, jewels, precious stones, and all the fittings of the temple, which we plundered as we desired and set the rest on fire. As the greatest affront that could be offered to the place, we slaughtered within it some cows, this being a stain which could not be purified without the most elaborate ceremonies." The sixth place to suffer destruction was Chilaw.

Rajavalia, pp. 310-311

Whilst the towns along the coast were being thus destroyed, a native of Peradeniya named Konappoo Bandar, who was a political refugee in Goa, and had there distinguished himself as a fencer, had been sent by the

Viceroy to his native district to raise a rebellion against Raja Singha, which he did successfully.

King Raja Singha, astounded by the intelligence of these disasters, disheartened by the failure of his repeated assaults on Colombo, and alarmed by the intelligence of the arrival of large reinforcements to the garrison from Goa, suddenly abandoned the siege and drew off his forces to the interior. With regard to the fortifications which he had raised around the Portuguese fort, De Couto says: "Our wonder was beyond words at the marvellous fortifications which the king had constructed; indeed it was hardly possible to believe that they were the work of human hands."

During this war the Sinhalese used firelocks which they had learnt to manufacture for themselves. De Couto says the Sinhalese "came to cast the best and handsomest artillery in the world, and to make the finest firelocks of which they had more than 20,000." *De Couto, Dec. 5, lib. i., ch. v. Dec. 10, lib. x., ch. vii.*

1591 A.C.

In 1591 A.C. the Portuguese invaded the territory of the King of Jaffna, on the ground that he disfavoured the conversion of his subjects to Christianity. The king's army stubbornly resisted the invaders, but was ultimately defeated, and the king and his eldest son were slain. The Portuguese left the place after they had secured a deal of plunder, and placed the second son of the deceased king on the throne.

In 1592 Raja Singha advanced with his army with a view to crushing the power of Konappoo Bandara, who, as a result of the baptism he underwent whilst he resided at Goa, was known to the Portuguese as Don Juan. Konappoo's forces met those of Raja Singha at Kukulbitra-welle near the Kadugannawa Pass and completely defeated them. During his retreat a thorn happened to enter the foot of King Raja Singha, which brought about his death before he could reach his capital (Sitawaka). He spent his last few days in bitterly lamenting the departure, in his old age, of that good fortune which had signalised his military career ever since he was eleven years of age. *Rajavalia, p. 312.*

Wimala Dharma, 1592-1604 A.C.

Konappoo Bandara (Don Juan) now ascended the throne of Kandy taking the name of **Wimala Dharma**.

Although his reign was a continuous struggle with the Portuguese, he did all in his power to promote the cause of learning and the Buddhist religion, which had received a staggering blow at the hands of his predecessor Raja Singha I., who, professing Hinduism, had built temples at Avisawella for Brahmin priests, had bestowed the shrine at Adam's Peak on certain Andi Fakiers, and had destroyed Buddhist libraries wherever he found them.

King Wimala Dharma had the sacred Tooth which was at Sabaragamuwa removed to Kandy. He held a great festival in commemoration of this act, and invited 2,140 priests from Arracan, in whose presence he celebrated the Upasampada Ordination. The poem *Dalada Katawa* was written at this period describing this function.

The Portuguese Viceroy at Goa, on receiving the news of Raja Singha's death, deeming it a good opportunity for extending the influence of the Portuguese into the interior of the Island, made extensive preparations for a military expedition as against King Wimala Dharma. An ostensible excuse for such an expedition was to be found in the fact that Donna Catherina, the daughter of the late King Jayaweira of Kandy, was the rightful heir to the throne. Accordingly an experienced officer named
1594 A.C. Pedro Lopes was sent over with a large Portuguese force with instructions that he should take Donna Catherina along with him on his expedition against Wimala Dharma, and, after subduing him, marry her to his (Pedro Lopes') nephew, and place them both on the throne of Kandy as king and queen. By this means the Portuguese hoped to secure a permanent hold of the kingdom, the king-to-be-created being of their own race. However, all these plans were doomed to end in failure, inasmuch as General Pedro Lopes, his nephew, and the whole of his Portuguese force were annihilated by the forces of
Ribeiro, King Wimala Dharma at Danture. Donna Catherina was
ch. viii. taken alive, and Wimala Dharma married her on the battle-field in the presence of his whole army there assembled.

When the news of this disaster reached Goa, Dom Hieronimo de Azevedo was sent out to Ceylon "with all the forces the State could afford." Azevedo resorted to violent measures of retaliation, and a war of extermination ensued unsurpassed in atrocity and bloodshed. Faria y Souza, in his review of the character of this commander which ended in a dungeon at Lisbon, says his reverses were a judgment from the Almighty for his barbarities in Ceylon. In the height of his success, he beheaded mothers after forcing them to cast their babes betwixt mill-stones. Punning on the name of the tribe of Gallas or Chalias, and its resemblance to the Portuguese word for cocks, *gallos*, "he caused his soldiers to take up children on the points of their spears, and bade them hark how the young cocks crow!" "He caused many men to be cast off the bridge at Malwané for the troops to see the crocodiles devour them, and these creatures grew so used to the food, that at a whistle they would lift their heads above the water."

Faria y Souza, vol. iii., pt. iii., ch. xv.

The war lasted for years, the Portuguese in successive forays penetrating to Kandy, and even to Uva and Sabaragamuwa, burning towns, uprooting fruit trees, driving away cattle, and making captives to be enslaved in the lowlands. These conflicts were, however, of uncertain success. On some occasions the Portuguese, overpowered by the energy of the Kandyans, were defeated and put to flight, followed by the exasperated mountaineers to the gates of Colombo.

Faria y Souza, vol. iii., pt. iii., chs. viii., ix., xii., etc.

In the midst of this terrible war died the Emperor of Ceylon, Don Juan Dharmapala. He expired at Colombo in May, 1597, bequeathing his dominions by will to Philip II. of Portugal. By this deed the Portuguese claimed title to the sovereignty of his kingdom. The immediate steps taken by the Portuguese to establish the rights of the King of Portugual are interesting. Ribeiro gives the following description :—"The death of the Emperor was greatly lamented by his own subjects and by us, and he was interred with all possible honours in the Convent of St. Francisco at Colombo, which was now a beautiful city, where many noble families lived. After his burial, and when his obsequies had been performed with the dignity due to his position, the Captain-General summoned the Captain of Colombo and the other counsellors to discuss the steps to be taken to induce the people to acknowledge his Majesty as their lord and king without having recourse to force; after several discussions they agreed to issue a notice to all the provinces (called Corles) of the kingdoms that they should send to Colombo on a certain day two delegates from each Corle authorised to take the oaths on behalf of the rest to the King of Portugal as their

Ribeiro bk. 1, ch. xv.

lord and king. They assembled on the appointed day, on receipt of the notice; and it was then proposed to them that as they were to be the vassals of His Majesty, it was but reasonable that they should receive the same laws as the Portuguese, and for the nobility to enjoy the same rights and privileges as they did.

"To these proposals they replied that such matters demanded careful deliberation; they had no doubt that they would be able to do everything which was required of them, but they should be allowed the opportunity to discuss them and to urge any reasons of their own; that always their duty was to look to what was most to the interest of the king, their lord. Two days were allowed them, and after deliberation they reported that they were Sinhalese brought up from their youth in the laws which they possessed and observed, and that it would be a very grave matter for them to abandon those laws and take in exchange what were now proposed; the result of so great a change would probably be that neither the one law nor the other would be properly observed to the great prejudice of His Majesty. They admitted the King of Portugal as their rightful lord and king, just as if he had been their own Emperor, born in their country, and as such they would serve him with the laws in which they had been brought up; but they must be guaranteed the continuance of those laws without any alteration at any time by His Majesty and his ministers; they would obey him and render him all the dues which they had at all times rendered to the kings who had reigned in the Island before, and they would take an oath to act accordingly; and as the king their lord had appointed them (*i.e.* the Portuguese Government and his Portuguese Consellors) to be his ministers, they too must take an oath on his behalf to preserve and defend their laws and privileges in their entirety.

"When we saw that there was nothing else to be done, a public instrument was drawn up, and confirmed by solemn oaths on either side. We promised, in the name of His Majesty, always to preserve for the kingdoms and vassals of Ceylon all their laws, rights, and customs without any change or diminution whatever. The natives similarly took another oath to serve the king our lord well and faithfully, as if he were their natural king, and to render to him the same taxes, dues, and other obligations which they had rendered to their kings in times past. Liberty was secured for the religious orders to preach in public when and where they pleased the faith of our Lord Jesus Christ; all who wished to receive their doctrine were not to be hindered in any fashion or manner, and there was to be no opposition even as between parents and children; if any one disregarded this condition he was liable to punishment at the discretion of the person authorised, and for the future no one was to be exposed to violence or persecution, but whoever voluntarily desired to be a Christian was to be at liberty freely to embrace the faith.

"With this agreement the council came to an end; the documents were copied and each delegate took away with him a copy to his province.........The Captain-General immediately sent for the archives of the Emperor, among which was found the *Tombo* of dues and services, not only of each kingdom and province, but also a detailed statement of the payments due from each village and household, and any further dues that they were liable to. All this was translated into our tongue with the same detail."

To protect the territories which they had thus inherited from the King of Cotta, as against the incursions of the Kanydans, the Portuguese were obliged to keep up two camps, one at Menikkadawara in Beligal Korle and the other at Sabaragamuwa on the confines of Uva. To garrison these and their forts at various points on the coast they were compelled to maintain an army of upwards of 20,000 men, most of whom were Sinhalese residents within the newly acquired dominion. The value of the trade carried on under such circumstances was incommensurate with the expenditure essential for its protection; the products of the Island were collected, it may almost be said, sword in hand, and shipped under the guns of the fortresses. Still tranquillity was so far preserved throughout the districts bordering on the coast from Matara to Chilaw, that the low-country husbandmen pursued their ordinary avocations, and the patriarchal village system still regulated the organisation of agriculture. The military were recruited by the feudal service of the peasantry; and the revenues in the same form in which they had been raised by the kings of Cotta were collected by the Governor of Colombo, who now styled himself the "King of Malwané." Trade was prohibited to all other nations, and even to the

Ribeiro, bk. 1., chs. x.-xi.

Sinhalese. Besides the royal monopolies of cinnamon, pepper, and musk, the chief articles of export were cocoanuts, cardamoms, sapan-wood, arecanuts, ebony, elephants, ivory, gems, pearls, and along with these there were annually shipped small quantities of tobacco and tree-cotton.

In quest of these commodities, vessels came to Colombo and Galle from Persia, Arabia, the Red Sea, China, Bengal and Europe; the surplus of cinnamon beyond that required by these traders was annually burned, lest any accumulation might occasion the price to be reduced, or the Chalias to relax their toil in searching the forests for the spice. The taxes were as a rule paid in kind.

THE DUTCH PERIOD.

1602 A.C. On May 28th, 1602, the Dutch Admiral Spilbergen arrived at Batticaloa with seven ships and captured four Portuguese vessels.

Of the reception accorded to Spilbergen on this occasion by King Wimala Dharma, Pridham says: "Nothing could exceed the hospitality and attention with which the admiral was received. Horses were brought to him daily, on which to take excursions, feasts in the European style were given on his account, and uninterrupted access was allowed him to every public building; the Emperor (Wimala Dharma) sought his opinion on the pagodas, which were of great magnitude and height, and asked if the Dutch churches were as much adorned with images and statues as those of the Portuguese; Spilbergen replied, that the Dutch loved better the sight of animate beings, and gave him to understand that they had no taste for the rites of the Church of Rome. The king appeared much delighted with his conversation, and listened with avidity to the state of the European politics. The tenets of his religion, the state of his nation, his friends, his fortune, his rank in the Dutch service, were all successively asked by the inquisitive monarch, but his chief delight was in the account of European wars and revolutions, and the political state of the United Provinces, of which he apparently could never hear too much. As a mark of high favour, the Emperor took him into the Empress's apartments. He found her in the midst of her children, and clad in the European manner.........Meanwhile, true to the national character, Spilbergen made every effort to obtain protection and commercial privileges for his countrymen. Full protection was offered, and free trade in cinnamon and pepper was likewise conceded. After this success, Spilbergen took leave of the Emperor, leaving him two of his musicians, and departed, laden with presents, for the squadron."

No sooner had the fleet of the admiral left the coast of Ceylon, than another Dutch expedition arrived under the command of Seebald de Weerd, who proceeded from Batticaloa to Kandy, and met with a kind and curteous reception from the Emperor. He left Ceylon for Achin, after having concluded a treaty with the Emperor for the purpose of making a joint attack on Point de Galle.

On returning to Batticaloa King Wimala Dharma hastened to meet him with a view to expostulating with him for having released some Portuguese vessels he had recently captured. At Batticaloa, Wimala Dharma was informed by the Sinhalese ambassador he had deputed to accompany De Weerd on his voyage out to Achin that he (the ambassador) had been treated by De Weerd with disrespect, inasmuch as the officers of the Portuguese vessels which had been captured and released were given seats of greater honour at table than he. This helped to further inflame the anger of the monarch. De Weerd, on meeting Wimala Dharma, invited him to visit his vessel, but was politely refused on the ground that the queen had been left alone at Kandy, his brother having departed for one of the provinces, and that consequently he could not delay. De Weerd, being a bit the worse for liquor, replied that she would certainly not be very long without having some one to fulfil his duties, and furthermore that he would not proceed to the attack of Galle till his wishes were complied with. Enraged at such impudence, the king turned his back on him, and walked off the scene remarking to the officers that stood beside him, "Bind that dog." A struggle followed, in which De Weerd and fifty of his men were slain. The king next addressed the following note in Portuguese to Jacob Pietersz, the second in command of the Dutch fleet :—"He that drinks wine is good for nothing; God has executed justice; if you desire peace let there be peace; if war, war." The reply of Jacob Pietersz consisted of an expression of approval of the conduct of the king, affording us a striking instance of Dutch passiveness under oppression, and the readiness with which they rendered subservient to the love of gain the passions which, in the case of a more impetuous people, would have been kindled to the highest pitch of excitement.

For six years the Sinhalese of the maritime districts remained faithful to the oath of allegiance which they had taken in respect of the King of Portugal. At length, roused to desperation by the miseries drawn down upon them in never-ending hostilities, and by the unspeakable atrocities perpetrated by the Portuguese soldiery, they cast in their lot with the Kandyans.

With reference to these atrocities Faria y Souza says:—"We had not grown odious to the Sinhalese, had we not provoked them by our infamous proceedings. Not only the poor soldiers went out to rob, but the Portuguese who were lords of villages added rapes and adulteries, which obliged the people to seek the company of beasts in the mountains than be subject to the more beastly villainies of men."

1603 A.C. Ribeiro, ch. 50, p. 179.

When the Portuguese found themselves thus deserted panic seized them. Soldiers mutinously resisted the orders of their officers, and the whole Island, with the exception of Mannar and Colombo, once more reverted to the hands of the sons of the soil. The Viceroy at Goa was appealed to for help.

1604 A.C.

Baldaeus' Description of Ceylon, ch. vii., contained in Churchill's Collection of Voyages, vol. iii., p 612.

Wimala Dharma, King of Kandy, died in 1604 A.C. Of him the Dutch historian, Baldaeus, says:—"Don John (Wimala Dharma) was a valiant and great captain, as his whole life sufficiently testifies. He was tall of stature and well-limbed, black, and rustical in his speech. He had gathered a vast treasure of gold and jewels, and had founded many forts, palaces, and resting places for the public (ambalams). He kept a strict hand in the government, and as he never pardoned crimes, so he was very liberal to all such as behaved themselves well in their civil or military stations, on whom he conferred honours and riches. He was a complete statesman, and stood firm to his engagements with all foreign princes, except the *Portuguese;* upon whom, looking with a jealous eye, he had conceived a mortal hatred. As he despised all religions, so he allowed the free exercise thereof to all without distinction."

King Wimala Dharma had a son and two daughters, and as they were all of tender years, a contest for the throne between the Prince of Uva and Senerat, Wimala Dharma's brother, became imminent. At this juncture the Queen-Mother Donna Catherina declared herself regent for her young son, and thus prevented a civil war, which would have undoubtedly been availed of by the Portuguese for extending their dominion over the whole Island. "As the Prince of Uva and Senerat were renewing their intrigues for the crown, the Empress (Donna Catherina) ordered the great body of nobility to make their appearance at court, all of whom obeyed the summons except these two aspiring chiefs. They were accordingly proclaimed rebels and their estates were declared forfeited. But they had sufficient influence to get this sentence revoked, and came to court as before each with a large body of retainers, being in mutual distrust. ....The rivals were proceeding to court to take leave of the Empress, and while with ceremonious politeness they were professing to yield the point of precedence, the Prince of Uva, as the eldest, consented to lead the way. He had gone but a few steps when Senerat stabbed him in the back, exclaiming, 'Lie there thou false traitor,' and his followers instantly carried off the dead body." Displeasing as this cowardly act was to Donna Catherina, now in the prime of life, yet the success of Senerat left her little ground for venting her displeasure, and such was his courtly grace that, though he had but recently relinquished the priestly robes, no long time elapsed ere Donna Catherina bestowed upon him her heart and hand and with them the sovereignty of Ceylon.

Valentyn.

Senerat, 1604-1632 A.C.

For eight years after **Senerat's** accession comparative tranquillity prevailed in the Island. In 1612 Marcellus de Boschouwer arrived at Kandy with two letters for the Emperor Senerat, one of which was from the States-General of the Netherlands, and the other from Prince Maurice of Nassau. They tendered the friendship of the Netherlands and offered, in the event of Portuguese aggression by land or sea, to assist His Majesty with ships, forces, and munitions of war. The result was a treaty by which, the Emperor, in return for the promised military aid, gave the Dutch permission to erect a fort at Kottiar, on the southern side of the bay of Trincomalee, and secured to them a monopoly of the trade in cinnamon, gems, and pearls. So eager was the Emperor to mature the alliance, and so impressed was he by the merits of the man, that be prevailed upon Boschouwer to remain behind at Kandy in the double capacity of representative of the Netherlands and his adviser. Boschouwer was created Prince of Migonne (Negombo*) and Anuradhapura, Knight of the Sun, President of his Military Council, and High Admiral of the Fleet. Alarmed by the dangerous character of these developments the Portuguese secretly despatched a force, across the Island, composed of 1,000 of their own nationality and 3,000 Indians commanded by a distinguished Sinhalese named Simon Corea, which surprised the Dutch garrison at Kottiar and put every man composing it to the sword. The Emperor immediately despatched a force of 5,000 men to avenge the massacre of his allies. The Portuguese who started a retreat were pursued day and night until they were met on the borders of the Seven Korles and routed. In this battle there fell twenty-three Portuguese and five hundred Indians. The victorious army returned to Kandy bringing with it much booty and many prisoners. Thereafter the Emperor summoned his Grand Council, which was composed of all the petty kings, princes, and chiefs within his dominions. The following list of those that assembled as well as did not is given by

Baldaeus, ch. xi. Baldaeus, viz.: "Idele, King of Cotiarum; Celle Wandaar, King of Palugam; Comaro Wandaar, King of Baticaloa; Corre Pitty Ralahamy, Prince of Ouve; Marcellus Boschouwer, Prince of Migonne; Meter Ralahamy, Prince of Vellane; Yalagode Ralle, Prince of Cotomale; Mewater Ralle, Prince of Mewater; Wik Venesinge, Earl of Quatre Korle (Four Korles); John Sangaiti, Prince and Lord of Podore; Cole Rale, Duke of Ode; Jattenore, brother of the Prince of Yalagode; Gael Heberad, Governor of the County of Harcipate; Kuruppu, Governor of the County of Odogo d'Askeri; Wanigasekere, Governor of the Province of Matara. In the same assembly appeared also the governors and commanders-in-chief of the lesser provinces and the ambassador of the King of Jaffnapatam, the King of Patania being the only one who, though summoned by a peculiar letter dated July 16, 1611, made several frivolous excuses for his not appearing there."

* Emerson Tennent, however, is of opinion that "Migonne was the Mangel Corle, north of the Deddera-oya"—Vol. II., p. 38, n. 3

There is a Magul Korle north of that river, but I have failed to discover any "Mangel Corle" in any of the available maps of Ceylon.

At this meeting it was resolved to raise an army of 50,000 men and make a simultaneous attack on Galle and Balane. The attack on Galle was to be led by the Prince of Uva, that on Balane by Boschouwer. In the event of success both armies were to make a joint assault on Colombo. No quarter was to be given to any subject of Portugal *save women and children*, which shows that the Sinhalese, though cruel perhaps, were more chivalrous than the Portuguese, who were no respecters of sex.

This plan was however frustrated by the Portuguese taking the field, and compelling an engagement in the Seven Korles, in which the Sinhalese were worsted, and his new principality of Migonne wrested from Boschouwer.

During this reign there lived a celebrated poet named Alagiawanna Mohottala—a native of Sina Korle. Amongst his works are the *Kusajataka*, the *Subasitha*, the *Nitisara*, the *Maha Hatana*, and the *Sewul Sandese*.

Prince Mahastanne, son of Donna Catherina by Wimala Dharma, died in 1612 A.C., some say of fever, whereas others say of poison administered by his physician at the instance of Senerat, who was anxious to secure the throne for his own son. In the following year Donna Catherina died of grief. Before her death she entrusted the guardianship of her children to the Prince of Uva and Boschouwer. As mentioned above, the King of Patania (Panane) was the only person who did not attend the meeting of the Grand Council summoned by the Emperor. Ere long evidence was not wanting to prove that he had entered into an agreement with the Portuguese for the purpose of overthrowing the existing dynasty. Accordingly he was tried, in conjunction with fifty-two accomplices, before a court composed of "fifty lords of the Empire" on the following charge:—"That he had entered into an agreement with the Portuguese against the Emperor, and was to have married the young Princess Hantan Adaseen, and with her, as a dowry, the kingdoms of Batticaloa and Palugam. That he had despised the Emperor's order in not coming to court; and hired a certain ruffian for five thousand *larynes* to murder the Emperor, with a promise of twenty thousand more, and certain possessions, after the same was accomplished, as appeared both by his own handwriting and the confession of the ruffian." The only answer the accused king gave to this indictment was, that he was *1612 A.C.*

guilty, and that he craved for mercy, on the ground that he was descended from the imperial line, and that his ancestors had rendered many services in the past to the crown. The court having sentenced him to suffer capital punishment, he appealed to Senerat for a commutation of the sentence to one of imprisonment for life. Senerat having refused to do this, he was beheaded, but given a royal funeral. His accomplices, who had been sentenced to suffer death at the hands of the elephants, were accordingly thrown before the animals to be trampled by them.

Baldaeus, ch. xiv. Soon after this the Emperor, who felt the loss of Quen Donna Catherina keenly, and still more acutely grieved over the fact that he was suspected to be the cause of the death of Prince Mahastanne, fell seriously ill, and summoning a meeting of his Grand Council appointed by royal patent, the Prince of Uva and Boschouwer, guardians of his son Comara Singastanne, and entrusted to them the administration of the country in the event of his death.

Baldaeus, ch. xv. The Portuguese, on learning that the Emperor was ill, immediately made overtures to Gael Henerad, Dissave of Harasia-pattoo,—who had an imaginary grievance, viz., that he was not given the promotion he deserved by Senerat,—and succeeded in getting him to join in a conspiracy for the purpose of murdering the royal children who were in Kukulu Korle and their newly appointed guardians. By the promptitude of Boschouwer the conspiracy was discovered, and Gael Henerad placed on his trial at Kandy, where his guilt having been conclusively proved he was condemned to death and broken alive upon the wheel, so as to serve as a deterrent to others who may be minded to join the Portuguese.

1614 A.C. Baldaeus, ch. xvi. Thereupon the people of Harasia-pattoo rose in rebellion, and the royal forces gave them battle. In this battle there fell no less than 4,000 men on both sides. At length the Portuguese came to the assistance of the rebels and surprised and defeated the royal forces in a battle, in which both the Prince of Uva and Boschouwer were wounded, and five hundred Sinhalese were slain.

The Portuguese, imagining that after this defeat Senerat would be willing to accept any overtures on their part for the establishment of a treaty, sent Dom

Francisco de Menzes to Kandy with a letter from the Viceroy of Goa written in the name of the King of Spain (who also was the King of Portugal) authorising the bearer of it to act as a plenipotentiary on behalf of Spain in respect of a treaty. King Senerat, however, wished that any proposals for a treaty should be sent him in writing. This was accordingly done. As the proposals were such as would only be made to a thoroughly defeated and demoralised foe, and could not be accepted, the king sent the following answer after a consultation with his ministers :—"That his Imperial Majesty was not inclined to treat with the King of Spain, before all the lands and lordships taken from him were restored. That however the Spaniards should remain in possession of Galle and Colombo with the territories thereto belonging; but that his Imperial Majesty would by no means renounce his alliance made with the Dutch, but keep the same inviolably. Furthermore, his majesty required full compensation for all the damage he had sustained in this war, and was resolved to have custom dues paid him for all goods imported and exported."

King Senerat's reply to a letter from the Portuguese General at Colombo, which too was sent him through Menzes, was still more pointed. It was to the effect, "That he was resolved not to violate his oath with the Dutch; and that being sensible no faith ought to be given to the Portuguese, he intended to pursue them by force of arms; and that they might make their account accordingly."

Exasperated at so resolute an answer, the Portuguese marched with an army of 25,000 men in the direction of Kandy, but were met at Balane by the royal forces consisting of 29,000. A sharp encounter took place, resulting in the defeat of the Portuguese, who took refuge in the neighbouring jungle, leaving 2,100 Indians and forty of their own nationality dead on the battle-field. Seven hundred men fell on the side of the Sinhalese. Not only on land was the war waged by Senerat against the Portuguese. Baldaeus tells us :—"In the meantime the Prince of Migonne had not been idle to equip some galleys and *fustas* (small vessels), to cruise upon the Portuguese, between Cape Comorin and Ceylon. The same set sail on the 16th May, 1612, out of the harbour of Kottiar, under the command of a nephew of the Prince of Uva as admiral, and Wandige Nay Hami

6th August, 1614 A.C.

Baldaeus, ch. xiii.

as vice-admiral. The first galley was called the *Kandy*, one *Sanderappoo* captain; the second called the *Holland*, *Kistena* captain; the third the *Migonne*, one *Dingappoo* captain; the fourth called *Fortune*, one *Ordia* captain; fifth, the *Good Luck*, one *Marasinghe* captain; sixth, the *Faithful*, commanded by captain *Sanderappoo*. These ships returned on the 6th March, 1613, with great booty, amounting to nearly 500,000 livres. For they had taken two Portuguese vessels near *Chilaw* to the north of *Negombo* and *Mannar*, called *Patasios*, and three *Fustas*, besides twenty barks which they set on fire. Not far from *Calicut* and the *Cape of Comorin* they took another ship, whereof they threw (in accordance with orders) the *Portuguese* overboard, forced another ashore, and took a *Moorish* vessel richly laden coming from *Ormus*, and bound for *Cochin*, and another Portuguese ship coming from *Bengal*. The *Portuguese* and *Mistices* of all which they threw into the seas, keeping only the *Portuguese* women and *Negroes*. In the road of *Panaca* they met another *Portuguese* ship riding at *anchor*, deserted by the ship's crew which they brought into Kottiar. His Majesty (Senerat) ordered the booty to be distributed among the officers and seamen."

1615 A.C. Baldaeus, ch. xvii.

In 1615 Boschouwer was despatched to Holland by the Emperor to solicit reinforcements, pursuant to the convention of 1612. The States General, dissatisfied with the conduct and demeanour of the envoy, who approached them not as a subject of Holland, but as a prince and ambassador from the sovereign of Kandy, declined to send the required forces. Thereupon Boschouwer proceeded to Denmark, which had recently turned its attention to the benefits of a commercial connection with the East, and entered into a treaty with Christian IV. on behalf of Emperor Senerat. By him he was furnished with a man-of-war and a yacht, with which he set sail for Ceylon in 1618; and the Danish East India Company, conceiving that such an opening was not to be neglected, despatched, soon after, five other vessels under the command of Gule Gédde, a Danish noble. Boschouwer having died during the course of the voyage, on the arrival of Gédde with his fleet at Batticaloa in 1620, the Emperor, who liked the fleet but not the bill presented by the Danish Admiral for the equipment, etc., of the fleet, repudiated the acts of his deceased agent and declined to receive the proffered assistance. Thereupon Gédde seized all the belongings of Boschouwer which were to be found in his two ships which were anchored in the harbour of Trincomalee, stripped his (Boschouwer's) wife of all that belonged to her, and returned with his ships to Denmark.

The Portuguese availed themselves of the perplexity of the Emperor, occasioned by these occurrences, to renew their solicitations for a truce, which they succeeded in obtaining in 1624; but in violation of its conditions, they commenced, in 1627, to fortify Batticaloa, having previously, in 1622, erected a fort at Trincomalee. The Emperor, alarmed by these proceedings, apparently deserted by his Dutch allies, and seeing his kingdom encircled on all sides by Portuguese garrisons—they having established forts at Jaffna, Mannar, Negombo, Colombo, Kalutara, Galle, Weligama, Batticaloa and Trincomalee,—made a vigorous and successful effort to rouse his fellow-countrymen, and organise a national movement for the expulsion of the perfidious Portuguese. The flame of war was simultaneously kindled at opposite points of the Island; the most influential mudaliyars of the lowlands entered earnestly into the conspiracy with their brethren of the highlands, and the people of Colombo, exasperated by the treatment they had experienced at the hands of the common enemy, expressed their readiness to revolt.

In 1628, Constantine de Saa y Noroña, who had been for five years in command of the Portuguese force, perceiving the hostile disposition of the Emperor, put himself as quickly as possible in a state of defence. Every soldier whom he could press into his service, whether European or native, was enrolled, and with a large force he advanced into the interior. The pass of Balane was first forced, and the road then lay open to Kandy. Constantine de Saa did not permit the Emperor Senerat to recover from his surprise, but boldly pushed his way to Kandy, burning or destroying everything which came within the reach of his army on the way. The Emperor, who had taken up his residence at Hanguranketa, was in consequence compelled to seek safety by retreating to the inaccessible mountains of Uva. From here he sent his Attapatu Mudaliyar with a force to fall upon Jaffnapatam, which was sparsely

Ribeiro, bk. 2, ch. ii. Baldaeus, ch. xvii.

garrisoned by the Portuguese. Constantine de Saa, having received timely information as to this manœuvre, sent a large force towards the north, which after a terrific battle, in which no less than 3,000 Sinhalese were slain, defeated the Mudaliyar. At length, De Saa, discovering that little progress could be made in his pursuit of the Emperor in Uva, where the sympathy of the inhabitants were entirely with the latter, decided upon beating a retreat to Malwana, which was now the seat of government of the Portuguese. On his arrival there he received imperative orders from the Viceroy of Goa to reduce Ceylon to subjection once and for all, and in the same despatch he was accused of a certain degree of negligence. Accordingly he again advanced at the head of 1,500 Portuguese and 20,000 auxiliaries. After plundering Badulla, the capital of Uva, the Portuguese posted themselves on a lofty hill in the vicinity with the object of refreshing themselves after the exertions of the forced march which they had made. Here they remained two days. They were, however, towards the close of the second day, undeceived with regard to their fancied security. Thousands upon thousands of Sinhalese were observed defiling towards the neighbouring eminences, while the remainder occupied the plains. Ribeiro says: "That afternoon the enemy did nothing but shout at our men as was their custom, saying, 'This is the last hour you have to live,' and adding insulting words; and so night came on." The night was spent by the Portuguese in confessing before the priests who accompanied their army and in praying to God for help. But the fates had determined that they should suffer for the most unchristian enormities they had all along been perpetrating in the name of religion.

One of the first events of the morrow was the defection from the Portuguese ranks of a large number of the Sinhalese force they had enlisted. The battle was nevertheless fought with equal fury on either side. The Portuguese fought with the desperation of men determined on selling their lives at the greatest possible cost. Prince Raja Singha, though but seventeen years of age, was in the midst of the fray directing and controling the royal forces. The battle continued without rest or cessation during the whole day, and the contending parties only paused when the darkness of night rendered their exertions unavailing. Rain fell heavily during the course of the night and rendered the powder and cord of the Portuguese useless. De Saa was entreated by his companions to flee for safety with a suitable guard during the course of the night, but noble warrior that he was, he was resolved to live or die with his companions in arms. The following morn witnessed the total annihilation of the Portuguese army. (The *Rajavalia* tells us that this battle was fought at Randeniwela in Wellawaya.)

From this moment the hope of ever conquering Ceylon ceased to be entertained by the Portuguese. Emperor Senerat's army, commanded by his son Raja Singha, lost not a moment in recapturing the forts on the Mahaveli-ganga and in advancing to the investment of Colombo. Assault after assault was delivered, but no less resolutely received by the gallant garrison; on one occasion the fort owed its preservation to the resolute resistance of the native citizens and slaves. Ultimately, the siege was raised as a result of the arrival of reinforcements from Goa and Cochin, and a treaty was *1631 A.C.* entered into, by which the Portuguese undertook to keep the peace so long as two tusked elephants were given them every year by the Emperor.

1632 A.C. Journal of R.A.S. (C.B.), 1889, vol. xi., No. 38.

Baldcaus, ch. xviii.

The Emperor Senerat did not live long to enjoy the fruits of Raja Singha's labours. After a reign of twenty-eight years he died in his old age in 1632, leaving behind three sons to administer the Empire. To the eldest of them, Comara Singha Hastanne, he entrusted the administration of Uva; to the second, Vijaya Pala, he entrusted the principality of Matale; and to his youngest son, Raja Singha (Mahastanne), the kingship of Kandy. Comara Singha having died shortly after his father, a contest took place between Senerat's other two sons for his principality, resulting in one of them, Vijaya Pala, taking refuge among the Portuguese in Colombo. Thereupon Raja Singha assumed the title of Emperor and proceeded to administer the whole of his father's dominions as Emperor **Raja Singha II.** *1632-1687 A.C.*

A Portuguese trader having presented the Emperor Raja Singha with a box full of vials of rose water, some white sandal-wood and a beautiful horse, the monarch, not to be outdone in generosity, presented him with a fine tusked elephant in return. When the animal was taken to Colombo by the donee, the Portuguese officials seized it and gave as their excuse for so doing, that the Emperor was in arrears regarding his payment to the Portuguese of the annual tribute of two tuskers. When the poor trader related the story of what had befallen him to the Emperor, the latter was greatly enraged as he had punctiliously performed his share of the treaty of 1631. Having compassion on the trader, the monarch bestowed on him double the value of the elephant in precious stones and sent him away *via* Chilaw.

Ribeiro, bk. 2, ch. iii.

As for his feelings regarding the base conduct of the officials at Colombo, the Emperor suppressed them, and when the usual time arrived for the payment of tribute he sent the two elephants for the year. The Portuguese Governor, who styled himself King of Malwana, imagining that the trader had been given the handsome tusker in *exchange* for the horse he had taken, and that it was a pure business transaction between the trader and the Emperor, which showed what a high value the Sinhalese monarch placed on horses, had procured two splendid horses, which he despatched to Kandy with an agent in the company of the Emperor's men who had brought the elephants. As soon as the Emperor was informed of the object of the mission, viz., that the horses were to be exchanged for two tusked elephants similar to the one he had given the trader, he said to the Portuguese agent: "Tell the King of Malwana that he has taken from me an elephant of greater value than these horses; when he sends it back to me I shall return him these horses, and in the meantime I shall take care that they are well looked after."

On receiving this reply the Portuguese Governor flew into a temper, and, whilst making immediate preparations for war, sent a message to the Emperor to the effect that he was coming to Kandy to punish him as he deserved, and that his horses should be sent back without delay or reply. The Emperor did not waver, but with a humility and a quiet dignity, which bespoke confidence in his own power and might, informed the messenger that he took this step merely to get back what was his own; that so long as the elephant taken from the trader was not sent back to him, it was useless to ask him for the horses.

On receiving this reply, the Portuguese Capt.-General Diego de Melo set out with an army said by Valentyn and Baldaeus to have consisted of 2,300 whites and half-castes, 6,000 Negroes; by Ribeiro to have consisted of 700 Europeans, "the choicest men the Portuguese ever had in the Island," and 28,000 Indians. At the pass of Balané the Portuguese were met by a priest sent by Raja Singha with a request that they should desist from waging an unholy war in which the innocent would have to suffer. The reply given by the Portuguese General to the envoy was that the latter was to inform the Emperor that he (the General) had come there only with the object of getting the Emperor whipped for his insolence. Having said this he immediately ordered his forces to advance on Kandy, where they set the city on fire after they had plundered it, and slaughtered cows in the temples with the object of defiling them. The Portuguese next advanced to Gannoroowe, where they pitched their tents. Here the Portuguese General received information to the effect that Raja Singha had in the meantime adopted measures to obstruct his progress, by barricading the pass at Balané. When he found himself and his forces thus hemmed in on all sides and shot at with muskets and arrows by an enemy that could not be seen, he had to swallow his pride and sue for peace. The Emperor, determined to punish him for the barbarities perpetrated at Kandy, gave the two envoys to the custody of the Prince of Uva, and immediately ordered his men to charge the enemy. The whole of the Portuguese force was thus put to the sword, with the exception of thirty-three who were taken prisoners.

1638 A.C. Ribeiro, bk. 2, ch. iv. Baldaeus, ch. xxi.

Rajavalia, p. 324.

The Emperor, perceiving the difficulty that he would have to expel the Portuguese from Ceylon, had resolved to send an embassy to a Dutch Settlement in India, requesting assistance for the purpose of driving them from the Island. In pursuance of this design he had sent a long letter dated September 9th, 1636, to the Dutch Governor of Palliacatta. A Brahmin, who was the bearer of this letter, was for six months detained at Jaffna before he could meet with a safe opportunity of proceeding to the coast of Coromandel. On receipt of the Emperor's letter, the Governor of Palliacatta forwarded it to Batavia to "the

Baldaeus, chs. xviii.-xxi.

Great Council of the Indies." Envoys were forthwith despatched to Kandy, and eventually a treaty of alliance was entered into between the Dutch and the Sinhalese monarch. According to the stipulations of the treaty, the Dutch were to furnish troops for the expulsion of the Portuguese, the Emperor paying them all the expenses of the war. The Emperor was to be placed in possession of the fortified places which might be taken from the Portuguese, and the Dutch were to have the entire monopoly of the trade of the Island.

1638 A.C.

Ribeiro, bk. 2, ch. v.

Prior to signing the treaty, the king stated to the Dutch deputies the condition in which he stood in respect of the Portuguese local government at Colombo. He informed them that, although he had adopted every means in his power to preserve peace with his neighbours, and paid, with the utmost regularity, the tribute to the crown of Portugal, to which his father had submitted, his pacific intentions were frequently defeated. Owing to the caprices of the governors, there was no security in treating with them. Upon the most trifling occasion, they would march an army into his territory, pillage the country and burn the villages. Within a few years they had reduced to ashes Badulla, the principal town of the Province of Uva, together with Kandy, the capital of his dominion. He represented, that although he had repeatedly defeated them in the field, they were always ready for war, by which means he saw that, in a short time, he should not have an inch of territory in the Island; and, on that account, he had come to the resolution to enter into terms of amity with the Dutch, and to make such stipulations with them as might lead to their reciprocal advantage.

The deputies replied that they were well aware of the oppressive disposition of the Portuguese; that similiar complaints were made of their tyranny in the peninsula of India, and in the other Eastern countries where they had established colonies; that it was to liberate the inhabitants of these countries from the oppression under which they suffered that the Dutch had come so far from their own country; that the Portuguese had no right to any part of Ceylon; and that the Dutch East India Company were able and willing to expel them from the Island without exacting any remuneration for their services.

Emperor Raja Singha II. promised that, in addition to the expenses of the armament, he would pay a certain sum for each officer or soldier who died in the service, according to the rank he held in the army; and that another sum should be given for every man who lost an arm, a leg, or an eye, and that the sum should be somewhat higher for a right eye, a right leg, or a right arm than for a left eye, leg, or arm. The treaty having been regularly signed, the Dutch deputies left Ceylon. In compliance with this treaty, Batticaloa was attacked in 1639 and soon taken by Admiral Westerwold, who commanded a force of 600 men with six pieces of cannon. Trincomalee was next besieged, and although the Portuguese garrison there consisted of no more than 50 men, it did not capitulate until twenty-three of that number had been killed. Before the other Portuguese forts were captured the struggle was long and bloody. Philip Lucas, the Dutch Director-General of the East Indies, took Negombo for the first time on the 9th February, 1640. In March, 1640, Commodore William Jacob Koster took Galle by storm, but did not long survive the victory, in that he was put to death at the instance of Raja Singha II. for having behaved in an insolent manner whilst on a visit to the Emperor at Kandy. The insolence consisted in his having used strong words in respect of the Emperor's courtiers for not permitting him to interview the Emperor as quickly as he desired. Meanwhile, reinforcements having arrived from Goa, Negombo was recaptured by the Portuguese. In 1644 Negombo was taken for the second time by the Dutch. Kalutara fell in 1655.

Baldaeus, ch. xlii.

A temporary pacification took place between the Dutch and the Portuguese in 1646, during which the Dutch authorities at Negombo carried off some tame elephants belonging to the King of Kandy, who was so enraged at the circumstance, that he surrounded a body of their troops in Seven Korles, and after slaying their Commander Adrian Vander Stell, cut off his head, and sent it in a silk bag to his countrymen on the sea-coast, ordering, at the same time, 688 Dutchmen into captivity in the hill-country. The Dutch exerted all their address to effect a reconciliation with the Emperor, who already hesitated between the policy of uniting his influence with his former enemies or his recently acquired friends, but in the end the Dutch prevailed.

Colombo capitulated in 1656, having been besieged for seven months by the forces of Raja Singha, consisting of about 20,000 men, and the Dutch troops. During the siege of Colombo the Emperor held court at Rygamwatte (near Biyagama.) When the fort surrendered, he expected that it would be delivered into his hands in accordance with the stipulations of the treaty entered into by the Dutch, and in accordance with the repeated assurances he had subsequently received to that effect from Dutch governors; but the Dutch continued to hold possession of it in spite of his remonstrances.

Ever since the arrival of the Dutch in Lanka, the Emperor had treated them as no other than mercenaries engaged for the particular purpose of expelling the Portuguese. In most letters of his to Dutch officers he speaks of them as "my Hollanders." The Dutch, on the other hand, in every conceivable manner helped the Emperor to continue in the belief that they had no intention whatever of stepping into the shoes of the Portuguese, once the latter had been ousted out of the country. Their conduct all along towards the Emperor was that of servants towards their master. The Dutch historian Baldaeus gives us the following description of an interview which the Emperor accorded General Hulft at the imperial camp at Rygamwatte, immediately prior to the assault on Colombo:—On entering the reception hall the "Dutch fell upon their knees, till His Majesty was pleased to order them to rise by a nod. Then they began to approach the imperial throne, adorned with most precious tapestries of gold (called by then *Alcatives*); coming to the middle of the hall they fell upon their knees a second time, according to the custom of Eastern nations, till His Majesty was pleased to arise from his seat, and commanded the general to come nearer, who made the following speech to His Majesty :—

Baldaeus, ch. xxxv., pp. 671 and 672.

"Most Potent Monarch,

"Your most humble servant approaches your imperial throne with a most violent passion, in confidence of your generous inclinations and wonted clemency, which has encouraged me to address myself to Your Majesty, whose name is renowned throughout the world, with a most sincere wish, that God Almighty might be pleased to bless your most Illustrious Imperial

Majesty, and the prince with a long and happy life for the welfare and protection of your subjects, etc., etc."

"His Majesty appeared highly satisfied with what His Excellency had said, ordering him at the same time to rise; which he seemed not to understand, and at the same time offered certain presents, being, as he said, of little value in themselves; but nevertheless much regarded by the most potent Emperors and monarchs, to wit, some standards taken from those very enemies who had for many years together so cruelly and barbarously oppressed His Majesty's subjects, especially in the lowlands. His Majesty then speaking of the presents sent to His Excellency by the prince, his son, His Excellency acknowledged the same with extraordinary reverence, pointing at the same time to a jewel, he wore upon his breast, presented him before by His Majesty; and so approaching the throne he kneeled upon a cushion laid upon a step on the throne, and touching His Majesty's hand told him, that he thought it the greatest honour he ever was capable of receiving, to be admitted to kiss His Majesty's hands."

In spite of all similar demonstrations of respect and servility, the Emperor had for some time prior to the storming of Colombo begun to doubt the good faith of the Dutch, as a result of their hesitation to deliver up Negombo to him; and had endeavoured to take every precaution against furnishing them with any pretext for a breach of the treaty he had entered into with them. With regard to the expenses incurred by the Dutch, he was ever anxious to have them supply him with the accounts and wrote repeatedly to them asking for them, so that he may settle them; but the Dutch contented themselves with putting him off with various excuses and obtaining shiploads of cinnamon, pepper, wax, etc., on credit. With regard to these matters, we find the Emperor writing to the Dutch Captain-Major Van Kittenstein on the 15th August, 1653, to which he received a reply on September 2nd, "begging His Majesty to take in good part his displeasure regarding Colombo. His Excellency (Van Kittenstein) also protested that the Dutch had never had in their minds to appropriate to themselves a foot of land belonging to the king's crown, much less Colombo after its conquest, but that we (the Dutch) should prove the contrary by

Donald Ferguson's "Correspondence between Raja Singha II. and the Dutch," Journal of the R.A.S. (C.B.), No. 55, 1904, pp. 216-217. Also "The Dutch in Ceylon" in Journal of R.A.S. (C.B.) No. 38, 1889, p. 50.

adding it to His Majesty's crown. He (Van Kittenstein) had written to Batavia for His Majesty's account which he (Raja Singha II.) had asked for several times, in which he would see that all the expenses, besides the receipts on the other side, would be plainly set down (*except the fitting out of the fleets which had yet to be ascertained*)."

1656 A.C. After the capture of Colombo, the Emperor, finding that the Dutch had no intention to fulfil the treaty, wrote thus on the 11th May, 1656, to the Dutch Capt.-General :—" I would have you remember, that such as know not God, and do not keep their word, will, one time or other, be sensible of the ill-consequences thereof : I know I have God on my side." Thereafter he withdrew his support from them, and rather encouraged than repulsed the Portuguese. He was obviously doubtful as to which party was the more perfidious, as neither fulfilled the most solemn treaties, even though confirmed according to the usage of the age, by oath.

Baldaeus, ch. xli.

The Dutch having persisted in retaining their conquests and adopted a defiant attitude as a result of the arrival of reinforcements from Batavia, the Emperor Raja Singha attempted to wrest Colombo from them, but failed. Thereafter he contented himself with cutting off supplies from the fortress and renewing friendly relations with Portuguese who remained in the Island, whom he permitted to establish themselves within his dominions. Upwards of seven hundred Portuguese families, availing themselves of the opportunity, settled at Ruanwelle with their priests and secular clergy.

Valentyn, ch. xii, p. 146.

Ribeiro, bk. 3, ch. ii.

1658 A.C. Jaffnapatam, the last of the forts occupied by the Portuguese, was besieged and takan by the Dutch in 1658. When it capitulated a considerable number of soldiers laid down their arms, although during the siege, which lasted 3½ months, they had lost nearly 1,600 men by the sword and disease. Baldaeus preached a thanksgiving sermon on the occasion, the text being Exod. xvii., 15.

A large portion of the troops employed in reducing Jaffnapatam having been detached to besiege Negapatam, on the Coromandel Coast, the garrison chiefly consisted of Portuguese volunteers, although there was a considerable number of prisoners in the castle. The Portuguese volunteers and prisoners, together with some of the natives of the place, "not without the consent of Raja Singha," formed a plot to put to death all the Dutch officers in the castle during divine service. The guard was next to be attacked, by which means they hoped to make themselves masters of the castle. The conspiracy was divulged by a half-caste, and not long after, most of the conspirators having confessed their crimes, some were condemned to be hanged, others to be beheaded. The three chief conspirators were laid upon the wheel, and after each of them had received a stroke with an axe upon the neck and another on the breast, they were disembowled, and each had his heart placed upon his mouth. The priestly historian Baldaeus gives us a detailed drawing of this splendid example to the Heathen, of Christian civilisation in those days, of which he was a witness. A thanksgiving sermon was preached by him on this occasion "out of the book of Esther, ch. ix., 20-24." *Baldaeus, ch. xlv., p. 722.*

In 1659 Robert Knox and his father, sailing in the good ship Ann of the East India Company from Madras, were overtaken by a storm, and had to put in for repairs at Kottiar, in the Trincomalee district. They were captured and sent to the Emperor Raja Singha II., who had a strange fancy for detaining foreigners. Knox's father died in captivity at Bandarakoswatte in the Kurunegala district, and Knox himself escaped, after a captivity of 20 years borne with exemplary fortitude, to write his famous book "The Historical Relation of the Island of Ceylon." *1659 A.C.*

Unable, from his defective military resources, to direct any decisive measures against his enemies, the Dutch, in the lowlands, the Emperor's fury expended itself in savage excesses against his own subjects, whom he suspected of disaffection or of intercourse with the Dutch. At length, the limit of endurance being passed, the Kandyans attempted a revolt in 1664. At this time, the Emperor resided at Nillambé, fourteen miles to the south of Kandy, while the queen and the prince, his son, were at Kandy. The insurgents, having mastered the watch, marched to Nillambé in the dead of night, fell upon and captured the nobles in attendance at the palace, killing some and wounding others, but resolved to defer making an attempt to seize the Emperor till the morning had dawned. In the interval the Emperor, having been apprised of their design, fled to the mountains with a *Knox, pt. ii., ch. ii., p. 39.* *1664 A.C.*

small party of fifty attendants, who, on finding the road through the jungle impassable for horses, were obliged to force an elephant before them to break a way through the woods. The insurgents thereupon returned to Kandy, where they proclaimed the young prince, a lad of twelve, Emperor in the place of his father. The noble youth, preferring not to avail himself of the prospect thus opened for his ambition, fled with his aunt, the Emperor's sister, to his father—a course of conduct which so astonished the insurgents, that, throwing aside the plunder the majoity of them had collected, they dispersed in all directions whilst others more politic, seeing the ruin of the plot, killed their confederates and seized their goods. By this time one of the nobles had assembled a body of men, and declaring for the Emperor he killed all he caught, innocent and guilty alike. In this state of convulsion and internecine anarchy, the country remained for nearly a month, when the Emperor stepped in and stopped the slaughter which threatened to depopulate the country, by ordering the imprisonment of the remainder of the rebels until they could be brought to trial.

The constant strain on the nerves of the Emperor as a result of the prolonged wars he had had with the Portuguese and the Dutch, and the treacheries he had experienced at their hands, had begun to have a marked effect on him at this period of his reign. He had begun to suspect even his most faithful adherents of conspiracy against him. Even his own son, who, as we have seen, had behaved so magnanimously in respect of him, was put to death, lest his continued existence be the cause of a fresh outbreak.

During the period that followed their capture of Colombo—a period neither of war nor of absolute peace, but involving the expenditure of the one without purchasing the security ot the other,—the military policy of the Dutch had been purely precautionary and defensive. Ceylon was guarded as the most precious possession they had, every maritime possession was strengthened, and fortifications were either constructed or enlarged at Matara, Galle, Colombo, Negombo, Chilaw, and Jaffna. Batticaloa and Trincomalee were abandoned, not only from the want of troops to protect the east coast of the Island, but from the equally prudential consideration that cinnamon was only to be found on the west. There every preparation was made for defence; ammunition was largely stored, each garrison was stored for a year, and,

Valentyn, ch. xii., p. 148.

in addition to the command of the sea, the inland waters were rendered navigable at various points on the west coast between Bentota and Negombo, and boats were placed on the Kélani-ganga to maintain a communication by it with the confines of the Kandyan kingdom.

Thus prepared for sudden attack, trade at Galle and Colombo was carried on with confidence; and in addition to shipments for Europe, vessels from all parts of the East, from Mocha, Persia, India, and the Moluccas, were laden with the produce of Ceylon; but only at the government stores; trade in private hands, either in exports or imports, being rigidly prohibited.

The Emperors of Cotta, in order to procure supplies of cinnamon for the Portuguese, had organised the great establishment of the *Mahabadde*, under which the people of the Salagama caste were bound, in consideration of their location in villages, and the protection of their lands, to go into the forest and cut and deliver at certain prices a certain quantity of cinnamon properly peeled and ready for exportation. This system remained unaltered so long as Portugal held the maritime districts; and the Dutch, on obtaining possession of the ports, not only continued the collection in the hills by special permission from the Emperor of Kandy, but sought earnestly to encourage the growth of the spice in the lowlands surrounding their fortresses from Matara to Chilaw. In the latter district especially, the quality proved to be so fine, that in 1663 the cinnamon of Negombo was esteemed "the very best in the universe as well as the most abundant." But the woods in which it was found were exposed to perpetual incursions from the Kandyans, and the obstruction of the Chalias and peelers was a favourite device of the Sinhalese Emperors to annoy and harass the Dutch. Hence the cost of maintaining an army to guard the cinnamon country was so great as to render it doubtful whether the trade so conducted was worth the expense of its protection. Towards the close of their career, the company were compelled to form enclosed plantations of their own, within range of their fortresses; and here, so jealous and despotic was their policy, that the peeling of cinnamon, the selling or exporting of a single stick, except by servants of the government, or even the wilful injury of a cinnamon plant, although it be growing on one's private land, were crimes punishable with death.

Valentyn, ch. xv., p. 316.

Valentyn, ch. xiii., p. 166.

Tennent vol. ii., p. 52

Next to cinnamon, elephants were, in the estimation of the Dutch, the most important of their exports. The hunting grounds were the Wanny in the north, and the forests round Matara in the south of the Island. Those captured in the latter were shipped at Galle for the East coast of India, and those taken from the Wanny were embarked at Mannar for the west. But the trade in these animals does not appear to have been ever productive of any considerable gain, and latterly involved an annual loss. This was owing chiefly to the scarcity of tuskers. The headmen of the Matara district were under obligation to produce annually thirty-four elephants, of which four were to have tusks. At a later period (1707 A.C.) one of the instructions given by the Dutch Government to its dissaves was to bribe the Sinhalese subjects of the Emperor to drive down tusked elephants across the Kandyan frontiers towards the Dutch East India Company's hunting grounds.

Valentyn, ch. xv., p. 272.

Valentyn, ch. xv., p. 310.

The third article of export which the Dutch guarded with marked attention was arecanuts, which were shipped in large quantities to India, where, as in Ceylon, it is chewed by the inhabitants in conjunction with the leaf of the betel creeper. The story of the trade in this commodity is singularly illustrative of the policy adopted by the Dutch to crush their commercial rivals. As we have already mentioned, on the arrival of the Portuguese in Ceylon they found a large portion of the active trade of the Island in the hands of the energetic Moors, who not only maintained a brisk intercourse by sea with the ports on the opposite coast, but also, by virtue of their neutrality, were enabled to penetrate to the dominions of the Emperor, carrying up commodities from the low-country for the supply of the Kandyans. After they were freed from apprehension of the Moors as military allies of the Sinhalese, the Portuguese were utterly indifferent to their operations as traders. Not so the Dutch, with whom commerce was more an object than conquest, and not content with having secured to themselves a rigid monopoly of all the great branches of trade, they evinced a narrow-minded impatience of the humble industry carried on by the enterprising Moors.

Among the principal articles protected, were arecanuts, which, at the time when the Dutch took possession of Galle, the Moors were in the habit of collecting in the interior of the Island, to be exchanged on the coast for cotton cloths, to be sold at a profit to the Sinhalese. This traffic the Dutch resolved to stop, not from any design to profit by it themselves, but with the determination, even with the anticipation of a loss, to extinguish the commerce of the Moors, whose name is seldom introduced into their official documents without epithets of abhorrence. In order to crush their trade in arecanuts the Dutch conceived the plan of purchasing arrack on government account, sending it to Surat and Coromandel, and there exchanging it for cloth with which to undersell the Moors. But the scheme was not successful, and they adopted the bolder course of taking the arecanuts into their own hands as a government monopoly, and prohibiting the import of cloths by the Moors, except on condition that they disposed of them wholesale to the Burghers, by whom alone they were to be afterwards retailed to the Sinhalese. In order to further ensure their discouragement, the Dutch Government resorted to the singular expedient of imposing differential Custom duties upon goods according to the *religion of the importer*. The tax on cloth imported by Mohammedans was raised to double that imposed upon cloth imported by Christians, and other articles which Christians imported free, were taxed 5 per cent. if imported by Moors. With the exception of a limited number who were permitted to reside in Colombo as tailors, the Moors were prohibited from establishing themselves in the fortified towns. They were forbidden to hold land in the country. The celebration of their worship was interdicted. They were subject to a poll-tax. They were obliged to obtain a license, every year, to live in the villages. One-third of their property was forfeited to the government on their death. But notwithstanding all these devices, this patient and intelligent class, like the Jews of Europe, persevered in their pursuit, and continue to the present day, as they did throughout the entire period of Dutch ascendency, to engross a large share of the internal trade of the Island; bringing down to the coast the produce of the interior in exchange for manufactured articles, introduced from the Indian Continent.

Valentyn, ch. xii., p. 134.

Ib. ch. xiii., p. 137.

Ib. ch. xiii., p. 147.

Ib. ch. xiii., p. 166.

Ib. ch. xiii., p. 128.

At first, the arecanut monopoly, under the management of the Dutch Government, was comparatively unprofitable, but by degrees it became lucrative, and, in 1664, it was described as "extremely productive."

Ib. ch. xiv., p. 195.

The other productions which constituted the exports by the Dutch from the Island were sapan-wood *(Oldenlandia umbellata)* to Persia, choya-roots, a substitute for madder, collected at Mannar and other places on the north-west coast of the Island, for transmission to Surat. Cinnamon-oil, pepper, and cardamoms were sent to Amsterdam; timber and arrack to Batavia; and jaggery to Malabar and Coromandel. The cultivation of indigo was unsuccessfully attempted in the Seven Korles in 1646; and in 1664 silk was tried at Jaffnapatam, but with no satisfactory results. Very few of the articles which form at the present day the staple exports of Ceylon appear in the commercial reports of the Dutch governors. As to coffee, although the plant had existed from time immemorial on the Island (having probably been introduced from Mocha by the Arabs), the Sinhalese were ignorant of the use of its berries, and only used its leaves to flavour their curries, and its flowers to decorate their temples. It was not till nearly a century after the arrival of the Dutch that one of their governors attempted to cultivate it as a commercial speculation; but, at the point when success was demonstrable, the project was discountenanced by the Government of Holland, with a view to sustain the monopoly of Java; as the growth of pepper had been discouraged for some years before, to avoid interference with its collection in Malabar.

Valentyn, ch. xiii., p. 174.

Ib. ch. xii., p. 134.

Ib. ch. xiii. p. 173.

Ib. ch. xiv., p. 194.

It is said that "coffee succeeded very well in the western parts of the Island. It was superior in quality to the coffee of Java, and approached near to that of Arabia, whence the first coffee plants came." Cotton grew very well in the Wanny, but as the art of spinning it was unknown to any of the Dutch subjects (although it was, as we shall presently see, well known to those of the Emperor), the crop was neglected.

Mr. Burnand in his Memoir Asiat. Journ., vol. xii., p. 444.

Asiat. Journ., vol. xii., p. 445.

In addition to their ordinary trading operations, the Dutch had certain trading monopolies which served to realise revenue. They farmed the collection of salt at the leways and lagoons on both sides of the Island; the fishery of chank shells was conducted for them at a profit in the Gulf of Mannar; but the pearl fishery at Aripo, though perseveringly tended, was seldom productive of remunerative results. "It is a matter for reflection," says Baron Imhoff in 1740, "whether the company derives any advantage whatever from the fishery of pearls, and whether the whole affair is not rather *glitter than gold.*" Besides these sources of income there were other taxes, such as: a poll-tax payable in articles of various kinds, such as iron ore and jaggery; a land tax assessed on produce; a tithe on cocoanut gardens; a license for fishermen's boats, besides a fish tax on the capture; the proceeds of ferries; and an infinity of minor items collected by the Sinhalese headmen and their subordinates.

The intervention of Sinhalese officers was indispensable in a state of affairs, under which no European could live securely beyond the limits of the garrisoned towns. The policy of conciliating the chiefs of the country was therefore transmitted by each governor to his successor, with injunctions to encourage and caress the headmen; they were to be "nourished with hopes," and their attachment secured by gratifying their ambition for titles and rank. *Valentyn, ch. xv.* The "Instructions" extant in 1661, defining the functions and the powers of the Dissave of the Western Province, include every function of government, and show the absolute dependency of the Dutch on the personal influence of these exalted chiefs. To them was entrusted the charge of the *thombo* or registry of crown lands, their sale and management; *Ib. ch. xi., p. 151.* the assessment and levy of taxes; the superintendence of education; the decision of civil cases; the arrest and punishment of criminals; and, in short, the detailed executive of the civil government in peace, and the commissariat and clothing of the army in time of war.

Throughout all the records which the Dutch have left us of their policy in Ceylon, it is observable that no disinterested concern is manifested, and no measures directed for the furtherance of the welfare of the indigenous population; even where care is shown to have been bestowed upon the spread of education and religion, motives are apparent, either latent or avowed, which detract from the grace and generosity of the act. Thus schools were freely established, but the avowed object was to wean the Sinhalese from their allegiance *Ib. ch. xii., p. 130.* to their Emperor, and the better to impress them with the power and ascendency of Holland.

Churches were built because the extension of the Protestant faith was likely to counteract the influence of

Valentyn, p. 134. the Portuguese Roman Catholics, and the spread of Christianity to discourage the Moors and Mohammedan traders.

In the promotion of agriculture the interests of the government were identified with those of the peasants, and the time was eagerly expected, but never arrived, *Ib., p. 148* when the necessity would cease for the importation of rice for the troops from Batavia and the coast of Canara. But notwithstanding these partial efforts for the advancement of the people, successive governors were obliged to *Ib. ch. xii., p. 148.* admit the fact of habitual oppression by the headmen and Dutch officials, and to record their conviction that as the condition of the Sinhalese of the maritime regions *Report of Hendric Adrian Van Rheede, 1677; Valentyn, ch. xv., p. 273.* was no better under the Dutch than it had been under the Portuguese, so would they one day turn on them, as they had before shaken themselves free of their predecessors.

Nor was the discontent confined to the Sinhalese alone; disappointment was felt in Holland at the failure of those brilliant estimates which had been formed of the wealth to be drawn from Ceylon; the hopes of the emigrants who had rushed to the Island were crushed by the reality; and the company's officers and servants were loud in their complaints of the impossibility of subsisting on their salaries and perquisites. The former were absurdly small, the permission to trade formed the great supplementary inducement, and as trade was unproductive, discontent was inevitable. To this the *Valentyn ch. xv., p. 252.* condition of the governors formed an exception; for although their nominal income was but £30 per month *Bertolacci, p. 56.* besides rations and allowances, yet, according to Valentyn, such were the secret opportunities for personal gain, that in two or three years they became rich; a *Valentyn's Oud en Nieuw Oost-Indien, ch. i., p. 26.* circumstance observable also in the case of the commandants of Jaffna and Galle, provided they maintained a good private understanding with the governors of Colombo, and knew how to take and give.

In fact, from the commencement to the conclusion of the Dutch period in Ceylon, their possession of the maritime districts was a military tenure, and not a civil colonisation in the ordinary sense of the term. Strategically its occupation was of infinite moment for the defence of their factories on the Continent of India; and for the interests of their commerce, its position (intermediate between Java and Malabar) rendered it of value as an entrepôt. But all attempts to render it productive as a settlement were neutralised by the cost of its defence and establishments. For a series of years previous to its final abandonment, the excess of expenditure over income from all sources, involved an annual deficiency in the revenue, and Ceylon was compared to one of the costly tulips of Holland, which bore a fabulous nominal price, without any intrinsic value.

Valentyn's Oud en Nieuw Oost-Indien, ch. xv., p. 247.

Appendix to Lee's Ribeiro, p. 182.

To such lengths did misgovernment prevail, that Holland was at last threatened with the loss of the "jewel" altogether, by the treason of her own officers Vuyst, the Governor of Ceylon, in 1729, aspired to become sovereign of the Island, and visited with forfeiture, torture, and death every chief who opposed him. For this he was broken on the wheel at Batavia, and his body burned and scattered on the sea. Versluys, who was sent to supersede him, was removed for extortion and cruelty.

1672 A.C.

A new European power attempted to settle in Ceylon in 1672 A.C. On the outbreak of war between Louis XIV. and the United Provinces of the Netherlands a French squadron, composed of 13 or 14 ships, made its appearance at Trincomalee under the command of Admiral De la Haye, the Viceroy of Madagascar. It is said that the French were induced to turn there attention to the power and wealth accruing to the Dutch Republic from their Eastern possessions, by the representations of a man named Carron, who was once a Major in the Dutch service, connection with which he had severed as a result of having been slighted or suspected at Batavia, that Carron had become so alienated from the interests of Holland as to have made overtures to the court of France for the attack of Point de Galle, and that the safe arrival at this crisis of a Dutch East Indian fleet, valued at upwards of 16 millions of guilders, by offering an increased temptation to French ambition, at once determined their resolution. So vigorous a defence was offered, by the Dutch commander at Point de Galle, that the French Admiral judged it expedient to proceed to Trincomalee, which was easily taken, whereupon the Dutch in their panic abandoned the forts of Kottiar and Batticaloa. At Trincomalee the French contemplated forming a settlement, under a conviction of its importance in relation to their own establishments on the Coromandel Coast, and three envoys were despatched with presents to the Emperor Raja Singha II. These the Emperor received with the greatest honours and liberality, ordered the supply of the fleet with everything of which it was in need, and hoping that they might become embroiled with the Dutch, and thus assist him in ridding himself of that troublesome people, gave them permission to build a fort in the bay, assisted them in executing the work, and allowed them to enrol a number of his subjects for service in its defence. This fortification being nearly completed and garrisoned, the French Admiral set sail for the Coast of Coromandel, at the same time sending Monsieur Laisne de Nanclares de Lanerolle, a French nobleman of considerable consequence, with six other Frenchmen to Kandy to assure the king of his speedy return and of his unalterable devotion to his service. De La Haye, however, failed to fulfil his promise, inasmuch as he was met on his return by the Dutch under Admiral Van Goens, who took four of his ships and compelled the rest to take refuge in Surat. Van Goens, after this, made himself master of the fort which the French had erected at Trincomalee. "Meanwhile, Lanerolle, conducted himself with such singular indiscretion as to excite the indignation of the Emperor and bring great misfortunes upon himself and his suite. He persisted in making his entry into Kandy on horseback, and in that manner even passed the palace on his way to his lodgings, in direct opposition to the earnest remonstrances of the Emperor's courtiers, who represented that such a measure was not only unusual, but expressly forbidden by the Emperor. The Emperor, though highly incensed at this violation of his orders, yet seemed willing to overlook it in this instance; and the ambassador and his suite were provided three times a day from the royal kitchen with everything which they could need. After a short interval the ambassador was summoned to an audience of the Emperor. A magnificent procession was formed to conduct him by torchlight to the palace; but as he was kept in waiting for about two hours, according to the forms of the Sinhalese, the Frenchman regarded this as an intolerable affront, to which no consideration of policy or interest could induce him to submit. Some of the Sinhalese nobles, seeing him preparing to quit the palace, made a show of stopping him by some elephants which were stationed

Philalethes, (Rev. Mr. Bisset), ch. xv., pp. 127 & 128.

about the gate; but finding that he drew his sword and seemed determined to proceed, they let him pass, whilst his suite, surprised at his obstinacy, and alarmed for the consequences, left him and ran away."

"This outrageous insult on the grave decorum of his court, no sooner came to the ears of Raja Singha, than he ordered the ambassador and the other Frenchmen of his suite to be arrested, well flogged, and afterwards put in chains. The ambassador was kept in this situation for six months; but his companions were liberated upon an assurance that they had no participation in the indignity which had thus been wantonly offered to the sovereign."

Knox gives a detailed description of the life of Emperor Raja Singha II. and the state of the country over which he ruled. The following is his description of the Emperor:—"He is not tall, but very well set, nor of the clearest colour of their complexion, but somewhat of the blackest; great rolling eyes, turning them and looking every way, always moving them; a brisk, bold look, a great swelling belly, and very lively in his actions and behaviour; somewhat bald, not having much hair upon his head, and that grey, a large comely beard, with great whiskers; in conclusion, a very comely man. He bears his years well, being between seventy and eighty years of age; and though an old man, appears not to be like one either in countenance or action. His apparel is very strange and wonderful, not after his own country fashion, or any other, being made after his own invention. On his head he wears a cap with four corners like a Jesuit's, three tier high, and a feather standing upright before, like that in the head of a fore-horse in a team; a long band hanging down his back in Portuguese fashion; his doublet after so strange a shape that I cannot well describe it, the body of one and the sleeves of another; he wears long breeches to his ankles, shoes, and stockings. He doth not always keep to one fashion, but changes as his fancy leads him; but always when he comes abroad, his sword hangs by his side in a belt over his shoulder ....a gold hilt, and scabbard most of beaten gold. Commonly he holdeth in his hand a small cane, painted of divers colours, and towards the lower end set round about with such stones as he hath and pleaseth, with a head of gold."

t. ii., ch. i., pp. 64, 65.

The Emperor had a particular fancy for having his meals prepared for him by the fairest women in the

Ib. pt. ii., ch. i., p. 68.

land. Numbers of Sinhalese and Portuguese women were employed for this purpose in his kitchen.

As for his mode of taking his meals :—" He sits upon a stool before a small table, covered with a white cloth, all alone. He eats on a green plantain-leaf laid in a gold basin. There are twenty or thirty dishes prepared for him, which are brought into his dining room; and which of these dishes the king pleases to call for, a nobleman, appointed for that service, takes a portion of, and reaches in a ladle to the king's basin. This person also waits with a muffler about his mouth (lest he should breathe upon the food)."

Raja Singha II. had a very high code of morality, and he expected the same of his noblemen. "He allows not in his court whoredom or adultery; and many times, when he hears of the misdemeanours of his nobles in regard of women, he not only executes them, but severely punisheth the women, if known; and he hath so many spies, that there is but little done he knows not of. And often he gives command to expel all the women out of the city, not one to remain; but by little and little, when they think his wrath is appeased, they do creep in again."

Knox, pt. ii., ch. ii., pp. 72 & 73.

In the royal stables there were twelve or fourteen horses, mostly Persian; and some hundreds of elephants.

Ib. pt. ii., ch. ii., p. 81. Ib. pt. ii., ch. iv., p. 96.

With regard to religion, the Emperor was more or less indifferent, although he professed Buddhism. He was tolerant of Christianity.

Ib. pt. ii., ch. ii., p. 82.

With regard to the administration of the country, the Emperor was assisted by two chief officers called adigars. Subordinate to the adigars were the dissaves or governors of provinces who, together with the adigars, had to reside at the Emperor's court. The dissaves attended to the administration of their provinces through the agency of korle vidhans and their subordinate officers. All these officers had to perform both revenue and judicial duties. Cases that could not be satisfactorily settled by the korle vidhans were heard by the dissaves, and in case the latter failed to give satisfaction to the litigants there was an appeal to the adigars, who were the supreme judges in all cases except those involving capital punishment, where the Emperor was the sole judge.

Ib. pt. ii., ch. v.

With regard to the minerals and other commodities to be found within the Emperor's dominions, Knox says :—"Here is iron and crystal in great plenty. Saltpetre they can make. Brimstone, some say, is here, but the king will not have it discovered. Steel they can make of their iron. Ebony in great abundance, with choice of tall and large timber. Cardamoms, jaggery, rack, oil, black lead (plumbago), turmeric, salt, rice, betel-nuts (arecanuts), musk, wax, pepper; which last grows here very well, and might be in great plenty if it had a vend; and the peculiar commodity of the Island, cinnamon. Wild cattle and wild honey in great plenty in the woods; it lies in holes or hollow trees, free for any that will take the pains to get it. Elephant's teeth and cotton; of which there is good plenty growing in their own grounds, sufficient to make them good and strong cloth for their own use, and also to sell to the people of the Uplands, where cotton is not so plenty." With regard to precious stones, Knox says :—"In this Island there are several sorts of precious stones, which the king, for his part, has enough, and so careth not to have more discovery made. For in certain places where they are known to be, are sharp poles set up fixed in the ground, signifying that none, upon pain of being stuck and impaled upon those poles, presume so much as to go that way. Also there are certain rivers, out of which, it is generally reported, they do take rubies and sapphires for the king's use and cat's-eyes; and I have seen several pretty coloured stones, some as big as cherry stones, some as buttons, and transparent, but understood not what they were. Rubies and sapphires, I myself have seen here."

Knox, pt. ii., ch. vii., p. 61.

Ib. ch. i., pp. 60, 61.

It is interesting to note what the Dutch historian Baldaeus has to say with regard to the state of medical science in Ceylon during this period. He says: "For the rest, Ceylon is sufficiently provided with medicinal herbs, and they cure all their distempers with green herbs, in the use whereof their physicians are better versed, than many of our pretending surgeons, God Almighty having provided remedies suitable to the distempers of each country." As for the conduct of the Dutch towards the Emperor Raja Singha II. and the latter's disposition towards them, Knox says :—"The Dutch, knowing his proud spirit, make their advantage of it by flattering him with their ambassadors, telling him that they are His Majesty's humble subjects and servants, and that it is out of loyalty to him that they build forts and keep

Baldaeus, ch. l., p. 747.

Knox, pt. ii., ch. ii., p. 76.

watches round about his country, to prevent foreign nations and enemies from coming; and that as they are thus employed in His Majesty's service, so it is for sustenance, which they want, that occasioned their coming up into His Majesty's country; and thus by flattering him and ascribing to him high and honourable titles, which are things he greatly delights in, sometimes they prevail to have the country they have invaded, and he to have the honour. Yet at other times, on better consideration, he will not be flattered, but falls upon them unawares and does them great damage." The Dutch made frequent attempts, by embassies and presents, to lull the Emperor's suspicions, to soothe his animosity, and to conciliate his confidence. But these efforts were productive of little effect. He received their presents, and detained their ambassadors.

Philalethes, ch. xv., p. 125.

In the year 1679 the Dutch Governor Van Goens sent the Emperor a present of two black Persian horses, covered with green velvet trappings, reaching to the ground; and each horse led by two Malabar slaves. There were also sent ten beautiful falcons, each borne by a Malabar, dressed in white; six musk or civet cats, each in a separate basket borne by two slaves; six Tuticorin hens, in elegant cages, covered with green velvet; two Persian sheep whose tails weighed from 20 to 25 lbs. apiece; a case of Persian wine; a piece of sandal-wood weighing 200 lbs., covered with fine white calico and borne by slaves. There was also a letter for the Emperor in a silver receptacle, which was carried by a Dutch sergeant bare-headed, under a canopy resting on four pillars borne by four Sinhalese noblemen, whilst, at each corner, four large wax tapers were displayed in much state by four other noble Sinhalese. This magnificent present was escorted by a large party of Dutch and Sinhalese. At Ruanwella it was handed over to Raja Singha's people, who assembled in great numbers fully armed; and when part of the Dutch, after having executed their mission, had crossed the river, the Emperor's troops attacked those that were left behind, killing a lieutenant and two soldiers, and compelling the rest to seek safety by swimming to the other side. This clearly shows the terms of amity which at that time subsisted between the Dutch and the Sinhalese; and the contempt in which the former were held by the latter, and which neither their presents nor their flattery could remove.

Robert Knox escaped from Kandy after twenty years of captivity in 1679. At the time of his escape there were not less than fifty Dutch prisoners in the hands of Raja Singha II., some of whom were Dutch ambassadors. Of these latter, Knox gives us a description of five, and the names of two, viz., Hendrick Draak and John Baptista. The object of the Emperor in detaining them was to make them naturalised subjects of his and secure their services for himself. With this object in view, they were treated very well, and facilities afforded them to get married to Sinhalese women. There were also some English prisoners whose liberation Sir Edward Winter had in vain solicited by a mission from Madras in 1664. In the year 1680, Governor Lourens Van Pyl endeavoured to propitiate the Emperor by a present of two lions, three tigers, twelve musk cats, all of which were enclosed in beautiful cages, covered with green velvet. There were also two black Persian horses covered with the same, twenty falcons borne by Malabars, with a letter carried by the ambassador himself in a silver dish under a gorgeous canopy, which was borne by four Sinhalese nobles bare-headed. In this procession there was an ambassador from the King of Persia, who travelled in a singular car, drawn by two white oxen, covered with white calico.

1679 A.C. Knox, pt. iv, ch. xiii., pp. 365-370.

Valentyn, ch. xiv., p. 200.

The same year, the fortress of Malwana near Colombo was attacked by the Emperor at the head of 30,000 men, but owing to the defection of Thennekon, one of his generals, who went over to the Hollanders with part of the troops, he was compelled to raise the siege.

1680 A.C.

Of the people of this Island during this period, Baldaeus says: "The Cingalese are naturally active and ingenious, and good workmen in gold, silver, ivory, ebony, iron-works, etc.; arms inland with silver; eloquent, nimble, courageous, fit for warlike exploits; sober and watchful. They march one single man after another, by reason of the many narrow lanes in this country; their arms are a half-pike; their drums are small, but make a great noise, which may be heard at three leagues distance in the mountains; they are best in the pursuit of a routed enemy. Since they have conversed so much with the Portuguese and other European nations, they are grown so cunning that they must not be too much trusted, nor despised."........."The Cingalese are in shape and manners not unlike the Malabars, with long hanging ears, but not so black. The dress of the men is a

Baldaeus, ch. xlix., pp. 744 & 745.

vest, called, *Ropillo*, of woollen or linen cloth; their undergarment is a piece of linen wrapped about the middle, and drawn through both their legs like a pair of breeches. On their heads they wear a kind of red caps, such as we call rock-caps *(Jajalat-Toppi)*, which they look upon as a singular ornament; and in their ears rings and precious stones. The hilts of their swords or scimitars are commonly of silver, ivory, or gold with flaming blades."

It is interesting to note from the above that the Sinhalese *men* wore earrings, as did most *men* of the Aryan branch of the human race during this period of the world's history.

Writing about the inhabitants of Jaffnapatam, which was a Dutch settlement, Baldaeus says: "Besides the artisans and handicraftsmen, whereof there is great plenty in Jaffnapatam, they have certain persons who apply themselves to the law; and in the high court of justice, composed of Hollanders and Indians, were set always (besides the Modeliars) a certain person well versed in the laws and constitutions of his native country. They have also their advocates, who make very long speeches in their pleadings."

Raja Singha II. died after a reign of fifty-five years on the 6th of December, 1687, and was succeeded by his son Mahastanne, who, on ascending the throne, took the the name of **Wimala Dharma Suriya II.**

Wimala Dharma II., 1687-1706 A.C.

In accordance with the advice given him by his father while on his death-bed, Wimala Dharma, who was by nature a religious and unambitious man, lived at peace with the Dutch.* His reign of ninteen years was marked, in consequence, by the occurrence of no important political event. The monarch endeavoured to restore the national religion to its pristine splendour, and in this respect he was assisted by the Dutch, who, within their territories, were using every means in their power to stamp out the Roman Catholic religion, and thought this to be an additional means

Journal of R.A.S. (C.B.) vol. xi., No. 38, "The Dutch in Ceylon," pp. 85-114, also p. 120.

* Although no hostilities took place between the two powers, negociations were carried on throughout his reign with a view to securing for the Emperor's subjects the right to trade freely at the ports of Calpentyn, Batticaloa, and Kottiar, until at length in 1705 the Dutch agreed to buy all the arecanuts produced within the Emperor's dominions at the highest price they could be sold for in India, viz., 3 rixdollars per amunam. In the course of these negociations, whenever the Sinhalese Ambassadors arrived at Colombo guns were fired in their honour.

whereby they might attain that end. With their co-operation Wimala Dharma despatched an embassy to Siam requesting that a number of priests of the Upasampada (highest) order might be sent to Ceylon to revive the neglected rites and ordinances of Buddhism. Accordingly the High-priest Santana arrived, with thirty-three other priests, at Kandy, and the remainder of his reign was devoted by the sovereign to establishing the national religion on a firm foundation. It is recorded that this king made a pilgrimage *on foot* to the top of Adam's Peak and held a great feast, which lasted for seven days, at the sacred shrine, and that "he made an end of this great feast by covering with a large silver umbrella the footprint which the great Sage had left on the top of the mountain."

Mahawansa, ch. 97, p. 334.

He was succeeded by his son **Siri Vira-Parakrama Narendra Singha,** also called Koondasála, after the name of a suburb he built for the city of Kandy. He was 17 years old when he ascended the throne. *Mahawansa* tells us that "he was a temple of wisdom and valour and virtue." He appears to have been a very pious monarch, who, like his father, lived at peace with the Dutch and devoted himself to the furtherance of literature and religion. It is recorded that he made two pilgrimages in great state to worship at the dagoba at Mahiyangana and held great feasts and made great offerings there, that he also made pilgrimages to Anuradhapura and Adam's Peak, and that he had a fine two-storied building—erected at Kandy for the Toot-relic, "the doors whereof were ornamented with exquisite workmanship of divers kinds, and the plaster work shone with exceeding brightness as a silver hill. The roof thereof was ornamented. On the walls of the two enclosures thereof he caused to be painted with exquisite art (the deeds of) thirty-two Jatakas."

Siri Vira-Parákrama Narendra Singha, 1706-1742 A.C.

Mahawansa, ch. 97, p. 336.

The king conferred special favours on a novitiate priest named Saranankara, who was a poet, preacher, controversialist, and teacher of great renown. At the instance of the king, this priest composed the religious book named *Sárattha Sangaha,* consisting of 11,000 ganthas, and translated the *Mahá Bodhivansa* and the *Bhesajja Manjusá,* a medical work, into Sinhalese. Alwis gives us a sample paragraph from the *Sárattha Sangaha* relating to the Sinhalese computation of time, which he translates as follows:—"The time occupied in winking the eye is called 'sukshama,' a *second;* equal

Mahawansa, ch. 97, p. 337.

Alwis' Sidat Sagara, Intro., p. 224.

to the time necessary for the utterance of a *lagu*, or short letter; 18 seconds make a 'kashti,' or *minute;* 36 minutes make an *hour;* two hours one '*mohota*'; 30 mohotas make a day and night; 15 days make a '*paksha*'; two pakshas make one month; two months a season. From the month of Bak (11th April) commence the seasons Wisanti (spring), Greeshma (hot), Warsha (rainy), Sarath (autumn), Hima (dewy), and Sisira (cold), at the rate of two months for each."

In addition to the above mentioned books the monarch had the following compiled :—The *Rajaratnacara*, a history of Ceylon, and the *Warayoga-sare*, a medical work.

Following the example of his father, King Narendra Singha left the Dutch in quiet enjoyment of the maritime districts during his long reign of thirty-two years. He married a Princess of Madura, but had no issue.

In A.C. 1721, on hearing of the death of the Empress, Rumph, the Dutch Governor, sent an embassy to the Kandyan court to offer the condolence of the Dutch East India Company and of himself and his council on the mournful event. Cornelius Takel, the ambassador employed on this occasion, wrote a circumstantial account of his embassy which is preserved in Valentyn. He had arrayed himself and suite in mourning, as most appropriate to the occasion. When they had arrived at their lodgings, at a short distance from the Emperor's palace, two nobles were sent to conduct them to the audience. These messengers were dressed in white, and informed Takel that old times having passed away, and a new year commenced, it would be hardly suitable at such a season for His Excellency to appear before His Majesty in the garb of woe; and as he had ordered all his courtiers to put off their mourning, it would be proper for him to do the same, with which he complied. When the ambassador, attended by the first adigar and different officers of the court, had come in front of the hall of audience, four curtains were thrown open, and the Emperor was seen seated on his throne. The ambassador took off his cap and knelt. Thereupon the Emperor began by enquiring after the health of the Dutch Governor and council, and the treatment Takel had experienced on his journey through his dominions. The ambassador then made formal inquiries after His Majesty's health, and represented the ardent desire of the Dutch Government to cultivate his friendship and promote his interest. The Emperor expressed his great satisfaction at these proofs of respect from his faithful Hollanders, for whom he professed the most exaggerated regard, so long as the sun and moon endured. The ambassador then proceeded to state the principal object of his mission, which was to present to His Majesty the condolence of his government on account of the decease of his "late high-born, excellent, and all-accomplished queen," and in their name be implored the Almighty to comfort His Majesty in his affliction, and by other rich blessings to compensate his calamitous loss. They prayed also, that he might for a long course of years be preserved in perfect and permanent health upon his golden throne, and that his good subjects, the faithful and loyal Dutch, might long experience the favour and protection of His Majesty.

Some of the Dutch governors exhibited a greater regard for justice than others, thus the administration of Rump was distinguished by equal humanity and ability during the seven years it continued, but even he could not always repress the exactions of his inferior Dutch officials; and it is certain that long before the arrival of the British the Sinhalese had anxiously sighed for an opportunity to shake off the galling yoke. The death of this governor was precipitated by an insurrection of the slaves at Colombo, and the murder of some of the Europeans. One of his successors, Vuyst, as we have already noted, attempted, in 1729, to render himself an independent prince, and, in fur- *1729 A.C.* therance of that object, resorted to the most atrocious cruelties, endeavouring to extort confessions, by torture, of crimes which had never entered into the thoughts of his victims, and rid himself by this means of all, who from their wealth and influence were most capable of opposing his pretensions. At length, being made prisoner, Vuyst was sent to Batavia, where he was sentenced to be broken alive upon the wheel, and his body to be quartered and burnt, and the ashes to be thrown into the sea. His successor, Versluys, so far from being warned by his example and fate, raised the price of rice to such a pitch as to cause a famine, for the gratification of his avarice.* A new governor,

* An interesting account of an embassy sent to King Narendra Singha by Versluys in 1731, as contained in the Diary of Lewis de Saram, Maha Mudaliyar, and translated into English by Mr. Paul Pieris, is to be found in Journal No. 62, vol. 22, of the R.A.S. (C.B.).

Doemburg, was finally sent in his place; but to such a pitch of audacity had the officers in the service of the republic attained, that Versluys absolutely refused to resign possession of his charge, and ventured so far as to fire on the company's vessels in the ports. At length, however, he was obliged to yield to superior force and sent under arrest to Batavia. Although the Dutch governors in Ceylon were dependent, in general matters of policy, upon the superior government at Batavia, yet such governors appear to have enjoyed the privilege of having direct communication with the Government of Holland, which privilege appears to have had the pernicious tendency of tempting them to withdraw from the obedience due to the company and aim at becoming absolute princes. Galle, styled "a commandery," was considered a post both of honour and profit, and the commanders, from the opportunities offered them at this, the chief seat of the foreign trade of the Island, of gaining a practical insight into the operations of Eastern commerce, were usually selected to fill the vacancies in the chief government at Colombo. With the arrival in 1736 of the Dutch Governor, Baron Van Imhoff, returned good government, and with it the first gleam of prosperity in the Dutch settlements. Hitherto cinnamon had been the only profitable article of commerce, but now the cultivation of pepper, cardamoms, and coffee was successfully introduced.*

The Emperor Narendra Singha died in 1742 A.C., and was succeeded by his brother-in-law Sri Vijaya Raja Singha.

Sri Vijaya Raja Singha, 1742-1748 A.C.

Sri Vijaya Raja Singha was a man of considerable culture and devoted his attention almost entirely to the furtherance of the national religion. He procured for himself a bride from the royal family of Madura. The Empress was not long before she embraced the religion of her husband, and assisted him whole-heartedly in his efforts to resuscitate Buddhism. It is recorded that she caused religious books to be written,

---

"The Dutch in Ceylon" Journal of R.A.S., (C.B.) vol. xi., No. 38., pp. 120-129.

* In 1736, prior to the arrival of Imhoff as Governor, the Dutch had experienced great difficulties with the Chalias of Bellitota, Kosgoda, and Madampe. These rebelled against their authority and were joined by the inhabitants of Matara, Galle, Siyane Korle, Gangaboda Pattu, Kandeboda Pattu, and later by those of Hapitigam, Alutkuru, Salpity, Rygam, Pasdun and Hewegam Korles.

as did the Emperor. The latter appears to have entertained as high a regard for the priest Saranankara as did his predecessor on the throne, and to have caused him to write a commentary on the four **Bhánavāras* of the Tripitaka in Sinhalese. The event of this reign is said to have been the splendid feast held by the Emperor in honour of the Tooth-relic, when it was exposed to the gaze of multitudes of people, as he adorned in his gorgeous regal apparel, held it out before them "in his lotus-hand." The Emperor is said to have caused life-sized images of Buddha in sleeping, standing, and sitting postures to be cut in the rock caves in various parts of the Island, and particularly in the Aluvihare and other caves in the Matale district.

Mahawansa, ch. 98, pp. 340 and 341.

Having heard that Buddhism in its purest form was taught and practiced in Ayodhya in Siam, the Emperor sent an embassy thither with a letter and present, with a view to obtaining priests and books from that country.

The Emperor was very fond of listening to learned priests propounding the Buddhist scriptures. Accordingly he had a special hall built attached to his palace in Kandy for the purpose. Furthermore, he caused preaching halls and lodging places for priests to be built in divers places suited for the assembling of people in his desire to promote the welfare of his people.

He is said to have made pilgrimages to Adam's Peak, Anuradhapura, and Mahiyangana (Alutnuwera in the Bintenne district). He also caused stone bridges to be constructed for the convenience of travellers. He had ordered a magnificent casket to be made for the Tooth-relic, but died before its completion. He died in 1748 A.C., and was succeeded by his brother-in-law Kirti Siri Raja Singha.

Kirti Siri Raja Singha, 1748-1778.

Kirti Siri Raja Singha devoted the first sixteen years of his reign to the advancement of literature and religion.

We have already seen that the *Mahawansa*, from B.C. 543 to about A.D. 452, had been written by the priest Mahanaama during the reign of King Datusena.

---

* A Bhanavara = 250 verses of 32 syllables each.

In the reign of Parakrama Bahu of Dambadeniya, the priest Dharmakirtti continued the history till about the year 1262 A.C. It was again continued till about the year 1295 A.C. in the reign of Pandita Parakrama Bahu IV. of Kurunegala. During this reign the priest Tibbotuwawa, by order of the Emperor, made a comparison of the *Mahawansa* as it existed in Ceylon with that which had been procured from Siam, and continued it down to the year 1758 A.C.

Mahawansa, ch. 99, vv. 78-83.

Further, the Emperor caused copies to be made of the *Digha Nikaya* and the *Sanyutta Nikaya* and paid the writers thereof in money. And when others, whether priests or householders, made copies of books decently and brought them before him he was well pleased therewith, and showed them much favour by giving them gifts of money and the like. The example of the Emperor in this respect was closely followed by his two brothers who occupied the office of sub-kings, and on whom the Emperor bestowed liberally equipages and all other things that were necessary for kings.

Ib. vv. 31-35.

Ib. ch. 99., v. 80.

In 1750, the Emperor, with the assistance of the Dutch, despatched an embassy with presents and a letter to King Dhammika of Siam, requesting the latter to send some learned priests for the purpose of advancing Buddhism in Lanka. Accordingly there arrived in Lanka a learned High-priest, named Upali, with over ten. other priests, bringing with them books of *Dhamma* and the *Vinaya*, such as were not to be found in Ceylon. They were received with great ceremony and honour by the Emperor, and ere long the rite of ordination was conferred, amid great rejoicing, on the principal Samaneras of Ceylon. The Siamese priests were given the Malwatta Vihara (Puspharma) to reside in.* Another chapter of priests, together with the High-priests Maha Visuddhácariya and Varananamuni, was sent over to Ceylon during this reign by the King of Siam, and hundreds of Sinhalese underwent the Upasampada ordination.

Ib. ch. 100., vv. 61-72.

Ib. ch. 100, vv. 118-121.

Not only did the Emperor cause the Siamese priests to impart the doctrines of Buddha to the priests in Ceylon, but he availed himself to the fullest extent

* For further particulars regarding this embassy the reader is referred to the Translation of Mr. P. E. Pieris, as contained in the Journal of R.A.S. (C.B.), vol. 18, No. 54.

of their learning. Among the subjects he caused them to expound for his benefit was "the ten-fold virtues of kings," which consist of charity, moral conduct, liberality, freedom from anger, freedom from cruelty, patience, rectitude, meekness, self-restraint, and freedom from revenge.

The Emperor is said to have made arrangements for a pilgrimage to be made by the Siamese priests to the sixteen sacred shrines of Ceylon, viz., Mahiyangana, Nagadipa, Kelaniya, Adam's Peak, Divágubá, Dighavápi, Mutiyangana, Tissa Maha Vihára, the Bó-tree, Mirisavetiya, Ruanweli, Thuparama, Abhayagiri, Jetavana, Sela Chetiya, and Kataragama.

In recognition of the service done by the King of Siam towards the furtherance of religion in Ceylon, the Emperor Kirti Siri Raja Singha sent him a likeness of the Tooth-relic, an image of Buddha cut out of a very precious stone, which is still to be seen in one of the temples of Siam, and a conch-shell with the whorls to the right.

During this reign was built the Raja Maha Vihara (Gangarama) at Kandy; and the Hindus who had been placed in charge of Buddha's footprint at the top of Adam's Peak by Raja Singha I. were expelled and Buddhist priests placed in their stead.

We have already noticed that a jewelled casket for the Tooth-relic was being made at the time Emperor Siri Vijaya Raja Singha died. During this reign, the Emperor "caused a large and excellent diamond of great value to be set on the top of that beautiful gem-coloured casket made out of 2,000 *suvannas* (= gold coins about the weight of a copper cent) with seven *nikkhas* added thereto. And the ruler of men, with the object of gaining merit, caused the casket to be set with 168 diamonds of great brilliance and value, 171 beautiful topazes, 585 blue sapphires, 4,880 rubies, and 778 pearls. And, so that he might enclose this costly casket therein, he caused two other caskets to be made, and splendid precious stones to be set thereon. And the Emperor caused the large casket to be gilded that the famous Emperor Vimala Dhamma Suriya had made. And the lord of the land then held a great feast, and placed the Tooth-relic of the Sage in the self-same caskets."

Many other religious benefactions did the Emperor Kirti Siri Raja Singha perform, for which the reader is referred to the *Mahawansa*, chapter 100.

The learned Sinhalese priest Saranankara (Welliwitta) was during this reign raised to the office of Sangha Raja (Archbishop). He translated the *Milindapprasne* from Pali into Sinhalese.

As for other literary productions during this reign, we find that in 1768 a cultured Sinhalese chieftain in the Southern Province, named Dissanayake Mudaliyar, who was a great linguist, produced the well-known *Makaraddaja* and several other miscellaneous pieces of great beauty. He also translated into Sinhalese verse the *Wallimatákatáwa*, a Tamil tale.

A poet of Tangalle, who held the office of lekam, or writer,—a man who was confessedly born a poet—produced the *Kawmini Kondala*, the *Kindura Jataka*, and *Wiogaratnamála*, of which the first two works are poetical versions of Buddha's incarnations, and the third an original poem inspired by an attachment to a woman. Of this last work Alwis says: "Addicted to dissipation and gambling, and engaged at cards night after night, he seldom rose from his chair without composing a dozen stanzas of his *Wiogaratnamála*. It is indeed not a little surprising that he should thus have produced an admirable poem, when it is stated that the greater part of it was composed during moments snatched from the time devoted to cards, in which he seldom lost. The work breathes such tender sentiments as one can hardly believe were entertained by a libertine such as the poet is represented to have been."

In 1770 an inhabitant of Katuwana in Matara produced the well-known work titled *Kaw-minimaldama*. He also composed three little poems in Sanscrit, Pali, and Sinhalese and presented them to the Dutch Governor, who showed the poet his pleasure by conferring the rank of Muhandiram on him.

After the Dutch had succeeded in rendering their fortifications tolerably complete, they began to push their posts farther and farther into the interior of the Island, and to seize upon every spot which appeared adapted for their purpose. They also increased their demands upon the Emperor for the protection they afforded him as guardians of his coasts. Exasperated by the oppressions of the Dutch, who kept destroying the plantations of his subjects and butchering those that offered any opposition, the Emperor, in 1761, fell suddenly upon the Dutch settlements and committed great devastation. A long course of hostilities followed, without any lasting advantage to either party. Peace was never long-continued or secure between the governor on the coast and the Emperor on the hills.

The renewed incursions of the Dutch naturally led to a commencement of hostilities by the Emperor. He was twice driven from his capital (Kandy), and forced to seek refuge in the mountainous district of Digliggy (Hangurankete), which was supposed to be the most impenetrable in his kingdom.

Encouraged by the dissensions among the Kandyan chiefs, the Dutch took the field in 1763 with an army of 8,000 men, composed of Europeans, Sepoys, and Malays, and made themselves masters of Kandy and the adjoining districts of Matale, Doombera and Walapane. With regard to the seizure of Kandy by the Dutch on this occasion, the *Mahawansa* says that they, "like a fierce multitude of devils, entered the city and destroyed all the religious books and the sacred things." For about nine months the Dutch maintained a garrison at Kandy; but in consequence of the vigilant hostility of the Sinhalese, who intercepted their convoys and communications from the sea-coast, they were obliged to abandon their position and retreat to Colombo. After having suffered extreme privations, their provisions being nearly exhausted, and all communication with their settlements on the coast cut off for three months, the officer on whom the command had devolved, (Major Frankena,) a brave and experienced soldier, called a council of war, in which it was finally resolved, after much discussion, to endeavour to force their way to Colombo, as the only means of saving the wreck of the army from certain death. A retreat was forthwith commenced, during which the sick, and those who were unable to keep up with the main body of the troops, were killed by the Sinhalese. At Sitawaka (Avisawella), only two days' march from Colombo, 400 Dutchmen were overpowered and put to death. Few survivors at length reached Colombo, exhausted with hunger and fatigue.

The war was continued by a new governor, (Van Eck), who succeeded in repulsing the Sinhalese;

and, by harassing and forcing them into the mountains and forests, prevented them from cultivating their fields for some time. The Kandyan dissaves, it is alleged, were on the point of delivering up the Emperor, upon condition that each should be left an independent *6176 A.C.* sovereign in his own province, when Governor Van Eck died. On the arrival of his successor, Governor Falck, negotiations with the Emperor were set on foot with success, and a peace was concluded on the 14th February, 1766, by a treaty of which, although it was very favourable to the Dutch, they refused to fulfil some of the articles.

Governor Falck considered it would be dangerous, if not impracticable, at that time to occupy the interior of the Island, the productions of which could be purchased cheaper from the Kandyans themselves, than collected by the Dutch Government, even when in possession of the country.

Preface to the Miscellaneous Works of Hugh Boyd. In the wars of the Dutch with the Sinhalese, it is alleged that the former treated their prisoners, of whatever rank or age, with the harshest rigour, and heaped upon them every mark of degradation which the most ingenious cruelty could furnish, or the most brutal barbarity inflict. The rapacity of the Dutch gave birth to a succession of petty wars, in which, though they were generally successful, the Sinhalese were not subdued. Even in times of peace, it does not appear that there was ever much intercourse between the subjects of the two powers. The recollection of the grasping policy of the Portuguese, and the selfish conduct of the Dutch, induced the Emperors of Kandy to forbid their subjects to have any intercourse with Europeans of whatever nation; and they instructed them to hold in eternal abhorrence a race of people which, as appeared to them, no ties of honour could bind, and against whose teachery no prudence could guard.

1763 A.C. During the year 1763, the Madras Government had despatched a Mr. Pybus as ambassador to Emperor Kirti Siri Raja Singha, with instructions to assure him of the friendship of the English, then the most potent European power in the East, and to offer him ample succours to support a war with the Dutch. His reception is said to have been as favourable as could be expected, the ministers having declared that they would be happy to enter into terms of mutual friendship and alliance with the English Government. To the bitter disappointment of the Sinhalese monarch the negotiations were not followed up by the Madras Government, and the Sinhalese monarch was left to carry on a war single-handed with the Dutch, as we have seen above.

Emperor Kirti Siri Raja Singha died in 1778, and was succeeded by his brother **Siri Rajadi Raja Singha.**

Siri Rajadi Raja Singha, 1778-1798 A.C.

Hostilities having been declared between Holland and England, during the war of independence of the United States of America, Lord Macartney, Governor of Madras, resolved to seize the Dutch settlements in Ceylon.

Accordingly Admiral Huges, after overcoming the feeble resistance offered by the Dutch garrison, captured Trincomalee in 1782. The troops employed on this occasion were commanded by Sir Hector Munro. A Mr. Boyd, who had been deputed by Lord Macartney to the court of Kandy, left Trincomalee soon after it surrendered, and proceeded to Kandy. The object of Boyd's mission was to do away with the odium which had, from various causes, been affixed to the character of the English, and also to announce to the Emperor that the British were at war with his implacable enemy, the Dutch, and to endeavour to obtain his friendly disposition, if not his active aid, in the contemplated attack by the British on the Dutch territories in Ceylon. Remembering the experience of his predecessor in respect of the British, the Emperor showed a decided reluctance to have any thing to do with them, and for a time interdicted any communication between his subjects and the Britishers at Trincomalee.

The Emperor's ministers, however, informed Boyd, that they were extremely happy to receive the friendly offers of the Madras Government, and that it was their anxious desire to establish such a connection with the British as he had proposed; but, in order to render the alliance sufficiently fair and respectable in the eyes of the Emperor, it was necessary to obtain the approval of the King of Great Britain. Boyd having explained to the ministers the inconvenience and uselessness of such a proceeding, the latter related to Boyd their experience of Phybus' mission in 1763 and complained of its having had no practical result in their favour. They stated that Phybus had been deputed to the court of Kandy with offers of friendship, which had been accepted by them;

but that on his return to Madras, the business, instead of being proceeded with effectually, as they expected, seemed to have been entirely dropped, and from that time to this they had not heard a syllable on the subject; that this departure from a negotiation so favourably begun had greatly surprised and disappointed them, especially as they were on the eve of a rupture with the Dutch; that when that rupture took place, they were obliged to support the war themselves without any assistance or even communication from Madras; but that now, when a rupture had taken place between the Dutch and the British, the communication was renewed;—that these circumstances could not but induce them to think that the attention of the British to their interest was subservient to the interest of the British; that although the Emperor was glad to have received such offers of friendship, he was resolved that any proposal from the British should come to him direct from the King of England.

Boyd's embassy, although unsuccessful in negotiating a treaty of alliance with the Emperor, had the good effect of procuring a supply of provisions for the British troops at Trincomalee.

Admiral Huges returned to Madras to refit the garrison at Trincomalee, being, in the meantime, reinforced with 200 men sent from the Coromandel Coast, under the convoy of two ships of war. Before Admiral Huges was able to return to Ceylon, the French Admiral Suffrein dashed into the harbour of Trincomalee, summoned the fort, and, in order to procure a capitulation before the British fleet should arrive, offered the most honourable terms. The garrison surrendered on the 31st August; and on the 2nd September Admiral Huges, having on board a new commander with a body of troops, arrived, and discovered the French colours flying in the fort. Thus the attempts of the British to gain a footing in Ceylon were at this time frustrated.

By the treaty of peace concluded between the Emperor Kirti Siri Raja Singha and the Dutch in 1766 it was stipulated that the Kandyans might obtain salt at the Dutch salt-pans at prime cost; in return the Emperor agreed to permit the Dutch to cut cinnamon within his dominion, or to cause it to be cut and delivered to them at fixed prices.

1791 A.C. In 1791 the Dutch Governor Van der Graaff, being informed of hostile preparations being made by the

Kandyans, prohibited the supply of salt for their use, thinking that, by depriving them of so essential a necessary of life, he would reduce them to the utmost distress. As a substitute for salt, it is alleged, the Kandyans had recourse to a species of potash, which proving unwholesome, they were on the point of submitting to any conditions, when the superior Government of Batavia interdicted this barbarous mode of conducting hostilities, and recommended the adoption of conciliatory measures.

As a consequence of an alliance entered into by the Emperor with the French with the object of expelling the Dutch from the Island, every preparation was made by the Dutch for war, and hostilities were about to commence in the year 1792, when the Government of Batavia disapproved of the conduct of the local Dutch Governor. About this time, it is alleged that the Emperor assumed a haughty tone towards the Dutch ; so much so that the latter hesitated to send the annual embassy to Kandy, to solicit permission from the Emperor to cut cinnamon within his territories. In this dilemma, Governor Van der Graaff directed a dissave of the Dutch territory to communicate with Kandy, for the purpose of ascertaining whether, if no embassy was sent from the maritime provinces, the Emperor would allow cinnamon to be peeled within his territories. The reply received from the court of Kandy was to the effect that the peeling of cinnamon within the Emperor's dominion was usually allowed when the Dutch sent an ambassador to Kandy, and craved permission to do so ; and that unless an accredited agent of that rank was commissioned to Kandy, no permission to cut cinnamon would be granted. The Dutch were, for various reasons, unwilling to send an ambassador to Kandy at this time. They were afraid that the Emperor might decline to comply with their request. Besides, embassies were expensive and degrading under any circumstances, but more particularly so, as the Kandyan court insisted upon the ceremony of prostration being performed by their ambassadors. No embassay was sent to Kandy on this occasion.

Trincomalee, regained by the Dutch in the peace of 1783, was again attacked in 1795, when the union of Holland with the French Republic, and its consequent hostility with Great Britain, induced the Government of Fort St. George to prepare a more effectual means of reducing the Dutch settlements in Ceylon. General

Stewart was therefore sent with a considerable force, with which he landed at a distance of about two miles from the fort. The climate and the nature of the ground occasioned much fatigue and some loss. During the siege a sally was made by the Malays in the Dutch service, who, contriving to steal unperceived into one of the batteries, spiked the guns, and killed several artillerymen before they were repulsed and driven back into the fort. The operations, however, being conducted with great vigour, the fortress was surrendered by the Dutch commander, just as the invaders were on the point of storming it. This was the only real resistance made by the Hollanders to the British troops.

After refreshing his wearied forces at Trincomalee, General Stewart advanced round the north of the island of Jaffna, which was surrendered by its commander on the first summons.

On the 12th February, 1796, Col. Stewart landed a body of troops from a fleet that was at anchor off Negombo and marched towards Colombo. The passage of the Kelani-ganga was disputed by a corps of Malays led by a Frenchman, but they were repulsed with little loss on the side of the British. Colombo made no resistance, and capitulated on the 15th. Thus fell, ingloriously, the Dutch power in Ceylon, Galle and other fortresses having speedily followed the example of Colombo. Previously to the arrival of the British troops on the west coast of Ceylon, the garrison of Colombo had been considerably weakened by the loss of the Swiss regiment of De Meuron, a corps of mercenaries which had for a long time formed a part of it. The term of its agreement with the Dutch having expired, and Col. De Meuron having transferred its services to the British Government in India, the military force of the Dutch was consequently, so far reduced; but the chief cause of the hasty surrender of Colombo is alleged to have been a mutinous spirit which prevailed among the Dutch troops. The state of total insubordination of the garrison, the violence of a Jacobin party, and the fear of an internal massacre, induced the governor to enter with promptitude into a treaty with the British.

Speaking of the Dutch during this period, Pridham says: "Divided into parties, disunited and mutinous, they filled the different posts which they possessed with debauchery, conspiracies, and rebellion, so as to have rendered it futile for their commanders, even if they had had the energy and courage to make an effectual resistance."

The following is the list of Dutch governors of the maritime district of Ceylon, with the dates of their appointments, from the date of their occupation, March, 1640, till February, 1796:—

AT GALLE:—Willem Jacobson Coster, 1640; Jan Thyssen, 1640; Joan Matsuycker, 1646; Jacob Van Kittenstein, 1650; Adrian Van der Meyden, 1653.

AT COLOMBO:—Adrian Van der Meyden, 1656; Ryklof Van Goens, 1662; Jacob Hustaard, 1663; Commandeur Roothaes, 1664; Ryklof Van Goens (Snr.), 1665; Ryklof Van Goens (Jnr.), 1675; Lourens Van Pyl, 1680; Thomas Van Rhee, 1692; Paulus De Rhoo, 1695; Gerrit De Heer, 1697; Cornilis Johannes Simonsz, 1703; Hendrick Becker, 1707; Isaak Augustin Rumpf, 1716; Arnold Moll, 1723; Johannes Hertenberg, 1724; Jan Paulus Schagen, 1725; Petrus Vuyst, 1726; Stephanus Versluys, 1729; Gualterus Woutersz, 1732; Jacob C. Pielaat, 1732; Diedrick Van Domburg, 1734; Jan Maccare, 1736; Gustaff W. Baron Van Imhoff, 1736; William Mauritz Bruinink, 1740; Daniel Overkeek, 1742; J. V. Stein Van Golnesse, 1743; Gerard Joan Vreelant, 1751; Jacob De Jong, 1751; Ivan Gideon Loten, 1752; Jan Schreuder, 1757; Subhert Jan Baron Van Eck, 1762; Anthony Mooyart, 1765; Iman Willem Falck, 1765; Willem Jacob Van der Graaff, 1785; Joan Gerrard Van Angelbeck, 1796.

COMMENCEMENT OF THE BRITISH PERIOD.

Emperor Rajadhi Raja Singha, who had rendered assistance to the British in the expulsion of the Dutch, expected to derive considerable advantages from the accomplishment of that event. But he was doomed to disappointment in his expectations, and he soon found that he had only exchanged a week for a powerful neighbour. All territorial and political relations between the British and Kandyan Governments remained on the same footing as they had been under the Dutch.

The cinnamon found in the store-houses was sold by the British troops employed in the reduction of Colombo to the East India Company for £180,000.

The administration of the Governor in Council at Madras commenced on the 16th February, 1796. The civil administration of the maritime provinces was provisionally placed under a Commissioner, named Andrews, sent from the Presidency of Madras, who endeavoured to introduce the same regulations and system of collecting the public revenues which were in force on the Coast of Coromandel. For this purpose some Indians (dubashes) were brought over to Ceylon to fill the subordinate situations under the British Government. An annual tax of a fanam (1½*d.*) was at the same time imposed upon the produce of the cocoanut and other fruit-bearing trees. The inequality with which this tax weighed upon the proprietors, from the great inequality in the fertility of land, became insupportable, and in a representation made to government, they offered to pay in kind a certain proportion of the fruit of every tree. This proposal was refused, and an insurrection followed, with the result that government had to abandon the tax altogether.

The maritime provinces of Ceylon were transferred to the British Crown in 1798, and the Hon. Frederick North was appointed to administer the government under the control of the Governor in Council of the Madras Presidency.

The King of Kandy, Rajadi Raja Singha, died the same year. The *Mahawansa* tells us that he was a very cultured man who knew many languages, amongst them being Pali and Sanscrit. He was a lover of poetry and himself a poet, and "he composed and published the *Asadisa Jataka* in Sinhalese verse." He reconstructed the walls of the Uposatha Hall of the Malwatta Vihara.

Rajadi Raja Singha having died without issue and without nominating a successor according to custom, it fell to the lot of Pilimi Talawa, the first adigar, who was an able, ambitious, and intriguing chief, to select a successor to the vacant throne. Deeming it unseemly to propose to his fellow chieftains that he himself be placed on the throne, he proposed that one Kannesamy, a youth eighteen years of age, the son of a sister of one of the queens-dowager, be elected sovereign. In so doing he hoped that the chiefs would disagree with him in his choice and invite him to ascend the throne. Unfortunately, he was mistaken in his expectations, in that they, led perhaps through jealousy, unanimously agreed to have the foreigner as their sovereign. Accordingly he was raised to the throne under the name of **Sri Wickreme Raja Singha**. Thereafter Pilimi Talawa commenced intriguing with Governor North for the purpose of attaining his end.

In February, 1799, North interviewed him at Avisawella. On this occasion the adigar complained of the king's countrymen (the Malabars) representing them as instruments calculated to subvert his (Pilimi Talawa's) influence, and that of the Sinhalese chiefs at the court of Kandy. In December of the same year a second interview took place between North and Pilimi Talawa, at which the latter, according to Cordiner, "made a direct request to the governor, to assist him in taking away the life of the king and placing himself on the throne, on which conditions he would make the English masters of the country." *1799 A.C.*

During the first three months of 1800 Boyd, the Acting Secretary to the British Government, had numerous interviews with Pilimi Tatawa, but finding the latter too astute a politician whose interests by no means coincided with those of the British, inasmuch as though both parties wished to depose the king, each wished to have exclusive possession of his territory, it was decided to send an embassy direct to Kandy to treat with the king in person. Accordingly, on the 12th March, General Macdowal, with an escort consisting of 1,164 men, Europeans and Indians, started from Colombo on his way to Kandy, but only two companies of Sepoys and two companies of Malays were allowed by the Kandyan Government to proceed beyond Ruanwelle, the boundary of the Kandyan kingdom. Pilimi Talawa met the embassy in state and presented General Macdowal to the king. Although the articles of the treaty proposed by the general were discussed, they were not acceded to by the Kandyan court, the third article in particular being peculiarly objectionable to the Kandyan monarch, who, unconscious of the intrigues of his prime minister, considered himself quite capable of looking after himself and his kingdom without any foreign assistance. *Marshall's "Ceylon," p. 81.*

Article III. ran as follows:—"In order to secure the honour and safety of his Kandyan Majesty and his successors, his Excellency the Governor of the British Possessions in Ceylon shall send immediately into his Majesty's territories a detachment of seven or eight hundred men, which force may hereafter be increased as occasion may require; and as the troops are to be employed for the purpose of securing the king on his throne, and defending him against all his enemies, foreign and domestic, His Kandyan Majesty agrees to defray the expenses of four hundred men, with a proportion of officers of the said force; that is to say, etc., etc.......... The troops which are stationed within His Majesty's dominions shall only be considered as the defenders of him and his successors, and to support and maintain them in all their rights and prerogatives."

Having rejected the treaty proposed by Macdowal, the Kandyan court lost no time in making counter-proposals for a treaty consisting of eight articles, which was considered inadmissible by Macdowal, who considered the 6th article impossible of acceptance. It ran as follows: "Article VI.—The King of Kandy shall be permitted to have twelve ships or dhonies, as he shall think fit, which shall be allowed to sail from, and return to, the English ports, with such merchandise as is thought proper; and these vessels are neither to be examined nor to pay any duty whatsoever."

The acceptance of this article would have involved a heavy loss to the local British Government, seeing that whatever produce the Kandyans imported or exported passed through British custom-houses along the coast. Arecanuts, the principal article of Kandyan export, were charged 75 per cent.; and the tax on salt charged by the English Government was from 800 to 1,000 per cent. above the cost of production.

For two years subsequent to the failure of this embassy, negotiations were carried on between Governor North and the Kandyan court with a view to agreeing upon terms of alliance, but without success. After the peace of Amiens (1801) the control of the British settlement in Ceylon was transferred from the East India Company to the Secretary of State for the Colonies in England, a change which dates from the 1st January, 1802.

In April, 1802, some inhabitants of Putlam, having journeyed into the Kandyan territory for the purpose of trade, were, at the instance of Pilimi Talawa, forcibly despoiled of a quantity of arecanuts and cattle. Reparation was repeatedly demanded by the British from the court of Kandy; but as the representations of Governor North were all conveyed through the adigar, Pilimi Talawa, the king may have never heard of His Excellency's claims for that purpose. *1802 A.C.*

Under these circumstances the local British Government determined to march an army to Kandy, for the alleged purpose of enforcing a claim to full indemnification for the loss incurred by the Putlam merchants, and to exact sufficient security against similar acts of violence.

Accordingly two divisions composed of 3,000 men marched into the Kandyan territory. The first division, commanded by Major-General Macdowal, started from Colombo on the 31st January, 1803; the second under *1803.* the command of Col. Barbut started from Trincomalee on the 4th February. The two divisions met at a spot on the banks of the Mahaweli-ganga, three miles from Kandy, on the 20th February. On the following day the British forces marched into the capital, which they found totally deserted by its inhabitants.

Mootoo Swamy, a brother of one of the queens-dowager, having " demonstrated his claims to the throne" to the alleged satisfaction of Governor North, His Excellency deemed it expedient to have him brought from Minnery, whither he had accompanied Col. Barbut, to Kandy, and there formally crowned king. Accordingly he was conveyed to Kandy by a large detachment of British troops and crowned on the 8th March with all the forms of Eastern ceremonial.

No sooner had Mootoo Swamy been crowned king *Marshall,* than articles of convention were entered into between *p. 240.* him and Governor North, in which great concessions were made to the British.

Speaking of what followed these transactions, Marshall says: " The policy of Pilimi Talawa, in opposition to Mr. North, was crafty and successful. By artful representations he encouraged the English to attempt exhausting and fruitless hostile expeditions, obviously for the purpose of gaining time, and placing both parties entirely in his power. He had the effrontery to carry on a correspondence under the mask of friendship, with the commander of the British forces, who was sufficiently credulous to become his dupe. In this correspondence he endeavoured to cajole our government, which, being very easy of belief, fell into the snare placed for it by the adigar. He urged us to make an attempt to capture the fugitive king, who was at this time at Hanguranketty, a post about two days' march (18 miles) from Kandy ....Accordingly two detachments, one amounting to about 500 men, under the command of Col. Baillie, and another 300, marched on the morning of the 13th March, by different routes. The country between Kandy and Hanguranketty is excessively strong by nature, and great pains had been taken to strengthen it still more by art. Batteries were erected on every eminence which commanded the paths through which our soldiers were to pass, and marksmen were placed in ambush in the thickest coverts of the jungle, and wherever they could do us most injury. The detachments reached the place of their destination on the evening of the 14th, by which time the king had made his escape. On the 15th the troops, having burned the palace to the ground, commenced their return to Kandy, and met with the same opposition they had experienced in their advance. The loss incurred by killed and wounded in this expedition was considerable, and there can be no doubt that the measure was planned and carried into execution for our destruction by the adigar."

"In the meantime, the Kandyans hovered round our outposts in the neighbourhood of the capital. Concealed in the woods and thickets, they fired upon the guards and sentries during the night; and whenever any unfortunate stragglers fell into their hands, they put them to death. They knew their own weakness too well to emerge from their hiding-places during the day, or near to any considerable body of troops. A reward of ten rupees was given for the head of every European, and five for that of every other class of soldiers in the English service."

"Another communication was made by the adigar (Pilimi Talawa) to the governor, which led to a conference between the second adigar and General Macdowal on the 28th March. At this conference it was agreed that the fugitive king (when he was captured, it may be persumed) should be delivered over to the British

Government; that Pilimi Talawa should be invested with supreme authority in Kandy, under the title of *Ootoon Komarayen*, the Great Prince, and that he should pay an annuity of 30,000 rupees to Mootoo Sawmy, who would hold his court at Jaffnapatam; that Fort Macdowal (situated 16 miles from Kandy on the road to Trincomalee), with the surrounding district, the road to Trincomalee, and the province of the Seven Korles, should be ceded to His Britannic Majesty, and that a cessation of arms should immediately take place between the contracting powers."

On the faith of the fulfilment of this treaty, made with an avowed traitor and minister of the king, General Macdowal set out from Kandy for Colombo on the 1st April, leaving behind at the mountain capital a garrison consisting of 700 Malays and 300 Europeans of the 19th regiment, and Bengal and Madras Artillery, besides a considerable number of sick. *Cordiner, vol. ii., p. 197.*

With reference to this expedition Major Forbes writes as follows:—"Mootoo Swamy was proclaimed King of Kandy by the British; they brought him to the capital; they saluted him as king; they offered to support him with a military force; yet but a very few days after this, without any fault of his, or misfortune on their part, they deliberately conclude and afterwards ratify a treaty, by which he was to become a pensioner on one they knew to be a villain, ready to commit the worst of crimes, yet whom they were about to raise to supreme authority over the Kandyans." Mootoo Swamy had obviously much reason to complain. *Forbes' "Eleven Years in Ceylon," p. 27.*

Governor North met Pilimi Talawa at Dambadeniya on the 3rd of May, and fully agreed to the terms of the singular treaty which had been drawn up in Kandy by General Macdowal and the second adigar on the 28th March.

On the 23rd June, Major Davie, who commanded the British garrison in Kandy, received an *ola* letter from Pilimi Talawa, informing him that the Kandyans intended to attack him, and that he himself had lost the confidence and incurred the displeasure of the king. In consequence of this information preparations were made for the defence of the town, and four field-pieces were placed in different directions for its protection. *Marshall, p. 96.*

On the same day the Kandyans seized the two British posts of Giriagamme and Galgedera, situated about ten or twelve miles from Kandy, on the road to Colombo by Kurunegala.

Before daybreak on Friday, the 24th June, the Kandyan force attacked a British post situated on a hill immediately adjoining the palace where the British troops were stationed in Kandy and made the garrison prisoners. The palace was next attacked by some Kandyans. These were opposed by Lieut. Blakeney and some men of the 19th regiment. In this engagement both Lieut. Blakeney and the chief who commanded the assailants were killed. Capt. Humphries is said to have done great execution among the Kandyans by loading a field-piece with grape shot. The Kandyans occupied the hill adjoining the palace in great numbers, and continued to keep up an incessant fire upon the English by means of jingals. Lieut. Plenderleath was mortally wounded; a private of the Bengal Artillery and two Malays were killed, and the officers of the garrison became exhausted with fatigue. Under such circumstances "the European officers of the Malay regiment having become sensible of the inability of the English to resist the Kandyans, represented to Major Davie that they could not hold out much longer, and entreated him to enter into a capitulation with the enemy. This representation was made about 2 o'clock, at which time they had been warmly engaged for ten hours. After some time being spent in considering the subject of a capitulation, a white flag was displayed by the British and the firing ceased on both sides. A conference between the adigar and Major Davie ensued, when it was stipulated that Kandy should be immediately delivered up to the Kandyans, with all the stores, etc.; that the British should march out of Kandy with their arms, by the road leading to Trincomalee; that Mootoo Swamy should be permitted to accompany them, and that the adigar should take care of the sick and wounded, until such time as they could be removed to Trincomalee or Colombo."

Marshall, p. 97.

Accordingly at about 5 p.m. Major Davie, with the forces under his command, and Mootoo Swamy marched out of Kandy and proceeded to the Watapologa ferry on the Mahaweli-ganga, about three miles on the road to Trincomalee. The river, which in rainy weather is both wide and deep, not being passable, and there being neither boats nor rafts provided by which they could cross it, they were obliged to halt all night. It rained very hard, and the party, having no better means of covering, sought shelter under a *bo*-tree, on a green hillock near to the ferry. Here they remained exposed to very heavy rain. Next day, Saturday, the 25th June, the troops were employed in endeavouring to form rafts.

On the 26th June the adigar sent an invitation to Major Davie and two of his officers to meet him (the adigar) and two other Kandyan chiefs at a spot about half way between the ferry and Kandy, for the alleged purpose of finally arranging the measures required to convey the troops across the river, and to assist them through the Kandyan territory towards Trincomalee. Major Davie accepted the adigar's invitation, and, accompanied by Capt. Rumley and Humphreys and a Malay officer named Odeen (as interpreter), proceeded to the place appointed for the conference. Here they met three chiefs, but not the adigar. The chiefs informed Major Davie that the king wished to have an interview with the British officers at the palace, for the purpose of negotiating with them in person.

On reaching the town of Kandy, the three officers were made prisoners and confined separately. Odeen, however, boldly resisted the Kandyans in their attempts to secure him, and died on the spot, having been nearly cut to pieces. Thereafter the Kandyan chiefs sent a messenger to inform the British officers at Watapologa ferry that he had been directed by Major Davie to convey his orders to them to give up their arms to the Kandyans, and to return forthwith to Kandy, thence to be sent by the Gonarooa ferry and the route of the Four Korles, to Colombo, an agreement having been made to that effect with the king. On the delivery of this message, a council was held by the officers, at which Mootoo Swamy was present, and warmly remonstrated against the officers entertaining the idea of ordering the troops to give up their arms, and submitting to the king. The officers, however, determined to obey the orders of their superior. They ordered the troops to give up their arms, which was done, and the native troops, consisting of the Malays and gun-lascars, were made prisoners. Mootoo Swamy was at the same time given up to the Kandyans, who conveyed him back to Kandy and forthwith put him to death.

The above information regarding the seduction of Major Davie from his men at the ferry and the deception employed to induce the troops to believe that the Major had directed them to surrender their arms, together with the fatal result, was communicated to Simon Sawers, in 1823, by Mullegamme Dissave, one of the three chiefs who were employed on the occasion, whose information was confirmed by the family of Millawa Dissave, another of the three chiefs already mentioned.—(*Simon Sawers' MS. Notes.*)

Marshall, pp. 245 and 103.

The European soldiers having given up their arms, and been abandoned by the Malays and Sepoys, did as they were desired, and returned two by two along the road to Kandy for a short way, when they were led into a small hollow or dell, out of sight of their companions. Here they were put to death, mostly with the but-end of a musket or large club. One person only of the whole number, Corporal Barnsley, of the 19th regiment, escap d to tell the tale. This man was in his turn led into the dell with his companion; and when he reached the place of slaughter, was knocked down with the but-end of a musket, and desperately wounded with a tulwar, or large Kandyan knife, across the back of the neck. When he received the all but mortal blow he fell to the ground, and rolled over a precipitous bank into the water-course of a paddy-field, where he was left for dead. Here he lay for some time, and, in that situation, alleges he heard some desultory firing. Having so far recovered as to be able to move, he crept into the jungle, where he lay concealed during the night, and towards morning crawled to the ferry, with the view of endeavouring to cross the river and to walk to Fort Macdowal. By the time he reached the ferry, the flood in the river had in some measure subsided, and the ordinary ferryman had resumed his occupation with his small canoe. The heart of the ferryman having melted with compassion upon seeing the miserable spectacle Barnsley presented, at the risk of his own life he not only ferried him across the river, but also gave him the small portion of rice which he had in his canoe. On reaching Fort Macdowal, Barnsley made a formal declaration or deposition before Capt. Madge and other officers of the garrison stationed there, of the surrender of Kandy and the massacre of the Europeans.

On receipt of the news Capt. Madge beat a hasty retreat to Trincomalee, a distance of 126 miles; and

Ensign Grant, who was in command of the British post at Dambadeniya, in the Seven Korles, situated about sixty miles from Kandy on the road to Colombo, also retreated to Colombo, which was reached on the 2nd July.

Thus in the course of ten days from the retaking of Kandy not an inch of ground remained to the British beyond their original frontier.

In the months of August and September the Kandyans poured down from the mountains, and by cajoling some, and intimidating others, prevailed on many of the low-country Sinhalese to join them, their ultimate object being to accelerate the expulsion of the British from the Island. The irruption of the Kandyans into the British settlements extended from Hambantota on the south coast, round the whole west and north coast, to the small fort of Mullaitivoe, north of Trincomalee.

On the 20th August, the Kandyans captured the British fort at Hanwelle, about 20 miles from Colombo, and next day they advanced to within fourteen or fifteen miles of that city, at which the Burghers in the suburbs became alarmed and fled for refuge to the garrison. Just at this time reinforcements having arrived from the Cape of Good Hope and Bengal, the British commenced a war of devastation if not of retaliation.

Of this war Marshall writes as follows :—"When we *Marshall,*
read of British troops being 'employed in burning and *p 120*
destroying all the houses, stores, and gardens in the rich province of Saffragam'—one detachment having destroyed 800 Kandyan houses, and many other parts of the country having been exposed to similar scenes of plunder and devastation,—we turn from the recital with disgust, and our hearts will not suffer us to admit that the plea of vengeance could sanction such enormities. On one occasion we are informed that a detachment plundered a pagoda, or place of religious worship, in Saffragam, which contained a large quantity of copper and silver coins. The Malay soldiers belonging to the detachment refused to accept a share of the plunder, and the common coolies would neither enter the pagoda nor touch the coins. The offence of violating or profaning and plundering a temple held sacred by Buddhists was committed by the European troops, and by them alone. The reverend historian who records these atrocities expresses no commiseration for the sufferings of the unoffending inhabitants; inflicts no

censure on the detachment for committing sacrilege; indeed, he seems to regret that the party was unable to bring away all the beautiful elephants' tusks, and other curious articles which the temple contained.—(*Cordiner, vol. ii., pp. 256 and 258.*)"

The British force having been strengthened by the arrival of the 65th regiment from England, and reinforcements from Madras and Bengal, it was resolved by the local British Government in August, 1804, again to invade the king's dominion.

From the magnitude of the army about to be employed by the British, it was resolved to divide it into six columns or divisions, which should march separately from different stations, so as to concentrate in the vicinity of Kandy for the purpose of making a joint attack on the city on the 28th or 29th September.

General Wemyss, who had succeeded General Macdowal in the command of the forces, desirous of ascertaining by personal inspection the state of the detachments at the different stations and of inquiring into the practicability and eligibility of the different routes, made a tour of the maritime parts of the Island. At Batticaloa, he met Capt. Johnston, the commandant, and explained to him the meditated expedition. Later, Capt. Johnston received two letters from the general, one from Trincomalee dated 3rd September, the other from Jaffnapatam dated 8th September.

The cruel and barbarous nature of the contemplated campaign could be gathered from the following passage in the general's letter from Jaffna:—"You will, in junction with the other detachments, concert such measures as will best tend to effect the greatest devastation and injury to the enemy's country."

Capt Johnston, in compliance with what he considered to be the purport of both the letters he had received, started from Batticaloa on the 20th September with a force of 834, composed of Europeans, Malays, Bengal Sepoys, pioneers and coolies, and made his way through the woods and mountains of Uva to Kandy, which he reached on the 6th October. Finding that none of the five other divisions had arrived, he remained there for three days, during which time the Kandyans busied themselves with preparations to cut off his retreat to Trincomalee. "The Aitgalle Pass, and the whole line of road through the jungles of Matale, extending for sixty or seventy miles, were barricaded, in some places with breastworks, and in others by means of large trees laid across the road." In spite of all these obstacles Capt. Johnston succeeded in beating a retreat to Trincomalee, which he reached on the 20th October, 1804, sustaining 71 casualties in killed and wounded during the course of it.

"Those men who had escaped sickness and wounds on the retreat were emaciated, sallow, and debilitated to an extreme degree. They were almost all barefooted, the shoes having been completely worn out. This retreat was nearly as fatal to the Europeans of the detachment as the massacre of 1803 had been, for almost all died in the hospital; few, very few, survived." *Capt. Johnston's "Narrative of the Operations of a Detachment, etc., in the Year 1804."*

Regarding this expedition Marshall says: "Too much credit cannot be given to Capt. Johnston for the great military talents he displayed in conducting his detachment through a country so full of natural obstacles, and defended by a race of people so active and persevering in resisting invaders as the natives of the interior of Ceylon."

On his arrival at Trincomalee Johnston was surprised to learn that it was not intended that he should proceed to Kandy; that the general, on arriving at Jaffnapatam, had found obstacles to the combined attack, which he considered to be insurmountable; that the second letter he received was intended as a countermand of the plan; and that his having gone to Kandy was deemed a disobedience of orders; that it was merely meant that the divisions should enter those parts of the king's territory adjacent to their respective districts, and return after laying waste the country; that the other five divisions had accordingly made these incursions, and had long since returned.

Johnston was ordered round to Colombo, where a court of enquiry having been held upon his conduct, he was honourably acquitted. A desultory warfare of retribution, between the Kandyans and the British, continued until about February or March, 1805. The war was conducted by both parties, with savage barbarity. Numerous villages were burnt and large tracts of country reduced to desolation.

Within the British settlements, the disaffection of the inhabitants was punished by martial law with fearful severity. At Kokgala on the southern coast, for example, the inhabitants of which village had interrupted the communication between Galle and Matara, fifty boats were burned, and all the houses in the village destroyed. One " rioter " was hanged, and five others were condemned to receive each 1,000 lashes, a favourite sentence with courts-martial at that period, and for a long time after.

In February, 1805, an extensive invasion by the Kandyans of the British settlements took place; but the British, availing themselves of the large reinforcements that had just arrived, succeeded in driving them back with great loss.

On this occasion, the king intended to make an inroad into the district of Colombo, and, being confident of success, accompanied a detachment of his army into the maritime provinces. His forces having been defeated, he fled with great precipitation believing that he was followed by the British. By the time he reached the district of the Four Korles, his palanquin-bearers and attendants were exhausted with hunger and fatigue, and unable to continue the flight. In this state he was met by Molligoda, then a young man not enjoying any office under the king, who rendered his sovereign the most acceptable and beneficial services. From this time Molligoda was regarded by the king with great favour, and, as we shall see, was soon after appointed to an important office under government. Indirect advances were soon after made by the Kandyans, and accepted by the British for a tacit cessation of hostilities.

1805 A.C. On the 19th July, 1805, the Right Hon. Sir Thomas Maitland assumed the government of the maritime provinces of Ceylon. Apparently, there was no friendly intercourse between Sir Thomas, while he was governor, and the king; but no act of aggression was committed by either party, and this policy was continued by Major-General Wilson, who assumed the Government of Ceylon
1811 A.C. on the 19th March, 1811.

During this period of mutual respect and forbearance important events occurred within the king's dominion. The dissavony of the Seven Korles having become vacant in 1806 by the death of Migastenna, the second adigar, and dissave, of this district, it was divided between the two chiefs Eheylapola and Molligoda; a circumstance which greatly dissatisfied the people, two dissaves being supposed to require double the services and duties of one, and the arrangement, moreover, being contrary to custom. An insurrection resulted, which Pilimi Talawa succeeded in suppressing, the district having been transferred to him and his nephew Eheylapola.

The success of Pilimi Talawa is said to have excited the king's suspicion and jealousy, and heightened the aversion he had for some time entertained towards him. Other circumstances occurred, which increased the discord between this chief and the king; mutual hatred followed, coupled with mutual dread, each having good grounds for considering his life insecure from the machinations of the other. The adigar, having committed some breaches of duty, was summoned by the king to court to stand his trial before him and the chiefs assembled in Kandy. Here he was found guilty and sentenced to suffer a term of imprisonment. A short time after, he was liberated with permission to retire to his country residence. A life of degradation and inaction was but ill-adapted for this able, ambitious, enterprising, and vindictive chief. He soon entered into a conspiracy to assassinate the king. For this purpose he bribed the Malay Mohundiram and sixty Malays, composing the royal bodyguard, to perpetrate the murder; and he prevailed on the headmen of Udunuwara and Yatinuwara to raise the people of their respective districts to arms simultaneously. These two provinces rose in rebellion prematurely, and the adigar's plot was marred. Some of the Malays fled to Colombo. The insurrection having been suppressed and the ringleaders apprehended, Pilimi Talawa, together with his son and a nephew, were ordered to be brought to Kandy to be tried for high treason. The adigar and his nephew arrived together, and, in the presence of the king and chiefs, were confronted with some of the other conspirators; and being convicted were sentenced to suffer death. It is stated that the prisoners confessed their guilt. Pilimi Talawa and his nephew were immediately beheaded; and six petty chiefs were at the same time hanged and impaled, the dead bodies being tied to a post and exposed *1812 A.C.* in that condition near a public road to serve as a deterrent to possible traitors in the future. The son who was imprisoned at a considerable distance was capitally convicted; but as he did not arrive till after the execution of his relations, and as it happened on a sacred day, his life was spared, but his lands were confiscated.

Lieut.-General Sir Robert Brownrigg succeeded to the Government of the British Settlements in Ceylon in 1812.

Eheylapola, who had been appointed second adigar in 1806, succeeded his uncle Pilimi Talawa as first adigar, This appointment is supposed to have been in a great measure occasioned by the ascendency which Pilimi Talawa's family had established with the other chiefs, whereby the king was induced to acquiesce in their wishes, and to appoint him prime minister. It does not appear, however, that the king ever placed much trust in him. He seems never to have deserved the king's confidence, for no sooner was he appointed first adigar, and became the head of the influential family to which he belonged, than he entertained the same disloyal and ambitious designs for which his uncle had suffered. After a brief period, the king's suspicions of his fidelity were excited, by learning that he was pursuing a system of intrigue inconsistent with loyalty to his sovereign.

At this juncture, the king sent the chiefs—who according to custom, together with their families, resided at his court—into their respective districts to superintend the cultivation of the country and to collect the revenue. Eheylapola proceeded to his dissavony (Sabaragamuwa), where circumstances soon occurred, which amply proved his want of fidelity to his sovereign. In consequence of several charges of extortion and injustice having been preferred to the king as against him, he was ordered to return to Kandy for their investigation. The adigar failed to comply with the order of the king, and the reply he made was not calculated to satisfy or conciliate his sovereign. He forthwith prepared to set the king at defiance, and commenced a treasonable correspondence with General Brownrigg. An open rupture between the king and the adigar having taken place, the latter lost no time in assembling his adherents in Sabaragamuwa for the purpose of resisting the royal forces. His designs becoming known in Kandy, he was deprived of all his public offices, and his wife and children, who were considered pledges of his loyalty, were imprisoned. Molligoda was appointed his successor, not only as first adigar, but also as dissave of Sabaragamuwa. To suppress the rebellion, this chief proceeded to the disaffected province, the road to which, from Kandy, passes over the range of Adam's Peak. Eheylapola's force was soon routed, his adherents having made no effectual resistance. He fled to Kalutara, a British post, in May, 1814, whence he proceeded to Colombo with some of his followers. Molligoda returned to Kandy with the prisoners he had taken, forty-seven of whom, it is alleged, were executed.

The brother of Eheylapola, having been suspected of misprison of treason, was executed, as were also his wife and sister, together with Eheylapola's wife, sister, and children. In front of the Queen's Palace and between the Natha and Maha Vishnu Dewalés the wife of Eheylapola and his children were brought from prison, where they had been in charge of female jailors, and delivered over to the executioners. The lady with great resolution maintained her own and her children's innocence, and not less her lord's; at the same time submitting to the king's pleasure, and offering up her own and her offspring's lives, with the fervent hope that her husband's fate would be benefited by the sacrifice. Having uttered these sentiments aloud, she desired her eldest boy to submit to his fate; the poor child, who was eleven years old, clung to his mother terrified and crying; her second son, nine years old, with all the inspiration of martyrdom, heroically stepped forward, and bade his brother not to be afraid—as he would show him the way to die! By one blow of a sword the head of the noble boy was severed from his body; streaming with blood, and hardly inanimate, it was thrown into a rice mortar; the pestle was put into the mother's hands, and she was ordered to pound it, or be disgracefully tortured and defiled by the Rhodias. To avoid the horrid alternative the wretched woman did lift it up and let it fall. One by one the heads of all her children were cut off and one by one the poor mother had to perform the hellish operation. One of the children was a girl, and to wound a female was considered by the Sinhalese a monstrous atrocity; another was an infant at the breast, and it was plucked from the mother to be beheaded; when the head was severed from the body, the milk it had just drawn in, ran out, mingled with its blood. During this awful scene, the crowd, who had assembled to witness it, wept and sobbed aloud, unable to suppress their feelings of grief and horror.

Pridham, vol. i., pp. 185-186.

Palihapané Dissave was so affected that he fainted, and was deprived of his office for showing such tender sensibility. During two days, the whole of Kandy, with the exception of the court, was one house of mourning and lamentation, and so deep was the grief, that (it is said) not a fire was kindled, nor food dressed, and a general fast was held. After the execution of her children, the sufferings of the mother, who had displayed the most astonishing fortitude throughout the whole fearful trial, were not prolonged. She and her sister-in-law, and the wife and sister of the Dissave Pussilla, were led to the tank called Bogambaraweva and drowned.

It had been over two centuries (1597 A.C.) since the Sinhalese had experienced such barbarities practiced in their midst, and then it was at the hands of the Portuguese, who not long afterwards found to their cost that they had forfeited the allegiance and respect of their Sinhalese subjects in the maritime districts. Now when the Sinhalese discovered that the man whom they had been pleased to elevate to the throne had taken a lesson in government from Dom Hieronimo Azevedo, the then Capt.-General of the Portuguese, it was not long before they decided almost to a man to rid themselves of his yoke, though it be at the cost of losing their separate national existence for a time.

Sir Robert Brownrigg, perceiving that his opportunity for annexing the Kandyan kingdom to the British Crown had arrived, started to make extensive preparations for the invasion of the king's dominion. In these preparations he was greatly assisted by Eheylapola, who furnished him with important information regarding the resources of the Kandyan country and the feelings of the chiefs and people towards the government. Eheylapola also submitted a plan of hostile operations to Sir Robert, which was adopted almost in its entirety.

While the British were thus engaged in making preparations and tampering with Molligoda, the adigar and prime minister of the king (in the hope of winning him over to their side), information was received during
1814 A.C. the month of November, that ten cloth-merchants, subjects of the British Government, had been seized in the Kandyan country and severely punished by order of the king The travelling merchants or pedlars, in question, were plundered by some low caste Kandyans in the Three Korles, who, to prevent themselves being brought to justice, accused the men who had been robbed of being spies from

the maritime provinces employed by the British. Upon this charge, supported by the testimony of the men who had plundered them, the merchants were found guilty, and punished according to the common usage of the country.

This was considered by Sir Robert Brownrigg to be an act of aggression involving the honour of the British nation.

The army which invaded the Kandyan territory was arranged in eight divisions and commanded in the following manner :—

	Commanded by	To march from
1st Division ...	Major Hook, 2nd Ceylon Regt.	... Colombo.
2nd Division ... (reserve)	Lt.-Col. O'Connell, 73rd Foot	... Colombo.
3rd Division ...	Major Kelly, 4th Ceylon Regt.	... Galle.
4th Division ... (reserve)	Colonel Murray, 4th Ceylon Regt.	... Galle.
5th Division ...	Major D. M'Kay, 3rd Ceylon Regt.	... Trincomalee.
6th Division ... (reserve)	Lt.-Colonel Rainsford, 19th Foot	... Trincomalee.
7th Division ...	Capt. Anderson, 19th Foot	... Batticaloa.
8th Division ...	Capt. De Busche, 1st Ceylon Regt.	... Negombo.

Marshall, to whose admirable little history of this period the writer is largely indebted for his information, came to Ceylon in 1808 as Assistant Surgeon in the 89th Regiment and accompanied Major Hook's division in the war of 1815. He was Senior Medical Officer in the Kandyan provinces from 1816 to 1821.

The principal reasons assigned for invading the Kandyan kingdom were the alleged tyranny and oppression of the Kandyan monarch, his unwillingness to enter into any terms with the representative of the British Government, the punishment by mutilation of the ten cloth-merchants already mentioned, and the irruption of the Kandyans across the boundary river of Sitawaka, in pursuit of Eheylapola's fugitive adherents—which latter fact occurred after every preparation for war had been made by the British, and as Major Hook was actually on the march and about to cross that very river!

Appendix No. 7, p. 266, of Marshall's Conquest of Ceylon.

The object of the war is thus stated in the proclamation or declaration of war dated the 18th January, 1815:—"For securing the permanent tranquillity of the British settlements, and in vindication of the honour of the British name, for the deliverance of the Kandyan people from their oppressors; in fine, for the subversion of that Malabar dominion which, during three generations, has tyrannised over the country, His Excellency has resolved to employ the powerful resources placed at his disposal."

Of this proclamation Marshall says: "An improvement of the condition of the inhabitants of a State, by delivering them from alleged oppression, is sometimes assigned as a pretext for subjugating and taking possession of a country; but perhaps the principle of kindness and humanity towards a people is very rarely indeed the real cause of war, professions of this kind being frequently used as a cloak to cover visions of glory, renown, and grasping ambition."

During the course of his march to Kandy numerous communications were made to Major Hook by the Adigar Molligoda and other chiefs, all professing their willingness to promote the advance of the British troops, provided they could do so without openly renouncing the Kandyan Government.

At length Molligoda had an interview with Hook, at which the former promised to make as little opposition to the British troops as he could, consistently with the appearance of obeying the orders of his sovereign. With this object, he informed Major Hook that, although the people under his control would continue to fire upon his division, no bullets would be put in the firelocks.

That the adigar kept his promise is shown by the following statement by Marshall:—"Although they continued to fire occasionally upon this division throughout its progress to Kandy, not a man was either killed or wounded."

On the 14th of February the various divisions entered Kandy.

Information having been obtained that the king was still at no great distance from the capital, no time was lost in adopting means to interrupt his retreat to some distant province, more especially to the Province of Uva. A detachment of troops, accompanied by D'Oyley and Eheylapola, was, on the 16th, despatched to the district of Doombera, whither it was presumed the king had retired. On the 18th the king was taken prisoner, with two of his wives, in the house of a subordinate headman, about a mile from Meda Maha Nuwara. His two remaining wives and his mother were at Hangwelle, a short distance off; and being sent for, with conveyances and an escort, were brought to Teldeniya to join the king. It appears that the few Malabar attendants remaining with the king made some resistance, and wounded one of the assailants under the command of Eheylapola, on which the party fired upon the house. The king then appeared and delivered himself up. His pursuers forthwith bound and plundered him of whatever articles of value he had in his possession.

The following description by Marshall of the manner in which the news of the capture of King Sri Wickreme Raja Singha was received by the British Governor-General Brownrigg is interesting:—

"The report of the capture of the king reached General Brownrigg on the 19th February, while he was at dinner with a small party of officers. The intelligence being highly gratifying, and in many respects of utmost importance, His Excellency became greatly affected. He stood up at table and, while the tears rolled down his cheeks, shook hands with every one present, and thanked them for their exertions in furtherance of an object which seemed to be nearly accomplished, and which had been vainly attempted for nearly three centuries by three European powers in succession—the conquest of the Kingdom of Kandy."

The king was taken to Colombo on the 6th March, where he remained until the 24th January, 1816, when he and all his relations, dependents, and adherents, amounting to about 100 individuals, were transferred to India, first to Madras and finally to the fort of Vellore, in which place he died of dropsy on the 30th January, 1832, aged fifty-two years.

Of him, Marshall, who had frequent intercourse with him during his stay in Colombo, says: "Sri Wickreme Raja

Singha, the deposed King of Kandy, was about five feet nine or ten inches in height, slightly corpulent, stoutly made and muscular. He had a pleasant expression of countenance, a handsome beard, broad shoulders, and a full chest. His figure was manly, and his general appearance dignified. He did not appear to the writer to be deficient in intellect, and was generally much more affable and good humoured than could be expected of a deposed king in a state of confinement. Having been placed on the throne by a professed friend, but in reality an inveterate intriguing enemy, for the intriguer's own aggrandisement, his situation as king was attended with insuperable difficulties. Like a man blindfolded and in fetters, he could neither see nor move, but as the adigar directed him. With a faithless minister and a powerful, ambitious, hostile neighbour, who was ever ready to encourage traitors, provided he might benefit by the treason, his throne was surrounded by the most embarrassing perplexities—difficulties which would have required a person of great natural talents to surmount.........Like Peter the Great of Russia, he was a despot by condition and necessity. Even among the despotic governments of civilised Europe, some sovereigns have committed atrocious acts of oppression and cruelty without being considered unworthy to retain their crown. Frederick II. of Prussia, in some respects, evinced as much inhumanity, perhaps I may say as much barbarity, in punishing alleged delinquents, as has been recorded of Oriental despots. Without any previous examination by legal authority, a secular clergyman was hanged, and the Governor of Spandau was beheaded on the authority of a mere order by him. These and many other acts of similar atrocity were ordered by a European despot, whom the world dignifies with the title of "Great."

Some of King Sri Wickreme Raja Singha's most severe measures, it is alleged, were ordered to be carried into effect while he was in a state of inebriety, he having become liable to paroxysms of intemperance; and from the great quantity of Hoffman's cherry brandy bottles, which are recorded as having been found in the palace, it may be inferred that he was fond of that liqueur.

As for the events which took place in Kandy between the day on which the king was captured, the 18th February, and the day on which he was taken to Colombo, we find it recorded that immediately after the capture of the king measures were put in progress for permanently settling the government of the newly acquired territory. The proclamation which the Governor had issued at the commencement of the war promised to the chiefs a continuance of their respective ranks and dignities; to the people freedom from all arbitrary severities and oppressions, and to all classes the inviolate maintenance of their religion, and the preservation of their ancient laws and institutions; and it was now deemed expedient to convoke an assembly of the headmen, for the purpose of affixing their signatures to a convention, which was to secure to the British Government the possession of the Kingdom of Kandy.

As a preliminary measure to the signing of a convention, an official declaration of the appropriation of the Kandyan provinces by the British Government was promulgated. The declaration began as follows :—

"Led by the invitation of the chiefs, and welcomed by the acclamations of the people, the forces of His Britannic Majesty have entered the Kandyan territory and penetrated to the capital. Divine Providence has blessed their efforts with uniform and complete success. The ruler of the interior provinces has fallen into their hands, and the government remains at the disposal of His Majesty's representatives." The document then goes on to enumerate in detail the king's alleged delinquencies, and concludes with the following paragraph :—"Contemplating these atrocities, the impossibility of establishing with such a man any civilised relations either of peace or war ceases to be a subject of regret, since His Majesty's arms, hitherto employed in the generous purpose of relieving the oppressed, would be tarnished and disgraced in being instrumental to the restoration of a dominion exercised in a perpetual outrage to everything which is sacred in the constitution or functions of a legitimate government."

On these grounds a solemn conference or convention was held in the audience hall of the palace of Kandy, on the 2nd March, between Governor-General Brownrigg on behalf of King George III. of England on the one part, and the adigars, dissaves, and other principal chiefs of the Kandyan provinces, as alleged, on the other part on behalf of the people.

The following description of the conference is given by Marshall :—

"The conference was held in the great hall of audience in the palace; but the governor declined using the adjoining room, where the king usually sat, cross-legged, on an elevated throne on occasions of ceremony, and chose to be placed within the hall, at the upper end with his back to the door of that room, which was divided off by a screen. The troops composing the garrison of Kandy, together with the corps of Ceylon Light Dragoons, which had been brought to Kandy for the occasion, were drawn up at three o'clock in the great square before the palace, forming a lane through which the adigars and principal chiefs passed to the hall.

"The conference was conducted with great ceremony. Eheylapola, a remarkably fine, intelligent-looking man, was the first who entered the hall of the palace. He was received by particular marks of respect by His Excellency, and seated on a chair on his right hand. Molligoda, who had been appointed first adigar, then came forward, leading in the dissaves of provinces, and other principal chiefs, about twenty in number. The governor rose up to receive them, and, with Eheylapola, continued standing throughout the conference. The hall was lined on both sides by British officers.

"The conference began with complimentary inquiries on the part of the chiefs, which were graciously answered by the governor, and mutual inquiries made. His Excellency thanked the dissaves for the attention paid to the troops, in their progress to the capital, which gave occasion to the chiefs to observe, that they considered them as protectors, and that, by the arrival of His Excellency and his army, they had been rescued from tyranny and oppression. The governor observed, he was gratified in having been the means of their deliverance; he assured them of full protection in their persons, their property, and all their rights; and added, that while he had the honour of holding the administration of the Island, it would be his study to make them experience the blessings of his Majesty's benign Government.

"It was then intimated to the chiefs, that a document had been prepared, expressive of the principles by which the administration of His Majesty's Government of the Kandyan provinces would be guided, and that it was about to be read, which they requested might be done.

"The document inquestion—or treaty, as it has been called—was read in English by Mr. Sutherland, Deputy-Secretary to Government, and afterwards in Sinhalese. His Excellency's part of the conference was communicated to Mr. D'Oyley, and by him to Molligoda Adigar, who delivered it aloud to the audience.

"Millawa, Dissave of Wellassa, was the organ of the assembly: he seemed to collect the sentiments of the chiefs generally in silence, but with occasional explanation, and conveyed them to Molligoda. Eheylapola, though not officially engaged in the conference, appeared to take an interest in what was going on. His carriage was distinguished by a courtly address, politeness and ease, and he appeared to be regarded by the assembled chiefs with a high degree of deference and respect.

"After the treaty was read in Sinhalese, the Adigar Molligoda, and the other chiefs, proceeded to the principal door of the hall, where the Mohottales, Koralas, Vidanes, and other subordinate headmen from the different provinces were attending, accompanied by a few followers; and the headmen being called upon by the adigar to range themselves in order, according to their respective districts, the treaty was again read in Sinhalese, at the conclusion of which the British flag was hoisted for the *first* time in the town of Kandy, and a royal salute from the cannon, which had with infinite labour been dragged up the hills, announced His Majesty George III. Sovereign of the whole Island of Ceylon. That portion of the population which had returned to the town of Kandy evinced no concern in the business which was going on in the palace. They did not leave their ordinary avocations even to look at the troops which were assembled, in review order, in the great square before the audience hall."

The text of the treaty ran as follows:—

"At a convention held on the 2nd day of March, in the year of Christ 1815, and the Sinhalese year 1736, at the Palace, in the City of Kandy, between His Excellency Lieutenant-General Robert Brownrigg, Governor and Commander-in-Chief in and over the British Settlements and Territories in the Island of Ceylon, acting in the name and on behalf of his Majesty George III., King, and His Royal Highness George, Prince of Wales, Regent of the United Kingdom of Great Britain and Ireland, on the one part, and the Adigars,

Dissaves, and other principal chiefs of the Kandyan provinces, on behalf of the inhabitants, and in presence of the Mohottales, Koraales, Vidaanes and other subordinate headmen from the several provinces, and of the people then and there assembled, on the other part, it is agreed and established as follows :—

"1st.—That the cruelties and oppressions of the Malabar ruler, in the arbitrary and unjust infliction of bodily tortures, and the pains of death, without trial, and sometimes without an accusation or the possibility of a crime, and in the general contempt and contravention of all civil rights, have become flagrant, enormous, and intolerable; the acts and maxims of his government being equally and entirely devoid of that justice which should secure the safety of his subjects, and of that good faith which might obtain a beneficial intercourse with the neighbouring settlements.

"2nd.—That the Rajah Sri Wickreme Raja Singha, by the habitual violation of the chief and most sacred duties of a sovereign, has forfeited all claims to that title, or the powers annexed to the same, and is declared fallen and deposed from the office of king; his family and relatives, whether in the ascending, descending or collateral line, and whether by affinity or blood, are also for ever excluded from the throne; and all claim and title of the Malabar race to the dominion of the Kandyan provinces is abolished and extinguished.

"3rd.—That all male persons being or pretending to be relations of the late Rajah Sri Wickreme Rajah Singha, either by affinity or blood, and whether in the ascending, descending or collateral line, are hereby declared enemies to the government of the Kandyan provinces, and excluded and prohibited from entering these provinces, on any pretence whatever, without a written permission for that purpose, by the authority of the British Government, under the pains and penalties of the martial law, which is hereby declared to be in force for that purpose; and all male persons of the Malabar caste, now expelled from the said provinces, are under the same penalties, prohibited from returning, except with the permission before mentioned.

"4th.—The dominion of the Kandyan provinces is vested in the Sovereign of the British Empire, and to be exercised through the Governors and Lieutenant-Governors of Ceylon for the time being, and their accredited agents, saving to the Adigars, Dissaves, Mohotaales Koraales, Vidaanes, and all other chief and subordinate native headmen, lawfully appointed by authority of the British Government, the rights, privileges, and powers of their respective offices, and to all classes of the people the safety of their persons and property, with their civil rights and immunities, according to the laws, institutions, and customs established and in force amongst them.

"5th.—*The religion of Buddha, professed by the chiefs and inhabitants of these provinces, is declared inviolable; and its rights, ministers, and places of worship are to be maintained and protected.*

"6th.—Every species of bodily torture, and all mutilation of limb, member or organ, are prohibited and abolished.

"7th.—No sentence of death can be carried into execution against any inhabitant, except by the written warrant of the British Governor or Lieutenant-Governor for the time being, founded on a report of the case made to him through the accredited agent or agents of the government resident in the interior, in whose presence all trials for capital offences are to take place.

"8th.—Subject to these conditions, the administration of civil and criminal justice and police, over the Kandyan inhabitants of the said provinces, is to be exercised according to established forms, and by the ordinary authorities; saving always the inherent right of government to redress grievances and reform abuses, in all instances whatever, particular or general, where such interposition shall become necessary.

"9th.—Over all other persons civil, or military, residing in or resorting to these provinces, not being Kandyans, civil and criminal justice, together with police, shall, until the pleasure of His Majesty's Government in England may be otherwise declared, be administered in the manner following :—

"10th.—Provided always, that the operation of the several preceding clauses shall not be contravened by the provisions of any temporary or partial proclamation published during the advance of the army; which provisions, in so far as incompatible with the said preceding articles, are hereby repealed.

"11th.—The royal dues and revenues of the Kandyan provinces are to be managed and collected for His Majesty's use, and the support of the provincial establishment, according to lawful custom, and under the direction and superintendence of the accredited agent or agents of the British Government.

"12th.—His Excellency the Governor will adopt provisionally, and recommended to the confirmation of His Royal Highness the Prince Regent, in the name and on behalf of His Majesty, such dispositions in favour of the trade of these provinces, as may facilitate the export of their products, and improve the returns, whether in money or in salt, cloths, or other commodities, useful and desirable to the inhabitants of the Kandyan country."

Of the above convention, Lieut.-Col. Forbes, in his work titled "Recent Disturbances and Military Executions in Ceylon," says :—"The most important articles of the convention were, the preservation of the religion of Buddha, and the recognition of the local institutions; which were made a *sine qua non* of the voluntary submission of the Kandyan people to a European power."

After the banishment of Sri Wickreme Raja Singha, the administration of the Kandyan provinces, under the British Government, was conducted by a Board established at Kandy, consisting of a resident, and a judicial commissioner, together with the commanding officer of the troops in the interior. This Board, with the adigars and principal chiefs, formed the great court of justice, from whose sentence there was no appeal except to the Governor. Besides the Board, and subordinate agents of government in Uva, Sabaragamuwa, and the Three Korles, the civil authority of the country was exercised, as formerly, by the native dissaves and Ratemahatmeyas.

The military force which was kept in the interior amounted to 1,700 or 1,800 men, who were stationed at about eleven different posts.

Molligoda was confirmed in the office of first adigar, Eheylapola, to whom this appointment was offered, having declined to accept it.

In October, 1817, an insurrection occurred, which required all the power of the British Government to suppress.

"For many reasons," says Marshall, "the Kandyans of all grades disliked the English. Differing in race, language, religion, customs, habits, and modes of thinking the British rule could not but be for a long time highly unpalatable to them.........In the administration of justice the English authorities did not recognise any distinction of caste, or any privileged class. They were as ready to hear the complaints of the poor as of the rich, by which the advantages of the wealthy were curtailed, and the long recognised privileges of caste disregarded."

"Governments and governed are commonly more or less mutually adapted to each other; they become in some degree identified. A despot is admitted to be, in a certain sense, a possessor of unlimited power, which he may employ in the oppression of his subjects, but it is not necessary that he should do so. The British Government assumed the despotism of the fallen monarch; the people having no more legal power to control the decrees of the governor than they had to modify the order of the king. One despotism had given place to another; in practice the common people found that the alleged moderation of the British Government differed very little from the exactions of their former ruler."

"To an unlimited despotism, the Kandyans had voluntarily submitted for many ages, and, although unrestricted, the government had been generally exercised in accordance with certain recognised usages under an implied obligation to act for the good of the governed. The chiefs reprobated any charge in the forms of government, and the common people appeared to consider an alteration of their institutions as downright impiety."

Dr. Davy, who had peculiar opportunities of obtaining information regarding Kandyan affairs, thus describes the feelings of the people towards the British :—"There was no sympathy between us and them, no one circumstance to draw or bring us together, and innumerable ones of a repulsive nature. The chiefs, though less controlled than under the king, and exercising more power in their districts than they ever before ventured to exert, were far from satisfied. Before no one but the king was above them, now they were inferior to every civilian in our service—to every officer in our army. Though officially treated with respect, it was only officially, as common soldiers passed a proud Kandyan chief with as little attention as he would a fellow of the lowest caste. Thus they considered themselves degraded and shorn of their splendour. The people, in general, had similar feelings on this score, at least the respectable and most considerable portion of the population."

Notwithstanding the animosity with which the English were regarded by the Kandyans, the people were not, generally, prepared to submit to the regal control of one of their own chiefs owing to the mutual jealousy that prevailed among the wealthy families. In short, the outbreak of the rebellion in the province of Wellassa in October, 1817, was purely accidental, and the chiefs and people of the other provinces were as much taken by surprise as were the British authorities.

The Wellassa Moormen, an active, enterprising body of Kandyan merchants, were the first portion of the population of the Kandyan territory who became useful to the British, more especially by furnishing carriage cattle to the commissariat for the purpose of conveying stores and provisions from the coast stations. This class of the population formed an intermediate link between the traders in the maritime district of Batticaloa and the interior provinces.

They supplied, for example, all the salt which was used in the Kandyan country, and as this was an expensive article, being monopolised and highly taxed by government, the traders required to possess a considerable amount of capital.

Although the Moormen had petty headmen of their own caste, they were, like the other classes of inhabitants, completely under the subregal control of the dissave and other Sinhalese chiefs of the province of Wellassa. These chiefs levied heavy taxes and fines from the Moormen, and insisted upon obtaining from them whatever salt they required, as well as other articles of trade, at their own price, and sometimes, as is alleged, without any remuneration. In order to escape from these customary dues or exactions, the Moormen solicited Governor Brownrigg, through Col. Hardy, to be placed under a headman of their own religious persuasion, and their request was granted. Hadjee, a Moormen who received the appointment, was a person of superior intellect, and highly respected among his own caste, not only on account of his natural talents, but also in consequence of having made a pilgrimage to Mecca.

The Moormen forthwith practically renounced the authority of the Sinhalese or Kandyan headmen, and withheld some of the dues which they had been accustomed to pay, either in kind or in money. Being deprived of their usual revenue, the chiefs were greatly incensed with the Moormen, and more especially with Hadjee, who had in no small degree supplanted the dissave in his authority.

On the 10th October, 1817, Wilson, assistant-resident at Badulla, having received information that "a stranger," with two old and six young priests had recently taken up their abode in the jungle in the province of Wellassa, Hadjee, his brother, and a party of Moormen were despatched from Badulla to apprehend "the stranger." Whilst on his way through one of the passes into Wellassa, Hadjee's progress was opposed by the inhabitants, Hadjee was taken a prisoner, his brother wounded, and the rest of his party compelled to beat a hasty retreat to Badulla. After the captors had subjected Hadjee to a severe flogging, he was sent to the man who was called the "stranger," and sometimes "Deiyo" (god), an appellation which was occasionally given to a king.

Marshall, p. 182.

The news of Hadjee's capture reached Badulla on the 12th, and on the 14th Wilson set out for Wellassa with a party of Malay soldiers under the command of Lieut. Newman, and attended by an interpreter and some Sinhalese lascoreens. Having reached Wellassa on

Ib. p. 188.

16th, and failed in his attempts to confer with the insurgents, Wilson determined to retreat to Badulla by a different route to the one by which he had arrived from there. "The detachment returned to Badulla, having been much harassed during a great part of the way, by small bodies of the enemy." During this retreat Wilson was killed, and his interpreter and some of the lascoreens were taken prisoners. The latter were subsequently released.

For the purpose of ascertaining the feelings of the people of the province of Matale with regard to the British Government, Sir John D'Oyley, the resident, authorised Eheylapola to proceed from his usual residence in Kandy to that part of the country. Having large estates in that province, it was presumed that he was likely to have it in his power to acquire correct information in regard to the dispositions of the inhabitants.

On the 20th October Governor Brownrigg started from Trincomalee for Kandy, and on the 23rd at Kandally, about 16 miles from Trincomalee, received for the first time news of the revolt. Eheylapola, who was in the province of Matale, with a large body of followers, fell in with Ratwatte, uncle of the Adigar Molligoda and Dissave of Matale, who was proceeding to pay his respects to the governor, and accused the dissave of having failed to pay him (Eheylapola) the honours due to him. He forthwith disgraced Ratwatte, deprived him of the insignia of his office, and, in fact, virtually suspended him. Grave fears were entertained by the British authorities in Kandy that this offensive measure of Eheylapola was prepartory to his openly heading the insurrection, and capturing the Governor and Lady Brownrigg. Fortunately for the British the result turned out otherwise. At Nalande, a post about 31 miles from Kandy, Eheylapola, accompanied by a following of about 3,000 men and several elephants, met His Excellency and accompanied him to Kandy, which was reached on the 26th October.

It was decided by the British Government to relieve Millawa, Dissave of Wellasa, of his office on the ground of age and consequent inability to execute active duties, and it was further resolved to attach the dissavony under his charge to that of Uva, of which province Monarawilla, commonly called Keppitapola, was dissave. This chief was sent by the British to the disturbed province for the purpose of tranquillizing it. No military force accompanied him; but twelve of his own followers were each furnished with a musket and a few rounds of ammunition from the government magazine. Soon after he reached the seat of disturbance Keppitapola decided to head the insurrection, and deeming it dishonourable to use the arms furnished him by the British against them, he sent his twelve followers back to Badulla, whence he had started with the guns and ammunition, which they delivered over to the authorities.

From about the middle to the end of October the weather was very unfavourable for the march of troops, in consequence of heavy rains in the Kandyan provinces.

No sooner the weather permitted, Major Macdonald proceeded with a detachment of troops to Wellassa. Several other small bodies of troops moved towards the same district, both from Batticaloa, on the east side of the Island, and from the garrison of Kandy. In these marches they had to pass through narrow pathways, close jungles, and over steep hills, exposed to the missiles of the villagers who, although some of them were armed with muskets, were chiefly armed with bows and arrows. The inhabitants of this district were the most backward of the population of the Island.

The British detachments having formed a junction about the heart of the disaffected country, it was deemed advisable by Major Macdonald to inflict a severe and deterrent punishment on the inhabitants. Accordingly, their houses were forthwith set on fire and burnt to the ground, and their cattle, grain, etc., were either carried off by the troops or destroyed. Marshall says: "The inhabitants appeared to be horror struck at the devastation thus produced: they ceased to shout at the troops or to fire upon them; while they were seen on the neighbouring heights, and close to the skirts of the plain, gazing in silence upon the flames which consumed their habitations and the driving away of their cattle, they having had no time to remove any part of their property." The rigorous measures adopted by British instead of acting as a deterrent, acted like a match thrown into a barrel of gunpowder, upon the dissatisfied and disaffected population of the whole country, and in February, 1818, the whole of the Kandyan country was up in arms against the British, with the exception of the lower part of Sabaragamuwa, the Three and Four Korles, Udunuwara and Yatinuwara; and with the exception of Molligoda, the first adigar, every chief of consequence had either joined in the rebellion or was confined by the British for favouring, or being suspected of favouring, the insurrection. Keppitapola having accepted the office of first adigar at the hands of "the stranger"—who was no other than a priest by the name of Wilbawa, who had cast off his priestly robes for the purpose of heading the rebellion and had assumed the name of Durasamy—commanded the insurgents.

Numerous indecisive battles were fought during the months of February and March between the insurgents and the various British detachments under Major Macdonald, Lieut.-Col. Hook, Major Delatre, and Capt. Raper.

On the 2nd March Eheylapola was arrested and kept a prisoner in Colombo, upon a suspicion of his being disaffected towards the British. Although no charge was ever made against him he was never restored to liberty. He remained a prisoner in Colombo till 1825, and then it was considered expedient to remove him to Mauritius, where he died in April, 1829. About the beginning of April reinforcements to the extent of 7,000 men arrived from Bengal and Madras, and a reward of 1,000 pagodas was offered by the British for apprehension of Keppitapola, and an equal sum for the capture of two other principal chiefs. Marshall says: "For a considerable period during the months of May, June, and July the issue of the contest seemed to be very doubtful. Indeed, it is alleged that arrangements were in progress to withdraw the British force from the interior. Lady Brownrigg left Kandy under the charge of a large escort, comprehending the major portion of the garrison of Kandy, under the command of Capt., now Lieut.-Col. Frazer, and proceeded to Colombo. Fears were entertained that the inhabitants of the Three and Four Korles might join the insurgents, when the communication with Colombo would be cut off. Had this taken place, which was at one time probable, the troops, including the sick, would have been obliged to fight their way out of the country, with all the unfortunate results of former retreats from Kandy in prospect."

"Luckily," says Forbes, "the private animosity subsisting between Eheylapola and the first Adigar, Molligoda, induced the latter to exert his influence in support of the British supremacy, which he had good reason to identify with his own safety. By his influence in the district of the Four Korles, the people there were generally restrained from insurrection, a service of great importance at this period to the British interest, as through that province lay the principal defiles and mountain passes of the road which led from Colombo to the Kandyan capital." *Forbes' Eleven Years in Ceylon, vol. i., pp. 49 and 50.*

So serious was the situation of the British in Kandy that a large portion of the invalids in hospital, numbering between 300 and 500 men, were kept regularly supplied with arms and ammunition at sunset, with the view of enabling them to defend themselves should the hospital be attacked.

Towards the end of August, Wilbawa and Keppitapola were joined by Madugalla, an energetic and enterprising chief of Doombera, who persuaded Wilbawa to hold court at a palace constructed for him in Doombera. Here Wilbawa was treated by the chiefs and people with royal honours, and the usual respect shown to a king. On the 3rd September, the office of 2nd adigar and the appointment of Dissave of Matale was conferred on Madugalla. Shortly afterwards Madugalla discovered that Wilbawa, who had been elected or appointed king by the chiefs of Wellassa and Keppitapola, was not, as alleged, a relation of the deposed king, but a man who had until lately been a priest. Greatly offended by the deception that had been practised upon him and the whole Kandyan people, Madugalla seized both Wilbawa and Keppitapola and put them in stocks. How long they were confined or by what means they were liberated is not known; but it is recorded that as soon as Wilbawa obtained his liberty, he practically renounced his kingly office and sought refuge among the Veddahs of Bintenna. Although a large reward was offered for his capture, he was not apprehended until 1829. He was captured in consequence of information supplied by a Buddhist priest who knew him, tried and convicted;

but pardoned by orders from Britain. Some of the chiefs who had joined the insurgents had been captured during the months of July and August. Several of them were tried by courts-martial. Among others a distinguished chief, Ellepola Maha Nileme, was brought before a court-martial on the 17th October, by which he was found guilty of levying war against the king, and decapitated on the 27th of the same month.

It is recorded that on the occasion of his decapitation "he conducted himself with the greatest firmness." Although he had expressed a wish that his carcass should be left a prey to dogs and jackals, his body was interred by the orders of government.

Towards the end of the revolt, one chief, and one only, joined the British in a plundering expedition against the disaffected, namely, Eknelligoda, Dissave of Sabaragamuwa. He accompanied a body of troops, who were employed against the insurgents in Uva, with a number of people from his dissavony.

On the 30th October, Keppitapola and another chief, Pilimi Talawa, son of the notorious Pilimi Talawa, were surprised and taken by a detachment of troops, under the command of Col. Fraser in the neighbourhood of Anuradhapura. Madugalla, who had become reconciled to Keppitapola, and was acting in concert with him, was taken on the 1st November; and with his capture the insurrection terminated.

Keppitapola and Madugalla were tried by court-martial and sentenced to suffer death.* Accordingly both of them were beheaded on the 25th November, and Keppitapola's cranium was sent to the museum of the Phrenological Society of Edinburgh.

Marshall, p. 280.

A considerable number of petty chiefs were banished, either as a commutation of punishment or from being suspected of having countenanced the revolt.

"It would be difficult," says Dr. Davy, "to give the English reader an accurate idea of the manner in which, during the rebellion, hostilities were carried on on either side. When a district rose in rebellion, one or more

* A very interesting account of the execution of these two chiefs, containing a vivid description of the dignified bearing of Keppitapola, not only during the ceremonies that immediately preceded the execution, but also while he was being executed, is contained in Appendix X. of Marshall's History.

military posts were established in it; martial law was proclaimed; the dwellings of the resisting inhabitants were burnt; *their fruit-trees were often cut down;* and the country was scoured in every direction by small detachments, who were authorised to put to death all who made opposition, or were found with arms in their hands." "But, in a warfare of the kind in question," says Marshall, "where every inhabitant is a foe, persons who are not with us are commonly presumed to be against us, and treated as enemies. Hence the war carried on against the insurgents became characterised by devastation and extermination.........In the neighbourhood of the military stations, the central bud or cabbage of the cocoanut trees was sometimes abstracted, by which means the tree was effectually killed. The cabbage was used as food by the soldiers. The whole country was traversed in every direction by predatory military parties, who applied the torch to the cottages and whatever other property fire would consume, and which they could not carry away. Women and children were, as appears by general orders, sometimes captured and retained as prisoners of war."

"Driven from their villages," says Forbes, "their cocoanut trees cut down, their property and crops destroyed, and unable to till their land, the natives suffered severely from sickness and famine, besides those who fell by the fire of the British troops."

Dr. Davy estimates the loss of life incurred by the Kandyans during this insurrection at 10,000.

On the termination of the insurrection, Sir Robert Brownrigg took advantage of the breach of faith on the part of most of the chiefs, to modify the convention of 1815 by a proclamation dated 21st November, 1818.

The proclamation in question consisted of no less than fifty-six articles, and entered fully into apparently very small matters, *e.g.*: It decreed that Europeans were to show respect to the first and second adigars "by touching their caps, or taking off their hats," when they passed. "The chiefs holding the high offices of first and second adigars will be received by all sentries whom they may pass in the day with carried arms." "Dissaves, or chiefs holding the governor's commission, may punish offences by corporal punishment, not exceeding twenty-five strokes with the *open hand*, and by imprisonment for a term not exceeding seven days."

Sections 16 and 21 of the proclamation related to religion. Section 16 says, "As well the priest as all the ceremonies and processions of the Budhoo religion shall receive the respect which in former times was shown them; at the same time it is in no wise to be understood that the protection of government is to be denied to the peaceable exercise by all other persons of the religion which they respectively profess, or to the erection under due license from His Excellency of places of worship in proper situations." Section 21 says, "The governor, desirous of showing adherence of government to its stipulation in favour of the religion of the people, exempts all lands which now are the property of temples from all taxation whatever; but as certain inhabitants of those villages are liable to perform fixed gratuitous services also to the Crown, this obligation is to continue unaffected."

Section 28 says, "The services of the adigars, dissaves, and other superior chiefs to government shall be compensated by fixed monthly salarics, in addition to the exemption of their lands from taxation."

Section 56 says, "In all matters not provided for by this Proclamation or other Proclamations heretofore promulgated by the authority of the British Government, His Excellency reserves to himself and his successors the power of reforming abuses and making such provision as is necessary, beneficial or desirable; he also reserves full power to alter the present provisions as may appear hereafter necessary and expedient, and he requires in His Majesty's name all officers, civil and military, all adigars, dissaves and other chiefs, and all other His Majesty's subjects to be obedient, aiding and assisting in the execution of these or other his orders, as they shall answer the contrary at their peril."

Since the year 1818, when the insurrection ceased, no active opposition or resistance worth mentioning has been made by the Kandyans to the British Government; although indications of dissatisfaction occurred in the years 1820, 1834, and 1848, so as to excite a feeling of insecurity on the part of the British colonists.

With the developments in the Island both material and intellectual, under British rule, the author hopes to deal in a later work.

INDEX.